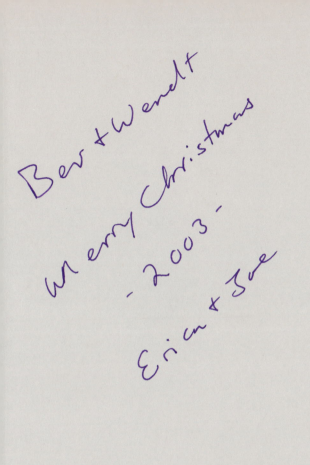

Bev + Wendt
Merry Christmas
- 2003 -

Eric + Joe

Ancient Wine

ANCIENT WINE

THE SEARCH FOR

THE ORIGINS OF VINICULTURE

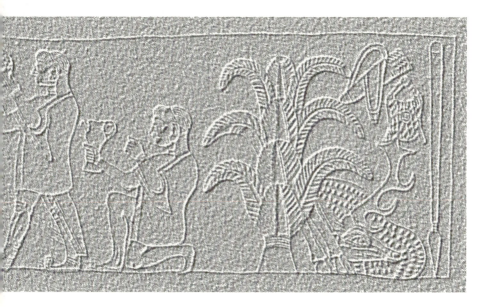

Patrick E. McGovern

PRINCETON UNIVERSITY PRESS

PRINCETON AND OXFORD

Library of Congress Cataloging-in-Publication Data
McGovern, Patrick E.
Ancient wine : the search for the origins of viniculture /
Patrick E. McGovern.
p. cm.
Includes bibliographical references and index.
ISBN 0-691-07080-6 (acid-free paper)
1. Wine and wine making—Middle East—History.
2. Viticulture—Middle East—History.   I. Title.
TP559.M53 M34 2003
641.2′0956—dc21   2002042714

British Library Cataloging-in-Publication Data is available

This book has been composed in Goudy
Printed on acid-free paper. ∞
www.pupress.princeton.edu
Printed in the United States of America

10 9 8 7 6 5 4 3 2 1

UXORI DILECTISSIMAE

· D O R I S ·

Then to the Lip of this poor earthen Urn
I lean'd, the Secret of Life to Learn:
  And Lip to Lip it murmur'd—"While you live,
Drink!—for, once dead, you never shall return."

Rubáiyyát of Omar Khayyám 35
(Edward FitzGerald, trans.)

CONTENTS

LIST OF ILLUSTRATIONS

Color Plates

1. The grapevine, *Vitis vinifera vinifera*
2. A reddish residue along one side of the interior of a wine jar from Godin Tepe (Iran), 3500–3100 B.C.
3. One of six jars that held resinated wine, excavated at Hajji Firuz Tepe (Iran), ca. 5400–5000 B.C.
4. A wine jar from a royal tomb at Abydos (Egypt), Early Dynastic period, ca. 3100–2700 B.C.
5. A Mesopotamian banquet scene on an impression of a cylinder seal from Queen Puabi's tomb in the Royal Cemetery at Ur (Iraq), ca. 2600–2500 B.C.
6. Bull-headed lyre from the "King's Grave" in the Royal Cemetery at Ur (Iraq)
7. "Peace Standard" from the Royal Cemetery of Ur (Iraq)
8. Phrygian jug from Tumulus W at Gordion (Turkey), early eighth century B.C.
9. "Autumn: Spies with Grapes from the Promised Land," by Nicolas Poussin (1660–1664)
10. Dionysos sailing the Mediterranean in a mid-sixth century B.C. painting by Exekias inside a drinking cup (*kylix*)
11. Bull rhyton from the Little Palace at Knossos on Crete (Greece), Neopalatial Period, ca. 1600–1400 B.C.
12. The Ayia Triada (Crete) sarcophagus, ca. 1400 B.C., showing bull sacrifice and presentation of a beverage
13. Tumulus MM (Midas Mound) at Gordion (Turkey), late eighth century B.C.
14. "King Midas" laid out in state

Figures

Maps

PREFACE

LIKE a well-tended vine or a well-aged wine, this book took many years to come to fruition. It has benefited from the advice and help of many colleagues around the world, freely given and appreciatively received. Although too numerous to list here, most of these individuals make their presence felt in the text, credits, and bibliography. The others know who they are. They all have my heartfelt gratitude.

The seedling for the book was planted at the 1991 conference, "The Origins and Ancient History of Wine," which was the brainchild of Robert Mondavi, who has done much to improve winemaking in the United States and to nurture a better understanding of wine's role in human history and culture. Without the impetus and excitement created by that conference, sponsored by the Robert Mondavi Winery, and the many programs and initiatives that followed, my research and writing would have long since withered on the vine. As it is, there is still much left to be done—perhaps trimming an overly luxuriant or misconceived growth or grafting on some new, exciting discovery.

I am especially thankful to my fellow participants and kindred spirits at the Mondavi conference, who have continued to share their specialist knowledge with me. Many of them encouraged me to write this book, a more popular and updated précis of the conference proceedings, published in *The Origins and Ancient History of Wine*. The latter volume remains an essential resource for specific topics, together with scholarly apparatus.

My first manuscript draft included a survey of the classical world of wine and details about the exotic wine-based concoctions of northern Europe. Because these developments are later and peripheral to the main thrust of the book or have been extensively treated else-where—as is true of Greece and Rome—they were severely pruned back, in the interests of giving a more intense, exciting flavor to what remained. The reader will still sense the potential importance of re-gions outside the Near East, such as northern Europe. My research is currently focused on Neolithic fermented beverages from China; other parts of the world may have equally impressive time depths, especially when something as consequential as a fermented beverage is involved. A future edition or a comparable investigation of the beginnings of winemaking by another writer might well be much less Mideast-centric than this book.

Most of the discoveries that have led to this appraisal of wine's earliest history would not have been possible without the support of the University of Pennsylvania Museum and its Applied Science Center for Archaeology (MASCA). Numerous funding agencies—the National Geographic Society, the National Science Foundation, the National Foundation for the Humanities, the J. M. Kaplan Fund, and the Wine Institute—have supported my research. Private indi-viduals, especially Robert and Beverly Brunker and Philip Schlein, and private companies (E. I. du Pont de Nemours, DuPont Merck, Rohm and Haas, and Thermo Nicolet) have been equally generous and crucial in developing the Molecular Archaeology Laboratory, within MASCA, and related programs.

Three dedicated volunteer chemists from private industry, who took up second careers in molecular archaeology, have been my mainstays in the laboratory: Rudolph H. Michel, Donald L. Glusker, and Gretchen R. Hall. They often devised innovative experiments and proposed incisive interpretations of the evidence. They were assisted by other extremely competent volunteers and students.

Well-deserved thanks are owed my editor, Joe Wisnovsky, and the staff of Princeton University Press, who spent many hours toiling in the vineyard of ancient wine. The perceptive critiques of three re-viewers also greatly improved the manuscript. The book was shep-herded through its production stages with exacting care by Helen Schenck, whom I have been privileged to know and work with for over 20 years.

ANCIENT WINE

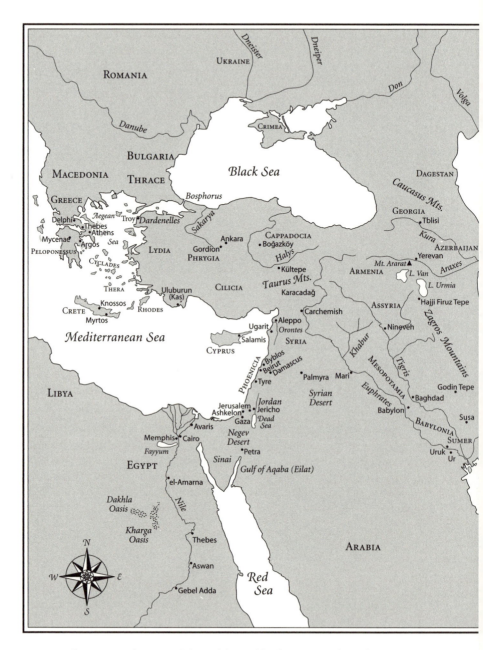

MAP 1. The principal areas of the Old World where viniculture began.

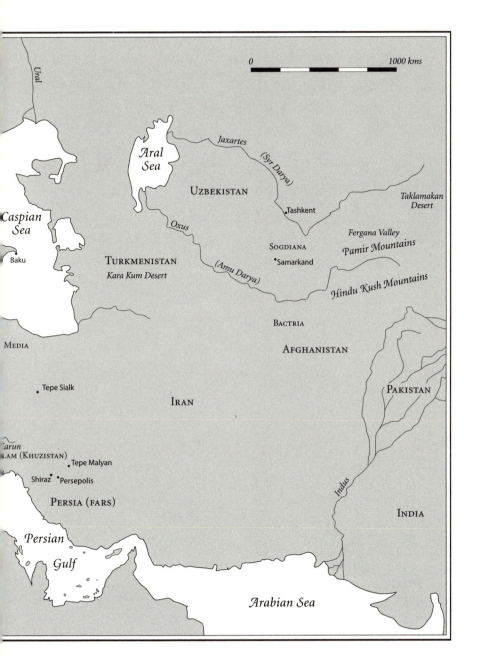

Ural

Aral
Sea

Jaxartes

(Syr Darya)

UZBEKISTAN

Taklamakan
Desert

Tashkent

Caspian
Sea

Oxus

Fergana Valley

Pamir Mountains

Baku

TURKMENISTAN

SOGDIANA

Kara Kum Desert

(Amu Darya)

Samarkand

Hindu Kush Mountains

BACTRIA

MEDIA

AFGHANISTAN

Tepe Sialk

IRAN

PAKISTAN

arun
.AM (KHUZISTAN)

Tepe Malyan

Shiraz   Persepolis

Indus

PERSIA (FARS)

INDIA

Persian

Gulf

Arabian Sea

0   1000 kms

CHAPTER 1

Stone Age Wine

A SINGLE Eurasian grape species (*Vitis vinifera* L. subsp. *sylvestris*), among approximately 100 that grow wild in temperate zones of Asia, Europe, and North America, is the source of 99 percent of the world's wine today (color plate 1). We may call the vine a Cabernet Sauvignon, a Gewürztraminer, or a Shiraz cultivar. We may be impressed by the varietal wines that are produced from the fruit of these vines, whether a dense red color, redolent of blackberries and cedar, or a flinty white with a hint of straw. The fact remains that we owe the seemingly infinite range of color, sweetness, body, acidity, taste, and aroma of this delectable beverage to one grape species.

The predominance of the Eurasian grapevine is all the more remarkable because the ancient inhabitants of the regions in which numerous wild grape species thrive today—China and North America, in particular—do not appear to have exploited the grapevine as a food source or to have brought it into cultivation. Leif Eriksson and his Viking compatriots were impressed enough by the proliferation of grapevines throughout the northeastern forests of the New World to call it Vinland. Yet, except for the occasional grape seed from an ancient village or encampment, there is as yet no archaeological evidence that Native Americans collected the wild grape for food, let alone domesticated the plant and made wine from its fruit.

Ancient Chinese sites are thus far similarly devoid of grape remains, although that picture is changing as more sophisticated techniques are used (see chapter 12). The earliest literary reference to

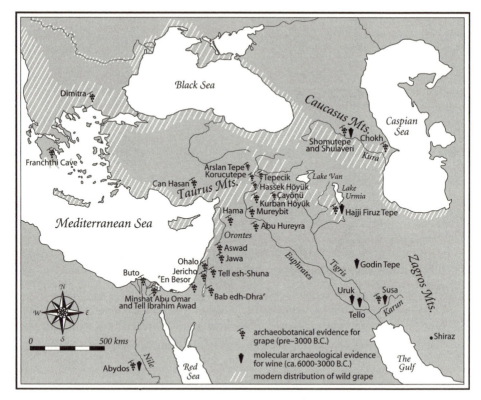

Map 2. The ancient Near East and Egypt. The distribution of the modern wild grapevine (*Vitis vinifera sylvestris*) is shown by hatching; isolated occurrences of the wild grape also occur in Turkmenistan, Uzbekistan, and Tajikistan, off the map to the east. The grape cluster symbol indicates wild and domesticated grape remains—primarily pips but occasionally skins and wood—that were recovered from representative sites primarily dating from the Neolithic to the beginning of the Early Bronze Age (ca. 8000–3000 B.C.) but sometimes much earlier (e.g., Ohalo, dating 20,000 years ago). The jar symbol marks wine jar types for the period from ca. 6000 to 3000 B.C., which have been chemically confirmed.

wine in China is the account of General Zhang Qian, who traveled to the northwestern fringes of the Western Han realm in the late second century B.C. He reported that there (in the modern province of Xinjiang), astride the Silk Road, and farther along in Bactria and Sogdiana in Uzbekistan whose grapes were already legendary in the

West, the most popular beverage was wine. Indeed, in the fertile valley of Fergana on the western side of the Pamir Mountains, the wealthiest members of the society stored thousands of liters of grape wine, aging it for a decade or more. Zhang was so impressed with the beverage that he brought cuttings back to the imperial palace, where they were planted and soon produced grapes whose juice was made into wine for the emperor. Zhang's vines, however, did not belong to any East Asian species, such as *Vitis amurensis* with its huge berries growing along the Amur River in Manchuria, but to the Eurasian grape species, *Vitis vinifera*.

How can the Eurasian grape's dominant position in the world of wine be explained? *Vitis labrusca* and *Vitis rotundifolia* (the latter also known as scuppernong or muscadine) eventually established footholds as wine grapes in the New World, despite their foxy or sour undertones and a cloying sweetness that seemed better suited to a Concord jelly than a Niagara or Manischewitz wine. By crossing an American species with the Eurasian species, experiments that were promoted by Thomas Jefferson and others, varieties that produce quite good wines were eventually established in Virginia and in the southeastern United States. In China, grapes with high residual sugar, such as *Vitis amurensis*, which can be further enhanced by raisining, can also produce a decent wine. But again, the Eurasian grape was crossed with Chinese species in recent centuries to provide the impetus for developing a native industry.

Sifting Fact from Legend

To understand why and how the Eurasian grapevine is central to the story of wine, we must travel back to a period in human prehistory shrouded in the mists of time. Barring time travel, would-be interpreters of the past are trapped within the fourth dimension. Time's arrow is pointed in one direction, and our task is to peer back millions of years and reconstruct the series of unique events that led to the domestication of the Eurasian grape and wine.

Archaeology—the scientific study of ancient remains—will be our principal resource and guide in proposing a plausible scenario for

Stone Age wine. Ancient records provide no signposts in this quest, because the earliest written texts, dating to about 3500 B.C., are much later and consist of brief, often cryptic records. Extensive treatises on wine—such as chapter 14 of Pliny the Elder's *Historia naturalis* (*Natural History*), written in the first century A.D.—are only as good as the writer's sources or experience and are refracted through the Weltanschauung of the time.

As intriguing and often exciting as the stories of the origins of viniculture (encompassing both viticulture—vine cultivation—and winemaking) are, this tangled "vineyard" needs to be trod with caution. Many books on the history of wine give undue weight to one legend or another and rely on dubious translations. If ancient Greek writers variously state that Dionysos, the Greek god of wine, came from Phoenicia, Crete, Thrace, Lydia, or Phrygia, one must plumb deeper. Another widespread view, shared by many ancient Mediterranean cultures, was that the vine sprang from the blood of humans who had fought against the gods.

A Persian tale of a king Jamsheed, otherwise unknown in that country's dynastic history, is very endearing. The monarch was fond of fresh grapes and stored them in jars to have a year-round supply. One consignment unfortunately went bad, and the jar was labeled as poison. Suffering from severe headaches, a harem consort then mistakenly drank from the jar and fell into a deep sleep, to awake miraculously cured. She informed the king of what had happened, and, in his wisdom, he discerned that the "poison" was actually fermented grape juice or wine with medicinal effects. He then ordered more such poison to be prepared, and thus humanity embarked upon its ages-long wine odyssey.

The Jamsheed story says nothing about how a mass of solid grapes could have fermented into a liquid beverage. Was the same procedure followed to make subsequent batches? There is also no mention of the domestication of the grapevine and vineyard management. In short, it is a simple tale, floating somewhere in time, like many other origin legends. If its historical details are suspect, it cannot be a basis for inferring that Iran is the homeland of winemaking, as has been done.

Archaeology, together with other historical sciences dealing with

geology and plant remains (paleontology and archaeobotany), is able
to provide a better starting point for hypotheses about the beginnings
of viniculture than ancient texts. Despite its narrow database and
mute testimony, archaeological evidence has a powerful explanatory
dimension. There is no hidden bias lurking in a pottery sherd or a
stone wall, as there might be in a written document. The archaeological artifact or ecofact (a term for a natural object, unmodified by
humans, such as a grape seed or vine) is there because it played a role
in the life of the community or was incorporated into the deposit by
some other natural agency. It represents unintentional evidence that
is contemporaneous with the events that one seeks to explain.

A host of scientific methods—ranging from radiocarbon dating to
high-resolution microscopy to DNA analysis—can now be used to
extract the maximum amount of information from archaeological remains. Increasingly, minuscule amounts of ancient organics, sometimes deriving from grapes or wine, have a story to tell.

Sufficient archaeological excavation has now been carried on
around the world to reveal that human beings, given enough time,
are remarkably adept at discovering practical and innovative solutions to life's challenges. Beginning as small bands, increasingly complex societies developed and led to the earliest civilizations of the
world—those in the Middle East, East Asia, South Asia, and Meso-
america and Peru in the New World. Although sporadic interactions
between these regions might have occurred from time to time, their
writing systems, monumental architecture, arts, and technologies are
largely explainable within their own contexts.

One example of human innovation that occurred in different regions is purple dyeing. It was most likely independently discovered by
humans living along the coasts of the Mediterranean Sea and on the
western and eastern shores of the Pacific Ocean in China and Peru.
The intense purple dye has only one source in nature: chemical precursors of the indigoid compound (6,6'-dibromoindigotin) contained
in the hypobranchial glands of certain marine mollusks. These animals, variously assigned to the genera *Murex*, *Concholepas*, *Thais*, and
Purpura, among others, live in saltwater bodies around the world.
Somehow, beginning as early as 1500 B.C. in the Mediterranean region, probably somewhat later in China, and about 700 B.C. in Peru,

human beings discovered by extracting the glandular contents in quantity and exposing the liquid to light and air enabled them to produce this unique color for dyeing textiles and other materials. Because it requires as many as 10,000 animals to produce a gram of the dye, it was very expensive to make. In each civilization, the molluscan purple dye eventually came to be associated only with the highest political authorities and was imbued with special religious significance. In first-century Rome, Nero issued a decree that only the emperor could wear the purple—hence, the name Royal Purple.

Some observers might argue that a transference of dyeing technology from a more advanced culture (e.g., the Near East) to a more fledgling one (China or Peru) accounts for the available evidence. Some might even go so far as to invoke a deus ex machina or extraterrestrial visitors. Another scenario is more likely for this example of convergent development, in keeping with Occam's razor or rule (the simplest, most straightforward explanation is often the right one). It runs as follows. The mollusks with the purple dye precursors were probably also a source of food in each region. The Mediterranean species, for example, are still a great delicacy in France and Italy, and the Chinese are renowned for exploiting every food source in their environment. When the animal is removed from its shell in preparation for eating, the hypobranchial gland, which is located on the outside of the creature, is easily broken. Once the liquid has seeped out, it will immediately begin to change from greenish to purple. A shellfish-monger's hands would soon be covered with the purple dye, which is one of the most intense natural dyes known and can be removed only by using a reducing agent. By no great leap of imagination, people began to collect the purple and use it as a dyeing agent. Although this scenario may never be proved absolutely, it accounts for the archaeological data and is in keeping with human inventiveness.

Food is a basic necessity of human life. It is also one of life's main pleasures and serves many auxiliary roles in medicine, social interactions, and religious symbolism. Just as people probably discovered the famous purple dye in the process of exploiting a food resource, humans have long been in search of that strange or exotic taste, texture, or aroma that will stimulate their senses, provide a sense of well-being, or even elevate them to metaphysical heights. Food is thus much more than simple nourishment, taken three times a day to survive. Because humans are omnivores who came on the world scene relatively late in the earth's evolution, they had an enormous range of plants and animals from which to choose. Yet they had to be willing to explore their environment and experiment to discover the delectable foods and beverages awaiting them, as well as to avoid danger.

Man Meets Grape: The Paleolithic Hypothesis

The wild Eurasian grapevine (*Vitis vinifera* L. subsp. *sylvestris*) grows today throughout the temperate Mediterranean basin from Spain to Lebanon, inland along the Danube and Rhine Rivers, around the shores of the Black Sea and the southern Caspian Sea, at the headwaters of the Tigris and Euphrates Rivers, and farther east in the oases of Central Asia. This distribution is likely only a shadow of what prevailed some 50 million years ago in warmer times, leading up to the most recent Ice Age in Quaternary times, starting about 2.5 million years ago. Pockets of the wild Eurasian grape managed to survive the four cold, dry spells of this Ice Age in lower-lying valleys and plains.

Fossil seeds and leaf impressions of the family Vitiaceae, including the American, Eurasian, and Asian groups, shared more physical features during the late Tertiary period, 50 million years ago, than now. Possibly, this plant even traces its ancestry back much earlier—to *Ampelopsis*, a climbing vine of 500 million years ago. With the breakup of the single landmass (Pangaea) and a gradual distancing of the continents from one another, however, the individual groups emerged. More recently, increasing desertification in Central Asia, North Africa, and North America and other natural barriers have isolated populations and led to the approximately 100 modern species thus far described.

Just as they were with the mollusks and their purple dye, humans certainly would have been acquainted with the wild Eurasian grapevine and its peculiar fruit at a very early date. Groups of human beings (*Homo sapiens*) migrated from East Africa about 2 million years ago, across the natural land bridge of the Sinai Peninsula into the Middle East. Their first encounter with the wild grape might have been in the upland regions of eastern Turkey, northern Syria, or northwestern Iran. Perhaps they saw the plant in a more southerly locale—the Hill Country of Palestine and Israel or the Transjordanian Highlands—because of moister conditions prevailing during interglacial periods than at present.

The general framework that brings human and grapevine together for the first time in the Paleolithic period also leads to a set of postulates about the discovery of wine, which is conveniently referred to as the Paleolithic Hypothesis. It was seriously entertained and debated at a watershed conference titled "The Origins and Ancient History of Wine" at the Robert Mondavi Winery in 1991 (see chapter 3).

One can imagine a group of early humans foraging in a river valley or upland forest, dense with vegetation, at some distance from their cave dwelling or other shelter. They are captivated by the brightly colored berries that hang in large clusters from thickets of vines that cover the deciduous or evergreen trees. They pick the grapes and tentatively taste them. They are enticed by the tart, sugary taste of the grapes to pick more. They gather up as many of the berries as possible, perhaps into an animal hide or even a wooden container that has been crudely hollowed out. A hollow or crevice in the rock might also serve the purpose. Depending on the grapes' ripeness, the skins of some rupture and exude their juice, under the accumulated weight of the grape mass. If the grapes are then left in their "container," gradually being eaten over the next day or two, this juice will ferment, owing to the natural yeast "bloom" on the skins, and become a low-alcoholic wine. Reaching the bottom of "barrel," our imagined caveman or -woman will dabble a finger in the concoction, lick it, and be pleasantly surprised by the aromatic and mildly intoxicating beverage that has been produced accidentally. More intentional squeezings and tastings might well ensue.

Other circumstances could have spurred on the discovery. Many animals, especially birds, have a fondness for grapes, probably as a result of their having occupied the same ecological niches as the grapevine since at least the Tertiary period. Under the right climatic conditions, grapes will ferment on the vine. The berries are attacked by molds, which concentrate the sugar and open up the grape to fermentative attack by the natural yeast, to yield an even higher alcoholic product than normal. As an aside, the deliberate use of a mold to a make a late-harvest, ambrosia-like wine had to wait another million years or more, when in the late seventeenth and eighteenth centuries A.D. both the Hungarians at Tokay and the Germans in the Rheingau took credit for discovering noble rot (*Botrytis cinerea*).

Observant humans, such as our prehistoric ancestors must have been to survive, would have seen birds and other mammals eagerly eating the fermented grapes. Their intrigue would have been aroused if they saw any ensuing uncoordinated muscular movements (robins have been known to fall off their perches). Sooner or later, humans would have carried out some firsthand experimentation.

Organisms as different as the fruit fly and the elephant gravitate to fermented fruits, and they have similar physiological responses. In the most general sense, their predilections are understandable because sugar fermentation (or glycolysis) is the earliest form of energy production for sustaining life. It is hypothesized that the earliest microbes dined on simple sugars in the primordial soup of 4 billion years ago and excreted ethanol and carbon dioxide. Yeast carry out a similar kind of anaerobic metabolism today, although they are hardly primitive; their single cells contain many of the same organelles as a multicellular plant or animal as well as a nucleus with chromosomes. Their ethanol production is like a signal sent up to the sugar lovers of the world, since this pungent, volatile compound leads back to a source of glucose or fructose.

Our common biological heritage with Stone Age humans, with a mental acuity similar to our own, strongly supports the Paleolithic Hypothesis. Yet it is extremely unlikely that the supposition will ever be proved. The greatest obstacle in the way of the Paleolithic Hypothesis is the improbability of ever finding a preserved container with intact ancient organics or microorganisms that can be identified as exclusively due to wine. In later chapters, we will see how fired clay (pottery) was ideal for absorbing and preserving ancient organic remains. The earliest fired clay artifacts—figurines in the form of pregnant females from the site of Dolni Vestoniče in the Czech Republic—date to about 26,000 years ago. Yet, the figurines were a serendipitous discovery, isolated in time and space; no evidence has been found that they were followed up by the making of any pottery vessels. The earliest pottery containers as such were produced toward the end of the Paleolithic period at about 10,000 B.C. in East Asia and Japan.

If pottery vessels were nonexistent, might tightly woven baskets, leather bags, or wooden containers have been used? Again, although the occasional plaited grass or reed textile fragment or impression on clay may be found, a preserved specimen is yet to be recovered from a Paleolithic excavation. Stone vessels have been found, and, if the stone was porous enough, they might retain enough intact organic material to determine what they contained. Rock crevices in the vicinity of an encampment are another possibility, but they would be exposed to weathering and degradation. As yet, none of the stone vessels have been tested by molecular archaeological techniques (chapters 3 and 4). It should be noted that most such vessels are open bowls and do not have a narrow mouth that might have been stoppered. Any Paleolithic wine made in such a receptacle must have had a very restricted production schedule, only during the fall when the grapes matured, and must have been drunk quickly before it turned to vinegar. We might imagine it as a kind of Austrian Heurige or Beaujolais nouveau. The latter is the intensely fruity wine of the Saône River region of France that is produced by carbonic maceration and released to the public a few months after the harvest. In this fermentation process, whole grape clusters are piled into a vat (as the Paleolithic Hypothesis proposes) and the accumulated weight of the grapes above crushes those below. The free-run juice then begins to ferment because of the natural yeast present, setting up an anaerobic, carbon dioxide–rich environment that triggers the whole grapes to alter their metabolism and to break down their sugar reserves into alcohol.

Paleolithic humans would have had little control over the fermentation process. Their vessels, whatever they might have been made of, were not airtight. Carbonic maceration might have taken place at the bottom of the vessel, but the overripe grapes and juice, harboring many other microorganisms, would have developed off odors and off tastes. The erratic fermentation would also have yielded less alcohol. Still, the final concoction or compote might have been quite stimulating and aromatic.

The analysis of Paleolithic stone vessels holds out the prospect of eventually determining where and perhaps how "Stone Age Beaujolais nouvaux" was made. Its discovery might have taken place at many times and in many places within the geographic range of the wild Eurasian grapevine. One thing we can be sure of: once the delights of this new-found beverage were known, roaming bands of humans would return year after year to the same vines.

Whence the Domesticated Eurasian Grapevine?

Winemaking, whether in the Paleolithic period or in today's wineries with all the tools of the trade and means to preserve the product, is very much limited by the grapevine itself. The modern wild vine of Eurasia exists only in areas with relatively intact woodlands and sufficient water, but it is fast disappearing because of modern development. Studies of *Vitis vinifera* L. subsp. *sylvestris* are important, because as the living progenitor of the domesticated species and its numerous cultivars, it accounts for nearly the entire stock of the world's wine.

Between 1950 and the present, wild grape populations were botanically described in the upper Rhine River region; at Klosterneuberg near Vienna along the Danube River; in the mountains of Bulgaria; in the lush, almost tropical, lowlands of Georgia along the eastern Black Sea (ancient Colchis, where Jason sought the Golden Fleece); and in the oases of arid Central Asia. Collectively, these investigations underscore the fact that the primitive forms of *Vitis* of Tertiary times were hermaphroditic plants like the modern domesticated *Vitis vinifera* L. subsp. *vinifera*. In other words, on either end of the long time span that *Vitis* has existed on the earth stands a grapevine that combines the male (stamen with anthers bearing pollen) and female (the pistil or ovary from which the seeds and fruit develop, after pollination) on the same flower. The advantages of this arrangement are obvious: the pistil is readily fertilized by wind and gravity and bears fruit that falls to the ground or is eaten (largely by birds). The seeds germinate in the area of the parent plant or are transported and take root some distance away, perhaps hundreds or thousands of kilometers distant.

For reasons yet to be explained and possibly related to harsh climatic conditions during the last Ice Age, the wild grapevine became dioecious throughout its range; that is, the sexes were segregated from one another on separate plants. Each still had stamens and pistils, but in males, a dominant mutation of a gene on one of the 38 small nuclear chromosomes, found in all *Vitis* species, suppressed the development of the female organ (denoted Su^F). In females, a recessive mutation (Su^m) impeded the development of the male stamen. Cross-pollination under these circumstances is more difficult than for hermaphroditic plants and must be helped along by insects or other animals, including humans. As a result, the male flowers rarely produce any fruit, and, to make matters worse, the female fruit is highly variable in its palatability because of the genetic polymorphism of the plant. In general, the modern Eurasian wild grape produces a rather astringent, small fruit with many seeds, hardly the kind of grape for making a good wine. Its sugar is relatively low and acids are high, as compared with the domesticated Eurasian cultivars, and the skin of its fruit is tough. Wild grapes are black or dark red, rarely white.

In contrast with that of its wild ancestor, the fruit of the domesticated Eurasian plant almost defies description. Its berries can be large or small; spherical or elongated and date-shaped, like the Mare's Nipple of Central Asia; of almost any color in the visual spectrum; and with varying amounts and endless combinations of sugars, acids, and a host of other chemical compounds. It is no wonder that a Wine Aroma Wheel had to be developed to deal with the plethora of tastes and smells of which this grape is capable. The wine taster performs an almost Herculean feat by characterizing the fruit (Is it a fresh, tart grapefruit; a clean, mild apple; or a rich, succulent blackberry?), together with its spicy accents, earthy or woody undertones, and more oxidative, even caramelized qualities. The sheer number of cultivars or clonal types, which has been estimated to be as many as 10,000 worldwide, further testifies to the plant's pliable, almost chimeric nature.

Much of this diversity, of course, is very recent, and the result of choosing those traits that are desirable and propagating them by cuttings or rootings. The grapevine growing tip actually consists of a core and an outer epidermal layer comprising different genetic systems. With time, mutations of one sort and another—often deleterious—accumulate in these tissues. After a vine has been dormant because of shorter days and lower temperatures, growth is reinitiated not at the old tip but at new lateral shoots with different genetic histories and different characteristics.

Horticultural methods of selecting and propagating desirable traits—whether size, shape, juiciness, color, skin toughness, taste, or aroma—were unknown to our Stone Age forebears. Each wild Eurasian vine is highly individual because it derives from a single grape seed with a unique genetic heritage, resulting from the combination of male and female gametes from specific polymorphic plants. Even before nuances of grape taste and aroma were made, however, a more basic decision had to be made by the first "viticulturalist." A single individual probably had an intuitive insight and acted on the idea, as has happened for many other advances in human history. He or she had to select plants that had reverted to their primitive hermaphroditic state. Such plants might have been observed to produce a large and regular supply of fruit. But how could a population of largely dioecious plant be converted to one that was hermaphroditic and a guarantor of greater productivity? If propagation by cuttings or rootings was not yet known, a very concerted effort must have been made, perhaps over generations, to plant and nurture seeds of hermaphroditic vines. In short, the wild vine had to be taken into cultivation, thus beginning it on its way to become the domesticated Eurasian grapevine that we know today. Once the basic principles of interbreeding and transplanting were mastered, additional crosses could be made or germ plasm chosen that produced the traits desired. The goal might have been a sweeter eating grape; a sourer, more bitter grape for vinegar; or a wine grape with balanced sugar content and acidity.

When and Where Was Wine First Made?

The wild Eurasian grapevine has a range that extends over 6000 kilometers from east to west, from Central Asia to Spain, and some 1300 kilometers from north to south, from the Crimea to Northwest Africa. Somewhere in this vast region, the wild Eurasian grapevine was taken into cultivation and eventually domesticated, perhaps more than once and in more than one place. The plasticity of the plant and the inventiveness of humans might appear to argue for multiple domestications. But, if there was more than one domestication event, how does one account for the archaeological and historical evidence that the earliest wine was made in the upland, northern parts of the Near East? From there, according to the best substantiated scenario, it gradually spread to adjacent regions such as Egypt and Lower Mesopotamia (ca. 3500–3000 B.C.). Somewhat later (by 2200 B.C.), it was being enjoyed on Crete. Inexorably, the elixir of the ancient world made its way in temporal succession westward to Rome and its colonies and up the major rivers into Europe. From there, the prolific Eurasian grapevine spread to the New World, where it continues to intertwine itself with emerging economies.

Winemaking implies a whole constellation of the techniques beyond taking the wild grapevine into cultivation. The plants must be tended year-round to ensure that they are adequately watered and protected from animals, which might trample them, graze on the vegetation, or eat the fruit. Pests, such as mites, louses, fungi, and bacteria that the vine is subject to, might have been invisible or just barely perceptible to Stone Age humans, but an early viticulturalist would have observed the tell-tale signs of disease and have tried to find a solution. Perhaps, suspect plants were rooted up, or the healthy plants moved and segregated elsewhere. With increasing knowledge of horticulture and natural contingencies, growers established new plants with the desired characteristics. The magnitude of this accomplishment is accentuated by the fact that it takes five or six years before a young vine produces fruit. Other prerequisites of the technology probably were developed in tandem with vineyard management. Airtight vessels were needed to control the fermentation and to prevent the beverage from becoming vinegar or otherwise spoiling. Subsidiary equipment, including hoes and cutting implements, vats for stomping out or pressing the grapes and separating the pomace from the must, funnels and sieves, and stoppers, were also essential.

The tool kit of a Paleolithic hunter-gatherer was well enough stocked with blades and pounders to squash grapes at the right time of the year and make wine. Yet the essentials of deliberate wine production—horticultural technique, pottery, and food-processing techniques such as fermentation—lay in the future. The Neolithic period, from about 8500 to 4000 B.C., is the first time in human prehistory when the necessary preconditions came together for the momentous innovation of viniculture. Numerous year-round villages had been established by this time in the Near East, especially in upland regions bordering the Fertile Crescent—the foothills of the Zagros Mountains bordering the Tigris and Euphrates Rivers on the east, Transcaucasia to the north, and the upland plateaus descending from the Taurus Mountains in eastern Turkey.

CHAPTER 2

The Noah Hypothesis

Hundreds, if not thousands, of years of experimentation in vine cultivation and winemaking technology were needed to achieve the level of sophistication displayed in the upland Neolithic settlements of the ancient Near East. The chemical evidence that Neolithic pottery vessels contained wine is marshaled in chapters 3 and 4. Other recent evidence from the fields of archaeology, genetics, ancient literary studies, paleobotany, and linguistics converge and point to the Neolithic period as the time when large-scale winemaking began. The moniker Noah Hypothesis encapsulates the main thrust of the argument, still to be proved.

Genetics and Gilgamesh

Strictly speaking, the Noah Hypothesis refers to the DNA quest for discovering when and where the wild Eurasian grape was first domesticated. It is similar to the Eve Hypothesis in that it purports a single original ancestor. The Eve Hypothesis claims that all of humanity can be traced to an original human mother in East Africa—whether 2 million or 200,000 years ago—on the basis of mitochrondrial DNA lineage trees. A similar investigation of the Eurasian grape would seek the ultimate progenitor of modern domesticated grape varieties.

The Noah Hypothesis is an apt phrase to describe a larger scientific quest for the origins of viniculture, because the biblical patriarch's first goal, after his ark came to rest on Mount Ararat, was to plant a vineyard (Genesis 8.4 and 9.20). It is not stated whether he used seedlings or rootings, but the "first *vigneron*" was adept enough to produce wine. The story focuses on Noah's moral character rather than his viticultural expertise, ending on the note that his youngest son, Canaan, and his descendants were to be condemned to perpetual servitude because Canaan saw his father naked and inebriated in his tent.

The biblical account of origins (Genesis 1–11) is a later version of a Mesopotamian epic of creation in which a hero survived a deluge. He was variously called Utnapishtim or Atrahasis in ancient Akkadian or Ziusudra in Sumerian. The bottom third of an early second millennium B.C. cuneiform tablet, written in Sumerian and from the city-state of Nippur in southern Iraq, provides the earliest epigraphic evidence for the Mesopotamian flood epic. Scholars believe that the story dates back another thousand years, much earlier than when the biblical account was put to writing in the first millennium B.C. By this time, the Sumerian poems had been incorporated into the grand Epic of Gilgamesh, recorded on 12 large tablets recovered from the library of Assurbanipal at Nineveh.

Gilgamesh undertook his bold exploits to discover the secret of eternal life from the flood hero, Utnapishtim. Like Noah, Utnapishtim was favored by the gods and told to build a huge ship, which saved him and his family from the inundation of rain that lasted seven days and nights. After Utnapishtim landed on Mount Nisir, he sent birds out to determine when the flood waters had subsided and whether it was safe to leave the boat. As a reward for their devotion, Utnapishtim and his wife were made "like unto gods" and placed in a distant abode "at the mouth of the rivers." The resonances with and similarities to the biblical accounts of creation and the flood are patent.

Noah's vinicultural and wine-drinking proclivities are paralleled by other details of the Gilgamesh story. For example, on his way to "the mouth of the rivers" along the road toward the sunrise, Gilgamesh enters a grove with vines bearing fruit like the precious stones carnelian (red) and lapis lazuli (blue). The colors suggest that the fruit was grape. Shortly thereafter, Gilgamesh meets Siduri, a barmaid or tavern owner, a female profession well-attested in the Code of Hammurapi. She has a jug and a bowl, standard vessels for serving and drinking wine, although one restoration of the damaged text reads "mashing bowl" for preparing barley beer. While she counsels Gilgamesh on how to cross the Waters of Death to Utnapishtim's home, Siduri dissuades him with more materialistic delights. Gilgamesh's companion, Enkidu, also succumbs to the wiles of a temple prostitute and drinks seven goblets of a strong beverage, eats prepared foods, and even puts clothes on over his shaggy body. Far from evidencing moral turpitude, Enkidu's indulgences mark him as "human" and "civilized."

The allusions to wine and grapes in the biblical and Mesopotamian versions of the Great Flood are intriguing, but they are interwoven with fanciful and legendary motifs that challenge historical investigation. The poetic epics represent the distillation of thousands of years of oral and written traditions and were intended to answer the great questions of human existence, besides providing an exciting tale of the hero who faces insurmountable challenges and emerges triumphant. Yet each story is partly set in time and space. Gilgamesh was the fifth king of the First Dynasty of Uruk (biblical Erech), a city-state in Lower Mesopotamia dated to about 2700 B.C. Noah's home is not specified, but it can be inferred from the biblical text that it was in the same region. Biblical chronology, if taken literally, would suggest a much earlier time period for Noah than for Gilgamesh.

Most of the vinicultural elements of each flood story are tied to geographic areas remote from Lower Mesopotamia. Noah planted his vineyard after his boat landed on Mount Ararat, which is almost certainly modern Büyük Agri Daği in the Taurus Mountains of eastern Turkey. This mountain, rising nearly 5200 meters and covered with snow year-round, is the most prominent landmark along the northern border of Mesopotamia and is a major source for the Tigris and Euphrates Rivers. On a clear day, it towers above the Armenian capital of Yerevan. Anyone who heard or read the story would have been familiar with this mountain, symbolically potent because of its size and as a source of life-giving water.

The Mount Nisir of the Gilgamesh Epic is more difficult to pinpoint. In one version of the account, Gilgamesh goes in search of the survivor of the Mesopotamian flood by traveling eastward toward the rising sun from the Mesopotamian lowlands. This description suggests that Mount Nisir is to be located in the southern Zagros Mountains, some of whose peaks are over 4000 meters high. Another reading of the story takes Gilgamesh through the Cedar Forest, a region that is usually located in the mountains of Lebanon. A journey in this direction might lead to Mount Ararat. Because of gaps in the Mesopotamian account and dubious translations, it is unwise to press the details. On balance, and if it can be assumed that the flood accounts contain reminiscences of the beginnings of viniculture—or at least a widely accepted view in antiquity—then Mount Ararat is a most appropriate locale. Lying near the center of the midworld fold belt stretching across Turkey and Iran, it is close to the earliest Neolithic settlements that have yielded the earliest evidence of the domesticated Eurasian grape. Settlements and ancient grape remains in the southern Zagros Mountains are of later date (chapter 3).

Transcaucasia: The Homeland of Viniculture?

Ancient records may hold some vinicultural secrets, but the real test of the Noah Hypothesis depends on scientific evidence. Nikolai Vavilov, a Russian botanist, was first to claim that the earliest "wine culture" in the world emerged in Transcaucasia, comprising modern Georgia, Armenia, and Azerbaijan. This region, stretching between the Black Sea and the Caspian Sea, is dominated by the high, snow-covered mountains of the Greater Caucasus Mountains, a natural barrier between Europe and Asia rising to more than 5600 meters. The major intermontane valleys of the Kura and Araxes Rivers, with their temperate, continental climates, especially invited early human occupation. Excavation in and around the modern capital cities of Tblisi in Georgia and Yerevan in Armenia has revealed an almost unbroken sequence of settlements, reaching back to the Neolithic period. Where the rivers meet and empty into the Caspian in Azerbaijan, south of the modern capital of Baku, a milder, wetter, almost tropical climate prevails. A similar ecozone of broad-leaved forests dominates the Georgian lowlands of Colchis and Rioni along the Black Sea.

Transcaucasia's dramatic scenery and diverse ecology are matched by more than 6000 plant species, many of which are also represented in Europe and western Asia. What is unique to Transcaucasia, however, is an enormous variety of wild fruit and nut species, such as pomegranate, plum, pear, hazelnut, and walnut. The trees and bushes grow along modern roads and are easily sampled and studied. Their domesticated counterparts are the mainstays of the native cuisines.

The wild Eurasian grape subspecies (*Vitis vinifera sylvestris*) still thrives throughout Transcaucasia. A student of Vavilov, M. A. Negrul, traveled widely in Transcaucasia, Europe, and Central Asia. Using the classical methods of botanical classification (or amphelography as applied to the grapevine), he distinguished three main families of the wild and domesticated *vinifera* grape: the *occidentalis* of Central and Western Europe, the *orientalis* extending from Central Asia to Azerbaijan and Armenia, and the *pontica* of Eastern Europe, southern Russia, Turkey, and Georgia. These proles, or ecotypes, are distinctly different. *Occidentalis* vines, for example, are more cold-tolerant and have smaller grapes, with lower sugar and higher acidity, than *orientalis* vines. *Pontica* varieties have larger berries, with smaller and fewer seeds, and are generally more fruitful than *occidentalis*. *Pontica* grapes also are of low acidity and moderately sweet, making them ideal for wine production. Red and white grapes are about equally represented in all the families.

Negrul's work was an important start in sorting out the history and ancestry of the Eurasian grapevine. His research showed that the families were interrelated and that cultivated varietals (*Vitis sativa* D.C., now classified as *Vitis vinifera vinifera*) were descended from wild *Vitis sylvestris* Gmel. (now *Vitis vinifera sylvestris*). He made a special attempt to search out and describe wild populations in the mountains of Bulgaria and along its Black Sea coast, in upland areas of Tajikistan bordering the fertile valley of Fergana, through which the Silk Road runs, and elsewhere. The modern forms, however, stand at the end of a long process, and it is often difficult to distinguish a truly wild vine from a secondary type. What appears to be a wild plant could have been previously cultivated, then abandoned; or the seeds of a cultivated varietal could have been spread by natural agency and produced plants that eventually reverted to what appears to be a wild or feral type, completely at home in its environment.

Domesticated vines can also interbreed with wild grapes, especially in disturbed habitats. What one really needs to know is whether the wild grapevine is an autochthon, that is, a plant that is indigenous to the area and has never come into contact with domesticated varieties.

Exploring Georgia and Armenia

In 1998, I traveled to Georgia and Armenia to put Vavilov's theory of the Transcaucasian origin of viniculture to the test. In the post–Cold War thaw, the political turmoil in the region had settled down. I was ensconced by my host, Tamaz Kiguradze, in a spacious apartment next to his in a restored wooden house atop the ancient city wall. The balustrades, courtyards, and winding streets of the Old Town of Tblisi are draped with Queen Isabella grapevines— a prolific import, a cross between an American *labrusca* and the Eurasian vine.

The first-time visitor to Georgia is overwhelmed by its century-old wine culture. Dinners are presided over by a toastmaster, or *tamada*, who coordinates the many toasts to the motherland, family, and life itself—impossible to imagine without wine—throughout the repast. With over 500 grape varieties grown throughout the country, Georgia today produces more than 60 wines, despite having its vineyards cut by two-thirds as a result of Gorbachev's crackdown on alcohol throughout the old Soviet Union. Wine is more than a social lubricant; it is a powerful symbol of Georgia's very early adoption of Christianity. The most common religious motifs are grape clusters and running vines, and the cross itself is entwined with grapevines and the hair of Saint Nino, the nun who brought Christianity to Georgia from Cappadocia in the Fourth century A.D.

Wine is still made in time-honored ways in Rioni and Kakheti, the principal wine-producing areas of the country. A small-scale farmer will usually have several *kwevris*, each holding as much as 1500 liters, in a corner of a barn, buried up to their mouths and covered with a stone or wooden board. The free-run and pressed must from the farmer's vineyards are fermented on the lees and aged for several

FIGURE 2.1. Experimental viticultural station, Georgian Agricultural University, Tblisi (Georgia). Revaz Ramishvili (left), Tamaz Kiguradze, Deputy Director of the Dzhanashia National Museum of Georgia (right), and Tamaz's sister, Medea, a wine educator (center).

years. The visit of a foreign specialist in ancient wine was reason enough to dip into the cache and toast my good fortune with a fragrant and refreshing glass of wine, hazy with unfiltered solids and yeast.

Besides experiencing the sensory delights of Georgia's modern wines, I was on an academic quest: were the modern Georgian *vinifera* domesticates, such as Rkatsiteli and Mtsvane Kakhuri, related to the wild grapevines of the country, and, if they were, could it be argued that they represented the earliest domestication of the Eurasian grape? A visit to Revaz Ramishvili, an amphelographer at the Georgian Agricultural University, was my first step toward answering these questions. Revaz had studied the range and characteristics of Krikina, a name that encompasses the many wild Eurasian grapevines still to be found in Georgia. He believed that the high morphological variability of the wild plant fit well with Vavilov's hypothesis that Transcaucasia was the world center of the domesticated Eurasian grape. Cross-breeding, by contrast, results in greater uniformity or genetic homozygosity.

Revaz was especially interested in the heritage of a distinct species, *Vitis sylvesatis ramishvilis*, identified by his father, also a professor of viticulture. This species is characterized by a relatively high proportion (10 percent) of hermaphroditic plants. One could not rule out the possibilities that *Vitis sylvesatis* Ram. represented a cross between *sylvestris* and *sativa* or the subsequent development of an escapee into the wild. Revaz enthusiastically offered me the young leaves of this species and many others, conveniently planted on the hill below his institute, for DNA analysis. Male and female wild vines of eastern Georgia (*Vitis sylvestris pontica* Negrul) rounded out the collection.

Revaz was able to help out in another way. Many DNA studies are hampered by a "shallow" temporal horizon, relying principally on modern samples. If enough intact DNA could be recovered from desiccated or mineralized archaeological specimens, it might be possible to establish a time line for genetic changes. In the collections of his institute, Revaz had grape materials from many Georgian excavations that he had studied, and he offered me grape seeds or pips from the Early Kura-Araxes site of Khizanaant-Gora, dated to about 3500 B.C., and from an enormous eleventh-century B.C. cemetery of 10,000 tombs at Samtauro inside the modern town of Mtskheta. He also gave me a piece of grapevine wood from the early second millennium B.C. site of Nosiri in western Georgia, an extraordinary piece of evidence for early viticulture, not only because wood is rarely preserved but also because the grapevine represents the parent plant. Pips, by contrast, are the progeny of male and female gametes and are more variable genetically.

Six pips from the Neolithic site of Shulaveris-Gora were the most important group of material in the university collections. This village of circular and oval domed houses in the hills south of Tblisi is one of the earliest known permanent settlements in Transcaucasia. The long, narrow shape of all the pips provided good evidence that they were seeds of domesticated grapes. If only one or two had had that shape, one might have argued that the inherent variability of seed size and shape in the wild grape, whose seeds are generally short and broad, accounted for the evidence.

The seed index measurement of breadth to length was established by A. Stummer at the Klosterneuberg Research Station outside of Vienna, Austria. He measured some 800 cultivar seeds and another 200 wild pips from Europe. Although there was a large overlap in the bell-shaped curves, the peaks differed (0.55 for the domesticated and 0.645 for the wild). An almost identical dichotomy was observed in ancient samples from the Middle East, although this observation has not been followed up by detailed studies of modern specimens. The limitation of this index, however, is highlighted by the "wild" look of modern Pinot Noir pips, which come from the fruit of the celebrated Burgundy cultivar. A single Middle Eastern varietal grape can also have a range of differently sized and shaped seeds.

The grape pips from the earliest levels of Shulaveris-Gora had been radiocarbon dated to about 6000 B.C. Revaz was nervous about giving someone he had just met what are very likely the earliest domesticated grape seeds of *Vitis vinifera vinifera* ever found, especially someone whose study would entail grinding the seeds up and destroying their morphological features. He left the room to think it over. On his return, I proposed that "it was for the cause of science." Again he left the room. When he came back, he presented me with one of the six pips that derived from the 8000-year-old grapes. He said that it was like "parting with his soul." In true Georgian fashion, an exquisite bottle of white Muscat Alexandrueli was then brought out and served. The aromatic, sweet muscat was especially appropriate, because it had been made and aged on the campus from what is believed to be an ancestral domesticated grape.

An eight-hour bus trip, over the very rough roads of the Lesser Caucasus Mountains at an altitude up to 2750 meters, took me from Tblisi to Yerevan. As it was in Georgia, the basis for a thriving wine-making industry in Armenia was probably laid in the Neolithic period. Unfortunately, early Neolithic sites, contemporaneous with Shulaveris-Gora, are yet to be excavated. The settlements that have been explored, including Khatunarkh and Engija dating to the fifth millennium B.C., are concentrated in the Ararat Valley and have cultural affinities with settlements north of the Lesser Caucasus range. No grape remains have been reported, but it is probably only a matter of time until this situation changes.

Ancient Armenian viniculture was so advanced by the eighth century B.C. that the Ararat Valley was described as the "land of vineyards" in inscriptions of the kings of Urartu, a highland empire extending from the upper Tigris River to Azerbaijan. Deep irrigation channels, still in use today, were dug through volcanic rock along the Razdan River (ancient Araxes) to water the grapevines and other crops.

The 35-hectare site of Teishebaini (modern Karmir-Blur), established by Rusa II around 700 B.C. on the left bank of the Razdan, reveals how important wine was to the royal household. A total of about 400 huge jars (Armenian *karas*, comparable to Georgian kwevris) were found half-buried in subterranean storerooms of the palace. When full, the jars would have contained some 35,000 liters of wine. Grape pips found in the jars and from other contexts were clearly of domesticated types, which could be assigned to modern varietals such as white Chachabash and red Chishmish. The nearby royal city of Argištihinili (modern Davti-Blur and Armavir) had even larger wine "cellars," which could have held as much as 400,000–500,000 liters. In the mind's eye, one can envision the valley carpeted with vineyards during the Urartian period.

Other Urartian sites, including Erebuni (Arin-Berd), from which the name Yerevan is derived, dot the length of the large, fertile Ararat Valley. Botanical materials at these sites have been excellently preserved. The masses of grape seeds, malted barley for beer, sesame oil cakes, lentils, peas, and grain from Erebuni are astounding. An excavator of the site, Felix Ter-Martirosov, provided me with hundreds of uncarbonized pips, dating to the late seventh century B.C., for analysis.

Ancient DNA

The recent successes of the Human Genome Project and Celera Genomics, as well as the complete sequencing of the nuclear DNA of the fruit fly (*Drosophila melanogaster*), the nematode worm *Caenorhabditis elegans*, and the brewer's and baker's yeast (*Saccharomyces cerevisiae*), have created a brave new world for finding out more about the origins of the Eurasian grapevine. Since 1998, I have collaborated with several of the principal DNA researchers on grape in the United States and Europe, and what has been dubbed the Ancient DNA Grape Project has taken shape. In addition to analysis of a range of modern cultivars and wild grapevines from the putative world centers, such as Transcaucasia, methods are now being developed to isolate and study ancient grape DNA.

The "library" of instructions for a grapevine to grow and function is contained in the unique sequence of complementary nucleotide base-pairs that bridge the phosphorylated carbohydrate backbone of the double-helix DNA molecule. The nucleus of each cell of a *Vitis vinifera* plant contains 38 such DNA molecules or chromosomes, along which are strung the discrete base sequences known as genes that direct the production of specific proteins. Shorter, often more strictly conserved, single strands of DNA are also found in other organelles: the mitochondria and chloroplasts.

One of the most fruitful ways of distinguishing individual grape cultivars from one another and shedding light on their ancestry has proved to be the analysis of nuclear DNA "microsatellites." These are short sequences of bases, interspersed between the genes and more readily duplicated or deleted because they are nonfunctional. The asexual transplanting of cultivars ensures that the microsatellites will remain intact for centuries. Applying powerful multivariate statistics for almost 30 idiosyncratic microsatellites (and the number of suitable loci continues to grow as researchers around the world apply the same techniques) has unequivocally established the parentage of some very well-known cultivars. At the same time, the wine world has been shaken to its foundations.

John Bowers and one of my collaborators, Carole Meredith in the Department of Enology and Viticulture at the University of California at Davis, have shown that Chardonnay, the principal white grape of Burgundy in France, was the result of a probable accidental cross between the famous Pinot of the same region and an undistinguished, obscure white variety, Gouais blanc, which has actually been banned several times because of its poor-quality wine. In one fell swoop, the honorable Appellation d'Origine Controllé (AOC) system, which

sets French wine standards and excludes hybrid varietals, was undermined. Another study by Bowers and Meredith demonstrated that
what is arguably the noblest red grape, the Cabernet Sauvignon of
Bordeaux, is a cross between another distinguished red variety (Cabernet Franc) and Sauvignon blanc, the principal white grape of Bordeaux and the Loire Valley.

The crosses that account for Cabernet Sauvignon and Chardonnay
probably occurred sometime during the Middle Ages. Because there
were no detailed descriptions or drawings of cultivated plants until
relatively recently, the names of varietals were often confused and are
a poor guide to how long and where a specific cultivar was planted.
The length of time since a varietal was established cannot be estimated by relating the genetic distance between parents and progeny
with the number of generations of a specific length that would account for the difference, as has been done for humans according to
the Eve Hypothesis. Grapes might cross annually or over longer periods, depending on environmental factors and animal vectors. Such
complex factors, as well as the plasticity of the grape genome, make
hermaphroditic wild plants of particular interest, because they should
be genetically closest to the vines that were taken into cultivation.

Once horticultural methods were well developed, a desirable cross
could be perpetuated by cloning for hundreds, perhaps thousands, of
years. Replication of the same somatic tissue means that a modern
cultivar can conceivably be the direct offspring of plants of the distant past. In that sense, when we lift a glass of wine made from the
fruit of that grapevine, we are "drinking history." Rare mutations
would have occurred from time to time, but these are generally deleterious and would have produced sports (accidental variations) that
could not survive.

Studies of modern plants projected back in time can be misleading.
A wild plant may have grown over a larger or smaller area, or its
seeds may have been dispersed and gained a foothold far from the
parent plant's habitat. Climates change, forests are cleared, and sheep
and goat grazing cause environmental deterioration. Ancient botanical remains provide a way around this problem, enabling the ancient
landscape and biosphere to be reconstructed from direct, contem-

poraneous evidence. They also provide an absolute time scale for genetic change.

The problems in obtaining relatively intact strands of ancient DNA, however, are legion. Upon death, an organism's DNA is broken down by its own enzymes, which are released in a process known as autolysis. Microbial decomposition continues the fragmentation process. The strictly chemical processes of oxidation and hydrolysis cause further damage to the molecule, including nucleotide base loss and helical distortion, which would have been corrected in the living organism. Free radicals and water can trigger the conversion of one base to another. The net result is that the few micrograms of DNA in an intact tissue are reduced to a hundredth of this amount, and what remains may be so extensively degraded that it is useless. The polymerase chain reaction (PCR), developed by Kary Mullis in 1985, can take very small amounts and quickly produce millions of molecules, but it balks at replicating damaged DNA.

The difficulties in analyzing ancient DNA have not deterred researchers, who have reported recovering it from a 20 million- to 35 million-year-old termite encased in amber and a 17 million-year-old magnolia leaf in a lake bottom deposit. Archaeological remains, such as the 8000-year-old brain of Windover man from a Florida peat bog and 2000- or 3000-year-old Chinese or Egyptian mummies, are modern by comparison, and the authenticity of such "Jurassic Park" DNA has been questioned. Yet, enough is now known from testing a variety of ancient materials—human bones and teeth, animal skins and feathers, charred and fossilized plant remains—to have confidence in the basic results.

Contamination by modern DNA must obviously be minimized at every stage in the process, from excavation to storage to laboratory. This problem can be partly obviated by using species-specific enzymes and primers. The latter are short known segments of the DNA molecule, which encapsulate a long strand on either end and enable PCR to fill in the missing nucleotide bases. If the sample has come into contact with a single source of modern DNA from the same or a related species, however, that strand will also be duplicated and compromise the analysis. Performing multiple runs of the same sample in different laboratories is the only way to rule out this possibility.

Casting a Wider Net in Anatolia

Another collaborator on the Ancient DNA Grape Project, François Lefort of the Higher Specialized College of Western Switzerland, has collected and analyzed the DNA of a large group of modern grape specimens from the Balkans, including mainland Greece, and the island of Crete. I was planning to attend an archaeological conference in Turkey and study materials from the site of Gordion in the spring of 2001, and he put me in touch with viticulturists on the agricultural faculty of the University of Ankara, including Professor Sabit Ağaoğlu, Ali Ergül, and Sümer Aras. François had not obtained material from this region (ancient Anatolia) between Greece and Transcaucasia, yet there were good reasons for thinking it was key to unraveling the earliest domestication of *Vitis vinifera*.

Botanists and archaeologists alike have discovered recently that important advances took place in the Taurus Mountains area of southeastern Turkey during the Neolithic period. The origin of three of the eight "founder plants"—einkorn wheat, chickpea, and bitter vetch—has been traced to this area. The founder plants comprise a group of cereals and legumes—also including emmer wheat, barley, pea, lentil, and flax—that were crucial in initiating the Neolithic Revolution, the millennia-long upheaval in human subsistence and culture resulting from the domestication of plants and animals.

A compelling DNA study of einkorn wheat, using 288 polymorphic fragments, has shown that wild stands of *Triticum monococcum* subsp. *boeoticum* growing today in the Karacadağ range of the Taurus Mountains are most closely related to the modern domesticated cereal (*T. m. monococcum*). Comparisons were made with wheat specimens over a 3500-kilometer swath from central Europe to western Iran and especially those from upland regions along the northern edge of the Near East. The fully dioecious plants retained enough of their genetic heritage in modern specimens for the establishment of precise links between domesticated plants and their wild precursors. The results were unambiguous: the Karacadağ wild einkorn wheat was the closest match to domesticated wheat, implying that the plant was taken into cultivation in this area approximately 10,000 years ago.

If agriculture began in the Taurus Mountains area of southeastern Turkey, then horticulture also might have had its beginnings there. Accompanied by Sabit, Ali, and Sümer, I traveled to the University of Ankara's experimental station at Kalecik, east of Ankara, where grape varietals from throughout the country are grown. The varietals include the red Boğazhere of the Karacadağ region; the red Ökükgözü from Erzincan, along the upper Euphrates; and the white and red Emir of Cappadocia. The fruit had just set on the plants, which were swathed in a profusion of fresh vegetation. Samples were collected, which I took the following week to François in Herakleion on Crete. He extracted the DNA immediately and sent some of the material to a Spanish colleague, José Miguel Martínez Zapater at the Autonomous University of Madrid.

After I returned to the United States, Ali went on the road in eastern Turkey, collecting more samples. We have also focused efforts on other regions of Anatolia that were eventually drawn into the orbit of early plant domestication. The rich archaeological finds from the Neolithic site of Çatal Höyük (chapter 4) and the early second millennium b.c. merchant colony at Kültepe (chapter 8) naturally suggested taking a closer look at the "native" grapevines of Cappadocia and the western reaches of the Taurus Mountains. The eventual transplantation of the domesticated grape to the Balkans and farther up into Europe meant that coastal western Turkey merited closer examination. The region from Muğla eastward along the coast to Antalya, where many ancient ships sank, has also been targeted. The wild *Vitis vinifera sylvestris* still grows in the pine forests there, as it does in eastern Turkey. Finally, samples from the corridor through the Hatay in southeastern Turkey, which represents a crucial connection to the wider world of the ancient Near East and Egypt (chapter 8), are now being analyzed.

The Indo-European Homeland

Sometimes, a plausible but as yet unproved postulate will gain support from an unexpected quarter. New evidence that is distinctly different from that on which the postulate is based and cannot have been contrived will give the postulate greater weight. A recent study of the ancestral Indo-European language by Thomas Gamkrelidze of the Georgian State University in Tblisi and Vjače- slav Ivanov, his Russian colleague who is now at the University of California–Los Angeles, has done just that for the Noah Hypothesis.

Like the genetic heritage of *Vitis vinifera*, which is the end result of millennia of accidental mutations and crosses and, more recently, of intentional human selection, the language that we speak has its roots in the largely arbitrary meanings assigned by our distant ancestors to specific sounds. These sounds can shift to other sounds with time or if a daughter language is cut off from its parent. By applying rules of phonology, or pronunciation, linguists have been able to interrelate living languages and construct "language trees." Thus, at the base of the Indo-European superfamily tree is a hypothesized proto-Indo- European (PIE) language, which is no longer spoken but which even- tually gave rise to English and the other Germanic languages; the Romance languages, which derive from Latin; the Slavonic and Bal- tic languages; the Iranian and Indic languages; Greek and the Old Anatolian languages; and even an extinct language far out in Central Asia in the Taklamakan Desert (Tocharian).

The Middle East can seem a hodgepodge of incomprehensible lan- guages to the Western ear. The predominant languages of Arabic, Turkish, and modern Persian (Farsi), are relative newcomers overlaid onto a patchwork of other tongues dating back thousands of years. Here and there, generally in isolated mountainous retreats, an an- cient language holds on; for example, Ossetian in the Greater Cau- casus Mountains has its roots in the language of the Royal Scythian nomads of the first millennium B.C. Indeed, the northern Caucasus range and the rich fertile valleys of Transcaucasia to its south in Georgia and Armenia harbor probably the most ethnically diverse and linguistically rich area in the world.

Jacob Grimm's "law" of consonantal shift (German *Lautver- schiebung*) was proposed as early as 1822 and was applied to determin- ing how the Germanic languages had evolved from PIE. The original Aryans were believed to have inhabited a large region between the Alps and the Baltic Sea. As more rules were worked out, a consensus emerged about the vocalization of PIE and how it had changed with time. Since the late nineteenth century, nearly a dozen ancient dead languages—including Hittite, Hurrian, Egyptian, Old Persian, Sanskrit, and the early Greek of Linear B—have been deciphered, and these could be shown to follow the same rules.

Even with this excellent start in reconstructing PIE, linguists were hard pressed to place it securely in time and space. The proto-language was dominated by words for a mountainous terrain with rivers and lakes and a cold climate marked by trees such as pine, fir, mountain oak, birch, and ash and animals such as bear and snow leopard. A large part of the PIE vocabulary was also taken up with agriculture and other crafts: "wheat," "barley," "apples," and "cherries"; "farmer," "fisherman," "potter," "weaver," and "metallurgist"; along with associated technical terminology. It was difficult to reconcile such words with a nomadic people. Nevertheless, some linguists argued that the first speakers were the Kurgan nomads, so named because of the large mounds (Russian *kurgan*) that marked the tombs of their leaders and male warriors. These nomads were envisioned as sweeping across Europe in a series of invasions during the fourth millennium B.C. A more cogent theory was that groups from south-eastern Europe, bringing with them well-developed agricultural methods, domestic architecture, and pottery technology, migrated during the sixth millennium B.C. and formed the basis of the wide-spread and advanced European *Linearbandkeramik* culture, literally translated from the German as "pottery with linear bands." Elaborate, incised geometrical decorations on ceramics characterized this homo-geneous, sedentary "proto-Indo-European" society.

Perhaps, it should not come as a surprise that a professor of linguistics at a Georgian University, Gamkrelidze, should have put PIE studies on their head and focused attention on the languages of the Caucasus Mountain region, particularly its southern Transcaucasian and eastern Anatolian branches, denoted Kartvelian. Gamkrelidze and Ivanov made the significant observation that glottal stops—voiceless sounds produced by interrupting breath flow through the glottis or vocal cords—are common in the Caucasian languages, whereas in most Indo-European languages they have been lost. They recast the linguistic rules for PIE, producing a system with much simpler and more understandable phonological shifts. Their reconstruction was in accord with Occam's razor, namely, the most economical solution is usually the correct one.

The reaction from other linguists was swift and generally very critical. Gamkrelidze and Ivanov's work, however, was favorably received by archaeologists such as Colin Renfrew of the University of Cambridge, who coupled the spread of a new agricultural subsidence base in Europe with a new language. Anatolia, in particular, evidenced very early agriculture, dating back to 8000 B.C. at Çayönü near the headwaters of the Tigris and Euphrates Rivers, and to the early seventh millennium B.C. at Çatal Höyük and Hacılar, farther west. It seemed more reasonable that peoples from this area, rather than from the Ukraine, where the evidence was meager, had radiated out from their home territory, perhaps under population pressure, and carried the seeds of a new civilization with its own vocabulary to Europe and elsewhere.

Gamkrelidze and Ivanov's hypothesis for placing the PIE homeland in the general region of Transcaucasia and eastern Turkey received further linguistic confirmation in a study at my home base—the University of Pennsylvania—by Donald Ringe, Ann Taylor, and Tandy Warrow. Feeding the essential information from numerous Indo-European languages into a database and applying multivariate statistical algorithms similar to those employed in DNA lineage studies, the Penn linguists also argued that the Anatolian languages were the first to branch off from the protolanguage. The results were so startling that the program was run and rerun, using different combinations of daughter languages. Each time, Anatolian emerged as the first-order relative to PIE. Without intending it, the researchers had arrived at a result from the primary linguistic evidence that was in excellent accord with the data from disparate lines of inquiry—such as the DNA findings for the southeastern Turkish origin of einkorn wheat—showing that this upland region of the Near East may well be key to explaining the Neolithic Revolution.

The Russian botanist Nikolai Vavilov, who first advanced the idea that Transcaucasia was the world center of the domesticated Eurasian grape and was where the earliest wine culture emerged, had an eye for more than grape plants. He also made a profound linguistic observation. The word for wine (PIE *woi-no* or *wei-no*, the asterisk indicating a reconstructed form) is shared by a host of languages, Indo-European and non-Indo-European, ancient and modern. Our English word wine, for example, clearly derives from Latin *vinum*, which also accounts for Italian *vino* and French *vin*. Old Irish *fín*, German *Wein*, and Russian *vino* (along with other Slavic forms) appear to have a more ancient pedigree.

When the dead languages of the ancient Near East are examined, one finds a remarkable cross-fertilization of the same PIE root. It is attested in the primary languages of Anatolia (Hattic *windu* and Hittite **wijana*), Mesopotamia (Akkadian *īnu*), the Levant (Ugaritic *yn*, proto-Semitic **wajnu*, and Early Hebrew *yayin*), Greece (Linear B *wo-no* and Homeric Greek *οἶνος*), and Egypt (Old Kingdom **wnš*). The equivalent in Kartvelian is **γwino*, which is still the spoken word for *wine* in Georgia today.

Gamkrelidze and Ivanov believed that the stable correspondences of *wine* and its cognates in many language groups of Europe and the Middle East were more than coincidence. They pointed to the extreme antiquity of the word as a "migratory term." In other words, at some very early stage in the formation of PIE, **woi-no* or **wei-no* was transferred to other languages and adapted to the dialects developing in other regions. The linguists also noted that the PIE word often was linked etymologically to "grape," "vineyard," "edible fruit" in general, and compound words such as "grape cluster" and "wine steward."

Because linguistics is a historical science, it is difficult to date precisely when daughter languages broke off from PIE. The correspondences of "wine" and "grape" in ancient texts that have been dated by an absolute method such as radiocarbon dating carry us back about 4500 years, but then we enter the realm of prehistory. On the basis of the mute archaeological record for early agriculture, metallurgy, and other crafts that are well represented in the PIE vocabulary, Gamkrelidze and Ivanov estimated that the first speakers of PIE had migrated some 2000 years earlier. Granting a wide margin for error, they envisioned agricultural groups leaving Transcaucasia and eastern Turkey in about 5000 B.C., heading eastward toward Iran, southward to Egypt, and westward to the Balkans. These migrants already tended the grapevine and enjoyed its principal product, wine.

"Noah's Flood"

The geologists have most recently joined in the search for the proto-Indo-European homeland. In a provocative and stimulating book entitled *Noah's Flood*, William Ryan and Walter Pitman of the Lamont-Doherty Earth Observatory at Columbia University have amassed a wealth of data for a catastrophic in-filling of the Black Sea basin by salt water from the Mediterranean Sea about 5600 B.C. Before that time, the Black Sea was cut off from the Mediterranean by a high natural dam at the Bosphorus Strait. After the last Ice Age, the level of the oceans gradually rose, as a result of melting of the glaciers, but remained below the top of the dam. Ryan and Pitman hypothesize that, on the other side of the barrier, freshwater rivers—the forerunners of the Danube, Dniester, Dnieper, and Don—fed a large inland lake. Around the periphery of the lake, villages sprang up surrounded by barley and wheat fields and the first vineyards.

According to Ryan and Pitman's scenario, the population of the region especially burgeoned during the period from about 6200 to 5800 B.C., when temperatures fell an estimated 5 centigrade degrees and rainfall declined precipitously. The Black Sea lake, located below sea level, would have provided a warm haven of perennially flooded rivers. Plants and animals, no longer able to survive in upland regions, would have continued to thrive in or to have been drawn to this habitat. With the return of a warmer climate after 5800 B.C., the region came face to face with its destiny. Oceanic waters began to rise again and finally breached the dam at the Bosphorus. Water is estimated to have flowed through the relatively small opening at speeds up to 80 kilometers per hour. Unlike a river dam, which has a finite amount of water behind it, the Bosphorus dam contained the unlimited resources of the oceans. When it broke, the noise would have been deafening—like hundreds of Niagara Falls—and audible hundreds of kilometers away. The villages closest to the dam would have been the first to go. With the surface of the water inside the relatively flat basin rising at about 15 centimeters a day, other villages must have been inundated within days or weeks. Still, many inhabitants could see what was coming and at least had time to escape with some of their belongings. Their houses, fields, and vineyards, however, were eventually covered by water up to 100 meters deep.

Ryan and Pitman did more than show how deep-water radar profiles and borings in the Bosphorus and Black Sea substantiated their claims. They also drew on coral reef evidence around the island of Barbados in the Caribbean to date the rise and fall of sea levels worldwide and on oxygen isotope and methane contents of glaciers on Greenland to illuminate ancient climates. Most important, a succession of freshwater and saltwater mollusks was recovered by coring into layers of mud and clay at the bottom of the Black Sea. Radiocarbon dating of the molluscan shells showed that the transition from freshwater to marine conditions around 5600 B.C. in the Black Sea basin had been extremely rapid.

Although not claiming to be archaeologists, linguists, archaeobotanists, or molecular biologists, Ryan and Pitman marshaled independent evidence from these disciplines, the combination of which bolsters their hypothesis that the proto-Indo-European homeland was located in the region around the Black Sea lake in the period preceding 5600 B.C. This represented a minor transposition in time and space of both Gamkrelidze and Ivanov's and Renfrew's proposals.

The ultimate proof for Ryan and Pitman's scenario of proto-Indo-European peoples' being driven from their homes by a flood and transferring their advanced way of life to other parts of the Old World would be the existence of Neolithic villages at the bottom of the Black Sea. Robert Ballard, noted for his discovery of the *Titanic* using a remotely operated submersible at a depth of 3800 meters off the coast of Newfoundland, has joined with a colleague of mine at Penn, Fred Hiebert, to explore the underwater shorelines of the Black Sea. Underwater archaeology is now a well-developed discipline, and we should eventually have the answer. The results of the first expedition, however, raised hopes only to dash them. It was excitedly reported in the press that log structures had been discovered in a part of the Black Sea that had long been submerged, presumably as far back as the Neolithic period. When pieces of the wood were radiocarbon dated, however, they belonged to the modern period.

Ballard continues his search, but, for now, Ryan and Pitman's theory of a proto-Indo-European homeland should be treated with cautious optimism.

Farther Afield

Some people, scientists among them, would argue that the search for the earliest domesticated grapevine or the first wine culture (that is, proof for the Noah Hypothesis) is futile. Given the genetic plasticity of the wild Eurasian grape subspecies (*Vitis vinifera sylvestris*), which is known to have grown over much of temperate Europe and the Middle East since the end of the Ice Age, it must have been taken into cultivation in more than one place at various times. Thus, it has been claimed that the grape was already domesticated at the western extremity of its distribution, at three aeneolithic (or Chalcolithic) sites in southern Spain, dating to about 3000 B.C. A large *Vitis* pollen rain at Laguna de las Madres was said to be due to local cultivation. A small percentage of grape seeds at El Prado de Jumilla had the long and narrow dimensions of domesticated pips. Fragments of grapevine wood found at El Prado and at Cueva del Monte de la Barsella, together with dried grape skin, pointed to intentional exploitation. Assuming the Eurasian grape had been domesticated in Spain 5000 years ago, it was even conceivable that the luscious Cabernet Sauvignon grape was a native Spanish varietal that made its way across the Pyrenees from Spain to the southwestern Bordeaux region of France at a later date.

At least some of these claims have proved to be exaggerated. A pollen rain at only one site hardly provides definitive evidence for grape domestication, because it mainly depends on ecological factors and is too localized. Unless a grape seed assemblage is dominated by specimens exhibiting the domesticated morphology, the argument for cultivation is weak. Such skepticism was justified by the radiocarbon dating of six seeds from El Prado, all of which were of modern origin (post–A.D. 1960).

Other evidence from Europe is equally unconvincing for an early domestication of the Eurasian grapevine there. The case thus far re-

lies on the dubious morphological differences between wild and domesticated pips. Excavated grape seeds in ancient Europe—from
Yugoslavia to Italy, to Switzerland, and as far north as Sweden—are
generally short and squat like the wild Eurasian grape. The shift to
the long, narrow pips of the domesticated grape occurred in the middle to late Iron Age, thousands of years later than in the Middle East.
Greece provides the only exception to this Europe-wide course of
development (see chapter 10).

Recent DNA microsatellite studies of more than 100 grape cultivars from Greece, Croatia, northern Italy, Austria and Germany,
France, Spain, and Portugal showed that the grape of each region was
genetically distinct, implying that the wild component in each area
had contributed to the genotype or was separately domesticated. At
the same time, cultivars in France and Austria-Germany were farther
removed from those of the Iberian Peninsula and Greece, whereas
those of Croatia and Italy were intermediate between those two
larger groups. As some of the researchers including François Lefort
and José Miguel Martínez Zapater, have pointed out, the testing of
ancient cultivars is needed to refine the assignments. The preliminary
results, however, might be interpreted as already pointing in the direction of the introduction of a cultivar from the eastern end of the
Eurasian grape's distribution and its subsequent interbreeding with
local wild grapes.

The popularity of the grape and wine undoubtedly resulted in a
complex genetic intermixing, which has accelerated in modern times.
Proof for the Noah Hypothesis can come only from more archaeological exploration, coupled with DNA and chemical research.
Grape pips or pollen rain alone cannot sustain a hypothesis of independent domestication of the Eurasian grapevine. Rather, a whole
vinicultural complex—winemaking equipment, storage containers,
even evidence for social and religious ceremonies in which wine
plays a major role—must be attested before it can be concluded that
the Eurasian grape was initially domesticated in more than one locale
of the Old World.

To date, the broad archaeological picture of viniculture in the Old
World is that of an industry that gradually spread out in time and
space, from small beginnings in the northern mountains of the Near

East, to become a dominant economic and social force throughout the region and across Europe. The earliest grape remains whose morphologies are consistent with domestication are those from early Neolithic sites in Transcaucasia, including Shulaveris-Gora and Shomu-Tepe, about 30 kilometers farther down the Kura River in Azerbaijan. Similar evidence comes from Chokh, a village of massive stone buildings situated in an isolated mountain valley at 1700–1800 meters above sea level on the northern side of the Greater Caucasus range in Dagestan. One wonders how many other Neolithic sites with grape remains and wine-related artifacts await discovery in the upland regions of the Taurus and Zagros Mountains.

The jury is still out on the Ancient DNA Grape Project. Special PCR protocols are being worked out. New primer pairs and more powerful statistical methods continue to be developed. Detailed sequencing of the nuclear, chloroplast, and mitochondrial genomes of the wild grapevine and a range of Middle Eastern cultivars may hold clues—perhaps, a rare gene or allele that occurs only in a wild hermaphrodite of one region and yet is shared by all the domesticated Eurasian grapevines worldwide. Though the Noah Hypothesis may be debated for years to come, the tantalizing notion that viticulture and winemaking had a unique beginning in real time has spurred on valuable research.

CHAPTER 3

The Archaeological and Chemical
Hunt for the Earliest Wine

AN archaeological excavation will often yield a set of data that appear to be linked together by a particular human activity, but convincing evidence for that activity may or may not be present. When organic materials are directly involved—as they often are since human beings and much of what they surround themselves with are organic—a satisfactory solution to an archaeological puzzle will be all the more elusive, because of the ease with which most organic compounds degrade, dissolve, and disappear. On the other hand, if an organic compound that is highly specific to a given plant or animal were preserved and identified, this evidence could well prove to be the missing link in a chain of reasoning.

Godin Tepe

In 1988, I had a telephone call from Virginia ("Ginny") Badler, with whom I had studied Akkadian many years earlier at Penn and who was hard at work on her doctoral dissertation on a Late Chalcolithic village at Godin Tepe. This site, located high in the middle Zagros Mountains of western Iran along the Khorram River, was the focus of a major archaeological expedition between 1965 and 1973 under the direction of T. Cuyler Young Jr. of the

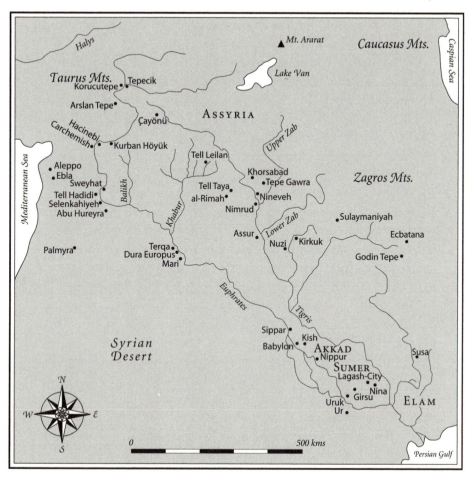

MAP 3. Upper and Lower Mesopotamia.

Royal Ontario Museum in Toronto, who was also supervising Ginny's dissertation at the University of Toronto.

Ginny wanted me to look at some pottery sherds from a large jar whose interior was partly covered with a reddish residue (color plate 2). She believed that the vessel had originally held wine, which had evaporated, leaving behind the dregs, or lees. I was very skeptical. The jar dated back to ca. 3100–2900 B.C., according to radiocarbon determinations. Was it possible that sufficiently intact organic material still remained after 5000 years and that it could be specifically identified as wine? If so, it would predate the earliest chemical evidence for wine from Roman amphoras recovered from shipwrecks off the French Riviera by almost three millennia.

My laboratory had already developed techniques for identifying very ancient biomolecules, in particular the earliest example of 6,6'-dibromoindigotin (DBI), the compound that yields the renowned Royal Purple dye. Before that discovery, I had been skeptical about whether any intact organics would be detectible from the purplish residue covering the inside of an ancient Phoenician storage jar, not much different in size and shape from the Godin Tepe jar. I eventually suppressed my doubts, and perhaps I would need to do so again. Nevertheless, I stressed to Ginny that there was no guarantee that our tests would yield ancient organic components to account for the reddish residue. Inorganic reds and purples are far more common in archaeological sites than are organic reds and purples. For example, red ochre or iron oxide was used as early as Mesolithic times (ca. 14,000–10,000 B.C.) to paint burials, and pyrolusite or manganese dioxide was early mined by the Egyptians and ground into a cosmetic for eye shadow. Ginny remained insistent: the Godin red was most likely a wine residue and would merit detailed chemical investigation.

Before embarking on any molecular archaeological project, one can often glean valuable clues from strictly archaeological considerations. Where were the pottery sherds found? Were they associated with other artifacts that might point to wine drinking or wine production? Perhaps most important, how did Godin Tepe fit into the wider world of the time? Was a mountain society advanced enough to support a winemaking industry or wealthy enough to have imported wine from elsewhere?

In the late fourth millennium B.C., Godin Tepe lay on the eastern edge of Lower Mesopotamia, where some of the earliest literate societies in the world had formed into city-states. The wide, rich alluvial plains of the Tigris and Euphrates Rivers had been harnessed for agriculture by canals and levees. Rulers, such as the semilegendary Gilgamesh, were faced with a harsh climate. During the summer, temperatures probably rose to as high as 49°C, as they do today, and barely 8 centimeters of rain fell during the year. Even more daunting, the lowland region was devoid of stone for making tools and of timber for fuel and building homes.

VITIS VINIFERA L.
Die weintragende Weurebe

PLATE 1. The grapevine, *Vitis vinifera vinifera*, showing three varieties of the domesticated grape: blue, white, and red (the Central Asian "Mare's Nipple").

PLATE 2. A reddish residue can be seen along one side of the interior of a wine jar from Godin Tepe (Iran), dating to 3500–3100 B.C. The deposit represents the lees of a well-aged vintage, probably as the vessel lay on its side.

PLATE 3. One of six jars that held resinated wine that were excavated in a Neolithic "kitchen" at Hajji Firuz Tepe (Iran), dating to 5400–5000 B.C.

PLATE 4. A wine jar from a royal tomb at Abydos (Egypt), dating to the Early Dynastic period, ca. 3100–2700 B.C., with a stopper impressed with the hieroglyphic *serekh* (inset) of Den, a Dynasty 1 pharaoh.

PLATE 5. A Mesopotamian banquet scene, the forerunner of the ancient Greek *symposion*, as depicted on an impression of a lapis lazuli cylinder seal from Queen Puabi's tomb in the Royal Cemetery at Ur (Iraq), ca. 2600–2500 B.C. A male and female imbibe barley beer through drinking tubes from a wide-mouthed jar, as dignitaries below raise high their cups, probably containing wine, which is served from a spouted jar.

PLATE 6. Bull-headed lyre, with a gold head and lapis lazuli beard, from the "King's Grave" in the Royal Cemetery at Ur (Iraq). The shell inlays of the sound-box show the "Master of Animals" and mythological creatures, like those in the Epic of Gilgamesh, who carry drinking bowls, goblets, and beverage jars.

PLATE 7. "Peace Standard" from the Royal Cemetery of Ur (Iraq), inlaid in shell and lapis lazuli. The plunder of a battle serves for the making of a great feast, to the accompaniment of music.

PLATE 8. Phrygian jug, from Tumulus W at Gordion (Turkey), early eighth century B.C., with an intricately painted geometric design and a stepped "waterfall" along the inside of the long, open spout. A beverage could be poured from the vessel or drunk directly by raising spout to lips, with an attendant phallic connotation.

Opposite page:

PLATE 9. (*top*) "Autumn: Spies with Grapes from the Promised Lands," by Nicolas Poussin (1594–1665). The French artist captured the ancient Israelites' delight with the fecundity of the Promised Land when the spies brought this gigantic grape cluster back from the Valley of Eshcol ("grapes") near Hebron (Numbers 13:24–27).

PLATE 10. (*bottom*) Dionysos sailing the Mediterranean, after he has miraculously grown a grapevine up his ship's mast and transformed his attackers into dolphins. Painting by Exekias inside a *kylix* or Greek drinking cup of the mid-sixth century B.C.

PLATE 11. A spectacular bull rhyton in carved black steatite from the Little Palace at Knossos on Crete (Greece), Neopalatial Period, ca. 1600–1400 B.C.

PLATE 12. One side of the Ayia Triada (Crete) sarcophagus, ca. 1400 B.C. The fresco shows the sacrifice of a bull and presentation of a beverage (a "bull's blood" wine?) in a beak-spouted jug, to the accompaniment of flute music.

PLATE 13. Tumulus MM (Midas Mound) at Gordion (Turkey), dating to the late eighth century B.C., seen here from the east. The 150-foot high mound covered a wooden burial chamber that held a royal burial, possibly that of King Midas himself.

PLATE 14. "King Midas" laid out in state on piles of purple- and blue-dyed textiles inside his cedar coffin.

PLATE 15. Bronze ram-headed *situla* or bucket, from the "Midas Tomb." Vessels such as this and its lion-headed counterpart (see figure 11.3) were used to serve out "Phrygian grog" to the mourners at the funerary feast of "King Midas."

PLATE 16. Jars excavated at Jiahu in Henan Province (China), seventh millennium B.C. According to a recent molecular archaeological investigation, these Neolithic vessels held one of the earliest fermented beverages in the world, with grape as a possible ingredient.

Slowly but surely, perhaps dating back to the period after the hypothesized in-filling of the Black Sea basin (chapter 2), humans had conquered this harsh environment and developed an integrated society, whose surplus food production supported royal courts, temples, scribal schools, and newly emergent arts and crafts. The people spoke a language called Sumerian, with no known linguistic affinities, that was transcribed as logograms—schematic pictures denoting the object or idea intended—onto clay tablets with a stylus. The great cities of Ur, Uruk, Lagash, and Kish were the legacy of the proto-Sumerians to humankind; the mounds or tells that now rise above the flat, arid landscape were once monumental ziggurats and palaces surrounded by lush gardens and fields. They represent the beginnings of complex urban life as we know it.

The urban development also spread eastward to the floodplain of the Karun River and to the city-state of Susa, in the foothills of the southern Zagros Mountains and downriver from Godin Tepe. There, another people, speaking a different language—proto-Elamite—had established themselves. Their material culture, however, can hardly be distinguished from that of their proto-Sumerian neighbors, and they shared the same cuneiform writing system of incising signs—although less pictographic in character—onto clay tablets.

Godin Tepe, situated more than 2000 meters above the alluvial lowlands and 300 kilometers north of Susa, might appear to have been a poor candidate for further expansion of an urban folk who had mastered their environment and become accustomed to a relatively sophisticated way of life. The main attraction of the Zagros Mountains was its rich resources, which included metals such gold and copper, semiprecious and other stones, wood, and a host of organic goods that were either unavailable in the lowlands or difficult to produce there. Sheep and goats, from which fine textile fibers and specialty dairy products were derived, were less efficiently raised in Lower Mesopotamia than by grazing herds in mountain pastures. Many plants—the Eurasian grapevine foremost among them—also cannot tolerate a hot, dry climate, but thrive in upland regions.

The lowlanders knew a good thing when they saw it. During the Late Uruk period, as the late Chalcolithic in Lowland Greater Mesopotamia is known, from about 3500 to 3100 B.C., they exerted their

control over a large area, from the Zagros, north into Upper Mesopotamia, west to Turkey, and as far north as the Caucasus. Although
independent traders and adventurers probably had a hand in the foreign ventures, the wholesale transposition of Lower Mesopotamian
building styles, even its bureaucratic apparatus as implied by the use
of pictographic tablets and cylinder seals, points to a royal enterprise.
Mesopotamia had not experienced such an explosion in trade since
the early Neolithic period. By setting up key trading posts and military bases, the rulers of Lower Mesopotamia could ensure a steady
supply of precious raw materials and finished products, including obsidian from Turkey and Transcaucasia, lapis lazuli from Afghanistan,
and, as can be inferred from the Gilgamesh Epic, wine from the
Zagros Mountains. As will be seen in chapter 7, the Lower Mesopotamian upper class had developed a taste—even a thirst—for the liquid elixir, which could not be slaked by the limited production of
small irrigated vineyards in the lowlands.

Godin Tepe fits all the criteria for a strategically placed Lower
Mesopotamian administrative center *cum* military base and trading
entrepôt for the central Zagros Mountains. It is located along the
"High Road" or the "Great Khorasan Road," the same route followed
by the famous Silk Road of later times. The proto-Sumerians, or
Elamites, or both, likely enlisted the local people to help build a
walled enclosure on the Citadel Mound; the summit of the mound
was stripped bare, beginning around 3500 B.C. (Early Period V at the
site), and a series of substantial mudbrick buildings forming an
"Oval" was constructed around a central courtyard. The structures
were laid out in symmetrical Lower Mesopotamian fashion, with off-
set-inset walls and niches. Pottery of lowland types, such as the ubiq-
uitous beveled-rim bowl, and as many as 43 tablets bearing numerical
notations, cylinder seal impressions, and pictographic characters also
signal the presence of lowlanders.

An intriguing assemblage of artifacts, including the sherds with the
reddish residue, were recovered from room 20 of the Oval in Late
Period V (ca. 3100–2900 B.C.). This room, although quite small,
yielded the most luxury items of any on the citadel. A rare necklace,
composed of more than 200 black and white beads, perhaps belonged
to the wife of a royal commandant. A curtain wall, shielding the

room from the courtyard, provided privacy. One's imagination about what went on here in 3500 B.C. could really take flight when the sherds with the reddish residue were reassembled to form two complete jars.

What immediately strikes one about these jars is their unusual design. The piriform shape occurs elsewhere in Mesopotamia. But the applied rope design of two inverted U shapes on opposite sides of each vessel is unique to Godin. The narrow mouth and tall neck, which contrast sharply with the style of other jars at the site, are best adapted to a container for liquids. If the jars had once held a liquid, they had been drained of their contents. The base of their necks had been carefully chipped away, apparently to remove neatly, and with a single blow, the clay stoppers that had sealed their contents. This method of "uncorking" a wine amphora and preventing the clay from contaminating the beverage is well attested 1500 years later in New Kingdom Egypt (chapter 6). One of the jars had an enigmatic small hole that had been drilled through its sidewall. The hole was about 10 centimeters above the base of the vessel, which stood about 60 centimeters high and had a capacity of approximately 30 liters. At the 1991 conference at the Robert Mondavi Winery, it was suggested that the hole might have been made to relieve gas buildup or provide a counterpressure for pouring liquid through the mouth. Vernon Singleton, a professor emeritus in the Department of Viticulture and Enology at the University of California at Davis, made the most plausible proposal: the hole was used to decant liquid without disturbing solid materials that had accumulated at the bottom of the jar. In fact, the hole was located just above the thickest accumulation of reddish residue.

Could the two jars have been filled with wine, to be consumed at a protohistoric drinking party? The festivities might even have reached a point that valuable jewelry was tossed aside and lost. We will never know the full story, but the combined archaeological evidence was enticing enough to try to find out more.

More jars like those in room 20 were excavated in an adjacent building complex. Room 18, which was surrounded by subsidiary chambers, was the focal point of the citadel. A large fireplace on its back wall would have provided heat during the cold winter months.

FIGURE 3.1. Wine jar from Godin Tepe (Iran), dating to ca. 3500–3100 B.C. After firing, a small hole was drilled a short distance above the base, possibly to decant the wine. The interior reddish deposit—the lees of the wine—is shown in color plate 2.

Two windows looked out onto the courtyard. The room had been left in disarray: carbonized lentils and barley littered the floor, and almost 2000 stone spheres, perhaps used as sling-stones to defend the Oval, were piled up in a corner. There was a wide-mouthed vessel with another unusual rope design. It has since been shown by molecular archaeological research in my laboratory to have been a container for barley beer; it has its own story to tell as the earliest chemical evidence for this drink of the masses in Lower Mesopotamia (see chapter 7).

Several jars with inverted U-shaped rope designs from room 18 were particularly intriguing. They had thick reddish deposits on their interior and belonged to an earlier phase of Period V, dating to ca. 3500–3100 B.C. These jars, with capacities of about 60 liters each, were more than twice the size of most of those from elsewhere on the citadel. When full, they would have been too heavy to move, and their liquid contents must have been ladled out.

Room 18 might well have been the central distribution facility for goods needed by the foreign contingent of merchants, soldiers, and administrators. Such rations as were needed for their home away from home—a replacement weapon, a clay tablet to write on, barley for bread and beer, or a fine wine for that special occasion—might have been parceled out from here through the two windows.

Directly across the courtyard, a very large funnel, about a half meter in diameter, and a circular "lid" of somewhat smaller dimensions were excavated in room 2. The funnel was a telling piece of archaeological evidence that the reddish residues inside the jars of rooms 18 and 20 might be related to wine. Similarly large funnels are known from well-attested winemaking installations of the Iron Age and later, and they have also been excavated at other upland Late Uruk sites in eastern Turkey and northern Syria, where the wild Eurasian grape grows today. Upon seeing the Godin funnel, McGuire Gibson of the University of Chicago's Oriental Institute opined that it would have served admirably as a strainer for grape must, especially if it were lined with a coarsely woven cloth (long since deteriorated). Grapes could have been heaped into the funnel, and the lid, weighing about a kilogram, then used to apply weight and pressure, to exude the juice and drain it into a jar. Sherds of two or possibly three jars with the inverted U rope appliqués were recovered from the room, but none had any visible reddish residue on them. It could be that they were "empties," waiting to be filled, or were from a part of the vessel where solids had not collected.

The scenario that room 2 served as a winemaking facility was plausible but lacked hard evidence. No grape pips, which are often well preserved, were reported from the room (although admittedly, the soil had not been screened or floated for archaeobotanical materials), and the funnel might have been used to transfer a liquid other than wine. The lid might have been just that—a cover for a wide-mouthed vessel. Only half of room 2 had been excavated when further work was brought to a halt by the 1979 Iranian Revolution. A rectangular "bin"—perhaps a treading platform—had begun to emerge, but any further clues about its function must await renewed excavations.

Was it possible that these seemingly disparate archaeological clues from Period V at Godin Tepe—involving a far-flung trading network of the world's first cities, upper-class orgies, and winemaking in the mountains of Iran—were interrelated and could be elucidated by chemically identifying the reddish residues inside the uniquely decorated jars?

Molecular Archaeology Comes of Age

In the time since the Godin Tepe sherds with the reddish residues were excavated in the early 1970s, the field of natural science–based archaeology has undergone a revolution. The physical and biological sciences, which are bolstered at their most basic level by an understanding of chemical composition and processes, have begun producing answers to archaeologically important questions at an ever-accelerating rate. Whether the task is to locate a site using false infrared images taken by a satellite or airplane, to decide where to dig using remote-sensing magnetometry or ground-penetrating radar, to date archaeological deposits and associated artifacts by radiocarbon or thermoluminescence, or to reconstruct the ecological setting of a site on the basis of its plant and animal remains, the natural sciences enter into almost every stage of a modern archaeological investigation. With the advent of high-powered computer graphics programs, capable of handling and enhancing enormous databases, it may someday be possible to "excavate" a site and analyze all the materials without even putting a spade to it.

In the last 20 years, the prospects for analyzing ancient organic remains have dramatically changed. A range of highly sensitive analytical tools—gas and liquid chromatographs, mass spectrometers, nuclear magnetic resonance instruments, DNA sequencers—has become standard laboratory equipment. Refinements in other techniques, such as infrared spectrometry, have also occurred. The upshot is that the modern archaeological scientist now has tools that can measure milli-, even microgram, quantities of ancient organics. The applications of this new technology in archaeology, what can be referred to as molecular archaeology, are virtually endless.

Whole new chapters in human and environmental history, including ethnicity and genetic development, diet, disease, cuisine, and materials processing, are being opened up. Lipids, resins, dyes, perfume ingredients, and drugs are some of the organic compounds that have been found to be well enough preserved in certain archaeological contexts—usually either in a dry climate or in a waterlogged environment where microbial activity and autoxidation is reduced—to be detected and characterized.

The Molecular Archaeology Laboratory, which I head in the Museum Applied Science Center for Archaeology (MASCA) at the University of Pennsylvania Museum has been at the forefront of these advances. Our first foray into this field was the discovery of the earliest chemically attested instance of Royal Purple, or DBI. Working closely with a retired analytical organic chemist from the Dupont Company and a research associate in MASCA, Rudolph ("Rudy") Michel, we focused on several sherds with a purplish residue on their interior. The sherds had been excavated in the early 1970s by a University of Pennsylvania Museum team, under the direction of James Pritchard, at the Phoenician site of Sarepta, along the southern coast of Lebanon between Tyre and Sidon.

The research held a particular fascination for me, because I was on the expedition and handled the pottery when it came out of the ground. Classical writers had credited the Phoenicians with discovering the purple dye, so it was possible that the sherds were covered with genuine molluscan purple. Nearby, piles of *Murex* shells had even been excavated. Moreover, according to radiocarbon determinations, the sherds belonged to the Late Bronze Age (fourteenth–thirteenth century B.C.), a period preceding the Phoenicians proper. If the purple residue was indeed Royal Purple, the sherds would provide definitive evidence for the dye's production by the Canaanite ancestors of the Phoenicians.

A very small piece of one sherd, with a thin purplish coating, was selected for the initial analysis. Because we had so little material, we first used nondestructive techniques—proton-induced X-ray emission (PIXE) spectrometry and X-ray photoelectron spectroscopy—which showed that the compound contained bromine, and this element had the same binding energy to carbon as the bromine in synthetic DBI. Diffuse-reflectance Fourier-transform infrared (FT-IR) spectrometry, which has been the workhorse of our molecular archaeology program and which is based on the principle that different chemical functionalities absorb infrared light at different wavelengths, revealed that the amino group in the molecule for DBI and the ancient specimen had identical infrared absorptions. With these data in hand, a spectroscopist would be satisfied that genuine molluscan Royal Purple had been identified.

A destructive wet-chemical test proved the presence of DBI beyond doubt. Royal Purple and indigo are the only known so-called vat dyes of antiquity. This family of dyes is characterized by their ability to be reduced to a soluble dye (the leuco base, which is yellowish) and then reprecipitated to the solid on exposure to air (oxygen). This chemical behavior of the indigoid dyes enables them to be used as fast textile dyes; after immersion of the textile in the leuco base solution, large dye molecules are encapsulated in the interstices of the material after they revert to the solid. DBI as the leuco base has another characteristic property: the bromine atoms will be lost if the solution is exposed to ultraviolet (UV) radiation, whether from daylight or a fluorescent bulb. Consequently, on exposure to air, the leuco base solution will change to a blue (indigo) color rather than the original purple. By dropping a warm reducing solution (alkaline hydrosulfite) onto a minute piece of the ancient Sarepta sherd, one observed the formation of the yellowish leuco base solution, which then started to reprecipitate as the purple-colored DBI, after which blue indigo began to form on further exposure to air and debromination by light. The ancient Royal Purple thus behaved exactly like a vat dye of synthetic DBI.

Just about the time that we were finishing our investigation of Royal Purple, Ginny showed up on my doorstep. She was proposing that we embark on the study of another important, high-end product of antiquity: wine. We now knew that at least one type of ancient biomolecule could be preserved intact, even though the specimens were 3000 years old. Why not see if ancient wine was another?

Identifying the Godin Tepe Jar Residues by Infrared Spectrometry

The possibility of identifying ancient wine using modern molecular archaeological techniques far exceeds that which was possible by wet-chemical methods only a half century ago. Although some excellent work on wine has been and continues to be done by older methods, irreplaceable material can be lost, with little to show for the effort. An instructive instance is the analysis of liquid samples from the Byzantine site of Niš in Yugoslavia, which were believed to be wine. The researchers took the bull by the horns and tasted the liquid on the assumption that their sensory organs were at least as good as any other available equipment. The taste test, as well as some other wet-chemical tests, proved inconclusive. The researchers concluded: "Der 'Wein von Niš' ist Wasser" (German: "The 'wine of Niš' is water").

The wine production and consumption scenarios proposed for Godin Tepe would stand or fall on whether the jars indeed contained organic substances derived from grapes, and, if they did, whether a grape juice had been intentionally fermented into wine. It should first be noted that wine is an unusually complex mixture of organic compounds, including alcohols, aldehydes, acids, carbohydrates, esters, proteins, vitamins, polyhydroxyaromatics including tannins, anthocyanins, flavonols and catechins. The range of compounds enhances the probability that some organics or their degradation products would have been preserved in an ancient context.

Diffuse-reflectance FT-IR has already been mentioned as a fundamental, versatile technique for ancient organic analysis. Particularly at the beginning of a molecular archaeological investigation, when it is not even known whether one is dealing with an organic or an inorganic residue, FT-IR is essential. In the diffuse-reflectance mode, it is not even necessary to extract or prepare the sample, as is often done, by mixing the material in an optically transparent medium, such as potassium bromide, for homogeneous light scattering. Instead, a small piece of the sherd with the reddish residue is placed in the path of the infrared beam, which nondestructively bounces off the sample and then is redirected toward the detector.

State-of-the-art FT-IR instruments in use today no longer measure the infrared absorptions at individual frequencies but use a statistical technique called Fourier transformation. By this method, multiple passes of infrared light are rapidly reflected off the sample and recombined with the reference beam by a moving mirror to yield an "interferogram." After Fourier-transform processing, the interferogram yields a precise absorption spectrum of the sample, with minimal background noise.

We specifically targeted tartaric acid, which, in the Middle East, occurs naturally in large amounts only in grapes. As a standard, we ran a synthetic sample of the naturally occurring isomer of tartaric acid—the so-called L-(+) form. Another reference sample, which had a high probability of being ancient wine, was also analyzed. This sample was a dark-colored deposit on the inside of an amphora from the ancient Nubian site of Gebel Adda, now submerged by the waters of Lake Nasser behind the Aswan Dam. There was little doubt that the amphora once contained wine. It was a specific pottery type for importing wine from Upper Egypt into Nubia during the late Byzantine period (fourth to sixth century A.D.). Whole villages in Nubia were composed largely of taverns, and empty amphoras, like the one tested, were piled in heaps around the taverns.

Our initial FT-IR spectrum of the surface scrapings of the interior reddish residue of the Godin Tepe jar gave evidence of organics but

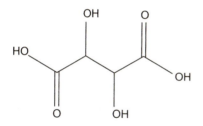

FIGURE 3.2. Chemical structure of tartaric acid, which occurs naturally as the dextrorotatory stereoisomer (causing polarized light to rotate to the right). At the plant's death, this isomer converts to a racemic mixture with two other forms.

was dominated by silicates from the pottery. More definitive results were obtained by extracting several sherds with boiling acetone. This procedure, yielding 6–7 milligrams of a resinous-looking solid, drew out the ancient organic molecules that were bound up in the porous matrix of the pottery. In general, these organics could be expected to be more representative of what the jar originally contained, having been absorbed in the pottery fabric and less subject to environmental contamination and degradation than surface residues.

The FT-IR spectra of the Godin Tepe jar extracts, the Nubian reference sample of ancient wine, and synthetic tartaric acid were very similar. Tartaric acid was present in the ancient samples, as revealed by doublet carbonyl peaks at 1740–1720 cm^{-1} and medium-intense bands between 1470 and 1385 cm^{-1} and at 1250–1240 cm^{-1}, associated with the two carboxylic acid groups of the compound. In addition, the absorption band at 1650–1600 cm^{-1} suggested the presence of some salts of tartaric acid.

A strong hydrocarbon band centered at around 2900 cm^{-1} pointed to large amounts of other organics in the Godin Tepe and ancient Nubian samples. In chapter 4, one very important component that was identified by liquid chromatography—a tree resin—is described in detail. Infrared spectrometric analysis of a complex mixture has the disadvantage that compounds are not unambiguously identified. Chromatography enables the separation and identification of individual organic constituents. Because the main objective of our pilot study was to determine the presence or absence of tartaric acid, we decided to forgo the chromatographic study and instead followed up the FT-IR analysis with a highly specific spot test, developed by Fritz Feigl.

In the Feigl test, as small a quantity of tartaric acid as a microgram in the mixture is converted with β, β'-dinaphthol and concentrated sulfuric acid to a compound that exhibits green fluorescence under UV light. Samples from the Godin Tepe jars and the Nubian amphora, as well synthetic L-(+) tartaric acid, all gave the same, characteristic green fluorescence. Here, we had again employed a wet-chemical method, which destroyed a small amount of valuable material, but it provided the all-important confirmation of the FT-IR results.

Archaeological Inference

The chemical confirmation of ancient tartaric acid in the Godin Tepe jars was the crucial link in the chain of archaeological inferences about winemaking, drinking, and trade at the site. Yet, the presence of tartaric acid by itself is not sufficient to establish what kind of grape product was in the jars. The archaeological clues did point to its being a liquid, from which solid materials had settled out to form the reddish residues. But had the goal been to produce wine or vinegar? Another possibility—a grape syrup—was ruled out because a thick, viscous liquid would probably have left a uniform coating of residue on the inside of the jars. Concentrating grape juice down by heating is still used to make the popular *shireh* of modern Iran and was known to the ancient peoples of Mesopotamia as well as the Greeks and Romans. It enables the fruit to be preserved, and, diluted with water, it produces a refreshing, nonalcoholic beverage.

On the assumption that the reddish residue in the jars represented a grape juice, it is a short step in making an excellent case that wine was the intended product. The warm climate and slow pressing methods of antiquity would ensure that the grape juice quickly fermented to wine, very likely in the first few days after the juice had been expressed from the fruit. Grape must fermentation proceeds rapidly owing to a variety of wild yeasts, especially *Saccharomyces cerevisiae*, which are present on some grape skins. Oxygen respiration is re-

quired for the growth and multiplication of the yeast cells and, consequently, for the course and degree of fermentation. The continued
availability of oxygen after fermentation has ceased, however, will
lead to the multiplication of acetic acid bacteria (*Acetobacter*), which
are responsible for the conversion of ethanol to acetic acid (vinegar).

Specific safeguards must be taken to prevent the dreaded "wine
disease" that results in mouth-puckering vinegar. For example, a liquid slurry of clay or a slip can be applied to the inside and outside of
the vessel, as was observed on several of the Godin jars. When the
pottery was fired, a barrier was created that prevented oxygen from
diffusing into the jar.

Stoppering the jar is even more critical for keeping wine. Seven
clay stoppers, several of which had been seal-impressed with lowland
Mesopotamian motifs showing processions of cattle, goats, and lions,
were found in the Oval, not far from the jars with the reddish residue. Unfired or sun-baked clay readily disintegrates, so it is possible
that more stoppers were represented in the debris of rooms 2, 18, and
20. The diameters of the largest stoppers recovered were slightly less
than the neck diameters of the smaller 30-liter jars. When wetted,
the clay stoppers would have expanded to form a tight seal and keep
air out. Moreover, although vinegar had its place in ancient cuisine
as a marinating agent, preservative, and condiment, it is unlikely that
several hundred liters of this liquid would have been needed in proto-
historic times. These were persuasive archaeological arguments that
the ancient winemaker, in collaboration with his fellow potter, had
made a deliberate effort to preserve his liquid as wine. The most
telling piece of evidence that wine was the intended product—the
addition of a tree resin to prevent the liquid from going to vinegar—
is reserved for chapter 4.

From Grape Juice to Wine to Vinegar

The line of argumentation needed to establish whether
an ancient jar contained wine and not another grape product, such as
grape juice or vinegar, bears repeating here, because it will enter over
and over again into the story that follows. The minimal requirements

are as follows. First, tartaric acid or one of its salts, or both, must be present, because the Eurasian grape (*Vitis vinifera vinifera*) is the only known, abundant natural source of this acid (produced during the maturation of the fruit) and its related compounds (formed during the winemaking process or in a postburial calcareous environment) in the Middle East. Tartaric acid is found farther afield in East Africa (the baobab tree) and South Asia (tamarind fruit), but it is highly unlikely that products of these plants were traded to the Near East before the middle of the first millennium B.C., if by then, and, in any event, that period falls near the end of the time span of interest here. Possibly, but again improbably, another significant natural source of tartaric acid might be discovered in the Middle East to account for the ancient chemical evidence. Tartaric acid is thus a fingerprint or a marker compound for grape and its derived products, including but not limited to grape juice, wine, and vinegar, in the Middle East.

My laboratory uses three independent analytical techniques to establish the chemical presence of tartaric acid and its salts in an ancient sample. Only if the compound is attested by all three analyses, as based on unequivocal observations and stringent statistical comparisons and a thorough search of large databases (comprising many relevant natural products and processed organic materials, synthetic compounds, modern wine samples, and "ancient wine reference samples" as identified by inscriptions on the outside of the vessels), is tartaric acid said to be present. In the Feigl test, a green fluorescence must be observed, because malic acid, in particular, yields a non-fluorescing green solution as a false positive. Results from the other analyses—chromatograms and IR and UV spectra—can be equivocal, because several compounds may be present or account for the evidence. Overlapping and similar absorption bands need to be carefully scrutinized and disentangled, or "deconvoluted," by statistical methods. Most of ancient unknown samples identified as containing tartaric acid and its salts chemically matched both the modern synthetic compounds and the ancient wine reference samples, a circumstance that is best explained as due to their sharing other degraded grape components.

As new, more sensitive methods of analysis have become available, we have applied those methods to samples already run. For example, my laboratory carried out and published the first gas chromatog-raphy–mass spectrometry (GC-MS) analyses of Royal Purple, and we now regularly use liquid chromatography–mass spectrometry (LC-MS) to study ancient foods and beverages. Yet, no single technique is a magic bullet for detecting every ancient compound. In the Royal Purple study, MS could not distinguish between dibromoindigotin and its isomer, dibromoindirubin, because the two have the same molecular weight; UV-visible spectrophotometry proved essential in that instance. Similarly, MS has not been able to provide confirmatory evidence for tartaric acid and its salts, even after conversion to the methyl ester, because of the insufficient volatility or polarity of the compounds.

Second, the fabrication and style of the vessel being analyzed must be assessed as to whether it held a liquid, a semiliquid, or a solid material. Narrow, high-mouthed jars and jugs, for example, were most likely used to handle and store liquids. Deep, open vats or bowls, on the other hand, are most convenient for processing more viscous materials or for serving solid food. The archaeologist bases his or her inferences on historical, ethnographic, and modern analogies.

Third, if it is probable that the vessel contained a liquid and if tartaric acid and its salts have been determined to be present, then fermentation of the grape juice to wine must have occurred, as argued above and as known from modern enological knowledge. Until the Roman period, the ancient winemaker lacked an inhibitor, such as sulfur, to stop the process. Fermentation will run until completion: that is, until the yeast can no longer survive in the high-alcohol solution.

Fourth, with the continued availability of oxygen, the ethanol will be further fermented to acetic acid or vinegar. Archaeological observation and inference are again the best guides in making this determination. If many jars, representing a large volume of liquid, are found in a single archaeological context—such as the Neolithic "kitchen" at Hajji Firuz Tepe (chapter 4)—and tartaric acid and its salts are attested in the ancient samples, then it is likely that wine rather than vinegar was the intended product. Vinegar is useful in food preparation but large quantities are not needed as they are of wine, which serves the same purposes and is eminently drinkable. If a jar of wine were to go bad, an inevitable occurrence in ancient time, it would provide more than enough vinegar for the householder.

The final piece of evidence in interpreting an ancient sample that tests positive for tartaric acid and its salts as wine is whether a deliberate effort was made to cut off the oxygen supply and prevent the wine from going to vinegar. Tight-fitting stoppers, relatively impermeable pottery fabrics, surface coatings, and the like were some of the means available to ancient winemakers. As will be explained in chapter 4, adding a tree resin to the wine was one of the most popular and widespread practices in antiquity.

As in any historical science, absolute certainty is unattainable. When any particular line of evidence—perhaps the archaeological context or the type of vessel or the detailed chemical justification—is pushed too hard, skepticism can arise. Chemists might request more evidence for the chemical compounds claimed to be present, and archaeologists might propose different interpretations of how vessels were used. The coherence of the archaeological and chemical data must be assessed in each instance and a judgment made as to whether the "wine hypothesis" best accounts for the available evidence. Then, necessary consequences if the hypothesis is true are deduced and tested further. Unfortunately, any alcohol in the ancient samples has long since evaporated, so it cannot be the basis for distinguishing wine from grape juice or vinegar. Acetic acid is sometimes detected in ancient samples, but it could have formed later. When DNA analysis (chapter 5) confirmed the presence of the "wine yeast" (*Saccharomyces cerevisiae*) in ancient Egyptian jar residues, however, the likelihood that they contained wine was strengthened.

Winemaking at the Dawn of Civilization

Once we had accepted the archaeological and chemical data for the jars recovered from the Oval at Godin Tepe as sufficient to interpret them as wine containers, we had to determine where the wine was produced. The unique decoration of the jars, as well as the difficulty in transporting the larger 60-liter type, are in keeping with local production. Yet, no grape remains were reported from room 2, which has been interpreted as a winemaking installation, or elsewhere on the site from the Late Uruk period. Grape pips belonging to the first millennium B.C., however, were recovered. The negative evidence for the earlier period is less compelling when it is remembered that no archaeobotanist was on site and that soil samples were not routinely sieved or floated.

The winemaking installation might appear to have been rather spartan, consisting of only a large funnel, a putative lid for pressing the grapes, and a possible treading vat. The actual processing of grapes into wine need not be very complex, as is well attested by later textual and pictorial evidence, especially from Egypt (chapters 5 and 6). Grapes were first treaded in crushing vats to extract the juice or must. A bag press or a funnel and weight might have been used to squeeze out any remaining juice from the solid residue. Pottery jars were then filled with the juice, which quickly fermented to wine by natural processes. The jars were completely stoppered only after most of the fermentation had occurred. A similar series of steps was probably involved in producing the wine contained in the Godin jars. Even the development of specialized pottery vessels and storage techniques for winemaking are not beyond the expertise of village or small-scale household vintners.

A more serious issue in the way of accepting local wine production at Godin Tepe is whether the wild vine or a domesticated transplant grew in the vicinity of the site in the late fourth millennium B.C. The wild vine is found today some 500 kilometers farther north in the Zagros Mountains, although sporadic occurrences have been reported around Godin. Moister, milder conditions in antiquity might have encouraged a more southerly distribution in the Late Uruk period. An even more probable scenario is that the domesticated grapevine had already been transplanted to the site from farther north. What can be interpreted as Transcaucasian pottery types first made their appearance in Early Period V and constitute as much as a third of the assemblage from the end of the period. The Caucasus and the northern Zagros Mountains (chapter 4) have produced the earliest evidence for viniculture, dating to the Neolithic period. Any contacts with that region might well have led to the transplantation of the Eurasian grapevine, along with the requisite knowledge of how to make wine.

If one were to go looking for an early center of wine production, well situated to grow grapes and supply the emergent city-states of lowland Mesopotamia, Godin Tepe is an excellent place to begin. It is centrally located on a major trade route through the Zagros Mountains. The area is extensively planted with the grapevine today and might also have been during the Late Uruk period. Larger scale production facilities than those already found, possibly overseen by royal officials on the citadel, might have been located closer to the vineyards; they are yet to be discovered and excavated. The entrepreneurial and experimental spirit of the period, so evident in the extensive trade connections, urban development, agriculture, and horticulture of the lowlands, might thus have found another outlet in highland winemaking.

The First Wine Rack?

Even in this highly technological age, the preferred method to store wine is in sealed bottles on their side, although we may prefer cork to raw clay stoppers. What was especially noteworthy about the reddish residue inside the Godin Tepe jars from room 20, the Late Period V residence which might have been the scene of a proto-historic drinking fest, was that it covered only one side of the vessel. In other words, the deposit was exactly where one would expect precipitates to have settled out from a liquid in a vessel that was stored on its side.

The interior reddish residue was also on the same side as one of the U-shaped rope decorations that had been applied to the outside of the jar. During the Late Uruk period, rope designs often indicate the placement of real rope that served practical purposes. Other jars, such as the beer container from room 18 (chapter 7), had rope appliqués that looped in and out of handles and even formed knots, as might have been done to hold down a covering over the mouth of the vessel or to enable it to be moved. The U-shaped rope design on the wine jars seemed meaningless until Ginny Badler suggested that it might have depicted how an actual strand of rope was used to support the jar on its side. Some simple experiments were carried out and quickly confirmed this as a possibility. With the jar lying on its side, the clay stopper would have been permanently moistened, thus preventing it from drying out, shrinking, and letting in air that would spoil the wine.

Of course, other explanations for the U-shaped rope appliqués can be entertained. Perhaps, they were purely decorative. There are also other reasons for placing or turning a vessel on its side. It can be a convenient, space-saving measure, as suggested by a horizontal wine rack that was mounted close to the ceiling in a tavern at Pompei, three millennia later. In attempting to get as much liquid as possible out of a container, one can turn a jar upside down, causing residues to slide along one side of the vessel. Or a jar might be deliberately tilted to scoop out the solid material. The uniform, thick accumulation along one side of each Godin jar, however, is more in keeping with a longer-term storage of the vessel on its side.

One could imaginatively re-create the ancient scene. Several wine jars had been stoppered and stored on their side in a cellar or dark recess of the Oval. After a year or two, the harshness of the young wine had mellowed out, and the solid lees of tartrate crystals and yeast had settled out. Then the day came when a royal courier or dignitary arrived from the lowlands or a special ceremony was called for, and the jars were brought out. They were set upright, with some of the lees running down the sidewalls and collecting on the bottom of the vessels. The mouths of the vessels were carefully chipped away and clopped off. A small hole was drilled near the base of one vessel, opposite the reddish residue on the other side, possibly to speed up the emptying process. The party (or ceremony) had begun.

A Symposium in the True Sense of the Word

The perforated Godin Tepe jar was the focus of another animated gathering at the Robert Mondavi Winery in the spring of 1991, albeit with serious academic overtones. Ginny Badler made a special trip from Philadelphia to the Royal Ontario Museum in Toronto, Canada, to pick up the vessel and accompany it by plane to California and back again to Toronto after the conference. Her adventures are amusingly retold in "Travels with Jarley."

FIGURE 3.3. Virginia Badler and the author presenting the Godin Tepe wine jar to the media at the 1991 Robert Mondavi wine conference.

With the generous support of the winery and its founder, many of the world's authorities on viniculture and ancient wine assembled to discuss the origins and ancient history of wine for nearly a week. A wide range of fields—archaeology, archaeobotany, food science, genetics, history, linguistics, art, and enology—was represented. Although each participant had a special perspective on the same topic, few had ever met before or benefited from an exchange of ideas. As two wines flowed at every lunch and four at every dinner, our discussions took on the spirit, even ferment, of a Greek symposium. Discussions went well into the night. I think that everyone who attended the 1991 conference left with the sense that it would be difficult to ever duplicate it. And what better way to put the ancient adage *in vino veritas* to the historical and scientific test?

The Godin discovery raised many more questions than it answered. Were the wine jars, which are of a type that is not known elsewhere, imported from a region that has not been explored archaeologically or at least that has not been reported in the literature? Or were the unique jars, in which wine apparently was stored in stoppered vessels laid on their side (greatly anticipating our modern wine rack!), rather evidence of local wine production, which might have been shipped out in containers made of an organic material, such as leather or wood, long since disintegrated?

Much broader questions could be posed. If cereal agriculture is known to have started as early as 9500 B.C. in the Near East, then what was the archaeological and archaeobotanical evidence for grapes and wine preceding 3500 B.C., the date of the earliest jars from Godin Tepe? At the end of the conference, everyone was sent off with the admonition to reexcavate wine-related artifacts and samples from older excavations and investigations in their museums, store-rooms, and laboratories. Possibly, even earlier evidence for the beginnings of viticulture and winemaking was right in front of our noses, waiting to be discovered and analyzed.

CHAPTER 4

Neolithic Wine!

AFTER the 1991 wine conference at the Robert Mondavi Winery, I was on the lookout for any Neolithic wine specimens. And what was a better place to look than my own University of Pennsylvania Museum, which has one of the best collections of well-documented excavated artifacts in the world? As a member of the Hasanlu Project in northwestern Iran, Mary Voigt had directed an excavation at Hajji Firuz Tepe, a Neolithic site in the northern Zagros Mountains, southwest of Lake Urmia, in 1968. It was a simple matter to ask Mary, now a professor of anthropology at the College of William and Mary, whether she had seen any prospective wine vessels among those that had come back to Penn as part of the division with the Iranian authorities. I also asked her whether she had ever noted any intriguing residues inside the Neolithic vessels that she had excavated. Yes, she told me, she did remember a curious yellowish deposit on several pottery sherds from Hajji Firuz that were later reconstructed into a complete jar. The residues were confined to the inside lower half of the jar. At the time, she had thought that the residue might be from milk, yogurt, or some other dairy product. After the jar had been dismantled, chemical analysis had been carried out. The test proved negative, and the sherds were consigned to the Near Eastern storage room in the museum's basement for the next 25 years. The effort to relocate them held out the prospect that more definite results could be achieved by using the more sophisticated chemical methods of the new molecular archaeology.

FIGURE 4.1. Mary Voigt excavating the Neolithic "kitchen" (ca. 5400–5000 B.C.) at Hajji Firuz Tepe (Iran). It yielded six wine jars.

A Momentous Innovation

The possibility of discovering chemical evidence for Neolithic wine provided an enormous incentive for reopening the investigation of the Hajji Firuz sherds with the yellowish residue. If winemaking is best understood as an intentional human activity rather than a seasonal happenstance, then the Neolithic period in the Near East, from about 8500 to 4000 B.C., is the first time in human prehistory when the necessary preconditions for this momentous innovation came together. Most important, Neolithic communities of the ancient Near East and Egypt were permanent, year-round settlements, which were made possible by domesticated plants and animals such as cereals and ruminants. With a more secure, even more restricted, food supply than nomadic groups and with a more stable base of operations, what might be termed a Neolithic cuisine emerged. Using a variety of food-processing techniques—fermentation, soaking, heating, spicing, and so forth—Neolithic peoples were, as far as we know, the first to produce bread, beer, and an array of meat and grain entrées that we continue to enjoy today.

Minor crafts, which are important in food preparation, storage, and serving, advanced in tandem with the new cuisine. Of special significance for winemaking are pottery and plaster vessels, which first appeared around 6000 B.C. The plasticity of clay made it an ideal material for forming shapes, such as narrow-mouthed vats and storage jars, for producing and keeping wine. The resultant pottery, after the clay had been fired to high temperatures, is essentially indestructible, and its porous structure helps to absorb organics—a boon for archaeological chemists. Clays belong to the family of hydrated alumino-silicates, which also includes the zeolite minerals. Zeolites and clays share the same property: they are excellent ion-exchange materials. More polar organic compounds will thus be "locked" in place in the silicate matrix of the ancient pottery, as long as the ground water does not introduce more powerful agents or upset the chemical equilibrium, and can remain intact for centuries.

Horticulture of grapevines and other Near Eastern plants (such as the olive, fig, date, and pomegranate) has often been viewed as a relatively late prehistoric development, beginning toward the end of the fourth millennium B.C. and rapidly expanding during the third millennium. Archaeobotanical remains (seeds, wood, skins, and so on) of horticultural products, which are more prevalent in archaeological contexts of this later period, provide the primary evidence for this hypothesis. However, systematic collection of botanical materials has been carried out at ancient Near Eastern and Egyptian sites only over the past few decades, and the morphological features that have been used to distinguish wild from domesticated types can be misleading.

Specifically for the grape, carbonized pips constitute the bulk of the archaeobotanical evidence, and the supposed domesticated grape seed has been argued to be more elongated (i.e., with a lower breadth to length ratio) than its wild counterpart. Experimental charring of modern pips has shown that a narrower pip can be expanded and rounded, blurring the distinction between the pips of the wild and domesticated subspecies.

The prospects for finding Neolithic wine seemed especially good, because many Neolithic sites are located in upland, mountainous regions of the Near East and this is where the wild Eurasian grape thrives. At an elevation of over 1200 meters above sea level, Hajji Firuz Tepe is located along the eastern periphery of the wild vine's modern distribution in the hill country bordering northern Mesopotamia.

Once Mary Voigt had "reexcavated" a pottery sherd with the yellowish residue from museum storage, our chemical investigation began in earnest. Only about 13 centimeters long and 5 centimeters wide, the sherd was covered with a thin yellowish deposit. It had once formed part of the base of a jar with a long, narrow neck, and a volume of about 9 liters. This jar was the best candidate for a liquid container at the site. It was plainer than the Godin Tepe jars (chapter 3); it lacked decoration except for a highly polished surface and even had a dowdy look with a pronounced bulge of the lower body (color plate 3). It was found together with five similar jars embedded in the earthen floor along one wall of a "kitchen" of a Neolithic mudbrick building, dated by radiocarbon determinations to about 5400–5000 B.C. The building, which was well made and not unlike modern village houses in the area today, was approximately 10 square meters in area. A large living room, which may have doubled as a bedroom, the kitchen, and two storage rooms might have accommodated an extended family. The use of the room in which the jars were found as a kitchen was supported by the findings of numerous pottery vessels that were probably used to prepare and cook foods and a fireplace.

After the extraction of the sherd with boiling methanol, my laboratory carried out the standard battery of infrared, liquid chromatographic, and wet-chemical analyses. The results clearly showed the presence of tartaric acid as well as calcium tartrate. Although the principal salt that precipitates from wine is potassium bitartrate, the even more insoluble calcium salt can be expected to accumulate with time in a calcareous environment such as exists around Hajji Firuz. Clay stoppers of approximately the same diameter as the Hajji

Firuz jar mouths were found nearby, so the expertise had been available to seal the jars and prevent any wine from going to vinegar. All the available evidence thus supported the conclusion that the Hajji Firuz jars had originally contained wine, as had the jars dating more than 2000 years later at Godin Tepe in the central Zagros Mountains.

Because we have no written texts, it is impossible to know whether the wine drinkers at Hajji Firuz Tepe were confined to the upper class. The Neolithic houses are similar in construction and layout to those in modern "middle-class" villages of the area, and, if their artifact assemblages reflect reality, the living standards of the ancient inhabitants were very much on a par with one another. Wine may have been a democratizing element in Neolithic Hajji Firuz society, as it is today among Georgians and Armenians, whether as a beverage enjoyed by the populace at large or, as part of the kitchen larder, a special ingredient used in cooking.

Liquid Chromatography: Another Tool of Molecular Archaeology

The analysis of the Hajji Firuz extract by high-performance liquid chromatography (HP-LC) pointed to a chemical component that made it virtually certain that the jar had originally contained wine. According to the FT-IR results (see chapter 3), this component was marked by infrared absorptions at frequencies of about 2900 and 2850 cm^{-1}, which are characteristic of hydrocarbon compounds that are composed essentially of only hydrogen and carbon.

The spectral peaks cannot be explained by tartaric acid or its salts, which absorb very little in the 2900–2850 cm^{-1} range. Depending on how well the wine had been filtered and fined, one can imagine that many chemical compounds from the ancient grape pulp, skin, seeds, and stems had been left behind in the dregs of the jar. Tannins, which are concentrated in the grape skins and give the wine much of its color and a good deal of its taste, might be responsible for the absorptions. Or the peaks might be due to scaled-down versions of the large, polymerized tannin molecules: pigments of the anthocyanidin or flavonoid classes of compounds. Media attention has focused on these healthy, or "good," compounds in wine lately, because of their polyhydroxyaromatic or polyphenolic structures. The double bonds of resveratrol and related compounds are able to "gobble up" oxygen and scavenge free radicals, thereby lowering cholesterol and protecting humans against cancers and other ailments. Their conjugated resonance structures have the added benefit for molecular archaeological investigations that the compounds are extremely stable and can survive intact for hundreds, if not thousands, of years.

Contrary to expectations, the HP-LC results did not implicate any of these compounds. Rather, the intense FT-IR hydrocarbon bands of the Hajji Firuz extract were caused by a resin from the terebinth tree (*Pistacia atlantica* Desf.), which is characterized by a group of polycyclic compounds called triterpenoids. Terpenoids, like polyhydroxyaromatics, are usually unsaturated and capable of acting as antioxidants. They are made up of a fixed number of units of isoprene, a five-carbon branched compound with a conjugated double bond system, which is also the building block for natural rubber. In the case of the triterpenoids, six isoprene entities are fused into four or five rings. Different triterpenoids vary in their side chains, where methyl groups are attached, the placement of their double bonds, and to what extent they are oxidized. The main triterpenoids of the terebinth family of resins are all acids, whose names—moronic, oleanoic, masticadienonic, iso-masticadienonic—suggest their uses, sources, and possible long-term effects.

We routinely use HP-LC in our laboratory to separate complex mixtures of chemical compounds. Microgram quantities of an ancient sample can be separated by HP-LC. The extract is dissolved in a solvent or eluent and passed through a column lined with a substrate of extremely fine particles (3–10 micrometers) of a material that can be more or less polar. Depending on the polarity and mass of the unknown components, as well as the polarity and flow rate of eluent, components come off the column at different retention times. The challenge is to determine the best set of conditions to separate fully the components of an unknown archaeological sample. As various fractions come off the separation column, they are passed through an ultraviolet- (UV) visible spectrophotometer detector. In the UV region of the electromagnetic spectrum, valence electrons and double bonds are particularly susceptible to excitation. The chromophores of some compounds have well-defined UV spectra, and identifications were made by searching our database of several hundred ancient and modern samples. Follow-up gas chromatography–mass spectrometry (GC-MS) analyses corroborated our findings.

The UV absorption spectrum of the unknown component closely matched that of terebinth tree resin, which was known as the "queen of resins" in Roman times. The relative amounts of the four triterpenoid acids distinguish terebinth tree resin from the famous Chios mastic, a more viscous oleoresin that is exuded from the "terebinth bush" (*Pistacia lentiscus*), growing only on the island of Chios in the Aegean Sea.

The terebinth tree, a member of the pistachio family, is widespread and abundant throughout the Middle East, occurring even in desert areas. A single tree, which can grow 12 meters high and 2 meters in diameter, can yield up to 2 kilograms of the resin in late summer or fall, at just about the same time the grapes are ready to be picked. Today, the resin is still used to make chewing gum and perfume in the Middle East. Although our word *turpentine* actually derives from the word *terebinth*, the natural resin, unlike the concentrated distillate, is not offensive in taste and smell.

Ancient Retsina: A Beverage and a Medicine

Pliny the Elder, the famous first-century A.D. Roman encyclopedist, devoted a good part of book 14 of his *Historia naturalis* to the problem of preventing wine from turning to vinegar. In fact, he wrote:

> There is no department of man's life on which more labor is spent—as if nature had not given us the most healthy of beverages to drink, water . . . and so much toil and labor and expense is paid as the price of a thing that perverts men's minds and produces madness, having caused the commission of thousands of crimes, and being so attractive that a large part of mankind knows of nothing else worth living for.

He went on to say that the best way to prevent the dreaded "wine disease" was to add a tree resin—whether pine, cedar, frankincense,

or myrrh, but most often terebinth—to the wine. Despite some negative sentiments about overindulgence, Pliny extolled the quality and
medicinal benefits of some 50 wines produced in Italy and abroad
(see chapter 12).

Another first-century A.D. writer, Columella, speaks of a *medica-
mentum* made of myrrh, terebinth resin, pitch, and various spices, in
his *De re rustica* (*On Agriculture*, 12.18ff.). The idea that was evidently being propounded here and elsewhere was that what was a
standard treatment or medication for a human wound could also preserve wine. The tree itself is protected by the resin; the sticky liquid
is secreted when the bark is gashed and solidifies as a protective coating. Pathogenic microorganisms are thus prevented from attacking
the tree, and loss of sap from the wound is kept to a minimum. The
pragmatic observation and practice of the ancients have been confirmed by modern chemical investigation. Triterpenoids and diter-
penoids, which predominate in pine tree resins, have been shown to
have bactericidal properties, which impede the proliferation of acetic
acid bacteria and other microorganisms.

The premier Roman wine additive was myrrh, the famed Arabian
incense, which also has analgesic effects. If the desired goal of preventing the wine from becoming vinegar failed, at least one's senses
were numbed. In general, the aromatics in tree resins covered up any
offensive taste or smell. However, myrrh and other exotic tree resins,
such as frankincense, were derived from trees that grow only on the
Arabian peninsula and the Horn of Africa. Before the rise of camel
caravaneering around 800 B.C. across the Great Sandy Desert or
Empty Quarter (Rub'al Khali) and north through the Hejaz, myrrh
and frankincense were not widely available to Middle Eastern cultures, and our Neolithic winemaker had to be content with terebinth
tree resin.

Neolithic peoples, such as those in the village of Hajji Firuz, probably already had an appreciation for the preservative and medicinal
properties of tree resins. Their use, particularly in combination with
wine, continued to expand in later periods throughout the ancient
Near East and Egypt, whose pharmacopoeias during literate times
were dominated by these ingredients. In an upland region such as
Hajji Firuz, where the wild grapevine actually grows on and is sup-

ported by the terebinth tree, fruit and resin would have been produced at about the same time of the year, during the late summer or
early fall. Mixing these products together might then have occurred
accidentally or as a result of an innovative impulse. The important
point, however it was accomplished, is that the Hajji Firuz sample
clearly was a mixture of a grape product and terebinth tree resin.
And that grape product was most likely wine, in light of later docu-
mentary evidence from the ancient world that highlights the prevalence of tree resins in preserving and enhancing wine.

The only country in the world that maintains the ancient tradition
of making resinated wine, or *retsina*, is Greece. Village winemakers
there claim special preservative properties for the resins of the native
Aleppo pine (*Pinus halepensis*) and the sandarac tree (*Tetraclinis articulata*), a member of the cypress pine family, which is imported from
the North African coast.

An appreciation for retsina has been said to be an acquired taste.
When the Neolithic wine discovery was first made, some writers, in
particular several from California, took me to task for seemingly bash-
ing retsina. Nothing could be further from the truth. In my experience, after spending several months roaming the Peloponnesus of
southern Greece and stopping every evening in an open-air restau-
rant to eat moussaka and drink retsina, while looking out across the
Aegean Sea, this taste wasn't hard to acquire. The Californians might
better ask why, if retsina is such a favorite on the West Coast, is none
produced there? Admittedly, a tree resin covers up the nuances of the
bouquet and taste of a modern varietal wine, and each person must
be his or her own judge of the finished product.

A Media Barrage

Fermented beverages did not hold a fascination only for
ancient peoples, and what had started out as a purely scientific en-
deavor soon became a darling of the international media crowd. To
be sure, the Hajji Firuz finding represented a major step forward in
our understanding of the origins of winemaking. Dating to approximately 5400 B.C., this well-aged vintage was over 7000 years old and

the containers predated the earliest known wine jars until this discovery was made, those from Godin Tepe (chapter 3), by more than two millennia.

Although often taxing, media attention can have its benefits. For example, a syndication group from London asked to photograph the Hajji Firuz jars when the discovery was announced. The division of finds had consigned two of the jars to the University of Pennsylvania Museum. The other four vessels in storage at the Iranian museum in Teheran, were inaccessible following the Iranian Revolution. The sherd that my laboratory had analyzed was pitifully small and not particularly photogenic. Yet, the second jar in Philadelphia was complete, as it had been reconstructed, and sat in a case in the Tokens-to-Tablets gallery of the museum. Because of the difficulty of taking objects off exhibit and getting permission to carry out chemical analyses, I had not had the opportunity to examine this vessel in detail. The request of the professional photographers eased the way. With intense lights blazing, I was asked to pose by peering into the jar, presumably to get a whiff of the ancient vintage. Because I had to hold this position for a time, I had ample opportunity to examine, at least by sight, every nook and cranny of the interior. There, unmistakably, were patches of a reddish residue, especially lower down on the inside of the jar.

After the photographic shoot, I was given permission to scrape out a small amount of the reddish residue. After extraction, our standard battery of chemical tests was carried out. The reddish residue proved to be a combination of calcium tartrate, relatively more tartaric acid than had been recovered from the sherd of the other jar, and terebinth tree resin. In other words, this second jar had also contained resinated wine. Was it possible that this was the red wine, to go with the white ("yellowish") wine of the first jar? Such a romantic idea will need to be confirmed by mass spectrometric analyses. Unfortunately, tests thus far have not been able to account for the colorations of the residues. If pigments, such as red anthocyanin (cyanidin) or yellowish flavonoid (quercetin), are present, they and any characteristic degradation products (e.g., gallic acid) must be in very low concentrations.

Wild or Domesticated Grapes?

It is not known whether the Hajji Firuz wine was made from the domesticated grapevine (*Vitis vinifera vinifera*) or the wild (*V. vinifera sylvestris*). The wild grape still grows here today, and, whereas the species status of the grapes at Godin Tepe, which lies farther south in the Zagros Mountains, is not known, pollen cores from nearby Lake Urmia have established that it grew around Hajji Firuz in Neolithic times. Neolithic inhabitants of the village would thus have had access to wild grapes once a year in the fall.

The quantity of wine in one kitchen of one house at the site— about 50 liters if all six jars contained wine and were nearly full— points to relatively large-scale production and consumption of wine. The same pattern probably repeated itself across the whole of the Neolithic stratum. Within the small area of the site that was excavated, the same kinds of houses, with numerous jars of the same type that tested positive for resinated wine, kept turning up. No grape seeds were recovered, but renewed excavation with a full complement of archaeobotanical recovery methods would probably produce grape seeds. If additional chemical analyses bear out the hypothesis that these jars held wine, it might reasonably be concluded that the grapevine had already come into cultivation. One might further conjecture that the domesticated grapevine had been transplanted from the northern Zagros Mountains to sites farther south, such as Godin Tepe, over the following two millennia.

But had the original domestication of the Eurasian grapevine occurred in the northern Zagros? Possibly, it represented one step along the way in the radiation outward of the more prolific and palatable fruit-bearing plant from a region farther north in the Caucasus or to the west in the Taurus Mountains.

More Neolithic Wine Jars from Transcaucasia

The tantalizing evidence for grape pips of the "domesticated" type from Neolithic sites in Georgia and Dagestan has already been presented (chapter 2). My trip to Transcaucasia in 1998 had another objective besides collecting samples of some of the earliest domesticated grape seeds in the world and embarking on the Ancient DNA Grape Project. Pottery vessels—suitable for processing, serving, and storing wine—were also essential to the beginnings of viniculture. A Caucasian "imprint" was detectible on the pottery from Chalcolithic Godin Tepe (chapter 3), but much earlier evidence existed in the "homeland" itself, going back to the beginnings of Near Eastern pottery making around 6000 B.C.

The Georgian National Museum in Tblisi kindly allowed me to sample pottery from the earliest Neolithic levels at Shulaveris-Gora, which had also yielded some of the earliest "domesticated" grape pips. The most interesting types were everted, narrow-mouthed jars with slightly flattened or disk bases, which held about 5 liters.

The jars that I examined in the museum often had a reddish residue on the lower half and base of their interior, which was highly suggestive of precipitates from liquids such as wine. Their exterior decoration was even more intriguing. Globules and strips of clays had been applied to the surface, to form triangular clusters and sticklike human figures, with legs spread out and arms, and sometimes the phallus, raised high. Small central indentations of individual globules looked like the attachment points of bunches of berries to their shoots. The evocation of grape clusters was intensified by what appeared to be schematic depictions of upraised arms and the drooping vines of an arbor or pergola, with semicircular strips opening upward or downward. When the two kinds of strips were combined, it had the appearance of a common motif seen on modern monuments throughout Georgia in which jubilant, dancing figures cavort under trellised grapevines. For instance, right across from my apartment in the Old Town, the national power authority building sported a comparable Bacchanalian scene on its elaborately carved stone facade. After I had spent a day in the museum staring at the motif on Neolithic pottery, its modern epiphany resonated forcibly in my unconscious as I sat on my balcony, with a glass of Kakheti wine in hand, and gazed at the sculptured relief.

Back home in my laboratory, one of the pottery sherds from an early sixth-millennium B.C. Shulaveris-Gora jar was shown to have contained resinated wine, making it an even older wine jar than those from Hajji Firuz Tepe. This was the first direct confirmation of

FIGURE 4.2. Fragment of Neolithic jar with applied motif possibly showing celebrant under a grapevine, from Khramis Didi-Gora (Georgia), mid-sixth to fifth millennium B.C.

the Noah Hypothesis for Transcaucasia. The congruence of this result with Gamkrelidze and Ivanov's linguistic reconstruction of proto-Indo-European, or PIE (chapter 2), can be carried a step further. The linguists stress the religious underpinnings of PIE viniculture as reflected in a common phrase, using the same vocabulary, for "pouring out" (libating) or "sprinkling" (offering) wine to a supreme deity, whether the Hittite Stormgod or the Greek Zeus. Is it possible that what I have interpreted as upraised arms beneath a grape arbor is the artistic counterpart to this literary expression? Perhaps, simple merrymaking is all that is intended, since no liquid is shown being libated. Yet, celebrations of the wine harvest or the first tasting of the new wine often had overt religious expressions, as is still true in modern Europe. The upraised arms might then signify adulation of a deity whose name and attributes, besides his marvelous beneficence of wine, are unknown.

The importance of viniculture in Georgian life certainly intensified in the periods following the Neolithic, and found new cultural ex-

FIGURE 4.3. (a) Silver goblet from Karashamb (Armenia), Trialeti culture, dating to the early second millennium B.C. (b) In the main register, hunting and fighting are climaxed by a festive banquet, in which the ruler sits with cup in hand, attended by a cupbearer (in front of the table), servants with fly-whisks, and a harpist (behind him).

pressions. For example, impressive and unique artifacts characterize
the so-called Trialeti culture of the early second millennium B.C.
Large burial mounds (*kurgans*) at Trialeti itself, west of modern Tblisi,
and other sites of the period, across the border into Armenia, have
yielded beautifully ornate gold and silver goblets, in some instances
inlaid with semiprecious stones. Banquet and drinking scenes or ceremonies are depicted in repoussé design. High officials or rulers, cups
raised to lips, sit on chairs. Processions of men carry large goblets.
Other figures with goblets attend to the goods laid out on high tables,
possibly enacting part of a rite.

Grapevine cuttings were even encased in silver by the Trialeti arti-
san, accentuating the intricate nodal pattern of the plant. These specimens, with their nearly 4000-year-old wood still intact, are on exhibit,
together with several Trialeti goblets, in the treasury room of the
Georgian State Museum. Until these finds are put on a firmer chronological footing and assessed within a larger regional framework, however, their significance for the prehistory of winemaking remains uncertain. Transcaucasia stands as a model of how a wine culture can emerge
and remain vibrant over centuries and millennia. Whether it is the
"home of viniculture" will require much more research.

Creating a Ferment in Neolithic Turkey:

A Hypothesis to Be Tested

Wild pips are the norm at sites along the middle Euphrates River, such as Mureybit, Abu Hureyra, and Dja'da, dating
back as early as the Epi-Paleolithic or Natufian period (ca. 11,000–
10,000 B.C.) and continuing down to the Early Bronze Age (EBA).
As more and more archaeological work has been carried out in the
Taurus Mountains of eastern and central Turkey, however, it has begun to take center stage in vinicultural prehistory.

Abundant archaeobotanical evidence for both wild and domesticated *Vitis vinifera* has been reported from the sites along the upper
reaches of the Tigris and Euphrates Rivers, including Korucutepe, Te-
pecik, Kurban Höyük, Hassek Höyük, Hacinebi, Çayönü and a num-

ber of sites in the Urfa region. These sites range in date from the Aceramic Neolithic period (ca. 8000 B.C.) down to the late Chalcolithic period (ca. 3500 B.C.).

Archaeobotanically, the sequence of finds from Kurban Höyük is most intriguing. There is a gradual increase of grape remains from the fifth millennium B.C. down to the early third millennium B.C. A pit of mid- to late third millennium date yielded not just masses of grape seeds but also stem and vine fragments, along with pressed cakes of the fruit itself, which imply the domestication of the Eurasian grape and winemaking on a large scale (compare a similar discovery at Tepe Malyan near Shiraz, chapter 7). The vinicultural skills exhibited at Kurban Höyük were likely characteristic of the region as a whole and were passed from there to areas farther south, bordering the Fertile Crescent. In view of the importance of adding tree resins to grape wine at a very early period, it is also significant that nutshell fragments of the terebinth tree (*Pistacia atlantica*) are attested at most of the sites in southeastern Anatolia and along the Tigris and Euphrates Rivers.

Moving farther west in Turkey, intensive archaeological work at sites such as Çatal Höyük, Can Hasan, and Hacılar has yielded a range of evidence that is even more highly evocative for the earliest stages of viticulture and beverage making in general. Çatal Höyük, in the Konya plain of Cappadocia, is the largest known Neolithic village in the Near East, with a succession of building levels from about 6500 to 5500 B.C. James Mellaart first carried out excavations here, and work was reinitiated under Ian Hodder of the University of Cambridge in 1993.

Çatal Höyük was situated in a marshy area at the time, and in the waterlogged, anaerobic conditions of the site, organic materials were well preserved. The tombs of its Neolithic inhabitants, which were under the floors of their houses, yielded textiles and elegantly contoured wood chalices. The most conspicuous discovery was some 40 shrines, filled with stone and fired-clay statues of a naked, amply proportioned "mother-goddess" with child, a bearded "god" mounted on a bull, leopards, and other figures. The walls were adorned with polychrome scenes showing "vultures" feasting on headless humans, huge plastered and painted animals in-the-round or sunk in relief, and the horns and skulls of bulls and rams mounted above niches or on benches and pillars. Artistic and religious fervor appear to have run rampant, and the combination of motifs and techniques differs in every shrine. The main focus of the cult—as seen in the bulls' and rams' heads emerging from the pregnant female statuettes—is to ensure the procreation of life now and in the hereafter.

Although some vessels from Çatal Höyük, such as the chalices, were intended for drinking, the lack of grape remains in the early Mellaart excavations and now the more recent expedition makes it unlikely that grape wine as such was drunk at the site. From the enormous quantity of hackberry (*Celtis* sp.) seeds found throughout the town, it is possible that a beverage was made from this fruit. Wood fragments of the shrub, which were recovered during the excavations, show that it grew locally. Domesticated barley and wheat were also well represented throughout the site, and beer might have been prepared and drunk from the vessels. A pottery funnel on exhibit in the Ankara museum shows that the Neolithic inhabitants of the site had the technical facility to transfer and refine liquids. Yet, if hackberry "wine" or beer was produced at Çatal Höyük, what was the source of the yeast (*Saccharomyces cerevisiae*) needed for the fermentation? Air-borne yeast are undependable, so possibly hackberry fruit itself harbors the microorganism.

The early beverage makers at Çatal Höyük might have relied on the osmophilic yeasts in honey (chapter 10) to start their fermentations and keep them going. Mellaart thought that he could discern bees foraging for nectar and depictions of honey and brood combs in the wall paintings. Today, Anatolia is famous for its delectable honeys. The fame is well deserved, a fact that Çetin Fıratlı, professor of apiculture on the agricultural faculty of the University of Ankara, demonstrated to me both descriptively and experientially. The European honey bee (*Apis mellifera*) is found throughout Turkey, including Cappadocia and the mountainous area of Karacadağ where einkorn wheat was first taken into cultivation according to the DNA evidence (chapter 2).

Çetin also described the flourishing modern honey industry to the west of Ankara, on the main road to Istanbul, where thyme, sunflower, acacia tree blossoms, and alfalfa are the sources for the honey.

To the east, not far from the university's grape experimental station at Kalecik, wild plantations are the rule, because wheat and barley, which are nonflowering and provide no nectar, are the crops. Far to the east, in the uplands around Mount Ararat, bee hunters still roam the evergreen forests in search of hives that are high enough off the ground to be protected from bears. Honeys from the west coast of Turkey in the Aydin and Izmir regions have a wonderful lemony taste and aroma derived from the citrus trees that the bees exploit there. The most sought-after and luscious honey, however, is that made from pine "honeydew," the sugar-rich product of an insect, *Marcheliana hellenica*, that feeds exclusively on the resin of the red pine tree. The tree, with its insect, grows along the southwestern Anatolian coast from Kuşadesi to Kaş, the site of several ancient shipwrecks (chapter 6). After our stimulating discussion, Çetin treated me to some of the dark citrus honey from Aydin and a deep golden commercial treacle. On my next trip to Turkey, I hope to taste the unique red pine honey, which is also made on southern Crete.

Even in the absence of grape and honey remains at Çatal Höyük and pending a molecular archaeological investigation, it may be hypothesized that some remarkable innovations in beverage making were taking place during the Neolithic period in central and eastern Turkey and that these changes had a profound impact on artistic and religious traditions for millennia to come. Only a short distance southeast of Çatal Höyük in the Taurus Mountains, Can Hasan is credited as having some of the earliest wild grape seeds of any archaeological site in Turkey, dating to a prepottery phase (ca. 7200–6500 B.C.) of the Neolithic period. Farther east along the mountain chain, aceramic Cayönü has yielded wild grape seeds from as early as 9000 B.C. Because these sites fall within the natural zone of the wild grapevine (*V. vinifera sylvestris*), the presence of the grape seeds could be due to fruit collection from their environs. Another possibility is that a range of fruit sources were being experimented with throughout the region, in the process of which it was discovered that certain fruits, such as grape, had the potential to ferment fruits with lower sugar content, such as hackberry, and grains such as einkorn wheat, once the polysaccharides had been broken down into simple sugars by malting. This scenario gains credence when it is recognized that grapes are not alone at Neolithic sites throughout Anatolia; they are often accompanied by raspberry, blackberry, cornelian cherry, elderberry, or bittersweet.

For significant fermentation to take place, a fruit with a minimum of 10 percent sugar content was needed. The principal wine yeast, *Saccharomyces cerevisiae*, will take that amount of sugar and produce a liquid containing about 5 percent alcohol. With higher sugar amounts, it will survive the increased alcoholic content in preference to other yeasts and molds, which can also produce undesirable off-flavors and aromas. Grapes and some other fruits are unique in having sufficient *S. cerevisiae* on their skin to cause a quick rise in alcohol and effectively eliminate any competing microorganisms (the "bad guys" for any aspiring winemaker). By trial and error, the ancient beverage maker must have come to realize that adding grapes to any mixture of other less sweet ingredients—berries, barley malt, wheat—improved the outcome. It is even possible that the frothy yeast that bubbled on the surface of the mixed beverages was skimmed off and used in later fermentations. Gradually, in this seemingly non-hygienic, experimental setting, one yeast came to predominate and was shared by the whole range of fermented beverages: *Saccharomyces cerevisiae*.

Saccharomyces cerevisiae is also the bread and beer yeast. Because it is not air-borne, one can only conclude that the knowledge of this yeast's activity in grapes, dates, figs, or honey preceded its use for grain-based foods and beverages. In other words, neither bread nor beer came first (chapter 7), but a sugar-rich material in which *S. cerevisiae* had established itself.

Other ingredients might well have been added to the "brew." For example, herbs and spices (e.g., anise, saffron, and fenugreek) abound throughout Turkey and were highly regarded in antiquity. This profusion of natural resources provided the ancient peoples of Turkey everything they needed to begin experimenting in beverage production.

The recently retired director of the Ankara museum, Ilhan Temizsöy, explained to me why grapes might be missing from the Çatal Höyük assemblage. As previously head of the museum in Karaman, a short distance north of the site, he often had occasion to travel there and in the surrounding region. He observed that grapes cannot be grown in the vicinity of Çatal Höyük because of poor soil conditions, possibly related to the bogs that long existed there. Yet, only 50 kilometers to the east at a higher elevation, large, succulent grapes grow in profusion, and today Cappadocia produces some of the finest Turkish wines.

Along with the knowledge of how to make various kinds of fermented beverages from fruits and likely honey and grains came a repertoire of serving and drinking vessels. At Hacılar, west of Çatal Höyük, hollow pottery vessels in the form of deer, bulls, and pigs, dating to the late sixth millennium B.C., are uncannily similar to those at early second millennium B.C. Kültepe (chapter 8), thousands of years later. Cups, sometimes in the form of a human head, and storage jars with a high, narrow mouth and sometimes shaped as a seated goddess, point to a highly developed drinking culture in which liquid libations were a regular feature.

The full measure of how a wine culture developed on the central Anatolian plateau was vividly brought to life for me during a visit to Ankara's Museum of Anatolian Civilizations in 2001. The museum, which traces Anatolian archaeology and history from the Paleolithic period through classical times, is essentially the largest collection of wine-related vessels and artifacts ever collected under one roof.

The ability to make fermented beverages and suitably display their splendor in drinking and ceremonial vessels can be traced from the Neolithic period through the Chalcolithic and EBA of Anatolia. Chalcolithic vessels might have been painted with more elaborate, geometric designs or include a unique shape such as the "churn" or "wineskin" (chapter 9), but the bowls, jars, jugs, and other types are not all that different from their Neolithic counterparts. The stupendous bronze and gold artifacts from third millennium B.C. sites on the central Anatolian plateau are the high point of the EBA exhibit. For example, a gold jug, bowl, and chalice from Alaca Höyük, constituting a drinking set, astound one by their beauty and craftsmanship. A bronze ladle from the same site—to serve the consequential potation—has an inlaid gold handle.

The EBA potters exhibited a similarly deft ability to replicate and elaborate on the styles of the past. The large eyes staring out from a jug in the form of a human face might easily be mistaken for the

mother goddess of Çatal Höyük, until one realizes that it was excavated at the site of Karataş-Semayük in the Elmali plain of southwestern Anatolia (ancient Lycia) and is dated to the mid-third millennium B.C. The arched side-handled cups, which Schliemann
dubbed *depata amphikypella*, had made their appearance in the central
and western parts of the country by this time, and their popularity,
together with a predilection for stylized fiddle-shaped mother goddesses, extended to islands in the Aegean (chapter 10). A vessel in
the form of a small wineskin (Greek *askos*) was made, and one-handled drinking cups were already being grouped together with intercommunicating channels.

The most extraordinary array of drinking-related vessels, however,
come from Kültepe (chapter 8). Beautifully contoured jugs have long,
open, and curved spouts, which suggest birds' beaks, and are highly
polished in uniform colors (scarlet, black, or cream) or intricately
painted. Birds, especially vultures, eagles, and other large birds of
prey, were important to the peoples of Anatolia from at least the
Neolithic period, as seen on the wall paintings of Çatal Höyük. Six
millennia later, the mother goddess of the Phrygians, Matar, is still
shown holding a bird or enwrapped in its feathers (chapter 11).

For an understanding of the emergence of ancient beverages—of
wine in particular—the important point that emerges from these
considerations of Anatolian archaeology and our present knowledge
of *Saccharomyces cerevisiae* fermentation is that the obvious differences between the beverages were less important than their shared
production method. According to ancient textual evidence from
around the ancient Near East, grapes most often entered into the
production of other fermented beverages. They appear to have been
the prime, preferred source of *S. cerevisiae*. Grapes could, of course,
have been prepared as pure juice and drunk as unalloyed wine. But
during the earliest stages of viniculture, grapes were a crucial component of most mixed fermented beverages, some of which continue to
be made today and others of which have disappeared or have gone
their separate ways, such as barley and wheat beer.

CHAPTER 5

Wine of the Earliest Pharaohs

THE wild grape (*Vitis vinifera sylvestris*) never grew in ancient Egypt. Yet a royal winemaking industry was thriving there in the wide alluvial plains of the Nile River Delta by at least Dynasty 3 (ca. 2700 B.C.), the beginning of the Old Kingdom. Is it possible to know when the first domesticated grapevines were transplanted to Egypt and to discern the prehistorical backdrop of an industry that eventually spread over the entire Delta and to the large western oases? Answers to these intriguing questions have important implications for the emergence and consolidation of one of the earliest literate civilizations on the earth.

A Royal Industry Par Excellence

The actual hieroglyphs meaning "grape, vineyard, or wine" are among the most telling pieces of evidence that Egyptian viniculture was highly sophisticated from the beginning. The logograms and other signs are incorporated into what are the earliest "wine labels" in the world, belonging to Dynasties 1 and 2 of the Early Dynastic period which is dated from approximately 3100 B.C. to 2700 B.C. Cylinder seals engraved with the hieroglyphs were rolled and stamped onto heavy clay stoppers that sealed elongated, handleless jars (color plate 4) of standardized shapes and volumes—on the order of 10, 20, or 30 liters each—and which were often decorated with rope appliqués running around the neck, shoulder, or base. The stoppers were made by inserting a round pottery lid into the mouth of the jar and then piling up a huge conical mound of clay and spreading the clay down onto the shoulder of the vessel to form a tight seal. Thousands of these jars were deposited in the tombs of the first pharaohs of Egypt at Saqqara (Memphis) and Abydos, the main centers of the recently united country in the north and south.

Because these are among the earliest written characters referring to the domesticated grapevine and wine from anywhere in the world, one is shocked to see how sophisticated the viticulture methods were. One hieroglyph, stamped on a stopper belonging to a jar of the Pharaoh Khasekhemwy of Dynasty 2, shows a grapevine growing up onto a trellis of vertical poles, forked at their upper ends to hold the vine. Large clusters of grapes hang down between the supports. This method of training the vine in an upright and linear fashion—enabling easy harvesting, as well as pruning of the plants and thinning out of the foliage as necessary—is still employed today. In a later manifestation of the hieroglyph, the grapevine is shown growing out of what appears to be a pottery vessel or basket. Because the vine needs to have ample space to develop its root system, this "vessel" is probably a small construction for irrigating the plant. The various forms of this hieroglyph demonstrate that viticulture was already very far advanced, as if it had sprung overnight from the brow of Zeus (or better, of the Egyptian god Horus).

Another hieroglyph has been interpreted as an upright mechanical device for twisting a bag filled with pomace and squeezing out the grape juice. It is recorded as early as the reign of Den, the fourth king of Dynasty 1. This sign is always associated with another that shows a two-handled jar, placed below the "press," presumably to collect the exuded liquid. The device is similar to one depicted in the Middle Kingdom tomb of Baqet III, dated ca. 2050–2000 B.C. at Beni Hasan along the middle Nile River, although it has never been found in an excavation. Possibly, the instrument was employed in processing another natural product. A small-scale olive oil press can be ruled out, because this tree was rarely grown in ancient Egypt, and nearby Levantine groves provided a plentiful supply for import.

A final hieroglyph of enological significance was used as a determinative or concluding symbol to specify the meaning of a foregoing word—whether expressed as a single logogram or a combination of syllabograms. In the case of "wine," the Egyptian word is *irp*, which is written out in syllabic form as early as the time of Cheops, the builder of the Great Pyramid at Giza during Dynasty 4. Although of uncertain derivation, onomatopoeically, it may reproduce the sound after overindulging in drink. The determinative sign shows two egg-shaped forms, side by side and joined together by a pair of horizontal lines. The ovoid shape immediately evokes the image of the standard elongated "wine jar," which filled the tombs of the first pharaohs. It is a mystery why two such jars should be conjoined by what might be interpreted as two encircling ropes or even a wicker basket. The former keeper of Egyptian Antiquities at the British Museum, T. G. H. Harry James, who enlivened the Mondavi conference with his ironic wit, quipped that "for the Egyptian 'wine connoisseur' 'the other half' was just as important as the first drink was for the devoted beer drinker." Of course, a good host always reserves the best wine for last. Even more romantically, perhaps the scribe was conveying the idea that the wine could be either a red or a white.

The earliest instance of the "wine" determinative is again on a label of King Den, referring to a vineyard or estate dedicated to Horus. The name of the vineyard is set within an oval, which probably defines a walled-in, protective enclosure. Horus, the falcon deity who represented the living pharaoh on the earth and in the afterlife, was prominently displayed on stopper seals in another way. The king's name in hieroglyphics was enclosed within a so-called *serekh*, the forerunner of the cartouche, which shows the paneled exterior of a palace on top of which a falcon stands in profile (color plate 4). The general location of the vineyard is sometimes marked by additional hieroglyphs on the seal, such as a crenellated rectangle marking the "White Walls" of Memphis, at the southern apex of the Nile Delta and the first capital of a united Egypt.

A good deal of subjectivity still swirls around the translation of individual seal inscriptions on stoppers at this earliest recorded stage in ancient Egyptian history and viniculture. All the seals name a pharaoh, thus providing a date for the "vintage" within the limits of a poorly established chronology for the Early Dynastic period and depending on how long the king ruled. Sometimes, the winery's name

and location are indicated. But more often, in lieu of the extra information, the king's name was repeatedly impressed on a stopper using
the same cylinder seal. The message is clear: This wine is owned or
was produced under the auspices of the named pharaoh.

Chemical tests have not yet confirmed whether any of the elongated jars, deposited in such vast quantities in the royal tombs of
Dynasties 1 and 2, contained wine. Examples in the University of
Pennsylvania Museum collection are available for testing, although
extractions of these large, complete vessels are out of the question.
Reddish residues, which have been observed on the interiors of several jars, remain to be scraped out with difficulty and tested.

Even without chemical analysis, the elongated jars can be shown
to have contained wine. Small holes had been punched through
some of the stoppers and later filled with clay plugs. These can only
have been "secondary fermentation locks," to allow fermentation
gases to escape after which the jars were permanently sealed. This
procedure for "bottling" wine—but not any other fermented beverage, such as barley beer—is well established by many later Egyptian
stoppers on wine jars.

Moreover, beginning in Dynasty 2, the tombs of nobles at Saqqara
are provided with stelae that show the occupant before an offering
table piled high with food—bread, beer, trussed fowl, and cuts of
beef—and other items such as bolts of cloth and natron, used in
mummification. An elongated jar, presumably containing wine, is
among the provisions. In an accompanying table listing all the offerings and specifying the amount of each that will be magically provided in the afterlife, a thousand such wine jars is the standard allotment. The ancient Egyptians had hit upon a wonderful solution for
providing sustenance for the dead: instead of physically burying hundreds of jars in the tomb, symbolic representation accomplished the
same thing much more neatly and economically. The list of necessary
offerings had achieved a canonical status by Dynasty 6, the end of
the Old Kingdom, about 2200 B.C. Beer, as the most common beverage of ancient Egypt, always stood ahead of wine, but five wines were
specifically named in the mortuary tabulations: "northern wine,"
"*abesh* wine," "*sunu* wine," "*hamu* wine," and "Imet wine." Most of
these terms are now understood as referring to wineries in the Nile

Delta generally ("northern") or circumscribed areas of this region (for example, *sunu* is equated with Sile, on the northeastern border of the Delta, where later some of the best vineyards were located and imported Levantine wines entered the country).

Other details of Egyptian viticulture and winemaking can be gleaned from the splendid paintings in the tombs of high officials at Saqqara and Giza, beginning in Dynasty 4, which provide another magical means for unlimited supplies of posthumous wine. The scenes, usually filling one or two parallel panels, follow the sequence of activities in the vinicultural year. Not every important occasion is illustrated, and many of the scenes become stock motifs that are repeated over and over by artists, some of whom may never have witnessed the actual events.

The first scene shows the trellised grapevines, heavy with grapes, being tended and watered. The grapes are shown at their ripest—always dark bluish in the earliest tombs—and squatting or standing men are seen picking the clusters. The vineyard workers do not use clippers, which in any case are not archaeologically attested until the later second millennium B.C. A sharp stone or metal blade would have served the purpose. My own experience in picking grapes in the steep, shaley vineyards of the Mosel River in Germany convinced me that even the best of tools will not prevent one's hands from being severely cut in the process. Fortunately, wine from last year's vintage is usually available to anesthetize both body and mind.

The grapes are then piled into open baskets and carried to the grape-treading area. The treading vats are round or rectangular and can accommodate as many as five standing men, who hold a horizontal rod with one hand while wrapping their other arm around the waist of their fellow stomper. With the slippery pomace and must under foot, firm grips were needed. To encourage and synchronize the men in their arduous task, which might continue for hours on end, two men beating rhythm with sticks are usually shown in a small circle, perhaps a mat, off to the side. These time-tested methods of bringing in the new vintage are still a part of traditional winemaking in the upper Douro River in Portugal, where Port wine is produced today. As yet, no treading vat has been excavated, probably because winemaking facilities would have been located away from living quarters, near the vineyards, and because the vats were made from relatively perishable materials. Unfired mudbricks or clay, covered with a plaster coating to give the whitish appearance seen in the tomb paintings, could easily be molded into shape and refurbished each year.

The must is not shown being siphoned off from the vat through a trough, as is later the rule for New Kingdom vintage scenes, dated ca. 1550–1200 B.C. (see figure 6.6). One can surmise that the juice was left in contact with the grape skins, seeds, and wood to produce a red wine. Even white or yellow grapes can be made to yield a red wine in this way. In the New Kingdom scenes, a reddish liquid is always shown running into a small side vat. Although ancient Egyptian artistic canons might be arbitrary (e.g., Egyptian men are always shown with a red skin, whereas females have yellow skin), the color of the must likely has a basis in reality, representing a tradition that may extend back to the Early Dynastic or Old Kingdom period. Again, unlike the more detailed New Kingdom scenes, the earlier paintings do not show storage jars in the background that could have been used to collect the free-run and pressed juice from the grape-treading.

The next stage in the Old Kingdom paintings shows the pomace being pressed a second time in a bag strung between two poles. Teams of as many as eight men, stationed at each pole, pull and twist the bag in opposite directions, as a dark-colored liquid cascades into a wide-mouthed vessel below. The skill of the Egyptian artist was challenged to the utmost, to depict in the two-dimensional medium the writhing and contorting bodies of the hard-working men, who could not let a single drop of the precious liquid go to waste. Another human—on occasion, a baboon—is also shown suspended in space and spread-eagle between the poles.

Then follow scenes of transferring the must from spouted jars into the elongated storage jars, like those so common in the Early Dynastic royal tombs. Potters are sometimes shown making the wine jars, and their sealing, after having been filled with the fermenting liquid, is a standard motif. Details, such as the stamping of the stoppers or inserting a reed for secondary fermentation, are usually lacking on Old Kingdom paintings.

The stopper wine labels give the overwhelming impression that the emergent Egyptian winemaking industry was operated by and for the benefit of the reigning pharaoh. Yet private production, albeit probably only among the upper echelons of society, who had property and could afford an investment with a delayed prospect for returns, had already begun. Metjen, an official under Snefru, the first king of Dynasty 4, is a case in point. He records in his autobiography, preserved in his tomb at Saqqara, that he had a walled vineyard of several hundred square meters as part of his estate, probably located in the Nile Delta. In addition to vines, from which he claims to have made "a great deal of wine," he also grew figs and many trees in the vicinity of a large lake. The mention of figs and other trees in the same breath with grapes and wines gains added significance when we turn back the clock to what was happening in predynastic Egypt.

An Amazing Discovery from a Dynasty 0 Royal Tomb

Our understanding of the prehistoric background for the Delta winemaking industry leaped forward with the discovery of some 700 jars of imported wine buried in a tomb of one of Egypt's first kings at Abydos, about 650 kilometers up the Nile River from Memphis. The name of this king was Scorpion, according to some of the earliest hieroglyphic writing from Egypt. His multichambered, mud-brick-lined tomb is about 100 meters north of the tomb of King Aha of Dynasty 1, in an area that served as the royal cemetery throughout the Early Dynastic period. It and neighboring tombs have been the focus of ongoing excavations, directed by Günter Dreyer of the German Institute of Archaeology in Cairo, for several decades. Dated to the Naqada IIIa2 period of Upper Egypt (ca. 3150 B.C.), according to radiocarbon determinations, the tomb is about 150 years earlier than that of Aha and somewhat later than the Late Uruk period of Mesopotamia (see chapter 3). The Scorpion I tomb is assigned to Dynasty 0, because it preceded the official unification of Egypt and because its occupant was unknown to the Hellenistic priest Manetho, who devised the canonical succession of later Egyptian dynasts.

The tomb, denoted U-j, was a virtual treasure house of provisions and accoutrements for the afterlife, in keeping with the close association of Abydos as the religious center of Osiris, a resurrection and fertility god, in later times. It was dug almost 3 meters down into desert sand and was laid out in the form of a model funerary house in which slits only 3 centimeters wide intercommunicate between the rooms. The burial chamber in the northwestern corner held the remains of a wooden shrine where the king was laid out with his ivory scepter. Seven other rooms were stacked high with goods—beer jars, bread molds, stone vessels, cedar boxes filled with clothing, ivory and bone objects, and much more—to accompany and provide for the ruler in the afterlife.

In several chambers, cylindrical jars, which likely contained an oil or a fat, had inked hieroglyphs on their sides. Small perforated bone and ivory plaques with incised hieroglyphs also had the appearance of labels, which were once attached by strings to other vessels. Depicting animals such as scorpions, birds, and bulls, these signs represent the earliest written records from Egypt and probably denote the Egyptian estate where the food in the container was produced.

One of the most amazing discoveries, which thus far stands alone in Egyptian archaeology, were three rooms in the southeastern corner of the tomb that were filled high with three or four layers of jars, stacked one upon the other. As our chemical analyses were to show, they had contained wine for the king's journey into eternity; these rooms were "wine cellars" for the hereafter. All of the goods in the tomb and the body had to be dropped down from above. Scorpion I's tomb was then roofed over with plastered beams and covered with a mound of earth. The desert sands took care of the rest, blending the tomb into the rolling dunes of its surroundings until it was discovered and opened by the German archaeological team after more than 5000 years.

Many small clay sealings were found associated with the wine vessels, which had jar rim and string impressions on their backs. They were probably once pressed onto covers made of an organic material, such as leather, that were tied over the jar mouths with string. On the sealings were hitherto unknown and extremely fine-cut cylinder seal impressions, depicting antelope, fish, and birds suggestive of storks and ducks. Two geometric motifs—nested lozenges and an X inside a rectangle—were reminiscent of seals and their impressions

FIGURE 5.1. Tomb U-j in Abydos (Egypt), ca. 3150 B.C., showing Chamber 10 filled with imported wine jars.

found at Khirbet Kherak, a site in the northern Jordan Valley, and Bab edh-Dhraʿ on the eastern shore of the Dead Sea. Only three seal designs of the same general type were attested for the numerous wine jars, possibly indicating a common registration procedure for the wine jars' importation into Egypt or their direct association with burial of the king.

None of the written signs on the tomb U-j jars, sealings, or labels can be related to winemaking or viniculture. Once the sand filling had been removed from the jars, however, rings of a yellowish crusty residue, which were slanted off from the horizontal, were seen on their interiors. These "tidelines" are best interpreted as the remains of a liquid that had gradually evaporated, with materials on the surface of the liquid agglomerating to form the rings.

My laboratory ran our standard battery of tests, including Fourier-transform infrared (FT-IR) spectrometry, high-performance liquid chromatography (HP-LC), and Feigl spot tests (see chapter 3), on the yellowish residues from three jars in two of the chambers. These analyses confirmed that the ancient material contained tartaric acid and its insoluble calcium salt, which had formed in the calcareous environment of the site. Moreover, strong hydrocarbon absorptions were noted in the IR spectrum, which the more definitive HP-LC analysis identifed as terebinth tree resin (*Pistacia atlantica* Desf.). In other words, we were dealing with a resinated wine almost identical to that found at Hajji Firuz Tepe more than 2000 years earlier in Iran (chapter 4) and only slightly later than that from Godin Tepe (chapter 3).

Our conclusion that all the jars had probably contained wine was borne out by the fact that 47 of 360 intact jars yielded grape pips, generally between 20 and 50 seeds in each jar. Incredibly, several desiccated grapes—raisins—were recovered, with their stem, skin, pips, and dried pulp intact. According to Friedel Feindt of the Botanical Institute of Hamburg University, the pips are morphologically most similar to those of the domesticated subspecies but not far removed from the more rounded wild shape. Eleven jars held the remains of sliced figs (*Ficus carica* or *sycomorus* L.), which had been perforated, strung together, and probably suspended into the liquid. A fig additive is otherwise unprecedented for ancient Near Eastern and Egyptian wine. It might have served as a sweetening agent or special flavoring; cutting up and stringing out the fig segments would bring more of the wine into contact with this horticulturally important fruit. Another possibility is that the fig skins were a rich source of yeast in fermenting the liquid (discussed later in this chapter).

The large number of jars from Scorpion I's tomb that yielded grapes was in keeping with our chemical findings. In addition, our analyses, which included one jar with grapes and two without, implied that most, if not all, of the jars had originally contained a grape juice, which would have quickly fermented to wine. The presence of terebinth tree resin, as well as the evidence that the vessels had been sealed, were additional strong indicators for wine.

With an average volume of 6–7 liters for each of the projected 700 wine jars in tomb U-j, Scorpion I could have drawn upon some 4500 liters in his afterlife. Where had such a large quantity of wine been produced? Abydos, located on the upper Nile River in an extremely dry terrain, did not support vineyards during this period. In the Nile Delta, grape remains of predynastic and Early Dynastic date are thus

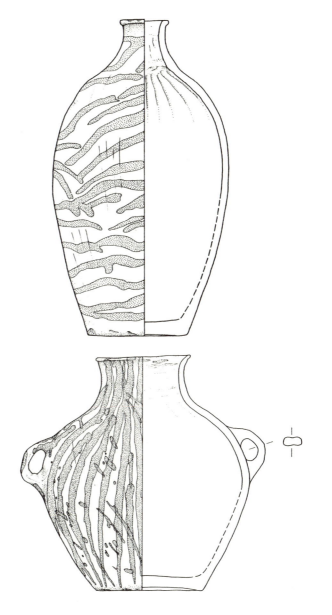

FIGURE 5.2.
Typical wine jars
from tomb U-j:
handleless and
with two loop
handles, narrow-
mouthed and
wide-mouthed,
with painted
"zebra" and
dripping designs.

far very sparse, having been confirmed only for Buto and Tell Ibrahim Awad in the east. The clay stoppered and sealed wine jars found in Early Dynastic cemeteries, which are of Egyptian type and made of Nile alluvial clay, remain the best evidence for the earliest Egyptian viniculture, but the Abydos jars predated this period.

The German archaeologists had never seen jars like those from Scorpion I's tomb in Egypt before, let alone at Abydos. Ulrich ("Uli") Hartung, an archaeologist who has long been associated with the German Institute's Abydos project, has made a special study of the pottery types. Many of the wine jars were bottle-shaped with a narrow mouth, which would have facilitated stoppering and ship-ment. The range of sizes, shapes, decorations, and other stylistic fea-tures, however, implied that they had originated from more than one place. Roughly smeared red and white slips covered the surfaces of many of the vessels, as is common in Early Bronze (EB) I. A smaller number of jars were decorated with various combinations of vertical, horizontal, oblique, and criss-crossing red lines. The most dramatic designs were swirling "tiger-stripes." A pair of ledge or loop handles was often placed symmetrically, one on each side, but other vessels had only a single loop handle on the shoulder, maybe even a second one set low down on the same side, or none at all. Short clay strips, possibly vestigial rope appliqués, had been applied to the neck of some vessels. The jars also appeared to be made from different pottery fabrics, in which varying amounts and kinds of mineral inclusions— so-called temper—had been mixed with the clay by the ancient pot-ter to improve its properties.

A careful survey of the published literature revealed that the best stylistic parallels, especially for the handled jars, were EB I vessels excavated at sites in modern Israel, the West Bank, and Jordan, in-cluding Tel 'Erani and Ashkelon along the southern coastal plain, Lachish and Beth Shemesh in the nearby lowlands, Megiddo, 'Afula and Beth Shan in the Jezreel Valley, Jericho in the Jordan Valley, Bab edh-Dhra' along the Dead Sea, and Lehun on the southern Transjor-danian plateau. Precise parallels for the bottle-shaped jars that lacked handles, however, are yet to be found. Possibly, this absence is due to the relatively small number of EB sites that have been excavated in the southern hill country of Palestine and in Transjordan. One might also propose that a specialized trade in wine would demand a special container and therefore be limited to a relatively few number of sites.

To find out where the Scorpion I wine jars had come from, I turned to another tool of modern archaeological chemistry: instrumental neutron activation analysis (INAA). In this method, small pieces of pottery, 50–200 milligrams in weight, are finely ground and subjected to high-energy neutron beams in a nuclear reactor. In the process, many chemical elements become radioactive, and, as they decay back to their ground state, their characteristic gamma-ray emissions are recorded and used as a measure of the amount of each element present in the sample. INAA is especially sensitive for a crucial group of elements known as the lanthanide series, or rare earths, beginning at cerium with an atomic number of 57 and extending through lutetium at 71. These elements and others serve to "fingerprint" the pottery and its presumed place of manufacture.

In the assignment of an ancient pottery sample to a given clay bed, two assumptions are usually made. One is what has become known as the Provenience Postulate, which states that the chemical variation within a given clay source is less than that between different sources. Enough analyses have now been made from clay beds around the world to show that this assumption holds true. Second, it is assumed that the inclusions in the pottery fabric, whether deriving from the original clay or added as temper by the potter, are relatively pure and do not skew the data for the clay itself. In the limestone-rich, sedimentary terrains of the Middle East, quartz, calcite, and organic material are the main inclusions, and they have a diluent effect on the chemical composition of an ancient sample that is spread across the range of elements. This effect can be corrected for by scaling up the INAA elemental concentrations. For igneous terrains, it may be necessary to identify the inclusions by heavy mineral analysis and to apply a more complicated formula according to the relative percentage and composition of each inclusion.

Huge amounts of INAA data are both the bane and the strength of the method. As can be imagined, the thousands of ancient pottery samples that have now been run, with upward of 35 elemental determinations for each sample, result in an enormous database. Besides an understanding of nuclear chemistry, a knack for computers and statistics is needed by the INAA practitioner. Consequently, a range of univariate and multivariate algorithms—means and standard deviations and correlational, clustering, and principal-component analyses of a range of elements—were developed. The programs are used to define local chemical groups of ancient pottery and to enable widely divergent samples, or outliers, to be identified and excluded. Archaeological and geological criteria are important in refining and testing these groups, whether well-dated pottery types, clays from specific geochemical regimes, or clay beds within a single deposit. For example, extremely large jars, as well as walls and kilns of mudbrick (sun-baked clay), are usually made of local clay and are not transported to another site. The INAA analyses of such samples should then serve to confirm a hypothesized local group based on other pottery types. This approach is essential when an ancient clay source has been totally exploited or systematic clay sampling has not yet been carried out in a region. But one must proceed cautiously. As my own studies have shown, large jars, clay artifacts such as sarcophagi, and cooking pots can be specialty items, produced by only a few workshops and distributed over an extended area. Moreover, the manufacture and even the clay that goes into a pottery vessel can be critical, because it is associated with a specific food or beverage. Any deviation from tradition will have direct effects, perhaps changing taste, texture, or some other quality.

I became interested in INAA and a whole host of related analytical methods—petrography, xeroradiography, heavy mineral analysis, and archaeothermometry—when I began studying ancient pottery in my graduate school days at Penn. In my position as a researcher in MASCA, I first focused on ancient inorganic materials, especially silicates (glass, faience, and frit) and aluminosilicates (clays). I became fascinated by how a glass or glaze had been colored and whether a cobalt or copper ion in a particular oxidation state had contributed the dark blue or aquamarine coloration to an ancient bead or pendant. At the same time, I was putting my academic background in archaeology to good use by directing excavations of Bronze and Iron Age sites in the Baqʿah Valley of Jordan, about 20 kilometers northwest of the modern capital, Amman. As huge amounts of ancient pottery came out of the ground, I began to wonder how it had been made and which pieces, if any, had been made locally or imported.

One of the first scientific studies I carried out involved using INAA to determine the origins of a diverse group of ancient pottery from a tomb in the Baqʿah Valley, dated from about 1550 to 1200 B.C. At the time, the scholarly consensus was that this period—the Late Bronze Age (LBA)—was a time of wandering nomads in Jordan and that any settled, civilized life was nonexistent. Yet the pottery coming from the burial had every appearance of being like that west of the Jordan River, where it was found in fortified towns or city-states and had most likely been made by local potters. Other pottery from the tomb was clearly affiliated with types from the island of Cyprus and even farther afield in mainland Greece (chapter 10). With burgeoning interest, I perused the available literature on provenience studies of ancient pottery using scientific techniques. By the time I had begun working on the Baqʿah pottery in 1976, INAA had established itself as the most straightforward method of choice, and some of its practitioners were not far away at Brookhaven National Laboratory on the eastern tip of Long Island.

I had met Garman ("Gar") Harbottle at the Archaeometry conference held in Philadelphia in 1977. He and several other scientists at Brookhaven, in particular Edward Sayre, had developed INAA for ancient pottery and glass studies as a peacetime use for nuclear energy after the war. I simply had to pick up the phone and give Gar a call to see whether he was interested in tracking down the origins of the Baqʿah pottery. He was very enthusiastic about the prospects, and from this small beginning, a whole series of ancient pottery studies blossomed in the years to come. Together with Christopher Wnuk, at the time a doctoral student in geology at Penn with an excellent eye for ceramic petrography, we soon had published a short paper of our findings in the *MASCA Journal*. In short, the pottery styles from the Baqʿah burial cave could be distinguished by their chemistry and petrology. Comparisons with modern clay samples that I had collected in Jordan, as well as published results for Greek and Cypriote pottery, made it clear that my hypothesis of local pottery production was cor-

rect. A sedentary community, with a well-established pottery industry, must have lived in the Baq'ah during the LBA and have been
tied into the international trade network of the time.

An INAA study of the Scorpion I wine jars was a natural development out of my collaboration with Gar over the years. As Brookhaven cut back on their peacetime mission, I also turned to Michael
Glascock and Hector Neff of the University of Missouri Research
Reactor in Columbia to analyze material. This INAA laboratory actually ran the Scorpion I samples. In statistically evaluating the data,
however, I drew on the Brookhaven Old World databank of more
than 4000 samples, with a heavy emphasis on the Eastern Mediterranean region and Egypt.

Eleven wine jars, representing all the major pottery fabrics in the
Scorpion I corpus, were tested at Missouri. Although three of the jars
had no chemical matches with any clay sample or well-defined local
group of ancient pottery in our databank, the other eight belonged to
or were closely related to well-defined groups for Southern Palestine
(the Gaza Strip and coastal plain and the adjoining lowlands, or
Shephelah, of Israel), the southern Palestinian hill country (Judean
Hills), the Jordan Valley, and Transjordan. None of the jars tested
were chemically close to any clay or ancient pottery sample outside
this region in our databank, which consisted of more than 5800 samples with excellent temporal and spatial coverage over the whole of
the Near East and Egypt. Of particular importance, no Egyptian clay
was indicated as having been used to make the wine jars from the
Abydos tomb. Thus, even though only a small proportion of the
Scorpion I jars have been tested, the INAA results pointed uniformly
to a region of the southern Levant where earlier (Chalcolithic) archaeobotanical evidence exists for the transplantation of the grapevine from farther north and where presumably large-scale production
of wine was in place by the time of Scorpion I (chapter 9).

In EB I, which is contemporaneous with Scorpion I's tomb, four
specific sites and areas of the southern Levant have yielded domesticated
grape pips and berries: 'En Besor near Gaza, Jericho in the southern
Jordan Valley, Bab edh-Dhra' on the eastern shore of the Dead Sea, and
Jawa in northern Transjordan. As mentioned above, these same sites
yielded jars like those recovered from Scorpion I's tomb.

The correspondence between the INAA, stylistic, and botanical results could hardly be more precise. The only possible conclusion was that the wine jars in Scorpion I's tomb had been manufactured in various regions of the southern Levant where they were used to collect wine produced in the same areas for storage and export.

One of the clay sealings associated with the Abydos jars was also analyzed by INAA. It was composed of Nile alluvial clay. Because of this clay's chemical heterogeneity, a precise geographic origin along the Nile cannot be determined. The finding does indicate that the final stoppering and sealing process, whatever its purpose, took place in Egypt, perhaps at Abydos before the jars were deposited in tomb U-j or, alternatively, at a site in the Delta where the wine entered Egypt and was then transported to the south.

Our combined study of where the Scorpion I wine jars were produced and what they contained is a good example of how powerful molecular archaeological techniques can be in establishing the trade routes for specific organic goods, wine in this instance. Additional archaeological considerations can take us even further in reconstructing this early phase in the development of Egyptian viniculture.

Archaeological investigation has established that the use of the northern Sinai overland trade route—"the Ways of Horus"—between Southern Palestine and the eastern Nile Delta intensified during EB I. The trip across the Sinai required about 10 days by donkey, and bones of this animal have been recovered from Maʿadi, a settlement near Cairo that was involved in overland trade with Palestine several hundred years before tomb U-j was built and Scorpion I had been laid to rest. An exchange of goods—even of technologies (pottery making and metallurgy)—can be documented going in both directions. Recent excavations at Maʿadi, begun anew by Uli Hartung of the German Institute, promise to reveal much more about this site's crucial role in the developing trade connections. Levantine merchants might have controlled the early trade, especially after the collapse of Maʿadi until the time of Scorpion I at certain sites, such as Minshat Abu Omar, along the most easterly Pelusiac branch of the Nile. Tel ʿErani probably played a key role on the Palestinian terminus of the trade route. Shortly after Scorpion I was buried in tomb U-j and until the beginning of Dynasty 1, the Egyptians themselves dominated the trade, founding trade stations along the route and in the southern Levant, most notably at 'En Besor.

A two-stage process in the EB I interactions between Egypt and the southern Levant may be proposed to account for the Scorpion I wine jars and the start of a native winemaking industry in the Nile Delta of Egypt in the Early Dynastic period. In the first phase, increasing Egyptian demand for horticultural products, especially wine and perhaps olive oil, spurred trade in these goods. Fig (*Ficus carica* L.), one of the additives in the Abydos wine jars, had probably also been taken into cultivation in Palestine by this time. The fascination of Egyptian rulers with wine created a perceived need for the beverage, although much of their wine unfortunately appears to have evaporated within the confines of their tombs. The kings, and probably other members of the upper class, began to import wine as a costly prestige item, not unlike what goes on today when we serve that special bottle of Pétrus to friends.

A leitmotif of this book is that once wine has established an economic foothold in a particular culture, it usually becomes institutionalized in its religious ritual and social customs, initially for the upper classes but eventually spreading among the populace at large. Mummification, for example, was first the prerogative of the pharaoh and soon became the fashion among his family and highly placed close associates. Eventually, only one's wealth (mummification required expensive spices, resins, and other materials, as well as a cadre of dedicated practitioners to carry it out) was the limiting factor. Similarly, in the Old Kingdom Pyramid Texts, the king's principle beverage after joining the gods in the western sky was wine. One text (§112c–d) reads that "He [the king] shall make his meal from figs and wine which are in the garden of the god." The wine in the Scorpion I tomb was laced with fig, so the dead king had essentially been provided with a complete and sancitified meal for the afterlife.

Once wine had established a foothold in a culture, the next logical step was to transplant the domesticated grapevine itself and begin producing wine locally to ensure a steady supply, at a lower cost and tailored to local tastes. Egypt's Nile Delta—with its extensive tracts of irrigated land, sunny days, and short rainy season—was ideal for this development and became the focus of a royal wine industry in the first two dynasties.

The domesticated grapevine could only have come from some region of the Levant that already was exploiting it. Many foreign specialists—farmers and horticulturalists, transporters and traders, pottery makers, and, above all, vintners—would have been involved and essential to the establishment and success of the nascent industry. The early hieroglyphs for grape, vineyard, and wine show just how sophisticated viniculture was at its inception in Egypt. Our INAA study pointed the finger squarely at regions of the southern Levant, stretching from Gaza in the west to the Transjordanian plateau in the east, where the experts could be found to set up an Egyptian winemaking industry.

Ancient Yeast DNA Discovered

The wine jars from tomb U-j have yet another fascinating detail to add to the history of ancient fermentation. Yeasts have been observed inside ancient vessels since the early part of the twentieth century. The German botanist Johannes Grüss noted their small elliptical shapes inside northern European drinking horns that held a mixed "grog" of beer and mead as well as inside ancient Egyptian "beerbottles." Grüss even commemorated one of his findings from a New Kingdom tomb at Thebes by naming the yeast *Saccharomyces winlocki*, in honor of the excavator H. E. Winlock, who had asked him to carry out the analysis.

As I pursued my molecular archaeological study of ancient fermented beverages, I often wondered whether more definitive evidence of the fermenting organisms themselves might not be detectible by the emergent DNA techniques that we were already beginning to put to use in tracking down the earliest domesticated grapevine (chapter 2). I did not have to look far. In early 1999, I received a letter from Robert ("Bob") Mortimer, a professor emeritus of Genetics and Development at the University of California at Berkeley. Bob had been instrumental in starting the project in the 1950s that led to the full nuclear genome mapping of the principal wine yeast, *Saccharomyces cerevisiae*, by more than 100 laboratories around the world in 1996. Sequencing the 16 yeast chromosomes from tip to tip, with a nearly 100 percent accuracy, was an accomplishment of unprecedented proportions that paved the way for the Human Genome Project. Some 12 million base-pairs and 6000 genes were determined by cloning overlapping chromosome sections.

Without hesitation, I started corresponding with Bob Mortimer and began picking his brain about modern and ancient yeast DNA. He wanted me to look over a section called "Yeast and Human History" that he was preparing for an article titled "Evolution and Diversity of the Yeast Genome." We were soon exchanging other articles on ancient beverage analysis and the peculiarities of yeast biology, reproduction, and genetics. For example, one intriguing theory that he and Mario Polsinelli, a colleague in the department of Animal Biology and Genetics at the University of Florence, had developed and garnered evidence for was that bees and wasps were the main vectors, or carriers, of yeast as they traveled from one piece of damaged fruit to another. The broken skin on grapes was especially enticing to the insects, because they could easily feed on the sugary juice that had been released. Careful measurements of the concentration of yeasts on grape skins throughout a vineyard showed that only a very limited number of grapes had been inoculated with yeast, and most of these were damaged fruit. When the grapes were trodden and pressed, these yeast were sufficient to begin the fermentation of the must en masse.

Bob Mortimer had another proposal for me. He was planning to spend a period of research in Florence, Italy, during the summer of 1999. He might find time to analyze some ancient samples to see whether any yeast DNA had been preserved in them. I bundled up and sent him samples of the "King Midas" beverage and "European grog" from the Danish Early Bronze Age and Roman period (chapter 11), as well as the yellowish flakes from a Scorpion I wine jar. The latter proved to be the most interesting.

Before the summer was over, Bob informed me that the team in Florence, which included an up-and-coming molecular biologist named Duccio Cavalieri, had isolated intact strands of what were almost certainly ancient yeast DNA from the tomb U-j sample. Microscopic analysis also revealed large numbers of dead yeast cells in the ancient material.

The 840 base-pair fragments of ribosomal yeast DNA that were isolated were some of the largest fragments of ancient DNA ever recovered. One 256 base-pair segment of the larger 840 base-pair fragment, after it was replicated by the polymerase chain reaction and sequenced, aligned most closely to modern strains of *Saccharomyces cerevisiae*. Only several important deletions set them apart. Other *Saccharomyces* yeast species, such as *S. bayanus* and *S. paradoxus*, were less comparable statistically and more distantly related to the yeast in the Scorpion I wine jar.

The most straightforward interpretation of these results was that the yeast in the Scorpion I jar was a precursor of *Saccharomyces cerevisiae*. If true, this was a finding that went beyond determining what yeast had been used in making some of the earliest wine in the ancient Near East and Egypt. The discovery also implied that the principal yeast in winemaking had an earlier history, which might explain why the same yeast came to be dominant in bread making and barley beer brewing. Grapes were one ingredient in an ancient Sumerian recipe for beer (chapter 7). In addition to its adding a special flavor or aroma, the grape additive might well have been intended to inoculate the brew with yeast. The chopped-up figs that had been added to or suspended in the Scorpion I wine might have been another rich source of yeast.

Ancient DNA studies have been dogged by problems of modern contamination. Was it possible that what had been identified as ancient yeast was an as-yet unidentified modern strain of *S. cerevisiae*, which deviated only slightly from known strains? Every precaution had been taken during the analysis. Positive and negative controls had been run alongside the Scorpion I sample. The work was carried out in a new isolated control room, with equipment that was not used to run other yeast DNA samples. The bench and equipment were thoroughly cleaned by UV irradiation and chemical methods. The samples were handled with clean latex gloves and transferred by new pipettes to sterile containers and tubes at every stage of the analysis.

If modern laboratory contamination is ruled out, how likely is other contamination, either during the postburial period of 5000 years or when the archaeologists collected the samples, admittedly without sterile gloves and masks? First, the large amounts of DNA obtained from the ancient Abydos samples cannot be the result of contamination. The residues were inside closed containers in an essentially zero-humidity, desert environment. The recovery of whole dried figs and raisins from some of the jars indicates how extraordinary the preservation conditions were inside the tomb and that there was relatively little activity by microorganisms once the air and water, available at the time of burial, had been consumed. Second, contamination by the archaeologists is also very unlikely because *S. cerevisiae* is not air-borne and is rare in nature, particularly in desert environments. The Florence laboratory and other researchers have shown that even grape skins rarely harbor *S. cerevisiae* cells unless broken to release the juice. Even more important, because yeast does not live on human skin, the probability that the archaeologists transferred modern *S. cerevisiae* to the ancient samples is very low.

There is little doubt then that the "precursor" of *S. cerevisiae* in the Scorpion I wine jar is an ancient specimen. Another fungus identified in the jar provides the capstone for the argument. It is a 540 base-pair DNA sequence that has an 87 percent probability of being the same as that recovered from the remains of the 5000-year-old Ice Man from the Ötztal Alps on the border between Italy and Austria. As yet, no other significant homologies have been noted between this ancient mold sequence and any modern sequence longer than 300 base-pairs. Most likely, both the Abydos mold and the *S. cerevisiae* precursor derive from ancient fermentation of the wine in the jars, a common enough occurrence even in modern wines.

Another 580 base-pair DNA fragment from the Scorpion I sample is probably a spoilage yeast such as *Ampelomyces humuli* or *Phoma glomerata*. It thus appears that the king's wines had been ruined. The wines probably were spoiled after they had been deposited in his tomb, since only the best wine would have been a proper tribute to the king or the right way to see him into the afterlife. Rather, once the ethanol in the wine had evaporated, mold spores probably germinated and caused the wine to go bad. Whether the wine were good or bad, the ancient yeast DNA inside the Scorpion I jars provided the tell-tale evidence that the grape juice, which we had already identified chemically, had been fermented to wine.

CHAPTER 6

Wine of Egypt's Golden Age

IN ORDER to track subsequent developments in viniculture in Egypt, as well as throughout the Near East and in the Mediterranean world and Europe, my laboratory of Molecular Archaeology at the University of Pennsylvania Museum has become a kind of repository of ancient wine samples, with well-aged vintages stretching back to 6000 B.C. and extending over a period of 8000 years, up to the present. Of course, there are many geographic gaps, and any vertical tastings (comparing vintages of different years), if it were allowable to add water to the ancient residues and reconstitute the wine, would need to leap over centuries.

The Hyksos: A Continuing Taste for Levantine Wines

The enigmatic "Hyksos"—Egyptian ḥḳ3w ḫ3swt, meaning "rulers of foreign lands"—controlled the Nile Delta and parts of Middle Egypt from about 1670 to 1550 B.C. Political dominance by non-Egyptians rarely occurred in ancient Egypt, because it was cut off from southwestern Asia by the Sinai Peninsula and by deserts from other parts of Africa. As a result, the origins of the Semitic-speaking Hyksos in Egypt and their rise to power has been and continues to be a hotly debated topic in scholarly circles. Were the ancestors of the Hyksos those Asiatic servants and other groups described in Middle Kingdom texts, who then increased in population and took advantage of native Egyptian weakness during the thirteenth and the ensuing dynasties of the Second Intermediate period? Or were they invaders from the Levant, as described in later accounts based on the now-lost dynastic history of a third-century B.C. Egyptian priest, Manetho? In a well-respected history written in the first century A.D. (*Contra Apion*, sect. 14), the Jewish historian Josephus wrote, citing Manetho, that the Hyksos were "men of ignoble birth out of the eastern parts [Syria-Palestine], and had boldness enough to make an expedition into our country, and with ease subdued it by force." A sixteenth-century B.C. Egyptian monument, purporting to be an eyewitness account of the military campaign against Avaris, the Hyksos capital, that led to defeat of the Hyksos bears out this interpretation. In the second stela of Kamose, the Theban ruler who set the stage for the final victory by his brother and the founder of the New Kingdom, Ahmose I, the Hyksos ruler is said to be the "vile Asiatic," "the ruler of Retenu [Syria-Palestine]." These phrases imply that the Hyksos at Avaris were closely tied to the Levant, whether having come originally from somewhere in that region or now exercising control there.

By an adventitious but sad chain of events in the late 1980s, I was handed a crucial link in understanding who the Hyksos were and their role in the evolving saga of ancient Near Eastern winemaking. I had collaborated with Joan Huntoon on an instrumental neutron activation analysis (INAA) project of pottery from Beth Shan, south of the Sea of Galilee in Israel. Joan had been taken under Gar Harbottle's wing at Brookhaven National Laboratory, where she became well versed in the intricacies of INAA (chapter 5). For her Ph.D. dissertation at Columbia University, she had begun analyzing Middle Bronze (MB) pottery, dated ca. 1900–1550 B.C.—in particular, the "Canaanite Jar"—from sites throughout the Eastern Mediterranean. Because half of her more than 1000 pottery samples came from the site of Tell el-Dabʿa in the northeastern Nile Delta, believed to be the Hyksos capital of Avaris, the prospects of finding out more about this enigmatic people and their foreign contacts were good.

Joan did not live to see the fruits of her labor on the Hyksos and the Canaanite Jar. Her health progressively failed and she died in the fall of 1987. Edith Porada, Joan's adviser at Columbia; Manfred Bietak, the director of the Austrian excavations at Avaris; and Gar proposed that I step in and complete the research. Overnight, I went

FIGURE 6.1. (Right)
Canaanite Jar from Tell el-
Dabʿa (Egypt), ca. 1700 B.C.
This pottery can be
compared with (bottom)
later Greek and Roman
amphoras from (left to right)
Rhodes, Knidos, Chios, and
Rome. The Market Hill of
Athens and the temple of
Hephaistos and Athena are
in the background.

from analyzing small confined groups of INAA samples, mostly from Jordan and Israel, to dealing with hundreds of samples from scores of sites in Egypt and up and down the Levantine littoral and inland regions.

A chemical study of the Canaanite Jar was very enticing, because jars just like it were to become *the* liquid containers and *the* export pottery vessels par excellence for Mediterranean trade. The ovoid jar—with two loop handles, a rounded or slightly flattened base, and a narrow mouth—is named from its probable region of origin, ancient Canaan along the northern Levantine or Syro-Palestinian coast. The earliest examples occur there, from around 1950 B.C., and were modeled on flat-bottomed Early Bronze (EB) types that had already been used to transport goods for a millennium. In the Late Bronze Age (LBA), the shape of the MB jar was refined into a piriform shape with a pointed or knobbed base and a narrow mouth— the amphora—which could be effectively sealed with a clay stopper. With relatively minor modifications of shape, the amphora continued to perform its economic function for thousands of years, through classical times and up to the Islamic period.

The Canaanite Jar was well-suited to transporting liquid goods by sea. Its curved base was stronger than the flat EB base, because the internal forces of a liquid were more evenly distributed and there were no weak joins between clay members. The base also served more effectively as a "third handle" for loading and unloading on and off of ships. Its approximately 30-liter volume was close to the maximum that could be handled by a single man. The contoured design enabled efficient storage in a ship's hold, because layers of jars could be intercalated one on top of another. Just such an arrangement of ancient amphoras was uncovered by George Bass of Texas A&M University in the hull of a late fourteenth-century B.C. merchantman that had gone down off the coast of southern Anatolia at Uluburun (Kaş).

"Avaris in the two rivers," as Kamose's second stela described the city's ideal maritime situation, lay at the confluence of two channels of the Pelusiac branch of the Nile River. Tell el-Dabʿa, which fits this description, holds a prime place in the ongoing discussion and debate about the Hyksos and the Canaanite Jar for good reasons. After 35 years of excavation, the Austrian expedition has uncovered numerous residences, palaces, temples, and tombs that can be attributed to the

FIGURE 6.2. Diver removing amphora from the late-fourteenth-century B.C. shipwreck at Uluburun (Kaş), off the southern coast of Turkey. Many of the jars contained nodules of terebinth tree resin.

Hyksos or their immediate predecessors. The cultural development of the "foreigners" can thus be followed in detail from the last days of the Middle Kingdom, around 1800 B.C., through the perilous times of the Second Intermediate period when the Hyksos came into power, to the reassertion of the Theban dynasts who founded the New Kingdom, about 1550 B.C.

At the same time that Avaris was going from a small town to a densely populated city-state extending over an area 2.5 kilometers on

a side, sites throughout the southern Levant were also being transformed. Both regions were rebounding from a kind of Dark Age,
which lasted for several centuries in the southern Levant at the turn
of the millennium. In Egypt, this hiatus—the First Intermediate Period—persisted for only about a hundred years. For reasons that are
still unclear, sites located farther north along the Lebanese and Syrian coasts and inland were less affected by the economic downturn
and social disruption. These regions also appear to have been instrumental in resuscitating urban life and foreign contacts in the southern Levant when the time was ripe.

The impacts of northern Levantine urban ways, as might be anticipated, were felt first at sites in northern Israel, Palestine, and Jordan.
For example, Hazor, north of the Sea of Galilee, expanded from
about 1 hectare to over 80 hectares during the course of the MB IIA
period from about 1900 to 1750 B.C. Fortified city-states seemingly
appeared overnight. They were built de novo, and the sheer man-
power and sophisticated technology that went into the new building
activity are awe-inspiring. During the transitional Dark Age of the
EB-MB period, the requisite skills and crafts for this kind of construction had been lost. These needs were most likely met by the influx
of craftsmen and peoples from city-states farther north, which had
weathered the hard times. The introduction of other new technologies supports this scenario. The fast wheel to make beautifully contoured pottery displaced hand and slow roulette techniques. A whole
host of new weapon, tool, and jewelry types were manufactured from
tin-alloyed copper or bronze for the first time.

If the MB IIA architectural boom and new technologies were introduced from the outside, what was the role of the native southern
Levantine peoples in this process? The massive fortifications of the
new settlements imply that the immigrants had a great deal to fear
either from the local people or from one another. They probably
feared both: individual city-states vied for power and attempted to
control the native population, who were a convenient and cheap
source of labor.

The INAA study on which I had embarked soon provided some
unexpected answers for the mystery of the Hyksos and Canaanite
urban renaissance. Gar Harbottle and I independently ran the INAA
data that Joan had already compiled against the more than 4000

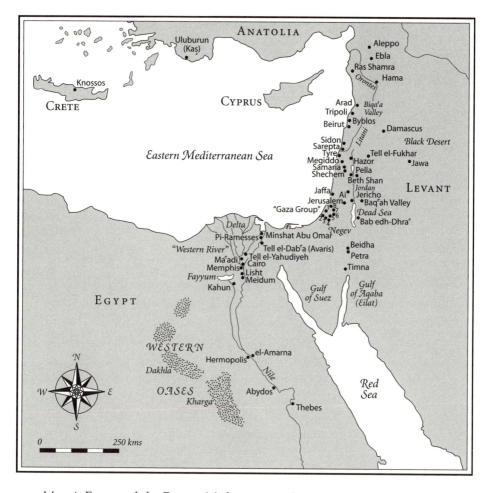

MAP 4. Egypt and the Eastern Mediterranean. Large quantities of wine were sent out from the Gaza region during the Middle Bronze Age. Numbered sites are: (1) Gaza, (2) Tell el-ʿAjjul, (3) Tell Jemmeh, (4) Tell el-Farʿah South, (5) Tel Haror, (6) Tell Beit Mirsim, (7) Lachish, and (8) Ashkelon.

samples in the Brookhaven Old World databank, employing univariate and multivariate statistical programs. In late 1988, we discovered virtually simultaneously that much of the Avaris pottery of Syro-Palestinian types had been produced in a well-defined region of Southern Palestine and exported from there to the Nile Delta. Among the sites in the approximately 3000-square kilometer area along the Mediter-

ranean coast were Gaza (largely unexcavated), Tell el-ʿAjjul (often
identified as ancient Sharuhen, a bastion that the Hyksos defended
for three years before surrendering to the Egyptians about 1550 B.C.),
and Ashkelon (a more likely candidate for Sharuhen because of its
large size). A red loess clay, with a distinctive chemical profile, had
been used to make the ancient pottery.

Gar and I excitedly communicated our results back and forth via
ARPANET, the pre-Web electronic mail system that had been set up
for use by the military, national laboratories, and research universities. We drafted and sent a detailed letter to Manfred Bietak of our
remarkable finding, who then confronted us with a conundrum.

Manfred had long advocated a theory that the Hyksos at Avaris
originally came from the northern rather than the southern Levant.
Specifically, he singled out Byblos as the home of the Hyksos. This
famous city-state of merchants and sailors was where Egypt had obtained its cedar and other goods, such as wine, during the Old Kingdom. After the ravages of the First Intermediate period had taken
their toll, Egypt soon resumed trade with Byblos during the Middle
Kingdom, at least by the beginning of Dynasty 12 around 1950 B.C.
The ties between Egypt and Byblos were so close that several Byblite
kings were interred in full Egyptian regalia. Their bodies were
adorned with intricately inlaid gold pectorals; two named the later
Twelfth Dynasty pharaohs Amenemhet III and IV, and a third bore
the Semitic name of the deceased ruler himself, Yapa-shemu-abi,
written in Egyptian hieroglyphs. Other exquisite burial goods of obsidian, silver, and gold combined Egyptian and Levantine artistic motifs and manufacturing designs.

Although the city-states of the northern Levant had not experienced the full impact of the Dark Age, many archaeologists had
noted a contraction in settlement and, presumably, in population
there, particularly at Byblos. If the population had, in fact, decreased,
where had the people gone? Manfred argued that a logical destination would have been the Nile Delta, easily reached in "Byblos ships,"
the Egyptian term for the best sea-going vessels, probably made of
cedar of Lebanon, that plied the Eastern Mediterranean.

Manfred's theory for the origin of the Hyksos was bolstered by an
intensive archaeological survey in southern Israel and the Sinai by

Eliezer Oren of Beersheva's Ben-Gurion University. Eliezer told me that very little pottery in the Gaza region or along "the Ways of Horus" to Egypt dated to MB IIA. Although I respected Eliezer's close familiarity with the archaeology of the region, the INAA results overwhelmingly painted a different picture and could not be dismissed.

In my doctoral dissertation, "Late Bronze Age Palestinian Pendants," I had dealt extensively with the elaborate Hyksos gold jewelry from Tell el-ʿAjjul, and I knew that it was one of the few sites in this region that had yielded MB IIA pottery from its "Courtyard Cemetery." My experiences in Jordan exploring the Late Bronze and early Iron Ages (chapter 5) had also taught me that some periods could be so deeply buried or were so small that they were not represented on the surface or in restricted archaeological soundings. Moreover, unlike pottery typology, which is more qualitative and subject to different interpretations, INAA is based on the chemical signature of discrete clay beds and powerful statistical techniques. If only a small number of the early MB IIA pottery imports at Avaris or elsewhere in Syria-Palestine had matched the red loess clay of Southern Palestine, then the INAA results might have been explained as a statistical fluke. But when hundreds of samples, representing the vast majority of the imports to Avaris, could be traced back to this region, another solution to the dilemma was needed. By contrast, less than 1 percent of the Avaris pottery corpus originated from sites farther north—including Sidon along the coast and Ebla in inland Syria.

The answer was not long in coming. Lawrence Stager of Harvard University, who was directing excavations at Ashkelon, a port city between Tel Aviv and Gaza, reported in 1992 that his team had uncovered an early MB IIA mudbrick arched gateway, similar to the one previously found at Tel Dan. The gate was part of an enormous glacis and moat fortification system that extended some 2 kilometers in circumference, enclosing an area as large as 150 hectares. Although the site has been encroached upon by the sea over the past three and a half millennia and was partly destroyed, it is clear that Ashkelon was one of the largest cities in Syria-Palestine during the period from about 1900 to 1750 B.C. If it were possible to excavate more of ancient Gaza or Jaffa, both of which are covered by modern cities, further evidence of an MB IIA city-state system in this region would probably emerge. Even at sites already extensively excavated (for example, Tell el-Farʿah South), MB IIA levels might not have been reached and still remain to be uncovered.

The early MB IIA city-state at Ashkelon provided a striking confirmation of our INAA findings. The site was located on the Mediterranean coast, not far from Avaris. Indeed, Ashkelon's large size made it a better candidate for the redoubtable Sharuhen, which put up three years of resistance to the Egyptian army, rather than Tell el-ʿAjjul, which covered an area of only 12 hectares.

What Gar and I took to be irrefutable testimony to Ashkelon and Southern Palestine's key role in the Hyksos controversy did not convince Manfred Bietak, who held out for his Byblite hypothesis. I proposed another test of the two competing theories. Manfred would choose Canaanite Jars from Avaris, mostly from early MB IIA levels at the site, that, on the basis of their style, fabric, or some other notable feature, he believed almost certainly originated in the northern Levant, and these samples would be subjected to INAA. Because Ashkelon material had also become available in the meantime, an additional seven early MB IIA samples from this site would be included in the new study.

The INAA results from the follow-up study were even more dramatic than what the original, larger project had already demonstrated. None of the Canaanite Jars that Manfred had selected could be matched definitively with any northern Levantine clay or local group in the databank. Instead, every jar that could be provenienced came from Southern Palestine, and most of those samples closely matched the Ashkelon chemical profile.

When a theory is confirmed time after time, both inadvertently and contrary to accepted wisdom, it gains credence. One can continue to argue about where the new settlers in Southern Palestine came from—Byblos and other cities in the northern Levant are likely possibilities—but there can now be no doubt that the major trading partner of Avaris in the northeastern Nile Delta throughout the Middle Bronze Age (MBA) was Southern Palestine. The lack of pottery imports from Syria or Lebanon, on the other hand, removes those regions from the Hyksos equation, at least in terms of having any direct or major role in the process.

Our Southern Palestine theory can be taken a step further. Relative pottery chronology suggests that Avaris was transformed into an Asiatic outpost during a later phase of MB IIA than that of the founding of Ashkelon and other southern Levantine sites. Because the MB IIA phases of Avaris were dominated by pottery imports from Southern Palestine, with only a few vessels coming from sites farther north, the stimulus for settling Avaris is best explained by an expansion of economic interests primarily from this nearby region. During a period of crisis in native governance, this development paved the way for the "migration" of Southern Palestinian peoples to Avaris and accounts for the tremendous growth of the city by the time of the Hyksos period proper, ca. 1650 B.C.

The wholesale transplantation of Syro-Palestinian culture to Egypt was manifested in the temple and palace architecture at Avaris. Burials, often a sensitive indicator of ethnic origins, at the latter site and at Ashkelon and Lachish in Southern Palestine are virtually identical. Tombs were made of vaulted mudbrick, accompanied by equid (ass) burials, and supplied with the same Syro-Palestinian pottery types (those at Avaris very often being imported from Southern Palestine according to the INAA results), metal weapons and luxury items, scarabs, and so on. Moreover, foodways and cuisine are among the most conservative elements of any culture, and the characteristic hand-made, flat-bottomed cooking pot of Syria-Palestine was used and manufactured in both regions over several centuries, from 1900 to 1650 B.C.

As Avaris grew, a more regulated trade, primarily with Southern Palestine, developed from about 1750 B.C. onward. Ship transport, especially for heavy loads, would have been an excellent alternative to laborious donkey transport across the Sinai, which Eliezer Oren's survey had shown to be unlikely. Both Ashkelon and Tell el-ʿAjjul were coastal sites, which had natural harbors for mooring and handling ships. The harbor at Tell el-Dabʿa, although long since silted up, was reached via the Pelusiac branch of the Nile. The reality of these maritime contacts is borne out by the contemporaneous Ka-

mose stelae, which describe ships docked together in the harbor of
Avaris.

The maritime transport of Canaanite Jars from Southern Palestine
to Avaris was an enormous enterprise. On the basis of how many
Canaanite Jars had already been excavated at Avaris, Manfred Bietak
estimated that as many as 2 million Canaanite Jars would be recovered from MB levels of the site, if fully excavated. If the INAA results are taken into account, at least three-quarters of these vessels
were imported from Southern Palestine, which converts to about
6000 jars per year or almost 20 jars per day over the 250-year lifetime
of the city. At about 30 liters to the jar, one or more commodities
were arriving at the Hyksos capital at a rate of about 600 liters daily.

Our molecular archaeological methods gave us the means of finding out what the Hyksos at Avaris craved. It will probably not come
as surprise to the reader to learn that all the jars that we have thus
far analyzed were filled with resinated wine. Our battery of chemical
analyses clearly showed the presence of tartaric acid or calcium tartrate, or both, together with terebinth tree resin, in 5 of 12 Canaanite Jars, which represented imports from Southern Palestine throughout the MBA. The lack of clear-cut evidence for wine in the other
seven jars does not prove that they never contained the beverage.
The preservation of organic remains at Avaris was poor, because of
the humid climate and high water table. The interior and exterior
surfaces of most of the pottery had irregularly shaped, dark-colored
blotches caused by mold growth. The "negative" jars had evidently
been subjected to harsher environmental conditions than had the
jars that gave positive results, because our HP-LC analyses did detect
possible traces of the marker compounds for resinated wine in several
of the them. On the other hand, some of these jars might have contained other commodities not readily detectible by our methods, such
as the various fats, honey, and olive oil mentioned in Kamose's second stela.

Canaan, especially the Gaza and Ashkelon regions of Southern
Palestine, was famous for its wine (chapter 8). If the Hyksos at Avaris
had indeed come from this region, they would have had a well-developed taste for the wine of their homeland. According to the INAA
and molecular archaeological results, they continued to satisfy that

taste for hundreds of years. We cannot know how refined their sensibilities were. If Levantine wines today serve as a measure—whether a cloying native varietal from the monastery at Latrun, in the hill country below Jerusalem, or a dry Cabernet Sauvignon from Chateau Musar, near Byblos—it could have been very eclectic.

Two other factors may help to explain why wine in particular needed to be imported on a regular basis from Southern Palestine throughout Hyksos times. The political upheaval and economic uncertainties of the Second Intermediate period had undermined the royal industry and curtailed wine production in the Delta. At the same time, the population of Avaris was growing, and along with it, the demand for wine.

A telling line in Kamose's second stela, after his victory over the Hyksos, states that he will "drink of the wine of the vineyard of [Apophis, the Hyksos ruler], which the *Asiatics* whom I captured press for me" [emphasis mine]. In a kind of recapitulation of the origins of the pharaonic winemaking industry, contacts with Levantine winemakers might have been mediated through the Hyksos at Avaris and have led to the resuscitation of the native industry in the Delta.

The return of the Egyptian winemaking industry to its former glory can be tracked by the INAA study. The Canaanite Jar, the ideal storage and transport vessel for wine, began to be replicated in Nile alluvial clay in the earliest MB IIA phases at Avaris. The number of locally made jars gradually increased in the centuries that followed, implying that the native winemaking industry was also expanding. Imports of Canaanite Jars remained at the same high level throughout the MBA, until the Hyksos were driven out of Egypt. Demand for foreign wine then dropped, as might be expected. After all, thanks to their Semitic interlopers, the New Kingdom towns and cities now had quantities of fine wine at their doorsteps in the Delta.

Significantly, the only winemaking installation in ancient Egypt predating Hellenistic times has been excavated at Avaris. A small plastered stone vat was found in a corner of an enclosed courtyard of a temple to the god Seth (or Sutekh, according to the Asiatic pronunciation introduced by the Hyksos), dating to the reign of the pharaoh Horemhab of the late eighteenth Dynasty. The god Sutekh/Seth was the patron god of both the Hyksos and the later pharaohs of the Nineteenth and Twentieth Dynasties (discussed later in this chapter), and was assimilated with the Asiatic storm god, Ba'al, during the New Kingdom.

Near the vat was a "garden" with an orderly arrangement of small dark depressions in the soil. These holes are believed to have held grapevines; they are too small for trees and too widely spaced to be a vegetable plot. The careful gridlike arrangement of the pits suggests a trellised vineyard, like those depicted in the tomb paintings. As described earlier in this chapter, the treading of grapes in ancient Egypt was often done in small plastered installations, with the grape must being directed into a side vat. The trough for the run-off of the must in the Avaris installation was bifurcated, so that juice could have been directed into two vats simultaneously or sequentially.

The archaeological discovery of a grape-pressing installation in the Sutekh/Seth temple was corroborated by our molecular archaeological study of its plaster surface that gave a positive result for grape. The Levantine origins and continued expansion of the Delta industry during the New Kingdom are reflected in the name of the famous Nineteenth Dynasty vineyard of Kaenkeme (Egyptian "vineyard/provision of Egypt"), located at the capital of Pi-Ramesses on the Waters of Re' (the Pelusiac branch of the Nile), modern Qantir, which is only several kilometers north of Avaris/Tell el-Dab'a. The root of this name, which is first used in the Kamose stelae, is probably of Levantine derivation and provided the later Egyptian words for "vineyard" (k3mw) and "vintner" (k3my). The wine of Kaenkeme is described as being "mellow . . . surpassing honey" in Papyrus Anastasi (III, 2, 6). Because reddish areas mottled the plastered surface of the vat in the Sutekh/Seth temple at Avaris, we might surmise that this was a sweet red, perhaps a genetic clone of an Iranian Shiraz rather than a yellow muscat (chapters 2 and 7).

Festival Wine at the Height of the New Kingdom

Although the Hyksos were expelled from Egypt, they had set in motion a series of events that culminated in a much-expanded Egyptian winemaking industry during the New Kingdom.

Hyksos influence was evident in the standard New Kingdom wine jar or amphora, the direct descendant of the Canaanite Jar. Many New Kingdom vintners also bore Semitic names, such as Khay, 'Apereshop, and Khoru(y), and were probably related to the Hyksos, even if they or their ancestors had recently arrived in the country as captives or immigrants from the Levant (chapter 9).

New Kingdom Egypt was a period of remarkable internationalism and cultural development, reaching its high point during the long reign of Amenhotep III, which lasted almost 40 years from about 1390 to 1350 B.C. This pharaoh was a devotee of wine, as shown by excavations at Malkata (Arabic, "the place where things are picked up") in southwestern Thebes, principally carried out by the Metropolitan Museum of Art's Egyptian Expedition between 1910 and 1920. At this site, a large complex of royal palaces, upper- and lower-class dwellings, and other facilities—storerooms, workshops, kitchens, gardens—was constructed over an approximately 500 by 700 meter area (35 hectares). An Audience Pavilion, where the king appeared on a balcony before the populace on major holidays, and a temple to the principal Theban god, Amen, were located to the north. More recently, the large artificial lake and harbor on the east, Birket Habu, some smaller structures of the complex, and additional buildings to the south have been excavated by the joint University of Pennsylvania Museum and Cambridge University excavations.

Among the many outstanding finds from Malkata were approximately 1400 jar shoulder sherds with black-inked hieratic inscriptions (referred to as ostraca), now in the Metropolitan Museum's Egyptian Art collection. These sherds shed light on goods supplied to Amenhotep III's palace, including wine, "ale," meat, fat, various oils, milk, honey, incense, and fruits.

The pottery vessels from which the ostraca came were almost exclusively storage jars or amphoras, derived from the well-known Canaanite Jar type. Hand-formed and wheel-made pieces had gone into their fabrication, after which the exterior was roughly smoothed. Their bases were generally made of a clay slab formed in a mold. Rims were made by folding the mouth outward, to create a rounded bulge to which a clay stopper would adhere. Handles were added after drying. By contrast, the bases of Levantine amphoras were wheel-

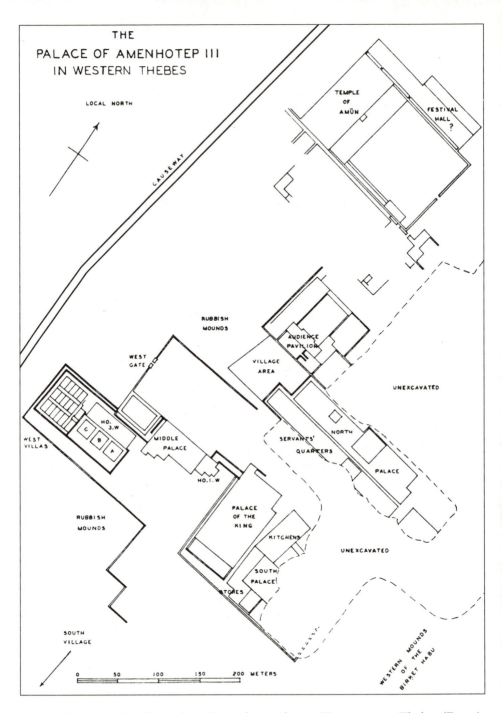

THE
PALACE OF AMENHOTEP III
IN WESTERN THEBES

LOCAL NORTH

CAUSEWAY

TEMPLE
OF
AMŪN

FESTIVAL
HALL
?

RUBBISH
MOUNDS

WEST
GATE

AUDIENCE
PAVILION

VILLAGE
AREA

UNEXCAVATED

WEST
VILLAS

HO.
3.W

C

B

A

MIDDLE
PALACE

HO.1.W

NORTH

SERVANTS'

QUARTERS

PALACE

RUBBISH
MOUNDS

PALACE
OF THE
KING

KITCHENS

UNEXCAVATED

SOUTH
PALACE

STORES

SOUTH
VILLAGE

0   50   100   150   200 METERS

WESTERN MOUNDS
OF THE
BIRKET HABU

FIGURE 6.3. Plan of Malkata, the palace of Amenhotep III, in western Thebes (Egypt), ca. 1350 B.C. Thousands of amphoras were found here. They had supplied celebrants of the *heb-sed*, a religious festival for renewing the life of Egypt and its pharaoh. Black-inked inscriptions on wine amphora fragments note the regnal year of the pharoah and, sometimes, the estate, vintner, and other winemaking details.

thrown and the remainder of the bodies built up by coils. Stylistically, the fully evolved Syro-Palestinian amphora of the LBA was characterized by a knob base, flat shoulders, low neck, and a more angular body than its Egyptian counterpart.

Except for meat, wine was the most frequent commodity listed on the ostraca, accounting for 285 examples, or 20 percent of the corpus. As do modern wine labels, the ostraca provided a host of important information about the production and kind of wine that each amphora contained. The Egyptian word for "wine" (irp) was sometimes modified by the words "genuine," "good," and "very good," even "very, very good," as additional guarantees of the high quality of the wine. The regnal year in which the beverage was presented to the pharaoh, presumably the vintage year of the wine, was also carefully noted on each ostracon. The vessel's volume was rarely included on the label, probably because the jars conformed to standard sizes.

The ancient Egyptians anticipated the French concept of a viticultural area—enshrined in the 1855 Bordeaux classification system and the 1936 appellation contrôlée law—by thousands of years. The ostraca marked out one region in particular, the "Western River," which encompassed the northwestern Delta region along the Canopic branch of the Nile, as the primary grape-producing and winemaking area. Other areas were Per-hebyt (modern Behbet el-Hajar) in the central Delta, Tjaru (Sile) in the northeastern Delta, Memphis, and the western desert oases, probably Kharga and Dakhla. Even "estate" names were provided, including those of "Nebmaatre" (the prenomen of Amenhotep III), "Amenhotep" or simply "the Pharaoh," and "the Royal Wife." Labels ending with "is-the-Splendor-of-Aten" refer to a religious establishment of the pharaoh, honoring the new god, Aten or the Sun Disk, that Amenhotep III's son and coregent in the last years of his reign, Akhenaten, had installed in place of Amen. The chief vintner was usually named: among others, Amen[hotep], Amenemone, Pa, and Ptahmai produced wine for the pharaoh.

The information on the ostraca surpassed that of a modern wine label by often stating the purpose for, or occasion at which the amphora was presented. "Wine for offerings," "wine for taxes," and "wine for merry-making" are self-explanatory. "Wine for a happy return" might have been served at a going-away party or might have been a final farewell gift to a deceased one preparing to embark on the trip into the afterlife. The two most important festive occasions commemorated by the ostraca were the "lifting up of the year," or the New Year's celebration, and particularly the *heb-sed* or *sed*-festival. Royal personages and high officials—such as the overseer of the treasury, the overseer of the fortress Thutmose, the royal scribe Huy—were sometimes named as the donors.

The Malkata ostraca were a molecular archaeologist's dream come true. Here were fragments of ancient vessels that gave the contents, the date of manufacture, place of origin, and additional details about quality and use. The ostraca provided an unparalleled touchstone for analyzing uninscribed vessels. An independent assessment of the place of origin of the amphoras and what they contained, using chemical methods and careful statistical evaluation, promised to refine, extend, and perhaps modify the existing understandings about the wine amphoras and related vessels.

My entrée to the unparalleled Malkata ostraca corpus came when I met Dorothea Arnold, co-curator with her husband, Dieter, of the Metropolitan Museum's Egyptian Art department. Dorothea has an absorbing interest in ancient Egyptian pottery, whose detailed study helps to round out the picture of life in pharaonic Egypt, which has often been dominated by monumental architecture, art, and inscriptions. Dorothea said that the Met's Malkata ostraca were being retranslated by Catherine Keller of the University of California at Berkeley, in the light of new information. The time was ripe to carry out a more detailed technological, chemical, and molecular archaeological investigation of the Malkata ostraca.

Dorothea's predecessor as curator in the Egyptian Art department, William Hayes, had already done a superb job of translating most of the Malkata ostraca, collating them, and interpreting them within a broader cultural context. As Hayes showed, nearly all the ostraca belonged to the last decade of Amenhotep III's reign. The stated use of their contents was for the "*sed* festival of His Majesty," and, amazingly, 711 of the 845 dated examples belonged to only three overlapping years—29–30, 33–34, and 37–38—when that festival was held. The *heb-sed* was a religious celebration, marked by ritual activity and feast days, that could go on for months and was often celebrated at fixed intervals in a pharaoh's reign. The main goal of the festival was to ensure a monarch's survival in later life and the country's welfare by guaranteeing the annual inundation of the Nile and the fertility of the land.

Hayes noted that the Year 29–30 and Year 37–38 ostraca were concentrated in the southern, older wing of the palace complex, whereas those of Year 33–34 came from rubbish heaps in or near the forecourt of the Amen temple to the north. This temple, together with a Festival Hall attached to its northern wall, had probably been specially constructed for the second *heb-sed*. In reinvestigating the main palace, a Japanese expedition uncovered part of a fresco that mentioned "wine for the *sed*-festival," which implied that these buildings had also served a special function during the first or third *heb-sed*. The University of Pennsylvania expedition recovered an additional 245 ostraca, most of which were wine dockets dating to the first *sed*-festival, in garbage dumps to the south of the main palace.

Hayes further observed that a large pile of sherds in one corner of the Amen temple's forecourt included 290 ostraca with excellently preserved meat labels. How could so many amphoras or larger-mouthed jars supplying food for a *heb-sed* feast have come to be in one place unless they had been used only once and then discarded? Why should so many jars in the corpus as a whole belong to just three years of Amenhotep's long reign? Hayes reasonably concluded that most of the amphoras in the palace had been specially made for the *sed*-festival and had been discarded after they had been emptied of their contents.

Hayes's hypothesis was supported by other considerations. It was common practice throughout the ancient Near East and Egypt to open a wine amphora by lopping off the stopper together with the entire neck, to prevent any contamination of the wine with the stopper materials. If that had been done at Malkata, those vessels could not have been refilled. In fact, only a relatively few examples of overwriting of one label over another, or palimpsests, were attested at the site, and those came from residential areas involved in the day-to-day functioning of the palace and were generally dated to non-*heb-sed* years (for example, an undated honey inscription written over a wine inscription of regnal year 9).

Under most circumstances—certainly among the lower classes—
an amphora was a technologically superior container and would have
been reused. Reuse on a very large scale, for example, occurred during
Persian times when the government collected hundreds of empty amphoras, which then were put to use as water containers along the
desert road to Syria (Herodotus, *History* 3.6–7). Such reuse of amphoras was the ancient equivalent of recycling soda or beer bottles
today. If Hayes was right, ancient Malkata was an exception to the
rule, and many scholars were hesitant to accept his hypothesis. Even
if we are accustomed to throw away a modern wine bottle, whether it
is fortified Thunderbird or a fine varietal, ancient Egyptians would
not have been so profligate.

The 35 wine ostraca that were chemically analyzed by INAA at
the University of Missouri Research Reactor cast a new light on
Hayes's hypothesis, as well as raising many other issues. The sherds
were selected to represent all the major geographic regions and many
of the named estates, officials, and chief vintners mentioned in their
inscriptions. In addition, 19 ostraca from jars containing other goods,
believed to have been either produced locally (meat and beer) or
imported ("ale" and *ben*-oil) and relevant to fermented beverage production, were tested.

The Old World databank was searched for the closest chemical
matches to the 35 Malkata wine ostraca. Except for four examples, all
the wine ostraca had extremely similar chemical profiles. No other
samples in the databank, representing many geographic regions of
Egypt and the Eastern Mediterranean, were as close as those from
Malkata itself. Similarly, the 10 meat ostraca, two probable "ale"
specimens, and seven additional samples from the larger area of
Thebes belonged to the same chemical group. The upshot of the
INAA study was stunning: the same clay had been used to make jars
that the inscriptions documented as containing several kinds of goods
and coming from the Delta, Thebes, and possibly farther afield (for
example, the "ale" or "beer" in one jar was from Kedy, often identified with Syria).

The INAA data and statistical analyses allowed for only one interpretation. A clay source in the Theban area had been exploited to
make the numerous jars belonging to the consistent compositional

group that included nearly all the wine amphoras. Yet, if this were true, why did so many of the wine labels mention the "Western River" (i.e., the Nile Delta) as the production area? Even more troubling, the hypothesized marl clay deposit has not yet been located in the Thebaid.

As was required to test the Southern Palestinian hypothesis vis-à-vis the Hyksos, a program of clay sampling and analyses in the Theban area is needed to resolve the second issue. Marl *tufle* or shale deposits have been reported at the entrance to the Valley of the Queens, as well as outcropping in many places along the limestone escarpment on both sides of the Nile. These fine-grained calcareous, marly sediments are ideal for pottery making, as are mixtures of *tufle* and Nile alluvial clay, which potters at a village near Malkata and across the river at Luxor are reported still to be using.

The problem of how the jars could have been made locally and the wine they contained produced elsewhere, especially in "Western River" estates, vanishes when the implications of Hayes's hypothesis are drawn out. If most of the amphoras in the Malkata palace had been specially made for the *sed*-festival—as borne out by the INAA study—then the wine and other goods produced in the Nile Delta, Memphis, the Fayyum, or possibly Syria, had been "rebottled" at Thebes. Amphoras made in uniform fashion—similar pottery fabrics, labels, stoppers, and stamped or painted sealings—were most appropriate for such a momentous occasion.

If this scenario is correct, wine and other goods coming from the north arrived in different containers from those used to present them at the *heb-sed*. A glimpse into the busy international trading world of the day is provided by a wall painting in the tomb of Kenamun (Theban Tomb 93), dating to the reign of Amenhotep II and presumably still in operation a half century later at the time of Amenhotep III. Amphoras are shown being unloaded from numerous Levantine merchantmen. Kenamun was the "Mayor of the Southern City, Overseer of the granary of Amen," and the scene in his tomb might well be a realistic depiction of activities in the harbor of Malkata (Birket Habu). After being carried down the gangplanks, the amphoras were weighed and registered. If a pottery vessel lacked a docket or sealing, this would have been the time to fill out a bill of lading or prepare a list of the vessel's contents on papyrus. Later, the information could be transferred to the dockets and sealings of the newly prepared and stoppered amphoras for the *sed*-festival.

This scenario also assumes that a royal pottery-producing center and central registration facility existed at Thebes, neither of which has yet been uncovered in excavations. Potters are known to have been active during Dynasty 19 at the village of Deir el-Medineh, whose workers were sponsored by the royal house to prepare and stock the tombs of the New Kingdom pharaohs. A unique, earlier, pottery workshop scene is depicted in Kenamun's tomb that very likely provides a glimpse into the royal potteries. Dorothea Arnold suggests that the reddish material in two large vats ("baskets"), and piled on the ground, is marl clay, probably obtained from a local quarry. A low "fast" wheel, which is operated by the combined hand and foot actions of the potter and with the help of an assistant, would have been ideal for mass-producing the range of pottery types that are shown being made. The Kenamun fresco documents a highly specialized, royal industry, in keeping with the large, thriving capital of Upper Egypt.

A royal administrative and registration facility must also have existed to register goods going into and out of the capital and the palace. Scenes in Dynasty 18 Theban tombs clearly show amphoras being sealed and stamped. A stamp for a fat label, obviously intended for an amphora sealing, was accidentally stamped onto a locally made mudbrick from Malkata, and a stamp reading "Wine from the Western River" was recovered from the nearby mortuary temple of Thutmose IV. These are excellent indicators that a royal registration center, which would have had a full collection of the necessary stamps for sealing the Malkata jars, existed in the area.

The more detailed ostraca or inked dockets would probably have been inscribed on the amphoras during the registration process, when the Malkata amphoras were sealed in Thebes. This activity is not shown in the tomb paintings, and discrepancies between the stamp and docket inscriptions on the same amphoras in Tutankhamun's tomb (discussed later in this chapter) are great enough to suggest that the jar labels were sometimes written at a different time or in another place. The handwriting of the hieratic script on New Kingdom ostraca and sealings shows that many scribes were involved in the labeling process over several hundred years.

As I pursued the INAA and molecular archaeological study of the ostraca, one peculiarity of the amphora stoppers found in Amenhotep III's palace struck my attention. It provided the confirming piece of the evidence that William Hayes had indeed been right when he hypothesized that the Malkata amphoras had been made in local potteries for the special occasion of the *heb-sed*.

Colin Hope of Monash University in Victoria, Australia, has carefully studied 53 stoppers that had sealed wine amphoras at Malkata. He has shown how reeds and chopped-up leaves and chaff had first been stuffed into the narrow mouth of the jars, sometimes along with a bowl or circular pottery sherd, to form a tight bung. In the final stage, wet clay was crammed into the opening and smoothed over the rim, to make a tight seal. As a further guarantee of the contents, the king's cartouches and a shortened version of the ostracon information in Egyptian hieroglyphs, usually mentioning the wine's quality, purpose, geographic or estate origin, were stamped or painted on the top and sides of the stopper.

What was curious about the Malkata stoppers was that none of them had been punctured by a small hole that would have served as a secondary fermentation lock. A young wine, especially one that was subject to movement or heating, would have continued to produce gases from unfinished or renewed fermentation and other chemical reactions. Puncturing the sealing—or in some cases perforating the base of a bowl that was tightly wedged into the amphora mouth— allowed the gases to escape and prevented the vessel from exploding. At the same time, it was important to seal this hole up again with clay as soon as possible, to keep the wine from being exposed to air and going to vinegar.

If the Malkata amphoras had been made in the Delta region, where most of their wine had been produced, why did their stoppers lack secondary fermentation locks? Any wine jar shipped up the Nile would be exposed to hot temperatures and excessive agitation. Ancient winemakers and their shippers would have taken the precaution of providing each amphora with the possibility to "breathe." Because they had neglected to provide this fail-safe device for the Malkata stoppers, it is reasonable to conclude that the wine was still—no longer biologically and chemically active—and had been transferred to new amphoras, which did not require secondary fermentation locks, for the *heb-sed*.

With the mystery of the ostraca's origins seemingly solved, we were on more solid ground when it came to determining the contents of the amphoras. According to our standard battery of analyses, all nine wine ostraca that were tested did indeed contain remnants of wine as attested by tartaric acid and calcium tartrate. Although the labels did not state it as such, they were also all resinated in keeping with Levantine and Near Eastern practice. As might have been anticipated, terebinth tree resin (*Pistacia atlantica* Desf.) was the most common additive. This resin was already being used 4000–4500 years earlier in Iran and the Caucasus, and Egyptians first whetted their palates on a similar blend shortly before 3000 B.C.

New Kingdom Egypt had a huge appetite for terebinth tree resin, which was used for incense, in medicine, and as a preservative to embalm the human body. The needs of the country could only partly be met by local production, and they looked abroad for additional supplies. Ships plied the Mediterranean, carrying loads of this resin and other goods. The late fourteenth-century B.C. wreck at Uluburun (Kaş) had been carrying a rich cargo, possibly bound for Egypt, when it sank along the southern Turkish coast. Some of the amphoras on board the merchantman were as much as a third full of terebinth resin nodules and chunks. In fact, samples of this resin provided the impetus for research to characterize fully the chemical composition of the resin—principally by John Mills and Raymond White of the National Gallery in London—and served us as excellent reference material. The MASCA laboratory took the investigation of the Uluburun terebinth tree resin a step further, since we discovered that the resin from the amphoras also tested positive for tartaric acid and tartrate. The best explanation for this result is that the amphoras had originally been topped up with wine. Only a finite amount of resin is dissolved into the wine, and, as a space-saving measure, it makes sense to ship jars of wine containing extra resin. Once the wine was decanted off, the extra resin could be used for other purposes.

The interiors of two Malkata ostraca were lined with a shiny black or dark brown deposit unlike the thin reddish residues of the tere-binth tree resinated wine. Our analysis of this residue proved to be chemically closest to myrrh (Egyptian ʿntyw). This extremely valu-able resin is exuded and collected from a tree (genus *Commiphora* of the Burseraceae family) that did not grow in Egypt. According to ancient texts, it had to be imported from Punt—probably Somalia—an arduous sea journey to the south. Much later in the Roman period (chapter 11), myrrh was the premier additive to wine and the most expensive. The Egyptians had scooped the urbane inhabitants of Italy on both counts.

Our analyses revealed that myrrh-laced wine had filled a "red lus-trous spindle bottle" from New Kingdom Egypt. A Cypriot archaeolo-gist, Kathyrn Erikkson, who has since published her doctoral disserta-tion on this important vessel type, arranged for it to be sampled at the Royal Ontario Museum in Toronto. Pieces of a dark brown de-posit—the liquid that had leaked out from the vessel through the clay stopper and congealed on the surface—were tested.

As the name spindle bottle implies, this one-handled jug form looks like an elongated yarn spindle, tapering toward the top and bottom. In its pottery incarnation, it can be over half a meter tall, and the surface was finished off with a red slip that was hand pol-ished. It is a stunning vessel, and many examples have been recov-ered from Egyptian tombs of the period. Waist-high examples found in central Anatolia (chapter 8) suggest that Hittite potters probably first got the idea to make such a vessel. The type probably influenced the development of the more bulbous "Syrian flask," soon imitated in Egypt and which Hayes believed was used to transport wine from the western oases to Malkata.

The tree resins in the Malkata wine were not specifically identified on the wine ostraca, perhaps because only a small amount of this material was customarily added to the beverage. Whether the addi-tive is equivalent to what is called "resin" (Egyptian *sft*) or "incense" (Egyptian *sntr*) on other Malkata labels is yet to be verified chem-ically. In addition to terebinth tree resin and myrrh, resins from pine, cedar, and various other conifers were in high demand for the mum-mification process and as aromatic substances in perfume and incense and had to be imported. It is perhaps no wonder that a captain of a commercial ship in the Mediterranean and Red Sea donated four of the six "incense" jars in the Malkata ostraca corpus.

Several wine ostraca at Malkata are modified by "blended" (Egyptian *sm3*) or "mixed" (Egyptian *mdg/mtk*). Yet, the labels do not state what was blended or mixed with the wine. Another dubious term is *šdḥ*, a prized beverage of the time, that is often translated pomegranate wine. This beverage is graded "good" and "very good," like some of the wines, and might well have been grape wine that had gone through a special heating or blending operation. On one Malkata ostracon, wine appears together with *ben*-oil. The moringa tree (*Moringa aptera*), from which the oil is derived, is probably indigenous to Egypt and thrives in tropical climates throughout northeastern Africa and the southern Levant. Moringa nut oil, a sweet, odorless liquid that does not easily become rancid, would be an excellent substitute for tree resin in wine. This wine, however, is said to come from Kharu, an Egyptian term for the Levant, so it need not represent common Egyptian practice.

Several vintage scenes from tombs at Thebes show a liquid being poured from a small jar into an amphora at a final stage in the fermentation process, before stoppering and sealing. A particularly evocative picture of how several liquids might be mixed together appears in the Dynasty 20 tomb of Kynebu (Theban Tomb 113). Three amphoras and two jars are placed on a high floral-decorated stand. Long tubes siphon the liquids from the three amphoras into a large two-handled bowl (krater) on a lower stand. A small jar, like those in the vintage scenes, is used to replenish one of the amphoras. This "mixed beverage" was probably prepared for immediate consumption.

What is being added to the amphoras in the winery, and what liquids are being mixed together at the celebration? Possibly, wine, beer, and mead were being mixed together to make an "Egyptian grog," like the concoctions that were common in Anatolia and Greece at this time (chapters 8 and 10). Other possibilities spring to mind: the ancient Egyptian winemaker might have blended different vintages, as in a modern sherry, or added special ingredients such as essence of blue lotus (*Nymphaea caerulea*). The simple truth is that, except for tree resins, we do not know what the ancient Egyptians added to their wines or how they mixed them with other liquids or

FIGURE 6.4. An additive is shown being poured into wine amphoras before they are stoppered with clay in this fresco from the tomb of Khaemweset (TT261) at Thebes (Egypt), dating to the fifteenth century B.C.

beverages. Ancient Egyptians had an empirical understanding and appreciation for natural products that had antimicrobial, medicinal, and aphrodisiacal, stimulant, and other psychoactive properties. Myrrh, for example, has analgesic effects, and one advantage of this additive in wine might have been that if the resin did not cover up any bad tastes or odors of the wine, at least it numbed your senses.

Wine and tree resins, together with beer, are the most frequently cited ingredients in the ancient Egyptian pharmacopoeia. They were applied externally to wounds and ingested to cure other ailments. In addition to wine's efficacy as a sterilizing and anesthetizing agent, its high alcoholic content served as a vehicle in dissolving other finely ground substances, particularly aromatics, that had their own benefits. Wine lees were considered especially healthful. It is now known that grapes are a rich source of antioxidants that reduce cholesterol and ward off cancers. These compounds are concentrated in the lees, together with vitamin-rich yeast.

The ostraca from Malkata and elsewhere in Egypt have only begun to yield their textual and chemical secrets about wine and other ancient Egyptian fermented beverages during one of the most prosperous periods of antiquity. Supplied by goods imported from other parts of Africa and the Eastern Mediterranean, New Kingdom palace life reflected the internationalism of the period and had profound effects on native Egyptian culture and technology. Fermented beverages were at the center of many of these developments, because of their expanding economic importance and uses in social, religious, and funerary contexts.

The careful labeling of wine amphoras and Egyptian realism in art, combined with molecular archaeological investigation, has provided us with a view of ancient winemaking available nowhere else in the ancient world. Of course, some details of the winemaking process may never be known, such as the particular grape varieties that were used by the Egyptian winemakers, whether their final products were sweet or dry as we understand the terms today, or whether they could effectively age their wines in pottery vessels. Molecular archaeology may eventually begin to fill in some of these gaps by analyzing for a range of constituents, including sugars, tannins and anthocyanins, and preservatives such as sulfite. Molecular biology may even be able to tell us a great deal more about grape varieties, as well as yeast and bacterial fermentation processes.

Wine as the Ultimate Religious Expression

Whatever its value as an earthly elixir, wine's special benefits were traced back to the gods. Wine served to invoke divine assistance and to bridge the chasm between this life and the next at many festivals, besides the *heb-sed*. One of the most important religious holidays, the so-called Wag-festival, came at the beginning of the New Year, when Sothis (Greek Sirius), the brightest star in the night sky, appeared shortly before sunrise, after having disappeared for 70 days. This auspicious event in summer was tied to an even more important natural event—the annual inundation of the Nile River that was essential for the fertility of narrow strips of land bordering the river and the Delta. The celebrations were held at Abydos, the religious center of the god Osiris and where Scorpion I had been buried with more than 4000 liters of imported wine in Dynasty 0 (chapter 5). An orgy lasting for three days was centered around a funerary feast to Osiris, who was called "The Lord of wine through [or during] the inundation," a title that had first been applied to this resurrection and fertility god in the Old Kingdom Pyramid Texts.

The rejuvenation of the vineyards in the Delta and elsewhere in Egypt was a key motivation behind the ritual celebrations of the Wag-festival. Like the grapevines that lay dormant, Osiris had been killed at the hand of his evil brother, Seth. Isis, his wife and sister, had gathered together his scattered remains and resuscitated him, so that he could father Horus, the falcon-god. Horus avenged Osiris's death by killing Seth and became ruler through his living representative on the earth, the pharaoh. By this intricate analogical "logic," the festival called to mind the mythological events that could ensure a "rebirth" of Osiris, who had been consigned to the western underworld, as well as renewal of the Egyptian vineyards and life in general. As was the Greek Dionysos (chapter 10), Osiris's resurrection was symbolized by the grapevine, which adorned the Theban tombs and was sometimes presented to the god.

The dark side of Egyptian wine was its symbolic association with blood, based on both materials' being red. When blood was shed, however, life was in the balance. It was no stretch for the Egyptian religionists and priesthood to imagine a terrible scene of death and destruction when the grapes were trodden out in the winepress. The god of the winepress, Shesmu, is described as a "slaughterer," and "red of timbers" because the supports of the press became stained with grape juice. The wrath of this god is especially directed against the enemies of the pharaoh. In one gruesome illustration in a New Kingdom papyrus, Shesmu is seen twisting a pressing bag to exact the last drop of the precious liquid. In addition to pomace, the bag contains three human heads, and two more dead bodies fall to the floor with the juice. The biblical Yahweh could not have exacted vengeance in a more dramatic way, when Isaiah (63:3) records that "I have trodden the winepress alone . . . I trod them [the enemies of Israel] in my anger . . . their lifeblood is sprinkled upon my garments, and I have stained all my raiment."

In Egyptian mythology, a female deity named Hathor wreaked the greatest havoc, which led to her appeasement by wine offerings and special celebrations. Several cycles of stories, including "The Destruction of Mankind" and "The Book of the Heavenly Cow," recount how the high-god Re was incensed at mankind's rebellion and decided to send his daughter Hathor in the form of a lioness, Sekhmet, to destroy them. At the last moment, Re retracts his awful judgment and fools Hathor into drinking "red beer," which has inundated the fields and which she believes is a sign of her successful campaign. Instead, she becomes drunk and forgets to kill what remained of mankind. Hathor's destructiveness and drunkedness are also paralleled by the frenzied behavior of the maenads in the Dionysiac cult (chapter 9).

In keeping with the symbolic salvation of humankind, the Egyptians celebrated a festival of the goddess, named appropriately enough "the Drunkenness of Hathor." It came one day after the Wag-festival and took place at Dendera, about halfway between Abydos and Thebes, where a large temple had been built to the goddess. The timing of the Hathor celebrations was no accident. They coincided with the Nile's inundation, which could be particularly violent at first, with a reddish iron-rich alluvium from the Atbara branch even giving a reddish cast to the floodwaters that fit with the "red beer" episode, and which then settled down, to set the stage for the renewal of the land. In like fashion, Hathor's wild Sekhmet nature could be calmed by the elements of civilization—drinking wine and other alcoholic beverages, making music, and dancing—and converted into its opposite— the milder, more benevolent feline Bastet. By offering the goddess wine and reveling in it, the celebrants were acknowledging Hathor's crucial importance in sustaining mankind.

Hathor was also known as the "goddess of foreign lands," and, as such, she was the patron deity of a host of natural resources and products that Egypt needed from outside its boundaries. The Nile's floodwater, of course, came from its East African tributaries, which flowed through the deserts of Nubia where Hathor dwelt. In the Sinai, a temple for her worship was built on a remote mountaintop, near the turquoise mines that the Egyptians mined and with an extraordinary view looking out across the rugged landscape. Hathor was the goddess of Byblos, the supplier of cedar and other goods from Lebanon. Because the grapevine had been transplanted from the Levant to the Nile Delta and foreign wines were much enjoyed, it was also natural to associate her with wine.

The earliest scene of a wine offering thus far discovered is at Memphis on the wall of the pyramid temple of Sahure, the Dynasty 5 pharaoh whose navy plied the Eastern Mediterranean. It shows the king making his offering to none other than Sekhmet, or Hathor in her terrifying aspect. A special bowl, often made of faience, was eventually developed to make offerings to Hathor. It was decorated with papyrus and lotus flowers and sometimes depicted Hathor as the heavenly cow or queen of the skies standing in the midst of the marsh.

Wines of the Heretic King, Akhenaten, and of Tutankhamun

When Amenhotep IV, the son and successor of Amenhotep III, ascended the throne in the mid-fourteenth century B.C., he undertook revolutionary changes. He laid out an extensive, new capital at el-Amarna, along the middle Nile, on virgin soil. It was named Akhetaten (Egyptian "The Horizon of Aten") after the new god Aten, or the Sun Disk, that he had devoted himself to. Amen and his priesthood had been ousted from their vaunted place, and, to mark this passage, Amenhotep IV took a new throne name, Akhenaten (the meaning is uncertain—"Glorified Spirit of the Sun Disk" or a similar sentiment to the deity). He swept away the complicated pantheistic religion in one fell swoop. All life and every blessing now emanated from the Sun Disk in his monotheistic re-interpretation of Egyptian cult and society. The "heresy" spread into the field of fine arts, which did not adhere to traditional Egyptian canons but boldly portrayed Egyptian life, including the paunchy effeminate-looking pharaoh, in a new realistic modality. The minor crafts, such as glassmaking and faience-making, drew on new sources of inspiration, especially from the Levant, to create masterly and colorful vessels, jewelry, statuettes, furniture, chariots, and other items intended for daily life or the tomb.

By contrast with his revolutionary thrusts into other areas of life, Akhenaten's taste in wine did not break with the past, nor did he encourage the development of new styles or technologies, as far as we know. After considerable excavation of his capital at el-Amarna, which was occupied for at least 12 years, only 165 wine ostraca have been excavated and published, far less in a relative sense than the more than 250 examples from three years of his father's reign at Malkata. Many explanations—the vagaries of archaeological exploration, the reuse of amphoras, a shift in religious priorities, or simply that Akhenaten never lived to see the celebration of a *heb-sed*—might be proposed to account for this difference. Except for some name changes of the religious estates producing wine in the Delta—those belonging to Amen had been confiscated by the adherents of Aten—little differed on the labels. Most of the wine came from the "Western River" or northwestern Delta region, but the eastern Delta, Memphis, and three western oases were represented. The wine was contributed by the king, his family members, and high officials. Some older vintages were dated to years 28 and 30, presumably of Amenhotep III since Akhenaten ruled only 17 years. Unless there was a co-regency between the two monarchs, a possibility that is seriously entertained by some scholars, these wines would have been as much as 15 years old when they arrived in Akhenaten's new capital. In the many domestic scenes from the Amarna tombs that show the royal family at ease, sitting in comfortable chairs in their diaphanous gowns, they drink their wine in cups and chalices, as had long been traditional in Egypt.

One of the most amazing discoveries of twentieth-century archaeology was made when Howard Carter and Lord Carnarvon broke into the tomb of Tutankhamun. Before their eyes lay the accumulated riches, some 5000 artifacts, that had been buried with the boy-king in the close confines of his burial chamber and three attached rooms. At 19 years of age, Tutankhamun, the son-in-law and possibly the brother of Akhenaten, had not had time to become a wine connoisseur. Nevertheless, he carried 26 amphoras to his grave. The dried reddish residues of the wine can still be seen inside some jars in the Egyptian Museum in Cairo. These vessels, which had been tightly stoppered and sealed, had burst open, possibly under the pressure of secondary fermentation gases that had built up in the hot tomb. Until the residues are analyzed, we can only surmise from the hieratic

FIGURE 6.5. Wine amphoras, stoppered and unstoppered, and a "Syrian flask" (no. 498), as found in King Tutankhamun's tomb in the Valley of the Kings, Thebes (Egypt), ca. 1330 B.C.

labels on the shoulders of the vessels what some of the finest wines produced in Egypt at the time might have tasted like and what additional secrets will be revealed by their chemical compositions.

Twenty-three amphoras date to just three years: years 4, 5, and 9 of Tutankhamun's reign. These must have been stellar years, at least in quantity if not quality. Otherwise, only a jar from the last year of the king (10) and another one dated year 31 were among the burial goods. If the year 31 amphora belongs to the reign of Amenhotep III, then it was particularly well aged for almost 35 years. Centuries later during the Ptolemaic period, Onkhsheshonqi wrote an aphorism to his son on a piece of pottery: "Wine matures as long as one does not open it." Perhaps, this jar in Tutankhamun's tomb represents an early attempt to apply this maxim.

Fifteen chief vintners are named on the Tutankhamun wine jar labels, and of those, two have Semitic names—Khay and 'Apere-shop—attesting to their Levantine roots from where so much know-how in Egyptian winemaking had come. With a half dozen jars to his credit, Khay was responsible for producing more wine than any of the other vintners. He is also the only vintner to whom is attributed wine from two years (4 and 5) and two estates (the "House-of-Aton" and the "House of Tutankhamun"). His expertise is further reflected in his making both wine of royal quality and šdḥ, likely a specially treated grape wine.

Predictably, every wine amphora, except two from Tjel (Sile) and Karet in the northeastern Nile Delta and a third from the Kharga, came from the "Western River." Most of the latter had been produced at the "House-of-Aton" estate, whose numerous vintners from the same years implied that its holdings were widely scattered. The two northeastern Delta wineries belonged to the same estate. When Tutankhamun changed his name from Tutankhaton (Egyptian "Living Image of the Sun Disk") in the middle of his reign, to curry favor with the priests of Amen, the Aton vineyards in the Delta did not change their names. A five-year lag is difficult to explain, unless Tutankhamun continued to share the faith of his predecessor. The priests and later rulers were not fooled, and Tutankamun's memory was carefully expunged from the record.

Very little information is provided on the Tutankhamun wine amphoras about the type and quality of wine that they contained. Šdḥ has already been discussed. "Sweet wine" (*irp ndm*) is listed on four labels, a pair each from the House-of-Aton estates in the northeastern Delta and in the "Western River." Similarly, at el-Amarna, the phrase probably connotes an especially sweet grape variety or the addition of extra sugar, perhaps as honey or figs.

In Tutankhamun's tomb, seven "Syrian flasks" were recovered, one of which was reported to contain "dried [wine] lees" and another of which had an intact sealing that was stamped with a wine label. They probably contained special Egyptian vintages, perhaps from the western oases. Tutankhamun had superb vessels for quaffing; an elegant alabaster chalice took the form of a white lotus, with open-work floral handles surmounted by *heh* (Egyptian "millions of years") hieroglyphs. A strainer in the shape of a one-handled bowl was a necessary part of any connoisseur's wine drinking set. Toward the end of the New Kingdom, bronze sets of a jar, ladle, strainer, and variously sized bowls were popular; they are also attested in Southern Palestine, on the northern coast of Israel, and in the Jordan Valley.

King Tutankhamun was ushered into eternity quickly but with decorum. His followers enjoyed a final farewell meal not far from his tomb. The remains of the funeral banquet had been buried there: they included broad collars made of flowers, bowls with the remains of the meal, and a long-necked jar with a floral design—similar in shape to a Syrian flask but lacking the handle—that no doubt held a fine vintage wine.

The Vineyard of Egypt under the Ramessides

Ramesses I, an obscure son of a "captain of the troops" in the northeastern Nile Delta became pharaoh at the beginning of Dynasty 19, in 1295 B.C. He reigned for only a year at the end of a life that had seen him rise through the ranks of the military and religious hierarchy to become vizier, the highest position in the court, with oversight over every aspect of Egyptian life. As ruler, he set in motion through his descendants, the great pharaohs—Sety I, Ramesses II, and Sety II—an unprecedented expansion of Egyptian prosperity at home and influence abroad.

As the name (Sety) of two of Ramesses I's famous heirs attests, the god Seth or Sutekh headed the pantheon of the Ramesside rulers. A more radical up-ending of Egyptian mythological thinking could not be imagined. Seth, the wild jackal-like god of the desert, had been worshiped by the Hyksos, who had been driven out of Egypt and expunged from the official history. He was the direct antithesis of Osiris and Horus, since he killed Osiris and injured his son's eye. Horus for his part had finally killed Seth, thus restoring order to the land. Even one form of the name Seth—*Sth*—is derived from the word *th*, meaning "intoxication" in a negative sense.

The Ramessides went so far in displacing Horus and Osiris by Seth that Sety I built a monumental temple to Seth at Abydos, where the other two gods had reigned supreme from time immemorial. In the final analysis, however, Sety and his son, Ramesses II, who completed the structure, placated the powerful priesthood at the religious capital by using the hieroglyph for Osiris in place of that for Seth, even in the ruler's name.

Ramesses II, who ruled for an extraordinary 67 years and sired hundreds of princes and princesses with his many wives, took his role as god incarnate on the earth a step further. He still stands in all his gigantic glory at Abu Simbel, above the second cataract, and the great Hypostyle Hall in the Karnak temple was completed by him. His ties to the northeastern Delta and Hyksos tradition, however, are exemplified by the new capital that he had built at Qantir, ancient Pi-Ramesses (Egyptian "House of Ramesses"; biblical "Raamses"), only several kilometers north of the Hyksos capital at Avaris. The extensive palace with multicolored faience plaques, showing prisoners of war, and geometric and floral designs, is now the focus of excavations under the direction of Edgar Pusch of the Pelizaeus-Museum in Hildesheim, Germany. In the so-called 400-Year Stela, which was discovered at nearby Tanis, where many of the monuments of Pi-Ramesses and Avaris were moved to adorn a later capital, Ramesses is shown standing before the Nubian Seth. The text below the figure relates how Ramesses' father, Sety I, honored the god in his 400th year at a celebration during the reign of Horemhab, the last pharaoh of Dynasty 18. Since the celebration in question can be dated to around 1330 B.C., the crucial anniversary of Seth occurred 400 years earlier, in about 1730 B.C. This date fits very well with the Hyksos rise to power in the northeastern Nile Delta. By erecting the stela, the Ramesside kings were proclaiming to the world that their power found its source in Hyksos culture and religion.

The northeastern Delta had long been a wine-producing area, although its production paled in comparison to that of the "Western River," the northwestern Delta. Ramesses II put the Waters of Reʿ, the Pelusiac branch of the Nile, on the vinicultural map as has never been matched before or since. The northeastern Delta truly became the Vineyard of Egypt, or Kaenkeme, as the ancient Egyptian referred to the region.

A century after the Amarna Age, the wine amphora ostraca from Ramesses II's mortuary temple in western Thebes—the Ramesseum—and from the capital at Pi-Ramesses tell the story of the expansion of the royal winemaking industry in the northeastern Delta, as well as throughout the country. Most of the vineyards were located at Kaenkeme, but other wineries throughout the Delta, at Heliopolis near Cairo, Meidum at the mouth to the Fayyum, and Hermopolis along the middle Nile, also supplied the royal house. According to Wilhelm Spiegelberg's definitive study of the Ramesseum corpus in 1923, 34 geographic locations and 34 vintners are mentioned in the 679 ostraca. Thirty years in the 67-year reign of Ramesses II are cited on the labels, but the overwhelming majority of the years fall within the first 11 years, probably when the temple was built and the main provisioning was carried out. Year 7 must have been a very good year for wine; it occurs 244 times. Because of the unevenness of the evidence, however, it cannot be concluded that later years in Ramesses II's reign were necessarily less good because they are less well represented in the Ramesseum. The generally high quality of the wine is emphasized by the repeated occurrence of "good" (nfr) and "very good" (nfr-nfr) on the labels. At his southern capital in Thebes, these wines were served up by a royal "scribe," or sommelier, who managed the "wine department of the Residence."

A splendid description of a small wine-producing estate in the northeastern Nile Delta, part of the extensive holdings of the royal house, was recorded by an apprentice scribe, Inena, around 1200 B.C. during the reign of Sety II. In Papyrus Anastasi (IV, 6.10–7.9), we learn that 21 individuals—6 children, 4 adolescent males, 7 mature

a.

b.

FIGURE 6.6. A cartoonlike series of vignettes captures both the serious and humorous aspects of ancient Egyptian winemaking, from the early Dynasty 18 tomb of Intef, Royal Herald under Thutmosis III, at Thebes (Egypt). In the first scene (a), the chief vintner, with an ample belly, plays the part of both taskmaster and fruit-taster. The grapevines have been trained to grow on an arbor or pergola, from which grape clusters are conveniently picked. In the second scene (b), a group of four exuberant men tread out the grapes, as they precariously hold on to ropes and the vertical struts of the vat. Their work is done to the accompaniment of a song to the Lady Rennutet, a cobra goddess and the patroness of winemaking. The third vignette (c) shows the final pressing operation, which yields a dark red must that cascades down into a deep vat. To the left, rows of amphoras are lined up, ready to receive

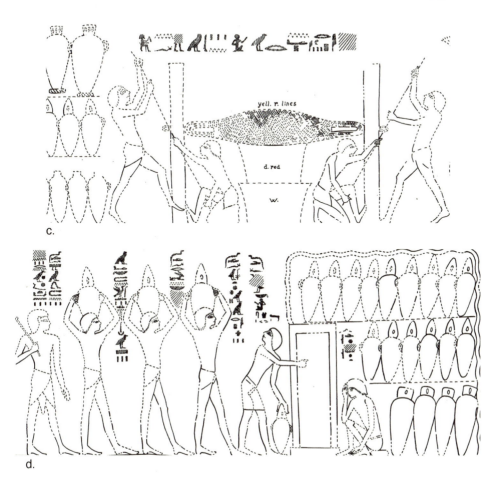

c.

d.

the juice and begin the fermentation. The amphoras in the lowest row are unstoppered, so the must in them is still undergoing fermentation. Those in the middle row have already completed the process because they are neatly stoppered and sealed. The amphoras in the top row are the most interesting, because their mouths are filled with some kind of material, perhaps the reeds, chopped-up leaves, or chaff that was stuffed inside stoppers of the period. Once all the fermentation gases had escaped through this loose stuffing, it could be covered over with clay and the identifying estate seal applied. The final scene of the series (d) takes us into the wine cellar itself, where the "guardian" of the wine has collapsed from overindulgence. The porter in front of the door says, "The servant is sleeping," but the keeper protests, "I haven't slept at all!"

males, and 4 older males—maintained an estate that produced about 1500 amphoras of wine, 50 amphoras of *šdh* (probably a specially prepared wine), and 50 amphoras of a particularly powerful-sounding beverage, *p3-wr* (Egyptian "the great one"), as well as fresh produce of grapes and pomegranates, in a single year. The winery's operation was overseen by Tjatroy. After the thousands of liters of wine were loaded onto two cattleboats, the scribe escorted the shipment up the Nile to Sety II's mortuary temple in western Thebes.

A new line of rulers was established by Setnakhte at the beginning of Dynasty 20, after a period of disruption after the death of Sety II, when it was said the "the land of Egypt was cast adrift, every man a law unto himself" (Papyrus Harris 75.2–5). Setnakhte's son, Ramesses III (1184–1153 B.C.), in both name and style reasserted the grandeur that was Egypt's in Dynasty 19. His mortuary temple at Medinet Habu in western Thebes is gargantuan, with its walls and pillars covered with reliefs of wine offerings to the gods—which were now more common than they had ever been in Egyptian history—together with his many military expeditions to the Levant, and his land and sea defense of Egypt against the "Sea Peoples."

Ramesses III, like every other Egyptian pharaoh, resorted to bombastic claims on his monuments. In the great Harris Papyrus (I.15a.13 and 18a.11), the longest papyrus (40.5 meters) extant from ancient Egypt, the king claims that he presented 20,078 amphoras of wine to Amen, the high-god of Thebes and Egypt, as well as another 39,510 jars to the deity at specific festivals. He also declares that he planted vineyards "without limit" in the western oases and in the southern part of the country. In the north, he planted hundreds of thousands of vineyards. Everywhere, he staffed the new facilities with workers and vintners, especially captives taken from the Levant. It is unlikely that he did anything on the scale that he claims. The Delta, for example, had already been closely planted with vineyards in his predecessors' reigns. Viticulture was difficult in the south, although eventually it was established there. The sheer scale of Egyptian viniculture, even if he took credit for what others had done, and the magnitude of Ramesses III's vision of wine's importance in life speak volumes about this very consequential beverage.

What we already know about ancient Egyptian wine provides a

tantalizing foretaste of what may eventually be discovered. The Pharaoh and the gods of Egypt, whose purview extended to the limits of the then-civilized world, would have expected nothing less than for us to pursue our research as far as possible. Who is to say whether wine like that produced in ancient Egypt cannot be made again. A Greek named Nestor Gianaclis attempted to re-create an ancient Egyptian wine in the northwestern Nile Delta, the "Western River" of old, beginning in 1903. The vineyard was laid out on well-drained, salt-free chalky soil. After he had planted some 73 grape varietals and even captured an award from a prestigious French gourmet society for his white wine, his efforts were cut short by World War II. The winery, which still bears his name, continues to produce mellow, delicious whites, such as ancient Mareotic wine, which Athenaeus (*The Deipnosophists* 1.33d) claimed was "excellent, white, pleasant, fragrant, easily assimilated." Horace (Ode 37) took a dimmer view of wine produced in this region, which he said had caused Cleopatra to go crazy. If the bottled "Cleopatra" that is available for sale today in Egypt is any indication, he might have been right. It is a rather sweet, cloying concoction. With time and the help of researchers on ancient wine and viticulture, it should be possible to produce a more fitting wine for a king or queen.

CHAPTER 7

Wine of the World's First Cities

O N THE OTHER SIDE of the Fertile Crescent from Egypt, civilization was also moving forward, and fermented beverages were near the top of the list of specialty items for royalty as well as the man or woman in the streets. As in Egypt, one's options— whether grape wine, barley beer, or date wine, which had established itself as the overwhelming Mesopotamian favorite by the first millennium B.C.—vastly differed, depending upon socioeconomic status, historical precedent, and the relative difficulty and expense of growing the necessary plants in the lowlands.

Wine and the domesticated Eurasian grapevine had already begun their odyssey southward from the highlands of the Caucasus, Taurus, and Zagros Mountains during the Neolithic period (chapters 2 and 4). By 3500 B.C., relatively sophisticated winemaking was in place at a key military and trading entrepôt, erected and controlled by proto-Sumerians or Elamites, or both, from the lowlands, at Godin Tepe in the middle Zagros (chapter 3). Standard-sized and well-fired pottery vessels, combined with wineskins, ensured that the wine could be transported by donkey the several hundred kilometers to the city-states of lowland Mesopotamia and Susiana.

The web of commercial enterprise during the Late Uruk period, from about 3500 to 3100 B.C., was masterminded by kings, entrepreneurs, and some of the earliest literati in the world from their palaces and temples at Ur, Uruk, Lagash, Susa, and elsewhere in the alluvial plains of southern Iraq. The tentacles of the proto-Sumerian city-states extended up into Syria and reached as far as Arslan Tepe in eastern Turkey. Large fortified settlements, such as the extremely well-preserved mudbrick structures laid out over an 18-hectare area at Habuba Kabira along the upper Euphates River, as well as smaller outposts and bases along the criss-crossing trade routes, were built de novo by "colonists" from southern Mesopotamia in the architectural styles of their homeland.

The sites had one strategic objective in view: to exploit this region and the adjoining uplands ("Hilly Flanks") for the natural resources that lowland Mesopotamia lacked—timber, metals, semiprecious stones, and the animals (sheep and goat) and plants that were native to those areas. When necessary, the proto-Sumerians and Elamites built a series of way stations that were strung out through the mountains to control access to more distant resources. Most of the goods that were shipped back to Lower Mesopotamia were raw materials, which were converted into jewelry, textiles, tools, weapons, and other finished products in the shops and "factories" of the city-states. In turn, these commodities could be exchanged for more raw materials, thereby fueling the "capitalist" engine and expanding trade. Grapes were an important resource at upland sites, and grape pips, which usually have been assigned to the wild variety, have been recovered from several late fourth millennium B.C. sites in Anatolia, Syria, and Iran. Can it then be assumed that wine was one of the goods imported into Lower Mesopotamia?

A Beer-Drinking Culture Only?

Unquestionably, barley beer and date wine were the beverages of choice in Mesopotamia from the fourth through the late first millennium B.C. There was a range of barley beers to choose from, including light, dark, and amber beers, sweet beers, and specially filtered beers. Sweet beers or wines, especially those made exclusively from dates, had become most popular by the first millennium B.C. For thousands of years, the upper classes and even royalty had a predilection for beer. A story even made the rounds in Greek society that Dionysos had fled from the "Land of Two Rivers" because the people there only drank beer.

The later caricature of a beer-drinking lowland culture is at odds with the use of pictograms for "grape, vineyard, or wine"—Sumerian *tin* and *geštin*—in the earliest texts. The *tin* sign shows a boomerang-like object, which might be interpreted as a grape cluster, set inside the sign for "jar" (*dug*), in the shape of a tall-necked vessel with a pointed base. The *geštin* sign is either a more schematic version of the *tin*-sign or a depiction of a stem and grape cluster. The Sumerian signs were later transformed into an Akkadian cuneiform (wedge-shaped) sign that was read *karanu*. Although the tablets say nothing about where and how wine was produced—to be sure, it was impractical to ship fresh fruit to the lowland cities for processing—there are tantalizing hints about its importance in the culture.

A jar full of *geštin* is mentioned in a text from Ur, and *geštin* is stored in rooms at Girsu (modern Telloh), which was the capital of the state of Lagash. *Geštin* is imported into Girsu from "the mountains of the East," presumably the southern Zagros mountains, and Hulbunu and Izallu, which are usually located in southern Elam (discussed later in this chapter). The phrase "the mountains of the East" may also be a reference to the Mount Nisir where Utnapishtim landed after the flood, as reported in its canonical version in the Gilgamesh Epic (chapter 2). *Geštin*, clearly understood to mean "vineyard," is also attested at Girsu; grapevines and other fruit trees—date, apple, and fig—were laid out in walled gardens, often in the vicinity of temples. By the end of the third millennium B.C., vineyards had been established at other cities in the same state, Lagash-City (al-Hiba) and Nina (Zurghul). A temple hymn of Gudea, a governor of Lagash around 2150 B.C., describes one of the orchards as "a mountain dripping vineyard . . . which is heaped up toward[?] the temple." This was the same Gudea who had told his donkey-groom "to make plenty of beer for the god Ningirsu" but to measure out six large golden chalices of *geštin* for the more important god, Bel-Marduk. At Ur, levees along waterways were dug out and "mounded up" to irrigate "acres" of vineyards in a farm named the "Garden of Vines," which was largely given over to grain production. Yet, as much as we might like to know more, the texts thus far published—constituting only about 2 percent of the total number known—are silent about whether grapes were served fresh, dried as grapes, or processed into wine or vinegar.

Whether to translate *tin* or *geštin* as "grape" or "wine" was left open in the texts cited above. At the 1991 Mondavi wine conference, Marvin Powell of Northern Illinois University made a strong case that the translation of *geštin* as "wine" in these and similar Archaic texts arose because of a misunderstanding of the compound ideogram "grape + sun" (*geštin hea*). Rather than reading it as "white wine," as the construct has usually been translated, Marvin translated the Sumerian literally as "dried grape" or raisin. He adduced several cogent arguments for his translation. First, unequivocal references to wine as a commodity, whether imported or locally made, are very infrequent throughout Mesopotamian history. Second, Nabonidus (555–539 B.C.), the last Semitic ruler of Babylonia before the Islamic conquest, went so far as to say that "wine, the excellent 'beer' of the mountain [regions] . . . which my country has none." Later Greek historians— Herodotus and Xenophon—paint the same picture of an alluvial culture wedded to date wine but lacking grape wine. An additional point in favor of Marvin's arguments is that "white wine" was rare in comparison with red wine in the ancient Near East and Egypt.

As Marvin himself would be the first to point out, there are many gaps in our knowledge of ancient Sumerian and Akkadian. It can be hazardous to project the dicta of a mid-first millennium B.C. king, which might be overstated, or of Greek historians, whose accuracy can be questioned, back thousands of years, to understand some of the first human writings ever put to clay. Winemakers likely had the necessary skills to make a white wine, in which the grape must has minimal contact with the skins and stems, as early as Neolithic Hajji Firuz Tepe (chapter 4). Moreover, the grapevine was certainly not at home in the harsh, saline conditions of southern Iraq, so why did the earliest rulers in this region make a special effort to plant vineyards? And why were these gardens so often connected with temples?

The answer to such questions probably has more to do with human vanity and ostentation than with the climate or any other unusual circumstance in southern Iraq. Like their counterparts in Egypt (chapter 5), the earliest kings of Mesopotamia might well have gravitated to wine, whether white or red, because of its éclat and high value. The earliest wine that was imported into the lowlands had to be transported overland from the Zagros or by boat from Upper Mesopotamia, 600 or more kilometers away, as was still being done in Herodotus's time (chapter 8). The relative rarity of white wine as compared with red wine would have added to its acclaim and made it more valuable and prestigious, as well as a more fit offering to the gods. Once the high-end market for wine had been cultivated among the rulers and upper class, the transplantation of the domesticated grapevine farther south in the Zagros Mountains followed in due course.

The Sumerian city-state was centered around temples to its principal deities. The temples were often placed at the top of ziggurats, the ancient equivalent of skyscrapers, which were built of mudbricks and towered over the cities. Reaching up to heaven, which the biblical writers (Genesis 11.1–9) took to be a sign of the overweening pride of the builders of Babel, the ziggurats were a kaleidoscope of color and geometric effects. In the "Painted Temple," south of Baghdad, a stunning display of black and white diamonds, separated by scarlet bands, was surmounted by painted figures of humans and "leopards." At Uruk (modern Warka) itself, the "White Temple" to the sky-god Anu sat like the Parthenon of its day, with its recessed niches and adorned pillars, atop a 12-meter ziggurat that was approached by steep ramps and stairs on all sides. Much later at Khorsabad in the north, the Neo-Babylonian kings built an even taller structure, with each of its seven storys painted a different color—white, black, red, white, reddish orange, silver, and gold.

The enormous expenditure of resources that went into the building, decoration, and furnishings of these temples was justified by the daily services and special celebrations that invoked the good will and blessings of the god who was worshiped in its inner sanctum. According to extensive textual evidence, the most important responsibility of the temple personnel was to attend to the provisioning of the god. The god was often represented in human form as a statue, which needed to be cleaned and dressed daily. Food was also needed for the god's survival. Wine, beer, and milk, in that order, were libated, and whole animals were sacrificed and cooked at a centrally placed fireplace and altars.

Prohibitions against priestesses' engaging in the wine trade or drinking wine outside the temple show how important wine was in the temple cult. The law code of Hammurapi, king of Babylon, was promulgated at the beginning of his 43-year reign in about 1790 B.C. on a tall slab of diorite, now in the Louvre Museum in Paris. Below a scene in which the ruler is shown receiving the law from the sun-deity and god of justice, Shamash, 282 legal provisions are detailed, along with their penalties if violated. The 110th paragraph reads: "If a hierodule [priestess], a 'nun' [exact meaning unknown], who is not living in a 'convent,' has opened [the door of] a wineshop or has entered a wineshop for a drink, they shall burn that woman." The severity of the penalty—capital punishment by burning being one of the gravest in the code—shows that priestesses, who had stepped down from their usual responsibilities, were expected to keep themselves "pure" by not indulging in common drinking or engaging in ordinary commerce, if that is what is meant by "opening the door." We are reminded of the temple prostitute in the Gilgamesh Epic who plied Enkidu with seven goblets of a strong beverage (chapter 2).

As the two preceding sections (108 and 109) of Hammurapi's Code make clear, wineshop owners are assumed to be female. We had already been alerted to this fact in the Gilgamesh Epic, when the hero met a woman, Siduri, who was a barmaid or tavern owner. Siduri is associated with both grapes and beer in this late text. The use of "wineshop" in the earlier texts may reflect the relatively higher status of wine at that time. One "wineshop owner," Ku-Bau, even rose to the heights of "queenship," to found the third dynasty of Kish around 2400 B.C.

Such provisions would be unnecessary in a major law code unless the temple priestesses regularly handled or imbibed wine, whether in the daily cult or at special religious rites. The most important celebrations in ancient Sumer were held over several days at the beginning of the New Year, probably in April or May. The festivities culminated in the sacred marriage (*hieros gamos*) of Inanna (Akkadian Ishtar), the goddess of love at Uruk, to the legendary, deified king of the same city-state, Dumuzi. A priestess of the temple reenacted this significant event with the reigning monarch yearly in the grand temple to Ishtar at Uruk, the Eanna, which was uncovered by a German expedition between the world wars. The ceremony had a pronounced fertility aspect; the three main deities in the various accounts that have been preserved—Inanna, Dumuzi, and Dumuzi's sister, Geshtinanna—all descend to the underworld, one after the other, to help each deity in turn return from "death" to "life." The New Year came in late spring, when the river waters were up and new life had begun to spring forth on the alluvial plains and in the surrounding desert, like the "resurrected" gods.

In one version of the sacred marriage story, a fly leads Geshtinanna to her brother, Dumuzi, who is living in a brewery ("beer-house") together with a group of wise beer-makers. As the observant reader will have already noted, Geshtinanna derives from the Sumerian word *geštin*, meaning "grape, vineyard, wine." The goddess's name is literally translated as "the leafy grapevine," and she is also referred to by her epithet, Ama-Geshtinna ("root of the grapevine" or the "mother of all grapevines"). According to the doyen of Sumerologists, Thorkild Jacobsen, this juxtaposition of beer and wine in a "resurrection" account of a brother and sister who are closely associated with the fermented beverages is related to the hiatus between the barley harvest in the spring and the vintage in the fall. The proper performance of the temple ritual ensured that each plant would mature at the proper time, so that the land, the people, and the king would prosper.

Beyond its rich literary remains, the archaeological record of Lower Mesopotamia has more to tell us about the grapevine and wine. The artwork may not be as graphic and exhaustive as that in the Egyptian temples and tombs, and its interpretation may be more debatable. Yet the realism of Mesopotamian art in depicting many facets of life in the alluvial plains—from the comforts of an upper-class existence to the more tedious duties of soldiering and dairying—is patent.

Cylinder and stamp seals were among the most evocative and prolific kinds of artifacts made in ancient Mesopotamia for thousands of years. The seals were rolled out and impressed into the wet clay tablets as marks of personal or corporate ownership. Every variety of stone, whether hard or soft—turquoise, hematite, lapis lazuli, steatite, basalt, limestone—had mythological creatures, heroic exploits, and scenes from everyday life carefully carved out in reverse design. Minute detail, flowing designs, and an exquisite balancing of motifs are most pronounced on the earliest seals from the Late Uruk period. An innovative tradition of glyptic art continued through Early Dynastic times, reaching its high point during the reign of Sargon the Great toward the end of the third millennium B.C.

One of the most common motifs on the seals is the royal banquet, which captures the essence and is the ultimate inspiration for the Greek *symposion* and Roman *convivium*, thousands of years later (color plate 5). We see men and women sitting on wooden chairs that have a short back and cross-struts like the "campstools" of Mycenaean Greece (chapter 10). They lift cups and goblets to their mouths or hold long tubes that are inserted into large jars. Stewards stand ready, with long-spouted jugs, to refill their goblets. In the background, a ram-headed lyre is strummed, and dancers and singers provide entertainment.

The earliest depiction of the splaying tube and jar motif is on an early fourth millennium B.C. sealing from the northern Mesopotamian site of Tepe Gawra, not far from ancient Nineveh. The stamped impression of the seal onto clay, now in the University of Pennsylvania Museum, shows two sticklike human figures whose dimensions are dwarfed by an enormous jar between them. The humans hold tubes, which are hinged at their middle. A careful examination of this and later seals and impressions, coupled with the discovery of actual examples of these tubes from excavations, has led to a plausible hypothesis: the tubes served as "straws" to suck up beer from the jar. The straw enabled a drinker to penetrate through an accumulation of grain hulls and yeast, floating on the surface, and reach the beverage below.

No inscription clearly identifies beer as the beverage being imbibed from the jars with the straws. It is also tacitly assumed that the same vessel was a combination processing-and-drinking jar. The best argument that the jars contained beer, which is a good one, is by analogy to modern practices that can still be observed in East and West

Africa. Native peoples there, such as the Bantu-speaking Masai of Kenya and the Kofyars of Nigeria, prepare sorghum and millet beers in large jars and drink the beverage directly from vessels using long reed straws. The parallel to ancient Mesopotamia can be carried a step further; beer-drinking through straws in African societies is usually associated with special celebrations and ceremonies marking rites of passage, such as birth, marriage, initiation into the tribe, and death. It is often an all-male affair in which a large group of men huddle around a jar of beer from which reeds sprout up and supply the drinkers.

The parade examples from ancient Mesopotamia of "straws" for drinking beer were discovered at the site of Ur, famous for its ziggurat approached by a triple stairway. Numerous tubes, made of lapis lazuli, gold, and silver, were found in a tomb of Queen Puabi by Sir Leonard Woolley, the director of the joint excavation by the University of Pennsylvania Museum and the British Museum that was carried out between the world wars. The precious materials had probably been applied around marsh reeds, which later disintegrated. Some examples clearly had sharp elbows like the tubes on the Tepe Gawra sealing. A silver jar, holding about 6 liters, was found near the straws, and it is hypothesized to have held the daily beer allotment of the queen. Most workers on large public projects in Mesopotamia normally received at least a 1-liter consignment each day.

Queen Puabi's burial was just one of many extremely rich tombs that were uncovered by Woolley in the "Royal Cemetery" at Ur, dating to the Early Dynastic II period from about 2600 to 2500 B.C. Puabi's tomb illustrates most of the key features of the cemetery. She herself, in keeping with her joint role as a priestess in the temple to the moon god Nanna at Ur, was decked out in all her finery, with headdresses, earrings, chokers, and necklaces of the most costly materials, which had been intricately worked into leaves, flowers, and geometric designs. A large collection of fluted—and sometimes spouted—cups and goblets of gold was buried with the queen.

Once the food and beverage offerings had been laid out in a tomb in the Royal Cemetery, the door was sealed with stone and mudbrick. The most astounding discovery made by Woolley, however, was in the ramped "death-pits" leading to the tombs. The royal personages

FIGURE 7.1. (Left to right) Gold spouted bowl, tumbler or goblet, and bowl with rosette design from Queen Puabi's tomb in the Royal Cemetery at Ur (Iraq), ca. 2600–2500 B.C.

had not gone to their graves alone. Placed in huge burial pits that had been excavated out of the alluvium were battle-carts pulled by onager-like equids and as many as 80 humans, including musicians with their instruments, soldiers, servants, and courtiers, some of whom wore ornate jewelry of gold, silver, and semiprecious stones. A pair of rams, rendered in gold, silver, lapis lazuli, shell, and red limestone over bitumen-covered wood, are among the amazing works of art recovered from the Royal Cemetery. Each ram is raised up on its hind legs, nibbling at a small shrub. The soundboxes of the bull-headed lyres are also noteworthy; their inlaid plaques depict scenes of the "Master of Animals" and fabulous creatures, like those in the Epic of Gilgamesh, who carry drinking bowls, goblets, and beverage jars (color plate 6). The trove of finds from the cemetery were equally shared by the University of Pennsylvania Museum and the British Museum.

A large copper pot, apparently filled with a liquid, had been set in the middle of the "death pit." According to Woolley, each retainer dipped a cup, perhaps poured out a partial offering to the deceased and the gods, and then drank what remained. The effect of a "drug" in the beverage was irreversible and fatal; as in a scene from a modern ritualistic suicide cult in Jonestown or California, the entire entourage of the ruler died at the same time. Arranged in neat lines, one after another facing in the same direction, the bodies were covered over by soil. Human sacrifice always seems gruesome, but if the goal is to continue this life—in particular the court service for a king or a queen—into another life to follow, it is at least understandable.

Banqueting the Mesopotamian Way

A banquet, literally "the place of beer and bread" in ancient Sumerian, was imbued with deep religious, social, and even sexual significance. The gods themselves often greeted one another and marked special occasions with a banquet, in which they might engage in drinking bouts and intellectual repartee. Enki, the god of wisdom and magic, used the bonhomie and the alcoholic haze engendered by such celebrations to his advantage. In a number of tales about this trickster god, he begins by sitting all the gods in their proper order at the table—from the sky-god An at the head of the table, his father Enlil next to An, and on down to the Anunna who had fallen from grace. After the food and drink have been blessed and toasts have been made, the party heats up and reaches a point in which high-ranking participants pose riddles to one another and engage in one-upsmanship. By astutely maneuvering around his adversaries, Enki is able to lay claim to creating mankind, official recognition for his temple at Eridu, and a host of women—mothers and their daughters through five generations—with whom he successively and successfully mates, sometimes after plying them with beer. Appropriately enough, a daughter from another union is Ninkasi, the goddess of beer. Enki also throws a feast in which wine is the main beverage, as recorded in a hymn to the sun-god, the earliest Akkadian (Semitic) literary text, from tablets found at Ebla and Abu Salabikh in Upper Mesopotamia.

Human kings and queens, acting as the gods' representatives on the earth, were as avid as any Celtic ruler, potlatch chieftain in the American Northwest, or Greek symposiast in hosting grand feasts. When Sargon the Great swept into Lower Mesopotamia around 2300 B.C. and established the first Semitic dynasty at Akkad, he solidified his rule by providing for "5400 men [who] ate daily before him." Women also played important roles in the royal house and at banquets. With the reassertion of Sumerian hegemony at Ur several centuries after Sargon, king Shulgi boasts about his lavish feasts and how he drank beer in An's temple and consorted with Inanna, the goddess of love, at a banquet. It is uncertain whether a feast always culminated in sexual licentiousness or the more exalted hierogamy of the king and a priestess, but Shulgi fathered more than 20 royal princes and princesses, exceeding any other Neo-Sumerian ruler. Sexual acts, counterbalanced by the drinking of a beverage from a large jar through a tube, are also portrayed on seals and plaques.

The royal banquet epitomized the complex interplay of social status, the ruler as the source of nature's fecundity, the symbolic import of the divine realm, and key events in the life and death of the individual, the society at large, and nature itself. The fealty owed to the ruler by his or her subjects, as well as formal legal arrangements for land transfer and other economic transactions, were ratified at feasts and by special drinking ceremonies. By the time of Sargon and Shulgi, the rulers and gods were regularly depicted on cylinder seals as seated and holding a cup in one hand, with the seal owner standing before his superior in the company of a mediating goddess. Gifts, especially rich clothing and drinking paraphernalia, including cups and jars made of gold, silver, and bronze, were presented at the feasts.

An elaborate banquet scene was depicted by inlaying shell and limestone pieces, with blue lapis lazuli as the background, onto a bitumen-covered box, which was excavated by Leonard Woolley in the Royal Cemetery of Ur, dating to about 2600–2500 B.C. On one side of the so-called Royal Standard, which was most likely the sound board for a lyre, the king sits placidly on his "campstool," basking in

the glory of his military victory; the other side portrays his army of
chariots and infantry. The king and his queen (partly obliterated)
have goblets in hand on the Peace Standard side of the box and are
personally attended to by servants (color plate 7). They wear expansive, multilayered dresses of lamb's fleece and face a line of six courtiers, all of whom are seated and holding goblets. As is the king, the
courtiers are bald-headed, which was a mark of religious fidelity, but
their attire is simpler and they are shown at a smaller scale. A male
lyre player and a female singer stand behind the courtiers.

All the elements are in place on the Royal Standard for a grand
celebration. The panels below the royal couple and their entourage
show many animals—goats, cattle, donkeys, and fish—being led and
carried, perhaps as booty from the military campaign and as a foreshadowing of the delicious meat entrées to be served at the feast. But
there is one troubling unknown: what was the beverage in the goblets that the king and his entourage raise to toast victory? And what
was being drunk from the goblets shown on the cylinder seals, and
why should a pair of individuals sit on either side of a large jar from
which long tubes are splayed out?

Wine, Too, Was Drunk in the Lowland Cities

A molecular archaeological study of a unique 50-liter
jar from the late fourth millennium B.C. Oval at Godin Tepe (chapter
3) by my laboratory provided the earliest chemical evidence—in the
form of calcium oxalate, or "beerstone" (chapter 10)—that barley
beer was drunk from the large jars with drinking tubes shown on the
Late Uruk and later seals. A small hole punched through the sidewall
of the jar might have accommodated the straw used by the chieftain
of the village or the foreign governor. Beer drinking in the ancient
world was a communal activity, and special jars, outfitted with two to
seven spouts evenly spaced around the rim of the vessel, have been
excavated at many third-millennium B.C. sites in Lower Mesopotamia, extending up to Mari on the Euphrates, across Turkey, and out
into the Aegean Sea to the Cyclades island of Naxos. The direct

correspondence with the beer-drinking scenes on the contemporary seals is impossible to miss.

Having accounted for beer drinking on the seals, we had to consider the distinct possibility that the goblets and cups had held wine. If they had, the wine must have been transported to ancient Sumer from its farflung domains. Large-scale local production was precluded by the hot climate in the south. Several jar types, which were widespread in lowland Mesopotamia and along the trade routes through the Zagros Mountains and up into northwestern Syria, are excellent candidates for the transport of precious liquids, such as wine, in the Late Uruk period. In particular, we focused attention on the "droop-spouted jar," an ovoid vessel with a narrow mouth and long, curved spout, which was similar to the spouted jugs used to fill the goblets and cups on the seals.

Droop-spouted jars are generally small—with volumes of a liter or slightly more—and their curved spouts, which could break off, would appear to be ill-suited for transport. Another problem in transporting a liquid in the droop-spouted jars is that, as yet, no stoppers have been found for the spouts themselves. Discarded clay stoppers for the mouths of the vessels, however, were found near the largest assemblage of these jars at Arslan Tepe, near the headwaters of the Euphrates River in eastern Anatolia. Presumably, the smaller spout opening was plugged with a piece of wood or other material. Apart from these difficulties, special commodities are often sent in small containers and, with careful packing, can be shipped without breakage. Arriving at their destination, the droop-spouted jars would have had the additional advantage that they could double as serving vessels, as shown on the seals. They might also have been hoisted aloft and the beverage drunk by pouring it from the spout in a continuous stream into the mouth, much as the spouted water jug is used today in the Middle East.

The hypothesis that the droop-spouted jars might have been used for wine was put to the test. Ginny Badler, who had provided us with samples from Godin Tepe to carry out our first wine analyses (chapter 3), made trips to the Louvre Museum in Paris and the University of Heidelberg, where the earlier excavated materials from Uruk are kept. She secured residue samples from three droop-spouted jars of the same type, one each from the important sites of Susa, Girsu, and Uruk. The residues were confined to the lower inside half or third of the jars, where materials and precipitates settle out from liquids. Our standard battery of chemical tests confirmed that all three vessels had contained a resinated wine.

Other candidates for transporting wine, both in pottery and other materials (e.g., the wineskin; see chapter 8), should not be overlooked. The piriform jar, the common wine jar type at Godin Tepe (chapter 3), is a prime example. These jars range in volume from 1.5 to 60 liters, usually with set capacities at fixed intervals. The 30-liter variety, which is comparable in size to the well-known Canaanite Jar and amphora of later times (chapter 6), is most suitable for long-distance transport because it is easily maneuverable by a single man and can be carried by pack animals or loaded into the hulls of ships.

The piriform jar type is attested at Uruk, Nippur, and Girsu in southern Mesopotamia and at Susa in southwestern Iran (Khuzistan) during the Late Uruk period. It also occurs at Tepe Sialk in north-central Iran, at Habuba Kabira, and elsewhere along the widespread tentacles of the Late Uruk trading network. The Godin Tepe wine jars have a shape similar to that of jars from other sites, but thus far they are unique in being decorated with inverted U-shaped rope appliqués. The organic residue analysis of one example of this jar type from Susa showed that it had originally contained wine.

Other jar types that my laboratory has tested also contained resinated wine as an ingredient, but because of their small size or unique styles, they again might have held specialty liquids. A miniature short-spouted jar of Late Uruk type from Girsu held about 15 milliliters. Another unique miniature jar was found together with numerous other examples of the same type at Uruk, in a sherd layer under an oven in the Eanna temple complex. This was the temple dedicated to Inanna, where the sacred marriage festival was celebrated each year. These jars, which date shortly after the Late Uruk period, have a narrow mouth and pointed base and range in volume from 10 to 30 milliliters.

A prima facie case can thus be made that viticulture was far enough advanced by the Late Uruk period in upland regions on the periphery of Lower Mesopotamia for surplus wine to be produced there and exported in vessels made of pottery or other materials to the emergent city-states. No chemical provenience study of their pottery fabrics has yet been carried out, so we cannot be sure whether the piriform jar, droop-spouted jar, or another type was the principal transport vessel. Local production of these jars for use as storage or serving containers cannot be ruled out. On the basis of the molecular archaeological results, however, we do know that these jars contained resinated wine. Consequently, the beverage being poured from the spouted jars into the cups and goblets at banquets and special ceremonies, as depicted on the seals, was almost certainly resinated wine.

Southern Mesopotamia offered poor prospects for producing wine because of its hot climate. Is it then possible to be more precise about where the bulk of this commodity was produced, which could have served the lowland needs? The northern Zagros Mountains, where winemaking dates back to at least the Neolithic period (chapter 4) and where the wild domesticated grapevine thrived, is a possibility. The eastern Taurus Mountains or the Caucasus, even farther away, are also conceivable locations. Goods, including wine, might have been transported overland until navigable waterways, connecting to the Tigris or Euphrates River were reached and allowed river transport to Lower Mesopotamia. We have seen that the lowlanders had established entrepôts at key locations in Upper Mesopotamia, much as was done in the early second millennium B.C. at Mari (chapter 8). Grape seeds, usually identified as those of the wild subspecies but likely including some domesticated specimens, have been recovered from late fourth-millennium B.C. sites over the extended upland regions of southeastern Turkey and northern Syria (chapter 4), so winemaking was probably well established there.

Long-distance trade in wine at this early stage of human civilization is an enticing, realistic scenario, and one that accounts for the evidence. Another possible development, however, needs to be explored further. If the demand for wine were great enough in the lowlands, transplantation of grapevines to closer locales in the central Zagros, such as Godin Tepe and possibly as far south as Susa, would be anticipated. We do not know whether the kings of the lowland Mesopotamian city-states were as ambitious as their Egyptian counterparts in establishing a royal winemaking industry nearby (chapter 5) but they probably had a strong incentive in this direction. The few irrigated plants in the gardens of southern Mesopotamia were not sufficient to satisfy their needs or those of a burgeoning upper class. If royalty did not pursue this initiative, then the slack might have been taken up by the private sector. When the Late Uruk trade routes were suddenly cut off at the end of the period, the pressure to establish productive vineyards closer to the major urban centers would have intensified.

Transplanting the Grapevine to Shiraz

The foothills of the southern Zagros Mountains near the ancient site of Susa are the closest region to Lower Mesopotamia that might have been productively planted with the domesticated grapevine to produce wine on a large scale. One of the capital cities of ancient Elam, Susa, is located along the Karun River, within easy reach of the other lowland city-states by boat or overland. During the course of the third millennium B.C., the city grew to be some 400 hectares in area, with two acropolises, one with a high mudbrick platform that presaged the development of the ziggurat.

Our molecular archaeological analyses of a range of vessels from Susa—including droop-spouted and piriform pottery jars and small specialty jars of stone—have shown that resinated wine was a popular commodity at the site, whether consumed as the beverage itself or mixed with other components in perfumes or oils. Yet, Susa has thus far yielded only a single grape pip from a Late Uruk context. This apparent dearth of evidence is explained by the fact that the French archaeological team had not yet adopted modern recovery methods when their excavations were halted in 1979 by the Iranian Revolution.

Susa's geographic location between the lowlands and the uplands made it ideal for launching out into the hill country and exploiting resources there. Partly for this reason, the excavators of Godin Tepe argue strongly that proto-Elamites, not proto-Sumerians, are responsible for building the Oval at the trading *cum* military post, which is approximately 250 kilometers north of Susa in the Kangavar Valley of the middle Zagros (chapter 3).

Susan merchants and other personnel, probably under royal aegis, also could have begun trading to the southeast, in the direction of Shiraz at an elevation of 1800 meters in the mountains of the modern province of Fars. This region was extolled for its fine wines in Persian times (ca. 550–330 B.C.) at the court of Persepolis (chapter 8), just north of Shiraz. Even during Islamic times and continuing as late as the fourteenth century A.D., Bacchic poets such as Omar Khayyam and Hafiz held sway.

Tepe Malyan—another University of Pennsylvania Museum excavation—served as the mountain capital of the ancient Elamite kingdom. The site, which is located several hundred kilometers northwest of Shiraz at an even higher elevation in the oak zone, was excavated under the direction of William Sumner. Anshan, as it was known to its inhabitants, has provided the crucial evidence for the domesticated grapevine that has thus far been lacking from Susa and the other city-states of Lower Mesopotamia. Grape seeds were recovered dating to as early as the late fourth millennium B.C., the Banesh period. By the middle of the third millennium, the domesticated grapevine and winemaking were well established. A refuse pit of the Kaftari period yielded masses of carbonized and uncarbonized grape pips, along with actual pieces of grapevine wood. A few seeds can always be viewed as the leftovers of some imported fruit or raisins, but the discovery of the plant itself in a region that did not originally support the wild grapevine is a strong indicator that it had been transplanted there. Aggregations of grape seeds are also unusual in archaeological excavations and are best interpreted as remains of pomace after the grapes have been crushed or pressed. When Iran opens up to foreign excavation again, further investigation of Zagros Mountain sites may well prove decisive in tracing the steady march of viniculture and winemaking from the north to the south at the same time that these significant developments in the history of civilization were occurring on the western side of the Fertile Crescent.

By the mid-third millennium, the kings of Elam ruled in both Susa and Anshan. Their cylinder seals tell the story of the centrality of grapes and winemaking in their history and culture. Foreshadowing similar scenes on Assyrian reliefs some two millennia later (chapter 8), the seals show male and female dignitaries or gods seated under arbors, dripping with large clusters of grapes, and drinking what is most likely wine from cups. Elam was also the traditional enemy of Sumer and Babylonia. These lands might have responded to Elam's stranglehold on the wellspring of wine nearest to Lower Mesopotamia by turning increasingly to barley beer and date wine production.

CHAPTER 8

Wine and the Great Empires
of the Ancient Near East

HERODOTUS, the "father of history," has a delightful account of his travels in Mesopotamia during the fifth century B.C. in book I (193–194) of his *History* (Greek "inquiry"). Although anecdotal, highly impressionistic, and moralistic in places, his description of the wine trade from the headwaters of the Tigris and Euphrates Rivers to the gates of Babylon has the stamp of credibility. He describes how the Armenian wine merchants fashioned circular "shield"-shaped boats by stretching animal skins over willow frames. After cushioning their vessels with straw, they loaded up their cargo. Two men were assigned to each boat, one to pull with an oar and another to push off with one. Live donkeys and, presumably, sleeping accommodations and food for the several-week trip downriver rounded out the supplies in each boat, some of which were quite large and could carry a weight of 5000 talents, or about 25 tons. Once their shipments had been sold and offloaded onto the docks of Babylon, the boats were broken down, because they were incapable of navigating the strong currents back to Armenia. After the straw and willow ribs had gone to the highest bidder, the skins were piled on the donkeys and the merchants began their arduous journey back upstream by foot. Back home, the skins could be used to construct new boats to export the next vintage.

A salient detail was omitted from this recounting of Herodotus's story. The wine cargo is said to have been carried in *bikos phoinikeiou*[s].

MAP 5. Anatolia and the Caucasus.

Most wine histories translate this phrase as "barrels made of palm tree wood." Yet, if barrels were used by the Armenian merchants for their wine, they would have had to be made in Transcausasia, and date palms do not grow there. The term *phoinikeiou[s]* might better be read as "Phoenician" or "red," referring to either amphoras of the Phoenician type or jars filled with red wine.

Wine Down the Tigris and Euphrates

Herodotus's description of the Upper Mesopotamian wine trade may stand at the beginning of what is considered "scientific history," but it provides no historical backdrop to a centuries-old phenomenon and also leaves out other essential information about the trade in his own time. He says nothing about exactly which Armenian towns or regions were involved in the trade, only that the merchants "live higher up than the Assyrians." How was the wine

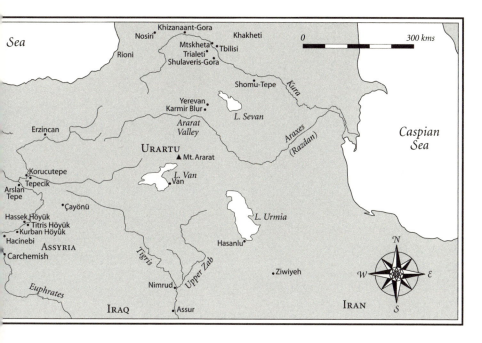

made? At what time of year did it arrive in Babylon? How much did it cost? Fortunately, large archives of cuneiform texts from cities in Upper Mesopotamia from much earlier periods enable us to fill in some of the gaps, assuming that, once the trading networks were in place, there was a large economic incentive to perpetuate them.

In chapter 7, a strong case was made for wine trade down the Tigris and Euphrates Rivers during the Late Uruk period at the end of the fourth millennium B.C. Twelve hundred years later, the great king Hammurapi of Babylonia attacked and burned the city of Mari, located along the Middle Euphrates. In the rubble of Mari's palace, covering about 2.5 hectares and incorporating hundreds of courtyards and rooms, French excavations under the direction of André Parrot discovered more than 20,000 cuneiform tablets. From this rich corpus of written records in Akkadian, a detailed picture of the wine trade can be reconstructed, captured at an instant in time around 1750 B.C.

An intricate network of trading connections emerges from the Mari archive. The main nodes in the network are the city-states of northern Mesopotamia, which are located at key locations along rivers or close to the Mediterranean Sea. The kings of these small principalities were a law onto themselves, but all stood to profit if they were able to work out agreeable arrangements of social conduct and trade. Ties between cities were often solidified by the marriage of a daughter of the king of one city to the king of another city in the network. The ruler of Aleppo, the main city in northern Syria, was related in marriage to the king of Mari and, on occasion, could be expected to send a "gift" of 100 jars. Each jar was about 30 liters in volume, so this largesse was the equivalent of 4000 bottles of modern wine, each with a capacity of 750 milliliters. Depending on how large a ruler's harem and the royal household were and how often he celebrated holidays and special occasions, this stock of wine might last weeks or months.

The Mari archives include correspondence between wine traders farther up the Euphrates River in the important entrepôt of Carchemish, now just over the border from Syria in Turkey, and buyers in Mari. Many of the letters are those of Ṣidqum-Lanasi, a highly placed merchant at Carchemish, who acted on behalf of the king of Mari as well as other private interests. The texts exude an entrepreneurial spirit, with huge profits to be made. With some educated guesswork, Marvin Powell at the Mondavi wine conference described how a shekel of silver, weighing about 8.5 grams, could procure six jars, or 180 liters, of wine, which in 2002 dollars would be about $130 per jar or $3.25 per modern bottle. Downstream at Mari, the same jar cost three times as much—$390 or $9.75 per bottle. This might still have been a bargain for the king or a wealthy citizen, but a common worker in Mari, who was paid in barley or beer, would have been hard-pressed to exchange as much as three-quarters of his daily wages to procure a liter of wine.

Ṣidqum-Lanasi's skill in bargaining and his business acumen can be seen from the ancient records in which he writes that he has been successful in getting a reduced price on a shipment of 180 jars of wine by including the cost of the boat, which often increased the price by as much as a third, in the overall deal. Once the boat had been used to transport the wine to a port downriver, it was essentially worthless. As were the skin-covered Armenian rafts, the cargo boats plying the rivers of Mesopotamia in the early second millennium B.C. were relatively flimsy affairs made out of wood and reeds. They were not intended to make the trip back upstream, but they had to be strong enough to carry tons of cargo. As Ṣidqum-Lanasi asked: "Am I going to buy a boat for ten shekels of silver when it won't bring one shekel of silver in Mari?" The cost of the boatmen who ferried the goods on such boats must have also been included in the price. In his composite transaction, Ṣidqum-Lanasi was able to get a 2 shekel, or 5 percent, reduction on what would have otherwise cost 40 shekels— 30 shekels for the wine and 10 shekels for the boat.

Another hidden cost of doing trade on the rivers of Mesopotamia was the tolls levied along the way. The situation differed little from that in medieval Europe in which each principality or city-state sought to exact exorbitant fees from trade through its territory. Among the tablets found in the Mari palace, one associate toll-taker upstream from the site issued some 39 notices of payment or outstanding debts, most of which involved wine shipments. Tolls were also levied on goods traveling downstream to Babylonia at Hanat. The wine then entered northern Babylonia at Sippar, where a group of merchants had organized themselves into a kind of guild to handle transactions on the upper Euphrates.

The king of Mari before its destruction, Zimri-Lim, must have understood the key role that his city had come to play in the economy of the Old Babylonian period (ca. 2000–1600 B.C.). Like Hammurapi, he belonged to the ascendant groups of western Semitic peoples known as the Amorites (or Amurru in Akkadian), which had gradually infiltrated Lower Mesopotamia and then assumed power over the Sumerians. One of his daughters even served as a votary of Shamash, the sun-god, in his temple at Sippar—the same god who is depicted presenting a staff and ring to administer the law to Hammurapi at the top of the famous stela of the Code of Hammurapi. Religion, law, and trade were all part of the formula to achieve political power in this period, and Hammurapi ultimately emerged as victor and ruler of a unified empire that encompassed Upper and Lower Mesopotamia.

The picture of Mari before its disappearance from the scene provides a glimpse of a wealthy society in which large stocks of wine were a natural accompaniment to the "good life." In the palace, rows of long rooms were set aside for *pithoi*, large lidded jars standing over a meter in height to store wine; this method of storage was common practice in Transcaucasia (chapter 2) as well as in Turkey (below) and Greece (chapter 10). Low mudbrick blocks were evenly spaced along the walls and sometimes down the middle of each room, and carbonized wood recovered from the depressions made by the pithoi showed that the jars had sat in racks. A specific Akkadian term, *kannum*, in the Mari texts likely refers to these racks, whether an ordinary potstand or a tall, ornate support with animals' heads and other devices that traces its origin back to the elaborate banqueting furniture of proto-Sumerian times (chapter 7). The word has also been translated as "cellar," encompassing the entire specially outfitted room for storing wine.

The Mari archives make it clear that the wine coming from farther up the Euphrates was sometimes transported in very large jars (Akkadian, *našpakum*), containing a 1000 liters or more. One can envision these jars being moved into the storerooms of the Mari palace, where they were stored in racks. When a feast was celebrated or foreign emissaries received, special portable stands to hold the jars were conveniently transported to the rooms and courtyards of the palace.

Wine was the property of the king, as Zimri-Lim tells his queen, Siptu, in a letter: "Fill ten jars with red wine and seal them with this seal; and give them to Bahdi-lim. However, send the seal on the chain back to me." Doors into the cellars were also sealed. These precautions were probably taken not just to prevent theft or the occasional nip by a palace functionary but also to guarantee high quality. The price differential of two grades of wine represented in the stores of the Mari palace is so slight (a tenth of a shekel per 30-liter jar) that we can assume that the king and his queen, for whom large quantities of wine were set aside, drank only the best. According to the texts, the wine was always red. Ageing of wines goes unmentioned, perhaps because the yearly allotment was quickly depleted. The sweeter wines were preferred and rated higher. "Blended" wines and beers imply that wine stewards or cupbearers were adept at enhancing flavors and aromas or covering up the faults in beverages that had started to go bad by adding spices, tree resins, or other ingredients, which had been common practice for thousands of years.

Another group of cuneiform tablets bearing on the wine trade of eighteenth-century B.C. Upper Mesopotamia was excavated at the nearby site of Tell al-Rimah, up the Khabur River (a tributary of the Euphrates) in the direction of ancient Nineveh. The texts describe a prosperous, regional wine industry, principally intended for royalty and visiting dignitaries. Today, this region is a dry wasteland except along the alluvial plain of the river, and it is difficult to imagine how vineyards could ever have graced its forlorn landscape. Yet, everywhere one looks, mounds of ancient settlements pop up—one of the highest concentrations of tells that I have seen anywhere—which attest to a rich, vibrant history. Karana'a, the ancient name of Tell el-Rimah, is fittingly related to the Akkadian word *karanu*, for "grape, vineyard, or wine." By a simple juxtaposition of the Akkadian with its Sumerian equivalent (chapter 7), one may suppose that the goddess Geshtinanna, the tutelary deity of wine, fertility, and the afterlife, was worshiped here.

Smaller jars, especially a type with one handle on its shoulder that could hold 10 or 30 liters, might also have been used to transport wine and, after delivery, to serve the wine. As do the droop-spouted jars of 1500 years earlier (chapter 7), these jars have a wide distribution, especially farther up the Euphrates (e.g., Terqa) and into southeastern Anatolia (Kurban Höyük). Their narrow mouth could easily have been stoppered. Molecular archaeology, which has not yet been applied to the range of pottery types from the important sites of the Old Babylonian period throughout Mesopotamia, waits in the wings and may eventually supply some answers.

Even without the chemical data, there is good reason to believe that a much larger area of the upper Euphrates and its tributaries was given over to grape production as early as the third millennium than is now possible. Carbonized grape seeds, often identified as the wild type but deriving from sites outside the modern distribution of *Vitis vinifera sylvestris* (e.g., Tell Taya, Tell Hadidi, Tell Selenkahiyeh, Tell Leilan, and Tell es-Sweyhat), imply that a milder, wetter climate prevailed then.

Wines of Anatolia and the Lost Hittite Empire

During the heyday of wine trade down the Euphrates River, when Zimri-Lim and Hammurapi ruled in Mari and Babylon, a fledgling power had begun to emerge along the Tigris River at Assur and up into the Zagros Mountains to its east. The Assyrians, who eventually came to control much of the Near East by the seventh century B.C., were attracted to the metal riches of central Turkey, some 700 kilometers from their homeland, as early as the eighteenth century B.C. It is difficult to imagine how they traversed the complicated political geography of the numerous city-states between Assur and the trading posts on the central Anatolian plateau, of which Kültepe (ancient Kanesh) is best known. By traveling overland with the famous Cappadocian black donkeys, the merchants might have been able to bypass the main cities and their tolls.

At the large 60-hectare site of Kültepe, which has been the focus of a long-term Turkish excavation under the direction of Tahsin Özgüç, the merchant colony (Akkadian *karum*) was brought to light in the walled outer town that encircled the citadel. In a precinct with large courtyard houses that was set aside for them, the Assyrians intermarried with the locals and adopted their ways. The merchants were nearly invisible, archaeologically speaking; the only evidence of their existence is the occasional Mesopotamian piece of jewelry, often buried in a tomb below the floor of a house. The native ruler of Kültepe held a tight grip on his foreign interlopers. As minutely catalogued in cuneiform tablets, still in their stamped clay envelopes and neatly arranged on shelves and in pottery jars of each merchant's house, taxes had to be paid on imported goods (principally textiles), prices set in silver, debts paid, and conflicts resolved.

The Old Assyrian Colony texts provide the first written testimony to grapes in Turkey. A grape harvest was celebrated at the time of the vintage (Akkadian *qitip karānim*; literally, "the picking of the grape"). These grapes were made into wine—this probably was one of the most stupendous "wine cultures" of all time—as evidenced by the native repertoire of pottery vessels (the "wine service"), many of which were found in the karum houses.

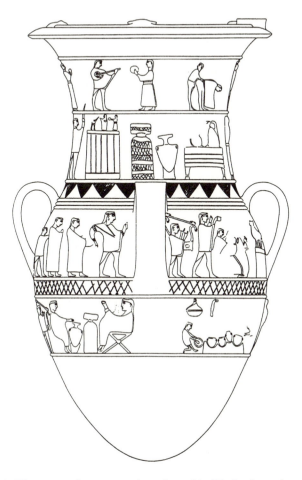

FIGURE 8.1. The magnificent vase from Inandık (Turkey), mid-seventeenth century B.C., depicts a sacred marriage (*hieros gamos*) ceremony in a series of molded panels. In the lowest vignette, the "king" and "queen" are seen enjoying "the great meal" on the left, while a wine-based beverage is prepared to the right. In the handle register, a procession of musicians and servants advances toward a bull sacrifice (at the far right). On the neck is depicted the proffering of the beverage and unveiling of the queen or "sacred prostitute" (partly destroyed). The culminating union is shown in the panel below the rim.

The Inandık Vase is the supreme example of this wine culture, showing how elegant beak-spouted jugs (chapter 4) and other drinking vessels were used in the royal celebrations and cultic rituals of ancient Anatolia. The mid-seventeenth-century B.C. four-handled storage jar from the site of Inandık, northwest of Boğazköy, stands in all its red, white, and black-slipped and molded splendor in the middle of the Assyrian Colony–Hittite room of the Ankara Museum of Anatolian Civilizations. The four running panels, or metopes, of the jar tell a fascinating story, as reconstructed by Hittitologist Sedat Alp.

The culminating moment shown on the Inandık Vase is a sacred marriage (*hieros gamos*) ceremony, which ensured fertility in nature and the well-being of the ruler and his people. In the top panel, the "king" and "queen," or "sacred prostitute," engage in a sexual act, as musicians play their flutes, harps, and cymbals, and dancers leap into the air in celebration. In the scene beneath, a procession of musicians, "sword-dancers," and other celebrants approaches a temple model and an altar, behind which the king and queen sit together on a couch. Because the Inandık Vase is broken away at this point, the details of what the couple are engaged in on the bed must be supplied from a similarly molded and decorated storage jar from nearby Bitik. On that vessel, the king pulls back a long cloak, such as is worn by devout Muslim women today, to reveal the face of the queen. He raises a cup to the woman's lips with his other hand. Sedat Alp interprets the storage jar, mounted on a stand in front of the couch, as a container for the "sacrificial bread." More likely, this jar—which has the same features as the Inandık and Bitik Vases (loop handles and a noticeably splayed rim)—represents the vases themselves, which contained the beverage proffered by the king.

In the third panel, the king or a god seated on a "campstool" is offered another cup of the beverage, which an attendant pours from a beak-spouted jug. Completing this metope, an entourage of musicians and attendants, carrying miniature altars, are shown approaching a statue of a bull, which represents the weather god. The group is led by a male figure who prominently displays a drinking cup; farther back in the line, a shorter individual, possibly the cupbearer, holds an animal-headed drinking horn. Although the portion of the vase in front of the bull statue is damaged, Alp proposes that the slaughter of a real bull is pictured here.

The lowest panel on the Inandık Vase depicts the standard Near Eastern royal banquet scene or "the great meal," as the Hittites called it. The king and queen sit on their campstools, with the queen at a slightly lower elevation and attending to the drinking needs of her husband, in a scene that is similar to the "*symposion*" of Assurbanipal and Assur-shurrat that is shown on the palace relief from Nineveh (discussed later in this chapter). The "queen" reaches out to a storage jar, again an exemplar of the Inandık Vase that would have held the "sacred" beverage, and the king holds up his cup. Food is available on a tall stand. Dancers, a lute player, and two strummers on a large harp provide entertainment.

The remaining vignettes on the vase go behind the scenes into the palace kitchens where the food and drink are being prepared. We see storage jars (Hittite *parīsu*) and a basket-handled vessel sitting in special racks and stands, which were the Anatolian equivalent of the Mari kannum. A "wine steward" either retrieves one of the jars from the "cellar"-full of jars, to replenish the stocks needed for the banquet and the ceremonies, or, if Alp is correct, he grinds out some cereal for the meal. Cuts of meat are suspended above him.

Finally, and most tellingly on the fourth panel, a tall figure stands next to a jar shaped like the Inandık Vase and "mixes" or stirs the beverage with a long stick. If the beverage being served and ceremonially presented in the other scenes of the vase was pure wine, why would such an operation have been necessary? The Inandık Vase itself may provide the answer. Its rim is lined with a hollow ring, and there is a large rectangular opening at one side. Four bulls' heads are mounted on the inside of the ring, with holes through their muzzles. Another liquid—perhaps honey, a berry juice, a raisined or herbal wine—could be poured into the large opening and automatically fed into the interior of the vessel. Once added, it would need to be mixed up and blended with the wine already in the jar. If a bull really was sacrificed, perhaps blood was one of the additives.

At approximately the same time, Minoan Crete was centered on a bull cult and had many bull-related artifacts, especially in the form of *rhyta* (elaborate funnel-like objects), that might have been used to

FIGURE 8.2. Beak-spouted jug with bird figurine from Kültepe (Turkey), ca. 1800 B.C. Ceremonial vessels for drinking and libations of wine were often in the shape of birds, especially of vultures, eagles, and other large birds of prey, which were associated with deities.

make a "mixed fermented beverage" (chapter 10). Central Anatolia also had the rhyton, but its "wine service" takes creative design and practicality in making "mixed" drinks to new heights. Stupendous drinking horns and rhyta were modeled three-dimensionally as lions, raptorlike birds, bulls, rams, pigs, rabbits, hedgehogs, and other animals. Smaller animal figures adorned large pithoi, tall stands, and "ritualistic" vessels in the form of boats and shrines, chalices, cups, and juglets. Multiple examples of the same pottery type were often combined together and fitted with column spouts and elaborate handles. Drinking horns were made in the shape of boots and shells. Tall jars had molded and incised faces of bearded males, similar to later Eastern Mediterranean designs. Sieves were incorporated into lids (which ingeniously moved along handles), spouts, and even bases, where particulate matter could be isolated from the liquid. Tubes were run down the insides of vessels, so that the drinker could insert a "straw" and avoid material floating on the surface. Jars were mounted together with intercommunicating channels, so that different ingredients could be mixed together. Multiple spouts enabled more than one person to be served at a time or to drink communally. Tour-de-force vessels were made to look like a single large grape cluster or multiple clusters mounted around a central spouted jar. Hundreds of years earlier than those of the Phrygians (chapter 11), the long-spouted jug, with its handle set at a right angle to enable easy drinking, was already being produced (color plate 8); the "waterfall effect" as the beverage rushed down the spout was highlighted on one example by the insertion of pieces of red, gray, and white stones in lines along a succession of projecting levels. Basket handles allowed for dipping into larger containers. The possibilities were endless for the innovative artist and potter, who was motivated and financed by a culture devoted to wine drinking, ceremony, and feasting. If the Assyrian merchants were not already enjoying wine that was served, poured as libations, and drunk from such an array of special vessels along the banks of the Tigris, they must have carried examples back with them and initiated their compatriots into the vinicultural world of central Anatolia.

As seen on the Inandık Vase and sculptures of the period, libations were made to theriomorphic and anthropomorphic images of the gods mounted on tall stands. As processions of functionaries filed by and musicians played their lyres and lutes, the rulers sat calmly on backless thrones and lifted cups to their lips. The motifs were encapsulated on a fine gold pendant from Kültepe that shows a "queen" seated on a chair, holding a cup, in front of an altar. Even more spectacularly, a small ivory box from Acemhöyük, a site located southwest of Kültepe, repeats the same scene on four sides: gold filigree, lapis lazuli, iron, and bronze studs accentuate the figures of lions, lionesses, and deer, as porters carry large jars on their shoulders to a seated dignitary with his cup in hand. The parallels with earlier Mesopotamian banqueting and worship are so evident from such artifacts, as well as from later Hittite artistic depictions of wine drinking and ceremonial presentations of wine, that one is hard-pressed to know which wine culture has precedence over the other.

The Kanesh merchant colony was the prelude to one of great civilizations of the ancient world, that of the Indo-European Hittites, whose existence was known from brief mentions in the Bible but whose language, culture, and cities were only rediscovered in the early twentieth century. The Hittite empire existed from about 1600 to 1200 B.C., reaching its acme between 1400 and 1200 B.C., at the same time that New Kingdom Egypt was flexing its political and military muscles in western Asia (chapter 6) and the Mycenaeans were ruling from their citadels on the Greek mainland and extending their power across the Aegean to the island of Crete (chapter 10).

The capital of the Hittites was at Boğazkale—ancient Hattusha—close to the modern village of Boğazköy, in a remote valley of the interminable expanse of the plateau, about 160 kilometers east of Ankara, the capital of Turkey. Located near the midpoint of a large bend in the main river of central Anatolia, the Halys or Kızıl Irmak, Hattusha was well situated to control an empire that encompassed Cappadocia, southern and eastern Turkey, and, for a time, northern Syria. In 1595 B.C., an early Hittite king, Murshili I, made a mad dash through Kassite-occupied territory and took the city of Babylon, thus ending the Hammurapi dynasty. The Hittite forces immediately retreated, but the point had been made: their culture could match anything that the rest of the world had to offer. Ironically, Murshili I was assassinated soon after his return to Hattusha.

The Berlin Assyriologist Hugo Winckler began excavating at Hattusha in 1905, and the German Archaeological Institute continued his work between the world wars and then every year from 1952 until the present, most notably under the direction of Kurt Bittel. What the German excavators unveiled at the site was little short of astounding. A massive fortification wall—6.5 kilometers in length by the time of the Hittites' greatest king, Šuppiluliuma, in the thirteenth century B.C.—encircled residential areas, an earlier Assyrian trading quarter (karum), five temples, and the palace atop the citadel. Three main gates have flanking figures of lions, sphinxes, and kings, sculpted in frontal and side views, which foreshadow similar developments on a monumental scale, centuries later, at Nineveh, Nimrud, and Khorsabad in Assyria and Persepolis in Persia.

Whole rooms were set aside in the palace as the royal archives, where 22,000 tablets had been deposited. Although they spoke an Indo-European language, the Hittite scribes wrote down their laws, hymns, myths, treaties, economic transactions, and other records in the cuneiform script of Mesopotamia. A careful study of these texts has shown that the Hittite civilization, at least at its upper socio-economic level, was preeminently a wine culture.

Hattusha and its kingdom were situated at a high elevation, more than 1000 meters above sea level on the central Anatolian plateau. Although freezing temperatures and low rainfall posed constant threats to the grapevine, the soil was rich, and the Hittites, like the Iron Age inhabitants of the Ararat Valley to the east (chapter 2), knew how to irrigate the land and increase its productivity. Vineyards, like those at Yazir, still line the hills around the ancient Hittite capital.

From the carefully worded Hittite Laws, which are a model of compensatory justice, it can be reasonably concluded that a 1-hectare vineyard was valued at nearly 120 shekels (each Hittite shekel of silver weighed about 12.5 grams, one and a half times that of the Babylonian shekel). A vineyard cost almost 40 times as much as other agricultural land, so it is not surprising that heavy penalties were meted out for human carelessness—such as allowing a herd of sheep to trample through a vineyard or accidentally burning it down—and for theft or wanton destruction of grapevines. Depending on who the offender was—a slave, a working man or woman, or a "free man"—each offense carried a specific corporal or monetary punishment. For example, when a whole vineyard was destroyed, the usual penalty appears to have been about a quarter of the value of a year's crop. In one sense, this penalty is not excessive, because it can take five or six years to establish a productive vineyard. On the other hand, the average hectare of vineyard yielded 1800 liters of wine, which sold for 30 shekels of silver figured at a half shekel per 30-liter jar (Hittite *parīsu*). To pay off the fine, a laborer needed to come up with 7.5 shekels or its equivalent (450 liters of wine or 1350 liters of barley), which probably took a half year or more of work, when it was to be had, at 10 liters of barley per day in wages.

The city of Hattusha has been extensively explored, but no wine-making installations have yet been found and excavated. Their absence can be explained, because it was more convenient to place industrial facilities close to the raw material being processed—grapes in this instance—and avoid extra transport costs. The Hittite texts describe vineyards nearby, probably on the hills surrounding the capital, but treading floors and vats were quickly silted up and are thus difficult to locate. Pressing operations could also have been carried out in small pottery "bathtubs," which have been excavated at the Old Assyrian colony at Kültepe and later Hittite sites, including Hattusha. These vats are similar to those associated with winemaking in Egypt and Greece (chapters 5, 6, 10, and 12) and were often situated in courtyards and kitchens where other foods were prepared.

My laboratory was directly involved in analyzing one of the few "bathtubs" for grape treading ever found in Anatolia. It dates to an earlier period than that of the Hittite empire—the second half of the third millennium B.C.—and rather than having been made of pottery, it was constructed as a permanent clay feature, lined with plaster. It was the principal installation in a separate room of a courtyard house on the acropolis at Titriş Höyük, a site that Guillermo Algaze of the University of California at San Diego has excavated along the upper Euphrates River in eastern Turkey. Ginny Badler, who has been so instrumental in obtaining other ancient organic samples for us, participated in this excavation. She noted suspicious reddish residues that mottled the plaster surface inside the small vat. Our analysis of the plaster showed that tartaric acid and its salts were present and thus confirmed its use in grape-pressing.

Given the expense of maintaining vineyards and making wine on a large scale, the beverage was the prerogative of the king, his household, and the gods. Royal wine suppliers oversaw the importation of wine from other towns in the empire, and a staff of wine stewards ensured that "pure wine" continually flowed "from a golden goblet" (The Blessings of Labarna). As was the wont of deities elsewhere in the Near East, they preferred wine at their banquets, sometimes used it to confound their enemies, and expected ample portions to be offered in their temples. At the Karaḫna Festival, for example, the celebrants "fill three rhyta ["large drinking horns"] with wine and place them back on the stele (for) the Sungod." After the deity has been sated, the assembled humans "drink three times." Wine was also used as medicine, to drive out evil thoughts, to sanctify new buildings and seal treaties, and to seal a warrior's loyalty to the king by pouring out wine that soaked into the earth just like blood. The king's role in guaranteeing the productivity of the land and propitiating the gods was symbolized by his enthronement on a backless chair, often a kind of campstool (see chapters 7 and 10), with a cup in hand.

The cuneiform tablets from the palace clearly identify wine as the beverage of choice in the royal court and cult. Enormous pithoi, which held between 900 and 1750 liters, were uncovered by the German excavators in the storage magazines attached to the large temple in the lower city of ancient Hattusha. Although some of these might have held grain, wine is believed to have been a high priority. Tahsin Özgüç also excavated similar "wine cellars" at Kültepe, which belonged to the first half of the millennium. As are the modern Georgian *kwevris* and Armenian *karas* (chapters 2 and 4), whose prototypes reach far back into Caucasian history, the pithoi of the Hittites and native Anatolian peoples were partly buried in the ground; underground storage helped to moderate the temperature of a wine that was aged in the jars. For transporting wine, the Hittites had a variety of storage jars, long-necked jugs, and multihandled ovoid flasks. Another important serving or transport vessel type was a straight-spouted version of the droop-spouted jar, which is attested as early as the late fourth millennium B.C. in eastern Anatolia and which probably supplied the Late Uruk cities with wine (chapter 7).

Besides the omnipresent cup, the Hittites drank and served their wine from rhyta in the shape of animal heads. Those of bulls, stags, and rams were most popular, and the most stunning specimens were made of silver and decorated with cultic scenes. A delicately rendered panel, encircling the upper part of a stag vessel in the Near Eastern galleries of the Metropolitan Museum of Art, illustrates the technical skill and inventiveness that went into these artistic masterpieces. Elaborating upon the standard libation scene in which a liquid is poured from a beak-spouted jug onto the ground, the special role of a raptorlike bird in Hittite iconography and religion is emphasized by showing both a deity, mounted on the back of a stag, and an enthroned "god," cup in hand, with this animal on outstretched arm in falconry pose. Such animal-head vessels are best described as

FIGURE 8.3. *Pithoi*, meter-tall storage jars that held wine, filled storage rooms in the palaces at Boğazkale (Turkey), the ancient Hittite capital of Hattusha, ca. 1400 B.C.

"drinking horns," because, unlike the proper Greek rhyton, which has a hole running through the animal's mouth, they were not used to transfer a beverage to another vessel for drinking or flavoring (chapter 10).

Even more magnificent, large-scale vessels in the shape of a whole bull were found in a "ceremonial" pit of the early palace at Hattusha, together with three red-burnished, long-spouted jugs. The bulls were nearly a meter tall and were decorated similarly with a highly polished red slip and distinctive cream-colored patches on their haunches and forehead. They were identical, except for their tails, which hung to either the right or the left. Kurt Bittel reasonably inferred that they were the famous sacred bulls Sheri and Hurri (literally "day" and "night") of the Hittite and Hurrian weather god. The weather god himself was represented by a gold-covered silver statue of a bull, according to a Hittite tablet found in the large temple of the lower city.

The usual Hittite libation vessel, as shown on stone reliefs and vessel panels, was the beak-spouted jug with a long, cut-away spout, which carried on the tradition of the Old Assyrian period. A similar

FIGURE 8.4. A silver drinking horn of the Hittite empire, 1600–1200 B.C. The libation or offering scene that encircles the mouth of the drinking horn shows a beverage being poured from a beak-spouted jug.

jug, made of highly polished red and black wares to imitate metal, was rapidly assimilated into the Eastern Mediterranean cultures, including that of the Hyksos (chapter 6), during the course of the Middle Bronze Age (MBA). The cut-away spout might have been packed with a piece of wool or cloth to filter the beverage or to add flavor—and possibly to produce other effects—by sprinkling on herbs or spices (see chapters 10 and 11). Long "libation" arms made of pottery, with a terminal hand holding a cup, could also have been stuffed with material and liquids poured through them. The Inandık storage jar and other vessels of its class expanded the possibilities: an intricate system of interior spouts enabled various liquids to be blended together. Phrygian serving jugs, more than a half millennium later, were as ingenious in their design, and we now have convincing chemical evidence that they held a mixture of wine, barley beer, and mead (chapter 11).

Mixing various beverages and ingredients together was an Anatolian specialty, which speaks volumes about where the earliest fermented beverages in the Near East were likely developed. The Hittite texts describe concoctions of wine, honey, fine olive oil, and sometimes tree resins. A perfumed oil could sometimes be in view, but a mixed fermented beverage (chapters 10 and 11) is a stronger contender in most instances. There is no question, for example, that kaš-geštin (literally "beer-wine" in Sumerian) was imbibed by the Hittites. It was supplied to the royal house only by the "wine supplier," a term that implies that wine was the stock beverage for the beer and other additives. In other words, the beverage maker began with grape wine, which provided a guaranteed source of Saccharomyces cerevisiae, and proceeded from there to add the wheat, barley, honey, raisins, oil, other fruits, herbs, or spices. "Greek grog" and kykeon, in which "Pramnian wine" was the essential beverage, are analogous (chapter 10). Because wine was the sine qua non of any Anatolian beverage, its amount could be increased, as recorded in a Hittite libation ceremony: "The wine is poured into the beer-wine, honey (and) water."

Centuries later in the wilds of central Turkey, a beverage similar to kaš-geštin was still being served. According to Xenophon in his Anabasis (4.5.26), the "barley-wine" served to the Greek soldiers, as they retreated from Persia, was harsh and needed to be watered down.

This barley-wine of 401 B.C. was drunk through straws or drinking tubes, as barley beer and date wine had long been consumed in Mesopotamia (chapter 7). A much earlier tradition for drinking a beverage—very possibly kaš-geštin—through straws is attested in Anatolia. On Hittite seals, a single individual, wearing the headdress of king or god, sits on a backless chair or "campstool" and sips from a jar mounted on an open-work stand. A tube on the opposite side of the jar suggests that the beverage can be shared with another celebrant. An attendant sometimes crouches nearby, with a cut-away spouted jug perched above the larger vessel—perhaps to refill it with kaš-geštin or to add a bit more wine or a special flavorant.

The diversity of traditional beverages in modern Turkey attests to both its rich history and the probability that they originated there in the distant past. Modern baqa is concocted by fermenting figs and dates together. Bazaq, which is made by reducing grape juice down to a concentrate and adding herbs, reaches a high percentage of alcohol after several years of ageing. Grapes are boiled down to a thick syrup or solid to produce basduk and kessme, which keep well and are diluted with water to make refreshing drinks as needed.

A more natural way of producing a high-sugar grape product is to allow the grapes to dry on the vine or to bake in the sun, and raisins have long been an essential part of Turkish cuisine and beverage making. The possibility that "noble rot" (Botrytis cinerea) was engendered on some of the fruit cannot be ruled out, especially when Roman writers such as Pliny the Elder (Natural History 14.241, 248–249) laud the raisin wine of Cilicia in southeastern Anatolia and speak so highly of Scybelites (Siræum) from Galatia in the central part of the country. The craving for sugar in the ancient diet set a high priority on these beverages, which entailed boiling down the grape must and adding honey. An especially powerful drink, known as tayf to the Ottoman Turks, was prepared by taking the first pressing of the raisins and combining it with the squeezings of wine-soaked pomace.

The raisin was a crucial part of Hittite life, whether as a dry ration on a military campaign or as a special offering for the king or the gods. These people had also perfected raisin wine, as one tablet puts it: "[Behold] the raisin. Just as it holds its wine in [its] heart . . . so

you [also] storm god, hold wealth, life, vigor, long years [and] joy of
the king, the queen [and] their children in [your] heart." The Hittite
texts are also replete with references to "honeyed wines" and "sweet
wines," and these were probably not confined to the usual reds but
included special white wines (see chapter 7). The possibilities for
making different kinds of beverages in ancient Turkey were endless.

What was once the "lost" Hittite civilization stands as a reminder
of what can be gleaned from the past by persistence and new methods of analysis. Even our well-worn phrase "Eat, drink, and be
merry!" owes its origin to the Hittites; it is attributed to the great
Hittite king Šuppiluliuma of the fourteenth century B.C., who finally
solidified control of southeastern Anatolia (Kizzuwatna) by treaty.
Several centuries later, after another "Dark Age," from ca. 1200 to
800 B.C., Hittite iconography is still apparent in the monumental
portrayal of a "Neo-Hittite" king, Warpalawa, and his tutelary deity,
the storm god, on a cliff side at İvriz in this same region. Appropriately, the god holds a grape cluster, with other clusters draped from
a live vine that encircles his body in Dionysiac fashion. A contemporaneous inscription on a royal statue at Sultanhan, near Kayseri,
speaks of "wine-gardens." Hittite enological skills had thus survived
the disruptive period at the beginning of the Iron Age. By the eighth
century B.C., Warpalawa and Mita of the Phrygians (chapter 11) were
growing grapes and producing wine. Competition that went far beyond wine production, however, had emerged on the eastern frontier
of the Neo-Hittite and Anatolian principalities.

Assyrian Expansionism: Cupbearers, Cauldrons,

and Drinking Horns

The Assyrian merchants who traversed the hill country
of northern Mesopotamia in the early second millennium B.C. and
traded metals and textiles—and intermarried and drank wine—with
the natives of central Anatolia have already been described. Their
descendants, beginning in the ninth century B.C., embarked on a
bold program of military conquest and ruthless suppression of their

FIGURE 8.5. The rock-carved relief of the storm god, Tarḫunta, at İvriz (Turkey), eighth century B.C., in which the god holds a grape cluster and is draped with a live vine in Dionysiac fashion.

enemies throughout the Near East. Their successes went hand in hand with a conspicuous growth in their wine industry in the northern Zagros Mountains, which bordered their homeland along the Tigris River, accompanied by banqueting on a huge scale to celebrate their victories and honor their gods.

Any doubt that the Assyrian kings were fully capable of conspicuous consumption was dispelled by Assurnasirpal II, who ruled Assyria from 883 to 859 B.C. He entertained 70,000 people when he inaugurated his capital at Nimrud, near the mouth of the Upper Zab tributary into the Tigris and some 100 kilometers north of the long-standing capital at Assur. The sheer amount of beverages to keep those people happy was astounding: 10,000 skins of wine, 10,000 units of beer, and 100 units of a "fine, mixed" beer, probably with wine and special flavorants added. The Assyrian kings called this "irrigating the insides" of their subjects.

The use of wineskins to transport the wine is a nod to the Aramaeans, who had become the ethnic majority in northern Mesopotamia by this time. Their status, however, was not necessarily affected by the Assyrians' adopting some of their ways, because the goal was to guarantee that tributes in wine were made from every corner of the empire—from Gilzani near Lake Van to Unki in the Orontes Valley of Syria. A liberal lifestyle demanded as much help as one's "neighbors" could provide.

The Assyrians embarked on an ambitious program of planting new vineyards in their own territories. In the "Assyrian Doomsday Book," which records a census of agricultural resources in the upper Balikh River to the east of Carchemish, tens of thousands of vines are enumerated. The operation described in the tablets was a royal enterprise, so it is not certain whether private estates in the region were similarly given over to winemaking. The conclusion that they were, however, accords with the fact that the same area had provisioned the entrepôt at Mari with wine a millennium earlier. In the eastern part of their territory, vineyards were planted at Yaluna, probably northeast of Nineveh, and up to an altitude of 1500 meters, in the land of Zamua in the district of Sulaymanyah. The latter wine was famous in the ancient world and might well have been transported by pottery jars to the main cities of Assyria, because one of the Nimrud texts (discussed later in this chapter) reports "a jar of Zamuan wine." Several hundred years after the Assyrians had passed from the world's stage, Xenophon in his *Anabasis* wrote of the plentiful vineyards that still grew in the region, especially on the east bank of the Tigris and along the Khabur River. Even today, small villages in hills east of Mosul (ancient Nineveh) are renowned for their vineyards.

Wild vines had long grown in the mountains of the northern Zagros, and the Assyrian kings were essentially capitalizing on and rationalizing an industry that had long existed in the area. Viniculture and winemaking were known to the Neolithic inhabitants of Hajji Firuz Tepe on Lake Urmia (chapter 4), 200 kilometers east of Nineveh but only reachable over the high mountains of Azerbaijan. Sargon II (722–705 B.C.) records in a letter to a god that his army traversed this territory during his eighth campaign. He describes a multitude of fruit trees and vines along the torrential stream of the Upper Zab. Reaching the mighty fortresses of Urartu, he was impressed by their extensive vineyards, and his army made short work of the quantities of wine stored in the forerunners of the modern kwevris and karas of Georgia and Armenia (chapter 2). Unfortunately, they also destroyed the vineyards, which was the usual Assyrian practice, presaging what Mikhail Gorbachev did at the end of the twentieth century A.D. Without wine, a king was effectively stripped of his prerogatives to propitiate the gods and ensure the welfare of his land and people.

Despite their destructive proclivities, the Assyrians could learn from conquered peoples who had such a long history of viniculture. They aspired to having "trees [that] were loaded with fruits like bunches of grapes," as Sargon depicted the Urartian city of Ulhu. They wanted cities that grew like wild grapevines on the mountainsides. The Assyrians were not beginners in the art of winemaking, but they took their holdings and expertise to a new level. They extended the vineyards throughout their territories and began to produce as good wine as anywhere else in the "civilized world." Their wine is described as "sweet," "good," "aged," and "strong," and both reds and whites were produced. As the Hittites in central Anatolia had done 500 years earlier and passed along to their successors, the Assyrians spiked some wines (*kurunnu* and *karanu duššupu*) with added grape concentrate, wheat, barley malt, and, undoubtedly, other ingredients.

Because the Assyrian capitals lay in the Tigris River plain, away from the mountains, the kings were obligated to re-create their own pleasure gardens in the accustomed manner of Mesopotamian and Egyptian rulers. Plantings, trees, and seeds were gathered from all over the empire. These miniparadises, similar to the grove with vines bearing fruit like precious stones that Gilgamesh entered in his quest for immortality (chapter 2), are said to have had pomegranate trees "clothed with clusters of fruit like vines." Since the grapevine grew up trees in the wild, with branches and the pendant fruits stretching from one tree to the next, it was natural for the Assyrians to plant their gardens and vineyards in the same manner—interspersing many tree species (date palms, pine and cedar, terebinth, pears, figs) with the vines—as illustrated in the stone reliefs that adorned their numerous palaces. These idyllic retreats were far from wild; as so vividly displayed on the walls of Assurbanipal's palace at Nineveh, they were populated by musicians, hunting dogs, and other accoutrements of civilization.

The stone reliefs and furnishings in Assurnasirpal II's new palace at Nimrud repeat the standard ancient Near Eastern artistic motifs that we have become accustomed to: the king, as the source of nature's fecundity and embodiment of divinity on the earth, is shown enthroned on his campstool and drinking wine from a cup. The king is attended to by a cupbearer, who carries an unusual serving cup ("ladle") with a nipple-like base and a long, curving handle that terminates in a serpent's head. In his other hand, the cupbearer extends a fly-whisk over the drinking bowl of the king. Just to make sure that no insect ends up in the obviously sweet beverage, another attendant stands behind the king and moves his fly-whisk over the ruler's head. The symbolism of the scene is accentuated by the elegance with which the king holds the cup outstretched on the fingertips of his right hand.

The drinking bowls or cups of the Assyrians, in keeping with ancient Near Eastern tradition, never had handles, unlike some Greek types (chapter 10). They were made of gold, silver, and bronze. They were often adorned with a fluted floral design and a distinctive belly button (Greek *omphalos*) by the seventh century B.C. The latter feature, which is well attested in the Midas Mound at Gordion (chapter 11), enabled the drinker to control his cup much better and perhaps avoid any appearance of inebriation. The whole hand wrapped easily around the outside of the bowl, and several fingers could be inserted up into the depression.

A 1989 discovery of two royal tombs at Nimrud, belonging to the seventh century B.C., mark an intermediary stage in the development of the drinking bowl. Whereas a simple hemispherical bowl is hoisted by Assurnasirpal II, the later bowls, which are inscribed as belonging to the queens of Tiglath-Pileser III, Shalmaneser V, and Sargon (II), are sharply carinated, or angled, and have horizontal fluting and exterior studding. One of these queens fittingly went to her death wearing a diadem bedecked with gold vine tendrils and festooned with grape clusters of lapis lazuli.

The celebrations at Nimrud brought together the upper class of the empire and foreign dignitaries for a limited time. During the remainder of the year, a royal household of 6000 had to be nurtured. From the queen on down through the various ranks of the administration and military to the "shepherd boys and assistant cooks," precise rations of wine were doled out. We know these details from two extraordinary groups of tablets: the Nimrud wine lists, dating to the successive Assyrian kings during the course of the eighth century B.C. The cuneiform texts were found by an expedition of the British School of Archaeology in Iraq, under the direction of Max Mallowan, in the "wine cellars" of the North West Palace and nearby Fort Shalmaneser. These cellars were laid out with large pithoi set into rows of mudbrick benches, which recall the kannum of the Mari texts and Hittite installations. In the Urartian city of Teishebaini, wooden planks between the rows of jars gave easy access to the thousands of liters of wine (chapter 2).

Whether the amount of wine at Nimrud was on the same order as that at a Urartian palace—with up to a half million liters in their cellars—is not known, especially now that the jars with inscribed amounts on them have disappeared. Mallowan estimated that the pithoi in the Fort Shalmaneser magazine could have held as much as 15,000 liters. The storeroom of the North West Palace was on the same scale, and, combined with other cellars that remain to be discovered, the wine supplies must have been adequate to meet the needs of the palace. The king's wives received the largest daily allotments, perhaps on the order of a *qa*, or 1 liter per day. By comparison, six skilled workers or 10 ordinary workers had to share the same amount. A harem of women from Arpad, a city of the realm, were given a *sappu* of wine each day, but the number of women and size of the jar are unknown.

The king's private guard was consigned 200 *homers*, the equivalent of about 20,000 liters of wine, which was presumably set aside for them over an extended period of time. Soldiers were known for their heavy drinking, which could sometimes turn ugly ("when they are drunk not a man of them will turn the iron dagger aside from his fellow") but was usually tolerated because it steeled their will in battle or, at least, broke down their inhibitions and relieved their pain. Despite the complaints of the mayor of Assur in a letter to the king that the commanders of the Ituaians were stirring up trouble outside the main gate, the heroics of these troops were legendary, and their highly placed leaders probably went on "eating and drinking wine" as before. The king himself had no such restrictions; quite the contrary, Esarhaddon's scribes became alarmed in the seventh century B.C. when he proposed to fast and counseled him to "eat bread and drink wine."

After Sargon had returned from his successful foray into the lands of Urartu, his victories were celebrated in regal fashion at his palace of Khorsabad (ancient Dur Sharrukin), a short distance upriver from Nineveh. Details of the most significant battles during his eighth campaign were depicted on the incised stone slabs of the halls and audience chambers. There, we see the temple of the god Haldi at the Urartian city of Musasir, with its gabled roof surmounted by an enormous spearhead and adorned with high columns, large shields, and helmets. In front of the temple stand two huge "cauldrons or vats," which sit in special open-work stands. The Assyrian soldiers are shown marching away with valuables from the temple—a high pedestal-based cauldron, a lion-headed *situla*, or bucket, and many other items—after its looting.

Back at the palace in Khorsabad, these valuables were put to another use at Sargon's celebratory banquet. Lion-headed buckets are shown on the reliefs being dipped into large cauldrons, mounted on floral-decorated pedestals, by a line of male attendants (see figure 11.2). Pairs of victorious leaders and their staff sit on ornate "camp-stools," opposite one another, and raise their lion-headed drinking horns in salute. The drinking paraphernalia are almost exactly matched by finds from the Midas Mound at Gordion, which date to approximately the same time (chapter 11). Except that a funeral

FIGURE 8.6. Wall relief from the palace of the Assyrian king Sargon II (722–705 B.C.) at his new capital of Khorsabad (ancient Dur Sharrukin) in northern Iraq. Two large vats or cauldrons, probably containing wine (similar to those from the Midas Mound; see figure 11.1), flank the entrance to the temple of the god Haldi at the Urartian city of Musasir.

rather than a military campaign was the focus of the Gordion assemblage, the Assyrian scene can easily be transposed to the highlands of central Anatolia.

Victor Place, the French excavator of Khorsabad and Nineveh, recorded a memorable incident in his 1867 publication of his findings. He noted a black resinous material inside the large, intact pithoi of a wine cellar in the Khorsabad palace. After a rainstorm, the solid turned to a violet-colored liquid, which looked very much like wine. Place was also overwhelmed by the peculiar smell of an "abandoned cave," which he associated with those caverns that were stocked with ageing wine and buried deep in the limestone hills of his homeland. He does not report whether he tasted the liquid to confirm his suspicion, but two of his associates and three local foremen were unanimous in agreeing with him that these jars had once held wine. During the nineteenth century, one had to be content with tests based on sight, smell, and taste. If the tools of molecular archaeology had been available, he might have been surprised to discover that the dark wine lees were laced with a tree resin.

The Urartians were noted for their elaborate wine serving and drinking apparatus, including gold drinking bowls, silver jugs, and bronze cauldrons. Highly polished red-slipped pottery vessels were made to look like horns or took the shape of high boots, with the stitching and buttons carefully rendered in white and red paint. When one's cellars are full of wine (chapter 2), the proper vessels are needed to serve and drink the beverage. Some vessel types, like the pottery boot-horns, were imitated by the immediately surrounding cultures, including the Phrygians, and their origins can be traced back to the early second millennium B.C. Other forms, such as the cauldrons that stand outside the Musasir temple on the Khorsabad relief, regularly appeared throughout the ancient world and eventually made their way to the far north of Europe. They are arguably a uniquely Urartian contribution to metalworking in the service of wine-drinking and ceremonial feasting.

Cauldrons from excavations in Urartu are adorned with bull's head and "siren" protomes like those from the Midas Mound (chapter 11). It can be argued that the bull is the embodiment of Haldi or is peculiarly Neo-Hittite in conception, rather than being associated with the chief male god, Assur, of Assyria. If it is, then such tour-de-force metalworking began outside Assyria, in the metal-rich area of eastern Turkey. At first, the Assyrians simply appropriated what they wanted in their military campaigns. As royalty and upper-class Assyrians came to appreciate the mixing of wine with other ingredients, they might have adopted the cauldron tradition. Rather than depend upon the uncertainties of wartime looting or tribute, foreign metalsmiths could be "exiled" to Assyria or elsewhere in the empire— Neo-Hittite centers in northern Syria and southeastern Anatolia at Carchemish, Zincirli, or Sakçegözü took over from the Hittite centers after that empire had collapsed around 1200 B.C.—and "made to produce" what was needed.

In keeping with the popularity of mixed fermented beverages in Greece and elsewhere in Europe (chapters 10 and 11), cauldrons are also very well represented there. The "orientalizing" motifs, including lotuses, griffins, and sphinxes, and the fact that the Greek and Etruscan cauldrons generally date to later periods than their Near Eastern counterparts imply that the primary impetus went from east to west. Peculiarities in style, however, show that local metalworking industries that specialized in drinking services were soon established on the Greek mainland and on some of the Aegean islands.

One of the richest tombs ever found on Cyprus—tomb 79 in the large necropolis of Salamis on the eastern coast of the island—illustrates the ever-broadening arc that was encompassed by the new drinking vessel types. The Assyrians took Cyprus in the same year, 709 B.C., that the Phrygians under Midas were brought in tow. The masonry-built central part of tomb 79 had been reused in Roman times for sarcophagus burials in niches. This chamber was approached by a wide *dromos*, or entrance hall, that was filled with amphoras and bowls—some containing ancient organic remains— four wooden chariots and wagons drawn by equids (probably horses), an ivory throne and bed, and bronze horse gear of blinkers, breast-plates, headbands, and side pendants. The burial goods were adorned with the rich iconographic repertoire of the Near East and Egypt, including winged solar disks, Hathor heads, winged genies holding situlae, the "tree of life," animals, palmettes, and lotus blossoms. All of these finds were associated with two burials in the dromos, dating to approximately 700 B.C. The most exciting discoveries for the history of wine, however, were two cauldrons near the facade of the main burial chamber.

One of the cauldrons from tomb 79 at Salamis had four sphinx protomes interspersed between four pairs of griffin protomes running around its rim; it was mounted on an iron tripod base with lily and animal-hoof terminals. The second cauldron was of the high pedestal-base type and had three bull protomes turned inward, below ring handles and mounted on plates that bore the wigged visage of "Hathor" or the "Lady at the Window," made famous from the Nimrud ivories, below a winged sun disk. These were extraordinary objects, especially in light of their being the first examples of cauldrons ever found on Cyprus. Moreover, the sphinx-griffin cauldron was filled with mushroom-lipped juglets of the Phoenician type (discussed later in this chapter) that were covered with tin metal, a rare technique that the Mycenaean Greeks had also mastered. We can imagine (but not prove, as yet) that the Salamis juglets had originally been filled with a "mixed fermented beverage," as the serving and drinking vessels in the Midas Mound at Gordion had been. Barbecued meats were probably also served at funerary dinners for the deceased; a pair of "firedogs," or pottery hobs, in the shape of ships, for suspending food over a fire, and 12 iron skewers were part of the dromos assemblage.

Individual cauldron styles have provided fodder for endless debates about where this vessel type was first made and which regions of the Near East and Greece eventually came to dominate production. Art historical arguments, with few chronological underpinnings, can be slippery, and more archaeological exploration of early Iron Age sites is needed to resolve these questions. One is on firmer ground in arguing that the ram-headed and lion-headed situlae from the Midas Mound must be of North Syrian, Phoenician, or Assyrian manufacture, because lion-headed buckets of precisely the same type as that from the tomb are shown being dipped into a large cauldron and carried by attendants to the waiting dignitaries at Sargon's victory celebration at Khorsabad. They are like carbon copies of one another and must have been made at a royal atelier.

Even if the ultimate inspiration for such exquisite metal vessels, used in drinking ceremonies and celebrations, remains uncertain, their stylistic spread throughout the known world of the time is remarkable. They were probably exchanged between the kings of Assyria and the small dynasts who emerged after the "Dark Age" in Greece, Anatolia, Phoenicia, Syria, and Palestine to seal diplomatic ties and cement relations. Especially in north Syria, each ruler strove to emulate his Assyrian overlord. At Carchemish, the important wine-producing center along the upper Euphrates, the reliefs that lined the walls of king Araras's palace show him battling the enemy, slaying lions, and, in true Assyrian fashion, celebrating and reveling in his good fortune. Along with scenes right out of the Epic of Gilgamesh, he sits on his throne, cup in hand, and is entertained by processions of dancers and musicians playing drums, lutes, pipes, castanets, and horns.

The apotheosis of palace interior décor, which reflects the central importance of wine-drinking during the life and times of the Assyrians, came during Assurbanipal's reign (668–627 B.C.) at the capital of Nineveh, just across the Tigris River from Mosul, the major city of northern Iraq today. Assurbanipal's grandfather, Sennacherib, had originally built the "Palace Without a Rival," as it was called in Akkadian, surrounded by wide boulevards, parks, and gardens. This magnificent 80-room edifice housed the king and his royal household—his wife and concubines, servants and bodyguards, and close confidants—in grand style. The Topkapi palace in Istanbul, home to the Turkish sultans from the fourteenth century A.D. onward, stands as a reminder of what the Assyrian palace might have looked like when it was in its glory. Now, nothing can be seen of the building itself, which has been covered over by mounds of earth and desert vegetation.

The wall reliefs of the palace at Nineveh, in the British Museum, provide visible proof of Assyrian greatness and tyranny. One scene, in particular, captures the dichotomy of opposites that made up the Assyrian royal psyche. Assurbanipal lies back on a long ornate couch, which is adorned with leaping lions, nude women looking out from windows that probably allude to the sacred marriage ceremony (chapters 7 and 9), and other motifs. While he holds a cup to his lips with one hand and holds a lotus flower in the other, a small table of delectables stands beside him within easy reach. Near Eastern monarchs had previously been shown sitting upright on their stools and thrones. The Assurbanipal relief is the earliest depiction of a "drinking party" in which a participant has assumed a more comfortable, reclining position, setting the pattern for the later Greek *symposion* and Roman *convivium*.

Asshurbanipal, however, does not share his drink with a group of men, as the Greek symposiasts would have insisted upon doing. Only his wife, the queen Assur-shurrat, is so honored. She sits on a throne in front of king, also holding a cup to her lips and looking up at her lord and master. Music is provided by a harpist, and attendants carry in more food and drink. The omnipresent fly-whiskers encircle the royal couple, to ensure that their perfect moment is not marred by an intruding insect.

The beverage that the king and queen drink is almost surely wine, as implied by the heavy clusters of grapes that hang down in profu-

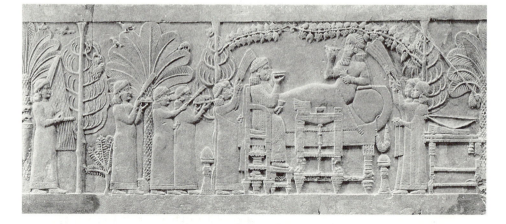

FIGURE 8.7. Wall relief from the palace of the Assyrian king Assurbanipal (668–627 B.C.) at Nineveh (Iraq). The king assumes the reclining banquet pose of the later Greek *symposion* and Roman *convivium*. The pair drinks wine beneath a heavily clustered canopy of grapevines. The tranquillity of the scene is shattered by the bloody head and hand of the king of Elam, which are suspended from nearby trees.

sion from the bower of vines above the pair. One notes that the grapevines have been trained by the gardener or vintner to grow up the trunks of evergreen trees and then across the space between them. Perhaps, the artist is using the trees as a symbolic device to convey the idea that the trees provided the resin for a "mixed" beverage. The significance of other details probably escapes the modern viewer. For example, a large multi-stranded necklace, hanging from one end of the couch, has been interpreted as belonging to the queen, who will don it in the ritualistic reenactment of the hieros gamos.

Against this placid scene, a bloodthirsty element intrudes itself. The head of the king of Elam, Te-umman, is suspended from the branch of a nearby tree. Birds are gathered around to pick off the flesh and pluck out the eyes. The hand of the Elamite ruler, still holding his sceptre, hangs from another tree. The symbolism of these images is clear enough. Assurbanipal has just defeated the hated enemy and has strung up the trophies of his victory to gloat over as he celebrates. The only thing missing from the realistic wall mural was for Assurbanipal to pour some wine over the body parts of his dead opponent, as he is often shown doing ceremoniously after he has killed a lion.

Within 15 years after the death of Assurbanipal, the Assyrian empire had disintegrated. The Babylonians, who were more used to drinking "date wine" than grape wine, had secured control of southern Mesopotamia, and the Medes had swept down from the Iranian plateau to capture Assur, the old capital, in 614 B.C. and then Nineveh in 612 B.C.

When I was a visiting scholar at the University of Copenhagen in 1995, I took advantage of my proximity to the mainland to travel to Berlin. There, the German Archaeological Institute kindly arranged for me to sample serving and drinking vessels from Nineveh and Neo-Babylonian Uruk in the basement storerooms of the majestic Pergamon Museum, which sits on "Museum Island" in the middle of the Spree River and proudly displays the "Ishtar Gate" of Babylon and other wonders of the ancient world.

Ancient organic residues were obtained for analysis from three vessels, including a bronze drinking cup from Nineveh and a bronze goblet and pottery "beer-jug," with a built-in strainer spout, from Uruk. All the vessels had been recovered from seventh to sixth century B.C. tombs, and all tested positive for resinated wine. This was a predictable result for a standard drinking cup from the heart of the Assyrian wine country. Wine inside an elegantly shaped goblet found in the lowlands of southern Mesopotamia, where most people drank date wine, also made sense, since it had been buried in a cemetery within the sacred precinct of Ishtar, the Eanna (chapter 7), and probably belonged to an official from the north. Even upper-class Babylonians were wont to celebrate with grape wine, that "excellent 'beer' of the mountain," according to Nabonidus. The "beer-jug," as we will see, was likely used to strain wine or prepare a "mixed fermented beverage" (chapter 9).

The Fine Wines of Aram and Phoenicia

The narrow strip of land that stretches along the Mediterranean coast from south of Mount Carmel northward to the modern Syrian city of Latakia, near where the French continue to excavate at the great site of Ugarit (Ras Shamra), was known to the classical authors as Phoenicia. The city-states of Dor, Tyre, Sarepta, Sidon, Berytus (modern Beirut), Byblos, Tripoli, and Arad hugged the shoreline, and from their well-protected harbors, the Phoenician ships carried wine, their famous textiles dyed purple, and other goods to Egypt, Greece, the far western isles, and beyond the "Pillars of Hercules" (Gibraltar) to Cornwall and the west coast of Africa. The Phoenicians and their ancestors before them, the Canaanites, deserved their fame as the seafarers of the ancient world: beyond transporting valuable physical commodities from place to place, they were responsible for transmitting the alphabet, new arts and technologies, and the ideology of a "wine culture" throughout the Mediterranean. Even the opponents of "Canaanite" culture made an exception when it came to their wine. Hosea, the eighth-century B.C. Israelite prophet, urged his listeners to return to Yahweh, so that "they will blossom as the vine, [and] their fragrance will be like the wine of Lebanon" (14:7). In classical times, Bybline wine continued to be renowned for its bouquet, which has led some scholars to propose that it was made from a muscat grape varietal.

An independent assessment of the Phoenician role in the ancient history of wine is presently impossible, because only one large-scale excavation of a Phoenician site has been carried out and because work in Lebanon ground to a halt after the outbreak of war in 1975 and has yet to recover fully. Before the devastating civil war, I participated as a pottery specialist in the last season of work (1974) at Sarepta, a major Bronze and Iron Age project directed by James Pritchard of the University of Pennsylvania Museum. It was not an easy assignment; dogfights went on overhead, as we excavated, and the main target of Phantom jet attacks coming from Israel was a Palestinian camp about 8 kilometers away on the eastern outskirts of Sidon. We had a boat ready to escape to Cyprus but fortunately never had to use it.

Most of my molecular archaeological research on the archaeological material from Sarepta has concentrated on the Royal Purple dyeing industry (chapters 1 and 3), a fascinating subject that bears tangentially on the wine industry. Both are luxury products, and if the Phoenicians were instrumental in establishing dye works elsewhere in the Mediterranean (e.g., Cyprus, Carthage, western Sicily, southern

Sardinia, and the Costa del Sol and inland Guadalquivir River valley of Spain), then they probably carried grapevine cuttings on board their ships, ready to plant vineyards where they went ashore and set up colonies. One of the first treatises on viniculture and other forms of agriculture was composed by a third to second century B.C. Carthaginian named Mago, who is quoted extensively in later Roman writings (Varro, Columella, and Pliny the Elder). Presumably, he drew upon older Phoenician traditions, extending back to the founding of the colony in the eighth century B.C. To date, however, the earliest excavated evidence for the domesticated grape at Carthage is from the fourth century B.C.

In the hot climate of north Africa, Mago had practical advice on how to aerate the soil and plant vineyards to take greatest advantage of the low rainfall. His recipe for raisin wine involved picking the grapes at peak ripeness, rejecting damaged berries, drying out the grapes in the sun for several days under a reed covering (taking care to cover them at night, so that they were not dampened by the dew), resaturating the raisins with fresh must, and then treading out the grapes. A second batch was prepared in the same way, and then the two lots were combined and fermented for 20–30 days, finally being strained into vessels with leather skin lids. The end result must have been a delicious, luscious elixir.

The Phoenicians competed with another wine-loving people, the Greeks, as both groups plied their ships throughout the Mediterranean and traded their goods. Together, they carved up the world marketplace and planted vineyards as they went. *Oenotria* ("the land of trained vines"), now Calabria in the toe of southern Italy, illustrates how seriously the Greeks took their task of promoting the "culture of the vine and wine" elsewhere. By establishing the domesticated grapevine on foreign soil—whether in the Black Sea or at Messenia in eastern Sicily—they stimulated and were better able to supply local demand. Some regions, such as the coastline extending from ancient Etruria up to Massalia (Marseilles), might be contested. The Etruscans, the native Italic peoples, were more than willing to learn about viniculture from the Phoenicians or the Lydians, but they also wanted and got a role in supplying wine to trans-Alpine Burgundy.

The role of viniculture in the homeland Phoenician culture of

Lebanon can be tentatively inferred from the limited archaeological evidence. Besides their Canaanite Jars and amphoras, Phoenician potters produced highly polished red-slipped bowls and decanters, with extravagant "mushroom" lips and a trefoil mouth, in imitation of gold and silver prototypes. These vessels, constituting part of the Phoenician wine set, were admirably suited to pouring out the wine with a flourish and drinking it in style or offering it as a libation. The famous coffin of Ahiram, a king of Byblos in the early tenth century B.C., shows the ruler seated on a "cherubim" throne. In standard Near Eastern fashion, he holds a cup in one hand and a lotus flower dangling from the other. Although women are seen tearing out their hair and beating their chests in mourning on the short sides of the coffin, the king's loyal subjects make certain that he has sufficient food and drink on the longer sides.

The image of Ahiram, sitting regally on his throne and indulging himself, is nearly identical to that of the high god of Ugarit, probably El, on a thirteenth-century B.C. stela found at Ras Shamra. Because similar artistic canons usually reflect similar social and religious conventions, scholars have turned to the large literary corpus from Ugarit, the important Canaanite city that was a short distance north of the Lebanese city-states, to illuminate the later history of the Phoenicians. The bulk of the literary evidence from Phoenicia proper consists of short funerary texts, including that on the Ahiram coffin, which provide only dull recitals of genealogies and threats against disturbing the dead.

At Ugarit, we are treated to a much larger, more dramatic picture of what a Canaanite or Phoenician feast was all about. The social institution of the *marzeah* is first attested in the fourteenth century B.C. at the site, and from there it spread out to Israel (chapter 9) and other parts of the ancient Near East, including Phoenicia and its Mediterranean colonies. Men and women of means gathered together in a *bet marzeah* ("house of the marzeah") on a regular basis where a *rb marzeah* ("prince of the marzeah"), a kind of Greek symposiarch, oversaw the festivities. The food and wine, which were served up at banquets for the gods and in commemoration of the dead, came from the properties of the marzeah's members. The land of a Ugaritic community could be divided up among many owners; for example, 81 vineyard holders from a single village were listed on a fifteenth-century B.C. tablet. The wealthy marzeah participants presumably controlled land throughout the territory of Ugarit, including inland regions, from whence they culled the best wines. Numerous amphoras of wine were transported back to the capital, where the French excavators found them packed into the storehouses of the city.

A marzeah banquet was not a genteel affair. We glean this fact from one of the Ugaritic texts that reads, "the gods ate and drank, drank wine until sated, new wine until inebriated." The head of the pantheon, El, drinks so much that he collapses into a state of incontinence, sitting in his own excrement. The gods were "models" for the living, so we can imagine that a marzeah feast of this world sometimes got out of hand. It is little wonder that the Israelite prophets sought to divorce themselves from these excesses and painted a different picture of Yahweh (chapter 9).

A marzeah in Phoenician Byblos, Sidon, or Tyre probably had much in common with the Ugaritic ceremonial feasting of the Late Bronze Age. Rich traders, entrepreneurs, and craftsmen would have owned vineyards backing up onto the mountains of Lebanon, which were well-watered, or in the rich inland Biqaʻa Valley, where the Litani and Orontes Rivers arise. The wild grapevine still grows throughout Lebanon and coastal Syria, and the transplantation of the domesticated vine there, perhaps as early as the sixth or fifth millennia B.C., would have gone quickly. The wild grape likely grew over a more extensive area in antiquity, because numerous grape pips have been recovered from aceramic levels at Ras Shamra, Hama in central Syria, and Aswad in the Damascus basin.

The kingdom of Aram arose in the early Iron Age to challenge the hegemony of the Phoenicians, Israelites, the Neo-Hittite states, and other peoples who had begun to consolidate political power in the Eastern Mediterranean area after the "Dark Age." The large, fertile oasis of Damascus was its "breadbasket," and the city controlled north-south inland trade. It was justly famous for its "Helbon wine" among the Assyrians and Israelites (Ezekiel 27.18). More than a half millennium later, Strabo claimed that the wine was so good that it was served to the kings of Persia. Helbon refers to the small town of Halbun, high in the hills west of Damascus, where ancient winepresses, hewn out of the limestone, can be seen. It, and the neighboring Christian villages of Maalula and Seidnaya, still produce good wines. Archaeological investigation in this region, combined with DNA analysis of the modern grape varietals, would be highly desirable.

Eastward to Persia and China

The discovery of wine by the Persian "Noah," Jamsheed, was dismissed in the first chapter of this book. Another Persian wag, one of the Bacchic poets of the Islamic period, said, "Whoever seeks the origins of wine must be crazy." This sarcastic *bon mot* nicely counterbalances the apocryphal story and suggests that it might be better to enjoy drinking the beverage rather than trying to determine where it came from and how it is made.

This book seeks a middle way, in the belief that an intellectual appraisal of the available archaeological, chemical, and other scientific data bearing on the origins and subsequent history of wine will lead to a better appreciation of its sensory delights and other benefits. Iran, especially the upland plains of the Karun River, where Susa is located, and the highland region around Shiraz have already figured importantly in our narrative (chapter 7). The domesticated grape was transplanted to these areas at a very early date and formed the basis for such a strong wine culture that it took centuries for Islam to shake off its influence.

Cyrus the Great, who conquered the Medes and Babylon in 539 B.C., hailed from Shiraz. Conspicuous consumption of wine was essential for this ruler of the largest empire that the world had ever seen. The skills of the Iranian metalsmith during the Persian period, as well as in the Parthian and Sassanian times that followed, were directed toward making extremely refined drinking sets—bowls, jars, ladles, mammoth horns with animal-head terminals, and so on—most often in silver and gold. The setting for feasts and celebrations was on a grandiose scale at the capital cities of the empire, first Babylon, then Ecbatana, Susa as the winter residence, and finally and most colossally at Persepolis, built by Darius the Great around 500 B.C.

The Persepolis Fortification Tablets, written in the Elamite language, track food rationing in the later capital for decades and give us some idea of how much wine was consumed by the "royal household." The thousands of texts were discovered in a northeast tower of the palace platform, which even today astounds the visitor with its sculptured panels and the towering columns of its audience hall. The ration lists consigned 5 liters of wine per day to the immediate royal family and progressively lesser amounts to high officials, the royal guard (the "Ten Thousand Immortals"), and functionaries. The nearby barracks of the army produced the tangible evidence for this level of consumption. Large pottery jars with pointed bases were set into depressions in the clay floors, and trefoil-mouthed pitchers and spouted bowls for serving and downing large quaffs littered the area.

If the firsthand observations of Xenophon in the *Anabasis* and *The Education of Cyrus* are to be believed, Cyrus the Great had a connoisseur's sensibility about wine. Whenever he discovered a particularly fine wine, he would drink only half of what he had been served—probably as much as 3 liters, or a good drinking horn's amount to start with—and would send the other half to a friend, with a note: "For some time, Cyrus has not found a more pleasant wine than this; and he therefore sends some to you, begging you to drink it today with those whom you love best."

One of the most endearing, and perhaps true, accounts of Persian wine drinking is told by Herodotus. "It is also their general practice to deliberate on weighty affairs when they are drunk; and in the morning when they are sober, the decision which they came to the night before is put before them by the master of the house in which it was made; and if it is then approved of, they act on it; if not, they set it aside." The proceedings are not exactly in accord with Greek democratic ideals, but they are reminiscent of the symposion!

Prodigious drinking at large banquets is the context in which the biblical writer of the book of Esther introduces Persian court life. Ahasuerus, probably Xerxes I, is said to celebrate his rule by inviting his satraps, army, and other subjects to a week-long feast in Susa. "Drinks were served in golden vessels—the vessels being diverse one from another—and royal wine in abundance, according to the bounty of the king" (1.7) The queen, Vashti, gave a similar feast for the women. Needless to say, everyone was feeling very merry on the last day (Esther 1.10), but the gaiety leads to complications in the biblical story and eventually a denouement.

Persian rule extended far to the east, out to Bactria on the north side of the Hindu Kush Mountains where the Oxus River (Amu Darya) begins its course down to the Aral Sea, and Sogdiana, with its capital at Samarkand and encompassing the fertile Fergana Valley. The Roman historian Strabo said that the grapevines of the Fergana Valley were huge and produced enormous clusters of fruit. The wine made from the grapes was excellent; it did not need to be resinated, and it could be aged for over 50 years with continual improvement. Strabo's account dovetails with that of General Zhang Qian, his Chinese counterpart who recounted a similar story about huge amounts of wine being produced and aged for decades in Fergana in the late second century B.C. (chapter 1). The cuttings that the emissary of the Chinese emperor brought back to the capital in Xi'an later produced the first grape wine in China, according to the literary sources.

Unquestionably, the domesticated grapevine had taken hold early on in the oases of central Asia. Wild *Vitis vinifera* also grows in the region today. But how early was wine made there, and did it have any impact on China before the second century B.C.? Very few excavations have been carried out in Uzbekistan, through which the main east-west route traveled between China and the Near East (the later Silk Road), so the picture is still extremely murky. The current consensus is that China, despite having more species of wild grape than any other part of globe, never got further than crossing a sweet indigenous grape with the Eurasian vine to make wine. New molecular archaeological evidence—showing that China was producing a resinated fermented beverage, with grapes as one of the likely ingredients, as early as the west (chapter 12)—has cast a shadow on accepted wisdom. Was this early Neolithic beverage discovered independently, or did some crucial ideas or technology flow from one area or the other through central Asia?

The available archaeological evidence suggests that the ancient peoples of Turkmenistan were consumed by a world of other drugs, not just wine. Several large fortified settlements, dating to the second millennium B.C., have been excavated by the Russians in the Kara

Kum desert, west of Bactria and Sogdiana. Pollen inside pottery bowls and engraved bone tubes from these sites were identified as deriving from *Ephedra*, *Cannabis*, and poppy (*Papaver*). All of these plants yield mind-altering substances—ephedrine, a powerful stimulant and vasoconstrictor, marijuana or hashish, and opium. The investigators suggest that the drugs were mixed into a drink and then consumed in a ceremony that foreshadowed a Zoroastrian rite in which *haoma* (Indian *soma*) was ingested. Later Persian kings adopted the monotheistic religion of Zoroastrianism, which centered around Wisdom and was based on a dualistic ethical system in which truth or evil in this life would be rewarded with heaven or a fiery hell in the next. Is it possible that the haoma drugs were consumed with the universal drug of humankind, alcohol? An alcoholic beverage like wine would be the best vehicle for dissolving the other substances, besides carrying its own symbolic import and creating additional mind-altering effects. The Persians and the oasis dwellers of eastern Iran were accustomed to wine. Because no grape remains are associated with the bowls and tubes, the mystery remains unsolved.

CHAPTER 9

The Holy Land's Bounty

It was a good land, called Yaa

Figs were in it, and grapes.

It had more wine than water.

Abundant was its honey, plentiful its oil.

(*The Story of Sinuhe*)

SINUHE'S tale is a classic of ancient Egyptian litera-
ture, and it captures the essence of life in the hill country of Syria-
Palestine (the land of Yaa or Upper Retenu) during the early Middle
Kingdom around 1950 B.C. As a privileged youth in the royal court,
Sinuhe had overheard the plot by eunuchs to assassinate the pharaoh
Amenemhet I and decided it was the best course to flee the country.
The land of the ʿamu, or Asiatics, had long been viewed as a margi-
nal area, inhabited by bedouin groups and small-scale agriculturalists.
Time and again, the Egyptians had invaded and milked the country
of its natural resources, only to be repulsed by the recalcitrant city-
states scattered throughout a diverse landscape of hills, valleys, and
streams, very different from the flat, alluvial Nile Valley. Sinuhe
blended in with the native people, but as he neared death, his final
wish was a characteristically Egyptian one—to be buried in the land
of his birth. He wrote the then-reigning king, Senwosret I, whom he
had known as a child, and humbly asked that he be forgiven for

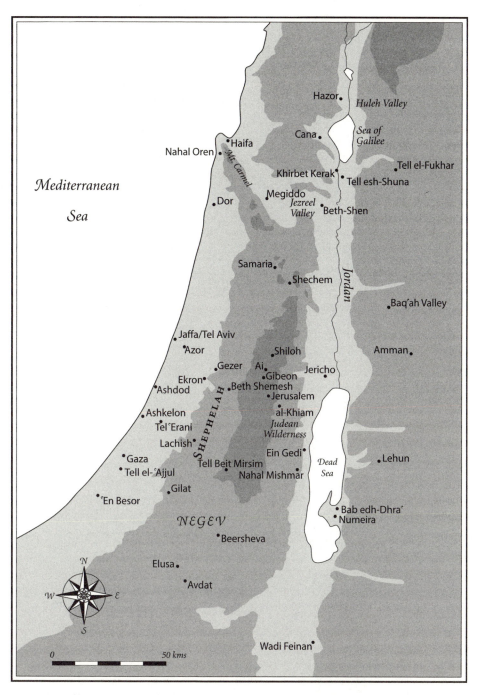

MAP 6. The Southern Levant, including Israel, Jordan, and the West Bank.

his errant ways. Although returning home like a bedraggled Setyu ("sand-dweller"), Sinuhe was given a royal welcome.

An echo of this story, couched in very similar horticultural allusions, occurs in Numbers 13.24–27, which was written down some 1500 years later. The 12 representatives of the tribes of Israel are said to have been sent out by Moses to "spy" out the land of the Canaanites. They returned with such a huge grape cluster that it had to be carried on a pole supported by two men (color plate 9). Figs and pomegranates also flourished in the Valley of Eshcol ("grapes") near Hebron, as they did in Yaa. The Israelite multitude had complained that there were no vines like those of Egypt in the wilderness of Sinai. The tangible evidence of the enormous grape cluster quelled their murmurings and convinced them that they were to conquer "a land flowing with milk and honey," or better, "with yogurt and grape syrup," as first proposed by Henry Frederick Lutz in 1922. In this felicitous translation, yogurt, a milk product of bacterial fermentation, is matched by a grape concentrate that might have gone into making an ethereal wine like a modern Sauterne.

Winepresses in the Hills, and Towers and Vineyards in the Wadi Floors

The wild grapevine (Vitis vinifera sylvestris) does not grow in the Holy Land today, which encompasses the modern countries of Israel, Jordan, and Palestine. Grapes grew there nearly 20,000 years ago during the Epi-Paleolithic period, as revealed at Ohalo II along the southwestern shore of the Sea of Galilee, or Lake Tiberias. The hunters and gatherers, who lived in the small huts at the site, cooked a range of meats (hare, fox, deer, fish, and other animals) over their open fires and accented their meals with olive, emmer wheat, barley, grape, and possibly pear. The terebinth tree (Pistacia atlantica) was also growing in the vicinity of the site, and its sap might have been collected and already used medicinally or for preserving food and drink. Drier conditions following the last glaciation, however, impinged on the habitat of Vitis, and wild vines survive today only along the coast of Lebanon.

The domesticated grapevine (*Vitis vinifera vinifera*) had taken hold in Palestine and Transjordan by the Chalcolithic period, at least by 3500 B.C. The earliest carbonized pips thus far found come from Tell esh-Shuna in the northern Jordan Valley. Toward the end of the millennium, whole dried grapes (raisins) are reported from Jericho in the southern part of the valley. Around the east side of the Dead Sea, the Early Bronze Age (EBA) city of Numeira yielded hundreds of raisins. More seeds were recovered from nearby Bab edh-Dhraʿ, ʿEn Besor near Gaza, and Jawa in the seemingly inhospitable Black (Basalt) Desert of northern Transjordan—all dated to Early Bronze (EB) I, ca. 3300–3000 B.C. Wood fragments of the plant were even excavated at Jericho and Numeira. Because *Vitis sylvestris* cannot have been growing in such arid regions, the conclusion is obvious: the domesticated grapevine had already been taken into cultivation there. Even though the shape and size of the pips accord best with the wild variety, the ancient grape remains must derive from the domesticated species that had been transplanted from areas farther north.

The ability to grow vines under such harsh conditions attests to the horticultural skills of the ancient vintner. Indeed, the rocky hillsides and limestone terrain of the land bridge connecting Asia with Africa, combined with a rainy season and months of sunshine, were ideal conditions for producing flavorful, fruity wines with solid textures and firm acidities.

If the 4500 liters of imported wine in Scorpion I's tomb at Abydos (chapter 5) are any measure, several centuries of transplantation, intensive cultivation, and honing of the winemaker's craft had led to a successful, profitable industry. The Levantine fig, which had also been taken into cultivation, flavored the wine exported to the Egyptian ruler in Dynasty 0. By EB I, wine was being produced throughout the southern Levant—in the sandy soils around Gaza, in the volcanic terrain of the Black Desert, along the steep wadi banks of the hill country, on the thick alluvium of the Jordan Valley, and on the high plateaus of southern Transjordan, where milder, wetter conditions probably prevailed than today. Trade to Egypt was coordinated through key maritime ports and entrepôts at the start of "the Ways of Horus," the land route that leapfrogged from oasis to oasis across the Sinai Peninsula. Goods were transported out from Tel ʿErani and Ashkelon, until the Egyptians inserted themselves as middlemen at ʿEn Besor toward the end of the millennium.

Very few Chalcolithic and EB I sites have been excavated, and the jury is still out on the density of settlement and land usage during these periods. Compared with EBA city-states in their heyday, EB I towns rarely exceeded 2–3 hectares in size, and they were widely separated across the landscape. Strange cuttings and cup-shaped depressions in the bedrock near many of these sites, especially in the highlands, have been interpreted as presses for grapes or olive or, even more dramatically, as "high places" for libations to the gods. Estimates of such installations, based on surveys and excavations, range in the thousands. Square-cut or circular basins, connected by channels in series along a hillside, were almost certainly used to separate grape must from its pomace of skins, seeds, and other matter. Outdoor stomping of grapes in rock-cut installations makes good sense. Large quantities of grapes could be handled at one time, and, because the winepresses were close to the vineyards, which were usually planted along terraced hillsides, transportation costs were kept to a minimum. Bare feet provided a gentle way to squeeze the juice from the fruit, even if they introduced some additional flavors not to everyone's liking. Despite their utility, these installations appear to date relatively late in the history of winemaking: pottery or other artifacts that have been recovered from them range in date from Iron II, about 900 B.C. at the earliest, to Byzantine times.

My own experience in excavating archaeological sites in the Baq'ah Valley of Jordan has taught me that the landscape today can be very different from what it was 5000 years ago. Especially low down on hills, crevices and hollows will erode out and later be filled in by soil, as rising and falling precipitation levels, animal grazing, and other activities take their toll. A magnetometer or other geophysical prospecting instrument was needed to discover the Late Bronze and Iron Age burial caves that we located and excavated because they had been completely silted up and lay hidden. How many well-preserved winepresses are still covered over? Those that were carefully hewn out and visible today could have been used and reused for millennia. The artifactual material inside such an installation reflects only its final phase. More careful excavation in the environs of a "winepress" might well reveal its earlier history, but such investigation has been rare.

One of the most amazing constellations of winepresses and pottery kilns for making amphoras to hold the wine produced is located along the coast of Israel between Ashdod and Gaza. High sand dunes covered many of the installations. Along the ridge of hard sandstone (*kurkar*) running parallel to the shore and several kilometers inland, mounds of sherds and pottery kiln debris are very obvious, rising 5–10 meters above ground level and spread out over many hectares. Some of these "tells" are composed wholly of sherds from well-known Byzantine amphora types—a long cylindrical variety known as the Gaza Jar and a short dumpier variety called the Ashkelon Jar—that were used to transport true Holy Land wine for the Eucharist throughout North Africa, Europe, and the Black Sea region. The eponyms were well chosen: Gaza Jars are concentrated at the kilns and pottery heaps around this city, and Ashkelon Jars at installations farther north. My laboratory has analyzed fragments from these jars and confirmed that they did contain wine and that it was resinated.

The potent combination of wine and religion had clearly attracted many new viniculturists to the southern coastal region in Late Roman and Byzantine times; they commuted between their villas and vineyards and nearby cities with churches, marketplaces, and workshops. The phenomenon spilled over into the drier climes of the Negev Desert, where numerous winepresses surround the Nabataean cities at Avdat, Elusa, and Shivtah. This final crescendo of making wine in the Holy Land represents the cumulative wisdom and expertise of many millennia, which then collapsed before the rising tide of Islam, which reserved the beverage for paradise, and the desert sands.

Given the ravages of nature and the fact that preclassical evidence for winemaking is often deeply buried, it is not surprising that relatively little archaeological or chemical evidence for winemaking has thus far been found and verified. Small spouted vats ("bathtubs"), like those used in Anatolia and Greece (chapters 8 and 10), have been recovered from Iron Age sites, such as Ashdod, north of Ashkelon along the Mediterranean coast. Like the metal pots and pans that Palestinian youth used to trample out the grapes in the early twentieth century A.D., the pottery versions were portable and well-suited to small-scale production, in city or countryside.

One of the most intriguing lines of evidence that can be related to the widespread planting of vineyards from an early period are the numerous towers that were dispersed in a seemingly random pattern, away from the main settlements, on rocky outcrops and in remote wadis. They are especially prevalent in the hill country, and, to the discerning eye of the explorer, flattened areas along nearby hillsides appear to have been intentionally terraced, perhaps to grow grapes or olives. In Transjordan, these buildings have been described as "megalithic," because they were made out of enormous boulders, weighing many tons each. The buildings could be circular or rectangular in plan and were sometimes combined together into more extensive complexes, with circular towers strategically placed along walls and at their corners, and with casement rooms surrounding courtyards.

From the limited evidence that has thus far been garnered, the smaller, isolated circular towers belong to an earlier phase of the Iron Age. They are very similar to the stone huts that are used by the farmers today, which are often two-story structures. Their advantages soon became obvious to our excavation team when we were invited back to a "tower" for lunch and a siesta. Their thick stone walls keep them cool, as much as 13 centigrade degrees cooler than the outside temperature during a summer's day, and they moderate temperatures at night and during the winter. The towers are close to the fields and orchards, so it is no problem to bring in the choicest produce and enjoy it right off the vine, tree, or plant. The upper floor can be sumptuously furnished with pillows and mats to lie down on, as a refreshing breeze blows through windows. Conversation and food are soon followed by sleep.

Ancient vintners might also have used the towers to store the freshly picked fruit before it was transported to the winepress. Wine production in jars could also have been carried out in the ground-floor "cellar." At least some wine must have been kept in reserve for celebrating the harvest. Guards to protect the vineyards from marauding humans and animals could stay overnight in the towers.

Isaiah, the late-eighth-century B.C. prophet of Israel, provides a set of practical guidelines (5.1–5) for the aspiring vintner when he compares Yahweh's love of his people to that of the viticulturist and his vineyard:

> Let me sing for my well-beloved,
> a song of my beloved touching his vineyard:
> My well-beloved had a vineyard in a very fertile hill;
> He dug it, and cleared it of stones,

and planted it with the choicest vine,
he built a tower in the midst of it,
and also hewed out a vat [i.e., a winepress] therein;
And he looked that it should bring forth grapes,
And it brought forth wild grapes [or fetid fruit].

Although the careful planting did not achieve its goal—the grapes were sour and set the peoples' "teeth on edge"—we do have an explicit mention of a tower in this poetic composition, which has come down to us from the middle of the Iron Age. The ancient text also makes it clear that winepresses were cut out of the bedrock. A less sturdy alternative to the stone tower is a seasonal shelter made of perishable materials such as cloth or animal skins over a wooden frame. The ancient Israelite festival of Succoth, "the festival of booths," probably harks back to the custom of a family's living among the vineyards and olive groves until the fruit was ready to harvest.

The earliest calendar of ancient Palestine, the Gezer Calendar, marks the two months of "in-gathering" of grapes and olives in September and October as the beginning of a new agricultural year, when the first rain arrives after months of drought. It is a time of joyous celebration and thanks for a bountiful harvest, with dancing and singing of women in the vineyards (Judges 21.19–23), like the Greek thyiads on Mount Parnassus; Chapter 10). The calendar, which was excavated by R. A. S. Macalister at the site of Gezer in the southern lowlands (Shephelah) of the Judean Hill Country, dates to the late tenth century B.C. and is one of the earliest inscriptions in early Semitic or Hebrew script ever found. Scholarly opinion is divided as to whether the text, which was roughly incised on a piece of soft limestone, is a kind of "Farmer's Almanac," a governmental record, or a child's school exercise.

The Success of the Experiment

As the clock is turned further and further back to trace the origins of winemaking in ancient Palestine, the literary and archaeological evidence gradually diminishes to a mere trickle. Molecular archaeology may have provided us with a tantalizing glimpse of a thriving winemaking industry in the late Chalcolithic period, but much more research is needed to fill out the picture. For example, when was the domesticated grapevine first established in the Jordan Valley and neighboring hills?

The archaeobotanical evidence from Tell esh-Shuna in the northern Jordan Valley is only a *terminus ante quem* (literally, "an end" or "date before which"), as archaeologists are fond of saying. Much more was happening in the Holy Land before the mid-fourth millennium B.C. At the southern end of the valley, the important oasis tell of Jericho, situated nearly 300 meters below sea level close to the Dead Sea, has a sequence of permanent human occupation going back to 10,000 B.C. Several thousand years later, during the Pre-Pottery Neolithic A period, a solid stone tower, which still stands 9 meters high and has an interior stairway, had been constructed to defend the site. Advances in architecture and town planning were matched by changes in burial and religious customs (such as the amazing plaster-molded skulls and figurines, best attested at Jericho and ʿAin Ghazzal on the Transjordanian plateau near Amman), trade (obsidian from eastern Anatolia and the Caucasus, shells and semiprecious stones from sea and desert), and a cuisine that reflected newly introduced cultivated grains and domesticated animals, including sheep and goat.

The Neolithic Revolution took more than 3000 years to work its way from more northerly regions into the varied Palestinian landscape—from ʿAin Mallaha (Einan) in the Huleh Valley and Nahal Oren on Mount Carmel to al-Khiam in the Judean Wilderness and Beidha and Basta, near Petra in southern Jordan. Even though the pace of technological change was slower than what we have come to expect today, this period was one of the most dramatic in human prehistory. Many things we take for granted today—Near Eastern and Mediterranean cuisines, clothing made of wool and cotton, but above all our fermented beverages—had their beginnings in this truly revolutionary time. Pottery, which we have seen is an ideal material for retaining ancient organics and tracking the course of fermented beverage production, made its first appearance around 6000 B.C. As yet, my laboratory has not analyzed any of the Neolithic pottery, which includes both crudely made as well as finely burnished slipped and painted cups, jars, and other forms that might have been used to make the various potables and, store, serve, drink, and pour them out as libations.

The Chalcolithic winemaking industry in Palestine owes its existence to the Neolithic Revolution. Many centuries were required to transplant the vine throughout the country, clone and nurture new cuttings, and successfully establish the far-flung vineyards and a prosperous export market. The characteristic pottery vessels of the period—cups, goblets and "cornets," "churns," handled and spouted storage jars—are reminiscent of some Neolithic forms. The extremely well-made Chalcolithic pottery types, with painted geometric designs and rope appliqués, are comparable to those found elsewhere in the Near East and Anatolia (chapters 3 and 8). Again, no molecular archaeological investigation has yet been carried out on this material, and we may be in for some surprises.

One peculiar jug with a basket handle and strainer spout is thus far unique to Chalcolithic Palestine. Although its provenience is uncertain—having been bought on the antiquities market and said to have come from a wadi in the Negev Desert—its style, pottery ware, and manufacturing details attest to Chalcolithic origin. Two free-standing bird figurines, set perpendicularly to the handle and spout and facing each other on opposite sides of the mouth, are the vessel's most distinguishing features. Similar birds appear on the elaborate "crowns" in the hoard of 429 bronze artifacts found at Nahal Mishmar in the Judean Wilderness. It is believed that these metal objects, which also included mace-heads, weapons, and tools, were produced of locally available arsenic-rich copper ores in the Wadi Feinan, south of the Dead Sea, or at Timna at the head of the Gulf of Aqaba (Eilat). Birds are a prominent feature of Near Eastern and Anatolian art (chapter 8), and it does not require a great leap of archaeological intuition to connect the rich hoard, which can be paralleled by similar tour-de-force metalworking in Iran, with an unusual "cultic structure" belonging to the Chalcolithic period that was found "empty" in the Ein Gedi oasis, 10 kilometers north on the western shore of the Dead Sea. The bronze artifacts, like the Dead Sea scrolls millennia later, had probably been wrapped in their straw matting and deposited under a boulder at Nahal Mishmar for safe keeping.

The bird-figurine pottery jug is similar to three bronze basket-handled vessels in the Nahal Mishmar hoard, although these lack the strainer spout and the birds. Other examples with spouts, but again lacking the birds and sieves, have been found at Ai in the Judean Hill Country, Azor near Tel Aviv, and Byblos in Lebanon, dating to either the Chalcolithic or EB I periods. Their differences apart, all these jugs were likely used for dipping into a large wide-mouthed jar, to transfer and filter a beverage for drinking or pouring libations. A simple plug of wool, cloth, or grass could have served as a filter in those examples that lacked the pottery strainer. In other words, this vessel type is very similar to the long-spouted and sometimes sieved jugs of Anatolia (chapter 8), which began to be made at the beginning of the Bronze Age and were transmogrified into strangely beautiful birdlike forms by the Middle Bronze Age (MBA). Phrygian renditions (chapter 11) represent an artistic climax in which the spout has become so long that any comparison with a bird beak is far-fetched unless it is that of a stork or a crane.

What was the beverage that was transferred and sieved using the basket-handled jugs? My suspicion, based on the molecular archaeological evidence that has already been obtained from the Scorpion I jars, is that it was wine. Most scholars have argued that such strainer-spouted vessels are more appropriate for processing barley beer. But wine also needs to be filtered, and the spouts might have doubled as a means to add herbs and spices or a tree resin, such as terebinth. Even the so-called churns, which got their name from similarly shaped leather bags used by modern bedouin to make yogurt or butter, can be viewed as "wineskins." The famous pottery sculpture of the naked lady from Gilat, north of Beersheva, who is shown balancing a churn on her head and holding a "drinking-vessel" under one arm, might then be a human or divine purveyor of wine rather than of a milk product.

Serving the Needs of a Cosmopolitan Society

By the Hyksos period between about 1750 and 1550 B.C., the winemaking industry of the southern Levant was firmly entrenched (chapter 6). We have seen how millions of Canaanite Jars, many of which probably contained resinated wine, were shipped out from the Gaza region to Avaris, the capital of the Hyksos in the northeastern Nile Delta. The huge exports of wine from their "home-land" were intended to quench the thirst of the Semitic rulers, who had originally come from Southern Palestine.

Middlemen in Gaza, Ashkelon, and other city-states in Southern Palestine, who presumably grew rich on the profits, handled the trade of goods coming from elsewhere in the country. Southern Palestine established itself early on as the commercial hub of the country, and exported pottery—whether utilitarian amphoras and cooking pots or fancy serving and drinking vessels—was most likely to come from here than anywhere else. The clay palette on which the potter and wine connoisseur could exercise their imagination had taken a huge leap forward. Indeed, I would argue that much of the MB and LB Palestinian pottery that we see in museum collections around the world represents either fine "dinner ware" or elaborate drinking sets. The real mark of distinction for the inland farmers, winemakers, craftsmen, and a growing upper class was to have an adequate wine service within reach and to emulate their rulers.

The introduction of the fast potter's wheel at the beginning of the MBA from the north made all of this possible. Some of the finest pottery ever produced in Palestine was made during the second mil-lennium B.C. Bowls, deep kraters, goblets, chalices, vases, jugs, and juglets generally imitated metal prototypes, as seen in their sharply angled and carinated forms, their ultrathin ("egg-shell") and high-fired wares, the highly polished red and black slips, and details such as applied rivetlike clay knobs.

The rich Jericho tombs, which John Garstang and Kathleen Ken-yon excavated in the twentieth century, illustrate how wealthy in-habitants of the Jordan Valley expected to be cared for in the after-life. Their body was laid out on a finely carved bed made from native tamarisk, cherry, and other woods, with a table within arm's reach that was laden with choice portions of sheep and goat, grapes and pomegranates, and drinking vessels, which could be filled from the nearby storage jars. Organic preservation conditions inside the tombs were excellent—even a desiccated human brain was recovered—but a molecular archaeological investigation and a full synthesis of the available evidence are yet to be done.

FIGURE 9.1. The Dolphin Vase, presaging the rise of the wine-loving Hyksos, was made in the southern Levant and imported to the capital of Lisht in Egypt between 1750 and 1700 B.C.

One tomb (J3) at Jericho, which dates to the earliest MB IIA phase of the cemetery, was unique in providing the resting place for a single individual: a young man whose military prowess was proclaimed by pairs of daggers and battle-axes. Other tombs at the site contain the commingled skeletons of 20 people on average, likely belonging to extended families. The male warrior was also accompanied to his grave by a pair of equids (asses), as was done in the

Hyksos burials at Ashkelon, Lachish, and Avaris (chapter 6). His funerary meal consisted of a side of lamb on a wooden platter and a drinking horn in the shape of a ram's head that might have been filled and balanced against the tomb wall.

Similar animal-shaped drinking vessels are well known from central Anatolia from about the same time (chapter 8). The contemporaneous Mari tablets from the important wine center on the middle Euphrates River are replete with references to these vessels and other royal gifts that were intended to seal relations between the powers of the day. Variations on the same theme—vessels in the form of an equid, lion, bull, bird, or a lowly rabbit—gained greatly in popularity in the centuries and millennia to come. During the Late Bronze Age (LBA; ca. 1550–1200 B.C.), specimens made of faience—a molded and fired quartz sand matrix that was overlaid with multicolored glazes—became all the rage throughout the Near East, Cyprus, and the Aegean. Some examples were true drinking horns; others had a spout running through the nose or mouth of the animal and are properly referred to as *rhyta*, which were used to transfer, filter, and possibly mix in other substances (see chapters 8, 10, and 11).

Two ivory strips from the palace treasury of Megiddo offer tantalizing clues of how crucial these vessels were to court life in the international world of the LBA. In celebration of a military victory, the king sits proudly upon his grandiose, cherubim-sided throne and raises a cup to his lips. A female attendant, perhaps the queen or a sacred prostitute, indicated by her high *polos* headdress and embroidered dress, stands before him, holding a "napkin" to catch any spilled liquid in one hand and a lotus flower in the other. Besides its symbolic import in ancient Egyptian religion and, by transference, in Canaanite cult, the blue lotus (*Nymphaea caerulea*) contains natural opioid compounds to soothe the body and the mind. A harpist provides background music in a gardenlike setting with birds and plants, and an armed warrior stands ready if anyone should try to disturb the festive occasion.

It is what is going on behind the throne that is of greatest interest. There, two male attendants are serving up the beverage from a large two-handled krater, much like an Iron Age cauldron from Urartu

FIGURE 9.2. A Late Bronze Age ivory plaque from Megiddo (Israel), ca. 1200 B.C. The ruler, seated on an imposing throne, quaffs wine being served up from a large krater behind him, using lion- and gazelle-headed drinking horns or *rhyta* (compare color plates 11 and 15 and figure 11.3).

(chapter 8) or Gordion (chapter 11). Right above the large container, drinking horns or rhyta shaped as lion and gazelle heads sit on a shelf or lid. They have either already been used to prepare the next round of drinks, which are being carefully carried in bowls to the king, or they stand ready for a later, more dramatic stage in the drinking ceremony.

The Egyptian armies, which regularly invaded Retenu or Canaan during the LBA, made certain that they brought back animal-headed rhyta and drinking horns as tribute. Two lion-headed examples in silver are depicted on the frescoes inside the Theban tomb of Amenmose, a commander of the infantry under Tuthmosis III and his son, Amenhotep II. The 14 campaigns of Tuthmosis III over his 54-year reign netted him fine oils, textiles, slaves, and wine, which "flowed like water." His soldiers are said to have been "drunk and anointed with oil every day as if at feasts in Egypt." The pharaoh's Annals also record that bull-headed, ram-headed, and lion-headed vessels were taken as booty. They were said to have been made in Retenu, and the styles of the many examples that have now been recovered from Levantine sites are clearly different from the rhyta or horns of other countries, also illustrated in the Theban frescoes. Immense bull rhyta, for example, are carried by porters, wearing distinctive "kilts with codpieces," from the island of Keftiu (Crete). Crosses on the rhyton surfaces suggest stone markings or the hair curls of a bull, such as are intricately rendered on the black steatite example from Knossos in the Herakleion Museum (chapter 10; color plate 11).

Wine for the Kings and the Masses

Egyptians and Canaanites alike enjoyed their wine mixed with other ingredients, whether an imported tree resin or a native herb or spice. Malt and other fruit beverages were also imbibed throughout the ancient Near East. The exact formulations of the various mixed beverages may still be conjectural, but wine likely entered into their preparation and was the sine qua non, especially in upland regions heavily planted with vineyards (see chapter 8). Kraters and rhyta are well-documented vessels that would have served admirably to prepare and filter such mixed beverages. The so-called beer-jug suited the same purpose. The long-spouted jug, with a built-in strainer and a basket handle or a loop handle set at a right angle to the spout, could be dipped into a larger mixing vessel and used to pour the refined beverage into a drinking vessel, or one could simply raise the jug and drink directly from the spout. The type, which has a long pedigree stretching back to the Chalcolithic period, became more prevalent in the Palestinian archaeological record toward the end of the LBA, probably because of increased contacts with Syria and Anatolia.

The fact that barley beer was strained through straws in Mesopotamia (chapter 7) misled William F. Albright, the dean of "Biblical Archaeology," when he first dubbed the jug with a strainer spout as a "beer-jug." Albright bolstered his theory on its prevalence at Philistine sites of the early Iron Age in the Gaza region, whose expansive coastal plains were imagined to have been planted with fields of grain. The Philistines' penchant for week-long feasts (Judges 10.10–19)—no doubt liberally provisioned with food and drink—fit with the picture of a bunch of "beer-drinking louts." The biblical text, however, makes no mention of beer, and vineyards actually provide the backdrop for the action. The Philistine "beer-jug" might better be called a "wine-jug," if that name did not also convey the image of uncultured boors. Current excavations, especially at Ashkelon and Ekron (Tell Miqne), show that the Philistines knew how to build a city, produce huge quantities of olive oil and wine for the export market, and play power politics.

Figure 9.3. A "beer-jug" of Philistine type from Cave A4 in the Baqʻah Valley (Jordan), ca. 1200–1050 B.C. Despite the name, the locally made vessel was more likely used to serve wine or prepare a mixed beverage.

The principal beverage of Southern Palestine had been wine for millennia, so it would have been insane for the Philistines to uproot the vines and begin growing only barley. That was a tactic that the Assyrians, sometimes even the Egyptians, employed to subdue an enemy, but it was counterproductive for anyone who planned on staying. As one of the Sea Peoples who invaded the country from the

Anatolian or Aegean region during the turbulent period at the end of the LBA and the beginning of the Iron Age, the Philistines rapidly assimilated, probably intermarrying with the locals, and adopted the customs and technologies of their new homeland. Once defeated by the Egyptians, they served as mercenaries and were settled in key garrisons in southwestern Palestine and at Beth Shan in the northeastern part of the country. In time, they came to rule the prosperous city-states of the coastal region—Gaza, Ashdod, Ashkelon, Gath, and Ekron—to such an extent that their ancestral name *Peleset*, from which "Palestine" is derived, became synonymous with the country as a whole.

The Philistines' predilection for wine is borne out by the finding of "bathtubs" at Ashkelon, of a type often used in Greece, Anatolia, and Egypt to tread out grapes or collect the must (chapters 5, 6, 10, and 12). The vats dated to the earliest phase of occupation, the twelfth to eleventh century B.C., when the Philistines were consolidating their power. Built within the city, one of the vats had been placed alongside a plastered mudbrick platform with channels to run off liquid. The installation, located directly beneath a later facility, set the pattern for what was to come later. Our molecular archaeological investigation of plaster sealing one of the vats showed that it had contained grape juice.

Besides the "wine-jug," the original home of the Philistines was betrayed by other elements of their wine service. A krater with uplifted horizontal handles was decorated in red and black paint with Mycenaean-like birds and geometric designs. A smaller version of the same type—a *skyphos*—was essentially a Mycenaean drinking vessel. At the site of Tell el-Fukhar in northern Transjordan, where I served as the pottery specialist, a piece of a Philistine skyphos was excavated in the vicinity of the eleventh-century B.C. city gate. Instrumental neutron activation analysis (INAA) confirmed that the vessel was made of the red loess clay of Southern Palestine. Thus far, it is the only true Philistine vessel found east of the Jordan River, and it also has the distinction of being a wine bowl.

On the other hand, a "wine-jug" that I recovered from an early Iron Age burial cave in the Baq'ah Valley, near Amman, had every appearance of having been just as well made as the skyphos from Tell el-Fukhar and being an import from Philistia. But INAA showed that it was made from the local clay, along with the 69 other vessels. Philistine styles, especially of wine vessels, had already penetrated into the heart of the country.

We know virtually nothing about Israelite production of wine until about 750 B.C., some 400 years later. One of the most significant epigraphic discoveries in a country notoriously deficient in writing, even though it produced the most famous book in the world, was made at the Israelite capital of Samaria. A Harvard University excavation in the early part of the twentieth century found 63 ostraca—broken pieces of pottery with inked writing on them—in a fill under the palace courtyard. Because the site was destroyed and the people taken captive by Sargon II in 721 B.C., the ostraca probably date to the mid-eighth century B.C.

Only two commodities are mentioned on the Samaria ostraca—wine and oil. A group of men from towns within a 15-kilometer radius of the capital are recorded as providing these goods to a smaller group of men living in the capital. One striking detail of the ostraca is that six of seven clan names of the tribe of Manasseh in Joshua 17 appear as town names in the ancient records. The quantities of wine involved are small—one wineskin, two at the most—so it is unlikely that the consignments were taxes in kind.

I take the view that the Samaria ostraca represent provisioning for members of the royal household from communities that were under their charge or that they represented as "family elders." Because the ostraca focus on only two commodities, something other than basic upkeep for a stay at the palace is implied. Indeed, the wine is always "old wine," presumably a well-aged vintage, and the olive oil is exclusively "washed oil," likely a cold-pressed, filtered fraction of the highest quality. These high-end products played an important role in a long-established social institution in the Levant—the *marzeah*—which was first attested at Ras Shamra (ancient Ugarit) in Syria in the fourteenth century B.C. (chapter 8) and continued down to the late Roman period at Palmyra, in the desert east of Damascus, and Dura Europus on the Euphrates River.

From diverse lines of evidence, the marzeah can be reconstructed as a family funerary cult, with a meal and a show of bereavement, on the one hand, to divine and royal banqueting on a grand scale, at the other extreme. At Ugarit, we have seen that the gods and kings heartedly indulged themselves in wine at a marzeah. In Israel, prophets such as Amos, Isaiah, and Jeremiah were duly alarmed at what they observed firsthand in the banquet halls of the palace and temple:

> Woe to those who lie upon beds of ivory,
> and recline upon their couches,
> and eat lambs from the flock . . .
> who sing idle songs to the sound of the lyre,
> and like David invent for themselves
> instruments of music;
> who drink wine in bowls
> and anoint themselves with the finest oils . . .
> the cry of revelry [*marzah*] of the recliners will pass away.
> (Amos 6.4–7)

This condemnation is specifically directed at the Israelite royal house in Samaria. Wine and oil are an important part of the festivities, in keeping with the allotments on the Samaria ostraca, as are music and other entertainment.

The "beds of ivory" for reclining came to life when one of the excavators of Samaria, Kathleen Kenyon, found wonderfully carved ivory plaques, highlighted with gold leaf and inlaid glass, in the late eighth-century B.C. destruction debris of the palace. These ivory pieces had adorned the furniture in Ahab's "house of ivory" (I Kings 22.39)—beds, couches, and thrones—perhaps the very ones denounced by Amos. They combined Near Eastern and Egyptian themes of the afterlife, mythology, and, most tellingly, the "woman at the window" motif—very likely alluding to the sacred marriage ceremony (*hieros gamos*), which had a long history in Mesopotamia and Anatolia (chapters 7 and 8).

Lounging on their ivory couches and drinking wine from their bowls, the Israelite kings and their fellow "symposiasts" were emulating the contemporaneous kings of Assyria, whose capitals and residences have yielded up fragments of numerous fragments of ivory beds, couches, and thrones (chapter 8). A large hoard of bronze bowls found at Nimrud had been inscribed individually with West Semitic personal names. Could these have belonged to members of a marzeah group there, like the wine bowls referred to in the Amos passage? The scraps and bits that can be gleaned from archaeological excavations and the biblical text are not enough to be sure, but they are highly suggestive that a similar institution existed in both Assyria and the Holy Land.

Although the marzeah feast was enjoyed by the living, it was intended for the dead, who had descended into Sheol, the land of darkness and shadowy ancestors. Even though the overindulgences of the northern Israelite kingdom had spelled their doom a century earlier, Jeremiah cried out with a similar message on the eve of the destruction of Judah, the southern kingdom, and its capital Jerusalem, by the Babylonians:

> For thus says Yahweh: Do not enter a house of marzeah,
> or go to lament, or bemoan them; . . .
> they shall not be buried,
> and no one shall lament for them
> or cut himself or make himself bald for them.
> No one shall break bread for the mourner,
> to comfort them for the dead;
> nor shall any one give him
> the cup of consolation to drink for his father or his mother.
> You shall not go into the house of marzeah to sit with them,
> to eat and drink.
> (Jeremiah 16.5–8)

The main problem with these feasts, according to their critics, was that they relied more on occult arts than on Yahweh. Far from being a way to receive divine revelation or communicate with dead ancestors, wine and strong drink caused the priests and prophets to "reel and stagger" (Isaiah 28.7). The continuing lure of this cult can be seen in the Phoenician inscription on a fourth-century B.C. bowl, decorated with a rosette design like those in the Midas Mound (chapter 11): "Two cups we offer to the marzeah of Shamash [the sungod]." Shamash, like his earlier manifestation Shapsh in Ugaritic mythology, was also a god of the underworld.

A more legitimate use of wine in the cult was to present it to the deity. At the temple in Jerusalem, a quarter hin of wine (about 1 liter) was presented with each sheep, a slightly larger amount for a goat, and a half hin (2 liters) for a bull (Numbers 15.5–8). The animals were offered as burnt sacrifices in the courtyard of the temple, where the liquid libations were poured out. A tithe of the new wine also went to Yahweh (Deuteronomy 12.17). The priests were expected not to drink before or during the temple service; once the offerings had been made, however, they were consigned specific portions of the animals and whatever wine was left over from the libations.

Nothing remains of the first temple on Mount Zion in Jerusalem, except some cuttings in the bedrock, but the biblical picture of its layout and the activities that went on there are consistent with what we know from excavated cultic installations elsewhere in the country and abroad (including Syria and the Hyksos Nile Delta), beginning a millennium earlier. At Hazor, the largest city in northern LBA Israel, for example, Yigael Yadin of Hebrew University uncovered four phases of a tripartite temple in Area H. Its "holy-of-holies" was outfitted with a fireplace for the burnt sacrifices, large kraters, and basalt libation and offering tables. Lion orthostats and two columns (like Jachin and Boaz of the Solomonic temple) fronted the building. The importance of wine in the cult was revealed by a small basalt statue of a male figure—perhaps a ruler or a tutelary deity—sitting calmly on his throne, with his cup in hand.

The Hazor temple and its cult partly laid the foundation for the first temple in Jerusalem. Before the king centralized worship in the capital, each town and city-state of the country had its own temple. Feasting and drinking sometimes took place in these temples, especially on the occasion of an annual harvest festival. In Judges 9.27, it is reported that at the time of the vintage, the inhabitants of Shechem first trod out the grapes and then celebrated with a feast in "the house of their god."

Huge quantities of wine were needed for these celebrations and the maintenance of temple worship, not to mention the normal sustenance of a community throughout the year. Even in areas removed from the centers of power, relatively large wine cellars have been excavated. The Jebusite and Israelite site of Gibeon (modern el-Jib), north of Jerusalem, had 63 rock-cut caves where some 100,000 liters of wine had been stored in 40-liter jars at a constant low temperature and in darkness during the eighth and seventh centuries B.C. James Pritchard, who excavated this site in the 1960s and called it the "Bordeaux of Palestine," sought out the winemaker, Brother Timothy of Christian Brothers, on a visit to Napa Valley. Brother Timothy confirmed Pritchard's suspicions that the temperature of the ancient cellars, which was 18°C, was ideal for storing wine. The Gibeon jars had inscribed early Hebrew inscriptions on their handles that referred to the vineyards and their vintners. Several hundred years later, the famous *lmlk* (Hebrew "to/for the king") inscribed jars transported wine and other goods from production centers in southern Judea to the palace in Jerusalem.

A megalopolis like the Philistine city-state of Ashkelon, whose towered walls extended over 2 kilometers, could accommodate larger, more permanent facilities. The city was destroyed by the Babylonian king Nebuchadrezzar in the winter of 604 B.C., as recorded in the Babylonian Chronicle, Jeremiah 47.3–5, and in an elegy by the Greek poet Alcaeus to his brother, a Babylonian mercenary killed in the battle. The literary evidence that the city was turned into a barren heap of ruins was confirmed in horrendous detail by Harvard University excavations under Larry Stager. The debris, however, held fascinating glimpses of a thriving winemaking industry, whose inception probably goes back thousands of years.

At the very center of the port city, a monumental building, with a hewn stone foundation and plastered mudbrick walls strengthened by timbers, was the focus of winemaking operations. Three winepresses in separate rooms had stomping platforms that were about 2 meters square. The must was run off into a medium-sized vat, followed by a deeper vat, which had a small sump in one corner to collect any remaining solid debris. Each installation was lined with some of the finest plaster yet observed on the site. Could this have been the headquarters of a firm of ancient winemakers, who, like modern Burgundy négociants, bought grapes from estates in the region and then processed the wine in their own facilities?

Other rooms of the structure held numerous fat-bellied storage jars, a type favored by the Philistines who ruled this area of the south-western Levant at the end of the Iron Age. The many perforated clay balls that were found near the jars and fit neatly into their mouths indicate that the must was fermented in the jars. A tight-fitting stick could have been inserted into the hole, to set up the nonoxidative conditions required for fermentation, and then easily removed to let gases escape. Unlike the heavy Egyptian stoppers (chapters 5 and 6) that were molded around the neck of each wine jar, the spheres were interchangeable and could be reused.

The Philistines had sided with the Pharaoh Necho II in his attempts to thwart the advance of the Babylonians. Finds from the monumental winery show just how "devoted" the Philistines were to the Egyptian cause. Along with a statuette of Osiris and a miniature offering-table plaque depicting libation jars, bread(?), and animals sacred to the Egyptians, a cache of bronze artifacts from the destruction debris yielded seven long, tapered *situlae*, or buckets. They were part of a set, held together by a chain and showing a procession of Egyptian deities, most notably Min or Amen-Re, the chief god of Thebes, with an erect phallus. While masturbating with his left hand, the god holds up his right arm in a triumphant or joyful gesture. Egyptologists have proposed that the situlae were filled with semen, milk, or water. Considering the use of such vessels in funerary and religious rites elsewhere (see chapter 10) and the place where they were found, they are more likely to have contained wine, to sanctify the harvest and ensure that the fermentation process went to completion and the wine did not turn to vinegar.

Dark Reds and Powerful Browns

What kinds of wine were drunk by the ancient Canaanites, Israelites, Philistines, and other peoples of the Holy Land. Unfortunately, little is yet known about the grape varietals, and molecular archaeological investigation has barely scratched the surface of what is hidden in ancient pottery fabrics. The intense reddish residue on the interior of a small MB II amphora from Beth Shan, displayed in the "Canaan and Ancient Israel" exhibit at the University of

Pennsylvania Museum, represents a beginning. Analysis by my laboratory showed that the jar had contained a resinated wine.

A range of wines were available to the discerning Bronze Age or Iron Age "connoisseur." At Lachish, an inland city of Judah, a jar was discovered with an inscription in early Semitic reading: "Wine made from black raisins." Drying the grapes on the vine or spreading them out on mats in the sun concentrated the sugar, and very sweet wines could be made by this method. An early Iron Age jug from the hill country site of Shiloh was accompanied by a sieve filled with grapes; either the grapes had been left in the wine and later filtered out, naturally drying to a raisinlike state during 3000 years since they were buried, or they were already raisins in antiquity and were used to flavor the wine that was strained into bowls or other drinking vessels. Perhaps, a kind of Tuscany "vin santo" ("wine of the saints") was made in which the must was squeezed out of the grapes, topped up with water in tightly sealed jars, and variously aged for years to a dry, semisweet, or sweet wine, depending on the climate.

Lachish, which was attacked and destroyed by Sennacherib in 701 B.C., was surrounded by vineyards, which are still there for all to see in the basement rooms of the British Museum in London. The stone reliefs from Sennacherib's palace at Nineveh show low-lying, unsupported vines lining the hills around the walled and turreted city, as the Assyrian forces mount their attack and the population is taken captive. Bush-shaped vines (also see Ezekiel 17.6) required less pruning and training, absorbed the heat of the soil and ripened early, and were relatively easy to harvest. Trellis support for the vines, as shown in the Egyptian tomb frescoes (chapters 5 and 6), was probably limited to flat, open tracts of land, along the coast and in the valleys.

Other late Iron Age jugs and jars are inscribed with terms such as "smoked wine" and "very dark wine." If we project later practice back into the past, we can understand "smoked wine" to mean either a "cooked" wine, in which the wine was concentrated down to a sweet syrup (Latin *sapa* or *defrutum*), or a wine that was prematurely aged by being stored in a room above a fire where the smoke could permeate the wine. Some of the best Roman wines, including the famous Falernian, whose vineyards grew north of Naples, were subjected to smoking and reserved for special occasions.

Mixed or spiced wines were also known to the Iron Age wine drinker. At least, we can infer this from the "Song of Solomon" whose female temptress had "a navel [like] a rounded bowl that never lacks mixed wine." Myrrh and frankincense, pomegranates and mandrakes, saffron and cinnamon are mentioned elsewhere in this book and were probably already being mixed with wine as was common in Roman and post-exilic Jewish times.

When it came to diluting their wines down with water, the residents of ancient Jerusalem and Judah parted company with classical civilization. Why else would Isaiah (1.21–22) cry out that "the faithful city has become a whore!" and compare its apostasy to silver dross and wine "cut with water?" The word for "very dark" (Hebrew and Arabic *kohl*) to describe the wine of a second vessel, a jug dated to about 700 B.C. from Hebron, conveys the same idea: *kohl* was the deep red eye-shadow of antiquity, prepared from manganese oxide ore, and a highly appropriate term for a rich, red wine. Ammonite wine from the central Transjordanian highlands was notoriously so strong that it "induced the body to sin" (Palestinian Talmud, *Sanhedrin* 17.2, 28d).

Up the street from the winery in the port city at Ashkelon, the excavators found what they believe was a commercial outlet for the factory—a seventh-century B.C. wine shop or wine bar. The building was strewn with storage jars of the Ashkelon type and dipper juglets for serving up the beverage. An ostracon found outside the front door of the shop might have been a merchant's invoice or a shopper's list. So many units of "red wine" and so many units of "strong drink" are incised onto the pottery sherd.

Overindulgence in "wine is a mocker," but imbibing "strong drink" [Hebrew *šekar*] is "riotous" (Proverbs 20.1). The upshot of this admonition is that *šekar* has a higher alcoholic content than wine. Barley beer can be ruled out; it runs at only 4 percent to 5 percent alcohol by volume. In any event, nowhere does the Bible claim that *šekar* was a grain product, whereas making wheat and barley into bread is a constant refrain. Distilling the wine or its pomace, in the manner that a brandy or Italian *grappa* is made today, is just as unlikely, because no archaeological or textual evidence for distillation exists before Aristotle. The related Akkadian word, *šikaru*, provides the best clue. It is usually translated as "date beer" or "date wine" (chapter 7). With twice as much sugar as grapes, dates could be fermented to a higher alcoholic content, possibly as high as 15% by volume. Date palms thrived in the warm, humid coastal plains and the oases of the interior. Their fruit could be concentrated down to a "honey" or made into a powerful drink with a brownish hue, as Mesopotamia had taught the world.

Wine: A Heritage of the Judeo-Christian Tradition

Whereas barley beer and beer goddesses reigned supreme in the lowlands of Egypt and Mesopotamia, wine was the preferred fermented beverage in the upland regions of the southern Levant. The Holy Land is where two of the world's major religions—Judaism and Christianity—originated, and their holy writings ("scriptures") are a testament to the centrality of wine in faith and practice. Wine is referred to some 140 times in the Bible.

Even God himself—in the male figure of Yahweh—is depicted as a vintner. In Isaiah (5.1–7), he is at pains to make sure that the vines yield the best fruit, just as he dotes over his people in Israel and Judah. When he sets out to destroy the enemy (Isaiah 63.1–6), the image changes to one of an angry grape-trodder, who tramples the fruit so ferociously that his clothes are stained red. The grape juice gushing in the winepress was like a blood-letting of colossal proportions. This powerful image is also invoked at the "end of days" when "blood flowed" from "the great winepress of the wrath of God" (Revelations 14.20).

The symbolic equation of wine and blood was brought home to the ancient Israelite by the regular sacrifice of animals in the temples, accompanied by the libation of wine. The apotheosis of the concept was achieved when the very body and blood of Jesus, shed for the sins of the world, were represented in the Eucharist by bread and wine.

Jesus' first miracle at the marriage in Cana of Galilee (John 1.1–11) anticipated his final sacrifice and last supper. When the wine was running low, he filled six large pithoi, each of which held about 100 liters, with water and converted it to wine. The wine steward was amazed at how drinkable the wine was. Usually, poorer wines were brought out at the end of the feast, when everyone was drunk, but this was as good as what had been served at the beginning. If a Mesopotamian or Egyptian cult, rather than an obscure one from the Levant, had been accepted as the official religion of the Roman Empire, beer or date wine would probably have been substituted for wine in the Christian liturgy.

Christianity had a difficult enough time defining itself in relation to the worship of Dionysos or Bacchus, as Dionysos was known to the Romans, and the more mystical manifestation of the "wine-god" in Orphism during the Roman period (chapter 10). Bacchus, like Jesus, was born of a god and a mortal woman. He miraculously changed water into wine. He was a savior figure who had been thrice born, and he was represented by the grapevine that renewed itself each year. Jesus is also reported as saying that he was "the true vine, and my Father is the vine-grower" (John 15.1). By drinking wine, the adherents of both religions hoped to attain eternal life.

The parallels between Jesus and Bacchus spilled over into the archaeological sphere. Images and symbols of the two cults were readily interchanged. Byzantine mosaics, frescoes, and icons show a baby on his mother's lap, a throwback to the Neolithic "mother goddess" of Çatal Höyük (chapter 4). Sometimes Mary and Jesus were the intended subjects, at other times Semele and Bacchus. Haloes were not specifically Christian, since this symbol of the sun's rejuvenation at the winter solstice had been adopted as a sign of beatification by both religions.

Jewish rituals and celebrations were much more down to earth, and still are today. Every major event in life was marked by wine, in keeping with the ancient Israelite "wine culture." One cup at circumcision, two cups at a wedding, four cups at the Passover seder, 10 cups at the funerary feast, and wine to begin and end the Sabbath were de rigeur. On the festival of Purim, which marked the downfall of an enemy of the Jews and the exaltation in his stead of the uncle and guardian of Esther in the royal Persian court at Susa, the observant were told by their rabbis to drink as much as possible, until they "can no longer distinguish between 'Cursed be Haman [the enemy]' and 'Blessed be Mordechai [the uncle]'" (Babylonian Talmud, *Megillah* 7b).

It is difficult to imagine a culture so permeated by wine—whether Christian, Jewish, or Bacchic—ever capitulating to the forces of prohibition. That is what happened in the early seventh century when the followers of Mohammed invaded the Holy Land. The bountiful Byzantine winepresses mostly stood idle and gradually silted up. Mohammed followed in the line of Judeo-Christian sages and prophets, accepting and elaborating upon many of their pronouncements, but he reserved the rich imagery of the vine and the literal drinking of wine to the houri-filled delights of paradise. In faraway Persia, some imaginative poets still sipped their wine (chapter 7). Small communities of Christians and Jews in Palestine made enough wine for their own needs. A resurgence of large-scale winemaking, however, had to wait more than a thousand years when the Carmel range, the Galilee, the Golan, and other parts of the Holy Land were replanted with the vine.

CHAPTER 10

Lands of Dionysos: Greece and Western Anatolia

IN the summer of 1996, my laboratory had just published an article in *Nature* magazine on the earliest resinated wine thus far attested by chemical analysis, a well-aged 7400-year-old vintage from Iran (chapter 4). In the midst of riding the wave of publicity, I got a telephone call from Holley Martlew, a Greek archaeologist. Holley had a proposition for me: Would I be interested in joining her and the then-director-general of Antiquities of Greece, Yannis Tzedakis, in a project entitled "Minoans and Mycenaeans: Flavours of Their Time," to be funded by the Hellenic Ministry of Culture and the European Union? I hardly hesitated in saying yes to this marvelous opportunity. Yannis and Holley had been intimately involved—whether directly or collaboratively—in the excavation of many Bronze Age sites on the Greek mainland as well as on the islands that dot the Aegean Sea, like so many sparkling gems. They had access to material, including much that was still unpublished, that promised to open up whole new vistas on viniculture in the ancient world. Plato's *Symposium* and Euripides' *Bacchae* may conjure up contradictory images of sedate intellectual discussions and frenzied midnight gatherings, but both reflect a culture that was consumed with wine. Now, I was being asked to pursue these developments, which had such far-reaching consequences for the civilization that we share in today, further back in time.

The project on the Bronze Age beverages and cuisine of Greece

MAP 7. Crete and mainland Greece, including the Aegean Sea and western Anatolia.

bore fruit beyond my wildest expectations, although it meant committing a large percentage of our research effort to one small part of the world. Our scientific findings were ultimately showcased in an exhibition at the National Museum in Athens during the fall of 1999, which drew crowds of visitors. Modern Greeks were intrigued to see what their Bronze Age ancestors had eaten and, especially, what they had drunk. The room where the drinking vessels were prominently displayed was almost always packed to capacity.

Drinking the God

In later Greek and Roman history, which is liberally interwoven with legend, the "wine-god" Dionysos (of Lydian derivation, later Roman Bacchus) is said to have come to Greece from overseas, bringing with him viticulture, winemaking, and his cult focused on wine. Dionysos' long journey achieves its highest poetic expression in *The Bacchae*, written by the fifth-century B.C. Greek playwright Euripides:

> I . . . am Dionysos, son of the king of gods, . . .
> I have come a long way. From Lydia and Phrygia,
> The lands of the golden rivers,
> Across the sun-baked steppes of Persia,
> Through the cities of Bactria,
> Smiling Arabia, and all the Anatolian coast,
> Where the salt seas beat on turreted strongholds
> Of Greek and Turk. I have set them all dancing;
> They have learned to worship me
> And know me for what I am:
> A god.
> And now,
> I have come to Greece.

Here, Dionysos in human epiphany announces himself to the Greeks of Boeotia, outside the walls of Thebes, where Kadmos ruled during the Mycenaean Age in the hills to the northwest of Athens. Lydia and Phrygia along the western coast of Anatolia are jumping-off points for Euripides, who follows Dionysos back in time and space to more easterly realms in Iran and Arabia. Previous chapters have documented that the initial steps in the odyssey of ancient viniculture were likely taken there, if one grants that Arabia encompasses Jordan and the Negev desert and if one allows Euripides some poetic license in omitting the Caucasus.

Euripides takes for granted that the domesticated grape and winemaking made their way to Greece from western Turkey by crossing the Aegean Sea, but perhaps another route was followed from the north or south. To get at the truth, we will need to follow the available signposts of current archaeological evidence and not rely too much on the complicated skein of ancient legends. In one way or another, you can make the oracles pronounce just about any origin for Dionysos and, by analogy, for ancient Greek viniculture that you want. Twentieth-century historians of wine were attracted to these stories, because they do hold a real fascination, and archaeological investigation was still subsumed under the traditional study of the classics. Readers must be constantly on guard not to be drawn into uncritically accepting their reading of the literary evidence, as they peel away the legends in search of the kernel of historical reality.

Several examples of this dubious methodology should help lay it to rest. One story of the birth of Dionysos runs as follows. King Kadmos is said to be the grandfather of Dionysos, because his daughter, Semele, bore the "thirteenth god of the Olympian pantheon" by being impregnated by Zeus in the usual way, or in parthenogenetic fashion with a pomegranate seed or an infusion of Dionysos's heart from a previous incarnation. As the story continues, Semele then asked Zeus to reveal himself in his full glory, and with a single bolt of lightning, she was incinerated. Zeus acted quickly to recover the child from Semele's womb and sewed it up in his thigh. The king of gods later gave birth to the "wine-god" on Mount Nysa, where he was raised by nurses, Kadmos's sisters, and his constant companion and tutor, Silenus.

Aside from the geographic reference to "Mount Nysa," which I will return to, some writers have teased another clue about the origins of Greek winemaking from the text. Because Kadmos was originally from Sidon or Tyre in Phoenica, modern Lebanon in the Eastern Mediterranean, Dionysos and viniculture must have been brought to Greece from that region. This interpretation also accords with another story in which the erstwhile daughter or sister of the king of Phoenicia, Europa, is ravished by Zeus in the form of a bull and carried off to Crete. As if anticipating the day when most of southern Europe would be given over to vineyards and the production of wine, Europa is often depicted with branches laden down with grape clusters.

The leap of fertile imagination from Phoenicia to Crete finds an echo in the sixth-century B.C. Homeric Hymn "To Dionysos," which explicitly states that Dionysos was a seafarer from Phoenicia. The sixth-century B.C. Athenian potter Exekias vividly portrays one adventure of the wine-god on the interior of a *kylix*, or Greek drinking cup, in vibrant scarlet and black (color plate 10). Dionysos is seen lying back in his single-man sailing vessel. A grapevine has grown up the mast, from which are suspended huge clusters of grapes. Dolphins frolic in the seas around him. The scene is a re-creation of Dionysos's encounter with pirates on his way to Egypt or Cyprus, in which he turned the tables on them by entrancing them with the miraculous growth of the grapevine, which showered fragrant, sweet wine down on them and turned them into dolphins.

The Homeric Hymn and Exekias's vase painting are intoxicating depictions from antiquity, but they provide little if any substantive basis for how winemaking arrived in Greece. The mention of Mount Nysa is equally problematic. Its location may be in Boeotia or in Thrace, farther north. If the latter, one can then buttress the argument with other Dionysiac stories. In a different version of the Semele account, a Phrygian goddess of the underworld was impregnated by Zeus, who came to her as a serpent, in a cave on Sicily. Hera, the queen of gods and Zeus's wife, was intensely jealous and called in the Kouretes, a Thracian tribe, to tear apart and burn the body of the newborn. As a result, grapevines grew up from the ashes. Homer also claimed that the most famous wine was the fragrant, heavy wine from Maronea in Thrace, which Odysseus used to lull the Cyclops to sleep before he and his men rammed a hot spear into the ogre's eye and escaped.

A Thracian beginning for Greek wine production gains added "support" from the story of Orestheus ("man of the mountain") and his dog, Sirius (the brightest star in the late summer sky). In the Thracian legend, the animal miraculously gave birth to a live vine cutting. When Orestheus planted it, the first grapevine grew up. Reminiscent of the biblical Noah and the Sumerian Utnapishtim, Orestheus was the son of Deucalion, who also survived a flood. The intricate—and possibly significant—interplay of culture hero, flood story, mountains, and the beginnings of viniculture was discussed in chapter 2.

These mythological accounts, which have the aura but very little of the substance of history, raise the crucial question: How can the grain be separated from the chaff, or, better, the pip from the fruit? Each story has gone through a long process of oral and written transmission, being elaborated upon and added to as each orator, writer, or editor saw fit. Who is to say whether Dionysos and winemaking came to Greece from Anatolia or Phoenicia, whether they came by land or by sea, or even whether the beginning and end points are correct? Perhaps, any transference of wine and its technology went directly from Phrygia to Sicily, if Dionysos's birth in a cave there is to be given credence. Or possibly, Naxos, an island in the Cyclades group, is the crucial link, because that is where Dionysos wed Ariadne, the daughter of King Minos of Knossos on Crete, once again emphasizing this geographic locale. With so many options to choose from, a skeptic could hardly be faulted for claiming that all the stories miss the mark and making a case for an indigenous origin.

A critical reader of the *The Bacchae* might also ask how Phrygia and Lydia could be the origin of Greek viniculture, when these kingdoms did not exist before 800 B.C. and the setting of story is the Greek Heroic or Mycenaean Age, over 400 years earlier. An apologist for the poet might answer: Phrygia and Lydia are anachronisms for western Anatolia. To be sure, Phrygia was known as the "land of vines," and, at another place in *The Bacchae*, Dionynos is said to descend from the "Phrygian hills to the broad streets of Hellas." A Dionysiac element is evident in what little is known about the early Phrygian cult (chapter 11). A "Great Mother" goddess named Matar (later Cybele) held sway, and nocturnal orgiastic rites and music figured prominently in her worship. Nevertheless, a Phrygian male deity is noticeably absent from the literary, pictorial, and archaeological record until the fifth century B.C., when a relatively minor god named Sabazios (later Attis), often identified with Dionysos, made his appearance.

A clearer perspective on the role of the wine-god in Greek history and prehistory is possible only by delving into the available archaeological resources. The earliest tantalizing piece of written evidence is a Linear B inscription of the Mycenaean Age that cites the name "Dionysos." The syllabograms *di-wo-nu-so-jo* in an early form of Greek appear on one of the more than 1000 clay tablets discovered and excavated by Carl Blegen in the archive of King Nestor's palace at Pylos in the southwestern Peloponnese. Some scholars believe that this is a reference to the god himself; others argue that it is a human by the same name. Another tablet from this archive enumerates donations to Poseidon (*po-se-da-o-ni*), later a member of the Greek

Olympiad and who sometimes interchanged roles with Dionysos. Wine is part of each donation, which might have been intended for a festival to the deity, amounting altogether to about 175 liters. Among other items including aromatic substances, honey, grain, cattle, and sheep, the provision of bulls by two of the parties brings to mind Dionysos's role as a wild animal in later Greek legend.

In *The Bacchae*, Dionysos transformed himself into a bull to incite three women in Boeotian Orchomenos to join the other maenads, the intoxicated women who were rushing up into the mountains to dance, sing, and worship the wine-god. The three Orchomenos women first responded by sacrificing a child to the theriomorphic deity. In the mountains, the congregation of women ferociously tore a wild animal to pieces and ate it raw. The great tragedy of the play comes when the prince regent Pentheus, who appears to the women in the guise of a lion, is similarly mutilated by his sisters and mother. Pentheus's head is proudly carried back by his mother to the palace in Thebes, where Kadmos recoils in shock and reveals the enormity of the crime.

One wonders whether such Dionysiac orgies ever took place, considering that it was not in the best interests of a town to have their women consumed with "Bacchic rage" and forgo their household duties. Numerous, scattered references in classical literature attest to their actuality, especially a biennial celebration on Mount Parnassus, near Delphi, by the thyiads, the Attic equivalents of the maenads.

A whole host of later Greek festivals imply that if Dionysos originally came to Greece as a foreigner, his worship was soon integrated into the native religion. Jubilant celebrations, called Dionysia, were held throughout the land, especially during the winter and spring. Like a country fair, they combined all manner of drinking, singing, dancing, and ribaldry. One game was to grease up an inflated wineskin and see who could balance on it the longest. People dressed up and paraded around, activities that eventually led to formal dramatic presentations. Other festivals—such as the Haloa in December–January and the Anthesteria in February–March—also developed into drinking fests to taste the first of the "new wine" from the previous year's vintage. In essence, these celebrations were harvest festivals, to enjoy the fruits of one's labor and encourage the earth to be bountiful in the coming year.

It is easy to understand why Dionysos might come front and center in any fertility or nature religion. The grape stands as a superb metaphor of the earth's fecundity, and its principal product, wine, is produced naturally, once the juice is exuded from the fruit and the yeast on its skins start the fermentation process. Besides possessing endless nuances of flavor and aroma, wine is the ultimate elixir, as Alcaeus of Mytilene wrote in the sixth century B.C.:

> Bacchus, son of Semele
> And of Zeus, discovered wine
> Giving it to man to be
> Care's oblivious anodyne

As if by infusion of a divine spirit, moderate drinking of wine heightens emotions and spurs the imagination. The grapevine itself is a metaphor of the cycle of death and renewal ("resurrection"). It must go into dormancy in the winter, from which it awakens in the spring to send out new shoots. The broader implications of this life cycle would not be lost on Greek villagers, who were tied to the land and highly observant.

The symbolism of the grape and wine was eventually incorporated into a less violent, more mystical religion, which is epitomized by the Eleusinian Mysteries, which were celebrated in September and October. Followers of this religion did not tear animals apart and eat their flesh (omophagy) or get roaring drunk to expiate and honor the wine-god. Rather, they believed that humans or Titans had killed and eaten a manifestation of Dionysos named Zagreus, thus accounting for man's evil nature. By being initiated into the Eleusinian Mysteries, a man or a woman was somehow identified with the sacrificial Zagreus, cleansed of sin, and assured of a happy afterlife. The rites of the religion—still shrouded in mystery—were associated with the gentle musician Orpheus, who was dismembered by Thracian maenads.

The references to Dionysos and donations to Poseidon on the Pylos tablets testify to a tangible, real-life backdrop for viniculture and the cult of Dionysos in Greece during the Mycenaean period. These enticing hints imply that wine was already a major product of the country, spurred on by "drinking the god." Other archaeological evidence is needed to carry us further back in time and fill out the picture within the limits of a fragmentary past.

A Minoan Connection? The Earliest Greek Retsina

The story that ties Dionysos to early viniculture on Crete is the one that culminates in his marriage to Ariadne, the daughter of King Minos of Knossos. Although none of the more than 3000 tablets from the latter site, excavated by Sir Arthur Evans early in the twentieth century, mention the king by name, the sheer elegance of the city—with its columned, multistoried villas decorated with frescoes—implies that a line of rulers was in power here from about 1900 B.C. to 1375 B.C. Without going into all the details, the Ariadne story starts with Poseidon sending King Minos a great white bull to sacrifice. Complications ensue, leading to the creation of a half bull–half man, called the minotaur, that Minos keeps in an elaborate labyrinth, perhaps modeled on the maze of rooms in his palaces. The gruesome creature is fed seven boys and seven girls, sent as tribute from Athens on the mainland, each year. Theseus, who has been selected as the flavor of one year, manages to slay the minotaur with the help of Ariadne who smuggled him a sword and gave him a skein of thread, which the hero unraveled as he first traversed the labyrinth and then follows back to the entrance to escape. When Theseus abandons Ariadne on the island of Naxos, Dionysos comes to her rescue.

The marriage of a wine-god from Phoenicia and a royal Minoan princess is certainly provocative—and is often cited by historians of wine—but it again misses the mark in not adequately accounting for the contemporaneous archaeological and textual evidence that has been uncovered over the past century. Our Greek project, which was to focus on Bronze Age beverages and cuisine by employing sensitive scientific techniques, was my entree into better understanding ancient Greek viniculture.

My laboratory analyzed and confirmed the presence of wine inside large storage jars, or *pithoi*, at Myrtos-Phournou Koryphe, which predated Minos and Ariadne by centuries. This site, excavated by Peter Warren of the University of Bristol, is an Early Bronze Age (EBA) village on the southern coast of Crete. The pithoi belong to the final destruction level of the site during the Early Minoan IIB period, ca. 2200 B.C., but occupation began near the beginning of the third

FIGURE 10.1. (Top) The Early Bronze Age village of Myrtos on Crete (Greece) as seen from the air. (Bottom) In rooms throughout the site, large-scale wine production is substantiated by numerous *pithoi*, dating to ca. 2200 B.C., with dark-painted "dripping" designs. (Top right) The jars—some of

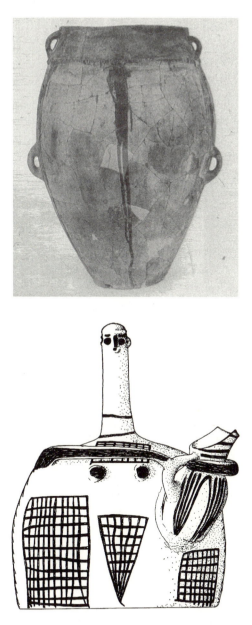

which yielded grape skins, stems, and seeds—held a resinated wine, according to molecular archaeological analyses. (Bottom) The "Goddess of Myrtos," a three-dimensional pottery figurine, holds a cut-away spouted jug—a type widely used to make and serve wine.

millennium B.C., and winemaking may go back earlier at the site. A minimum of 44 pithoi, with volumes of about 90 liters each, were excavated in storerooms and kitchens of houses and workshops constituting the small farming community. Similar vessel types are found as early as the mid-third millennium B.C.

Many of the jars had a reddish interior residue, and some contained grape seeds and even grapevine stems and masses of skins, seemingly the ancient organic remains of grape pomace. Intriguing dark-painted "dripping" decorations on the jars suggested that the vessels had once contained liquid. Rope appliqués, which often replicate the placement of real rope on Mediterranean pottery of Chalcolithic and EBA date, suggest that cloth or leather covers were originally tied down by rope over the mouth of each vessel. These organic materials had long since disappeared or been destroyed in the final conflagration of the site.

The six pithoi tested by our battery of analyses for tartaric acid and tartrate salts (chapters 3 and 4) yielded positive results. Moreover, the infrared and liquid chromatographic data showed the presence of a tree resin additive—whether pine, terebinth tree, or some other species is uncertain. Two of the jars might have held a barley product, perhaps beer, but that is another story (discussed later in this chapter).

A small hole had been punched through the sidewall of the some of the jars before they were fired, as has also been observed on late Chalcolithic wine jars at Godin Tepe in Iran (chapter 3) and at other sites in Transcaucasia and Turkey. The holes on the Myrtos pithoi were unusually placed near the base. It was difficult to imagine how wine could have been decanted or racked through them, as had been proposed for the Godin Tepe vessels, without contaminating the wine with the lees. Peter Warren has suggested that the holes provided an easy way to run water through and clean the vessels. Another possibility is that the hole was used to remove the lees themselves by popping a stopper out of the hole with a sure and steady hand and pushing it back in before the wine started flowing out.

The analyses of the Myrtos pithoi represent the earliest chemical evidence for resinated wine from ancient Greece: that is, retsina, as it is known in Greece today. Greece is the only place in the modern world that perpetuates the ancient tradition of adding tree resins to wine. Wine snobs may turn their nose up at it, but an appreciation for the beverage comes quickly after spending some time in Greece. My wife and I readily adapted to local custom, as we roamed the Peloponnesus of southern Greece in the 1970s, stopping every evening in a village to eat moussaka and drink the local retsina, while looking out across the beautiful "wine-dark" sea. Each person must ultimately be the judge of whether retsina is an appealing wine.

The sheer amount of resinated wine at Myrtos makes one pause: some 4000 liters, the equivalent of 450 cases of modern bottled wine, if all the pithoi were filled with wine. This calculation may be an overestimate; some of the jars could have been filled with other goods, such as olive oil. But, the minimum number of 44 pithoi represents only what has been excavated. Other vessels remain to be discovered, and others were disposed of for one reason or another. Conceivably then, the 4000 liters represents a lower limit for annual wine production at Myrtos during the later third millennium B.C. before it was destroyed. Why would a small farming community need so much wine?

One possibility is that wine was already being produced at this site for export to larger towns on Crete, such as Knossos. A large funnel, an essential tool of the ancient winemaker, was found at the site and is now on exhibit in the museum at Ayios Nikolaos. The impressions of grape leaves on the base of a circular pottery vat or pithos show that grapevines grew in the vicinity of the site. The Stummer size indices (see chapter 2) for the recovered grape pips fit better with that of a wild than a domesticated plant. Yet, circular vats ("bathtubs"), 10 of which were found along with pithoi in installations scattered throughout the site, would have been ideal for treading grapes on a fairly large scale. They are about 60 centimeters in diameter and fitted with spouts. A much later classical vase scene shows how they were used. In a busy wine cellar scene, a satyr merrily stomps away inside an open basket filled with grapes, from which the juice runs into a flat basin and from there by a trough into a large jar buried up to its shoulders in the floor. Similarly, one of the Myrtos spouted vats was elevated over a hollow in the floor, with just enough clearance to hold a pithos for collecting the must and beginning the

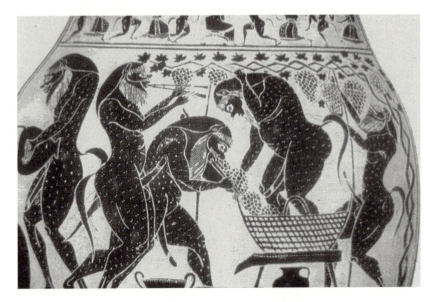

FIGURE 10.2. Black-figured vase by the Amasis Painter of the sixth century B.C. shows a busy wine cellar scene. A satyr merrily stomps away inside an open basket filled with grapes, from which the juice runs into a flat basin and from there by a trough into a large jar buried up to its shoulders in the floor. Use of wine-stomping vats (compare figure 10.3) and ageing in subterranean pithoi go back thousands of years.

fermentation. The vats could accommodate only one stomper at a time, and the work was arduous and tedious. By switching off from one vinicultural task to another, each worker could enjoy a change of pace and some rest, while many vats were kept going and churning out a large volume of juice.

Larger-scale production of wine, of course, would have required pressing floors spread out over a larger area, with collecting basins. The earliest evidence for such installations are in six townhouses and a countryside villa at Kato Zakros in East Crete during the Late Minoan (LM) I period, about 1500 B.C. Later, at nearby Palaikastro, a plaster pressing floor inside a house slopes down to a pithos buried in the ground.

I had a close-up look at an especially well-preserved LM I wine-making facility at Vathýpetro in the Archanes hill country, south

FIGURE 10.3. The Late Minoan IA (ca. 1550–1470 B.C.) winemaking complex at Vathýpetro on Crete (Greece). The spouted vat, often referred to as a bathtub, was commonly used in the ancient world to stomp out grapes.

of Herakleion. This region produces some of the best Cretan wines available today, made from traditional red varieties, such as Kotsifali and Mantilari, and white Vilana. My companions were the owner of the local Minos winery, Takis Miliarakis; his winemaker nephew, Nikos; François Lefort; and a businessman with a keen interest in the history of the island, Idomeneas Markakis. We traveled by car through the quiet countryside, past Knossos and vineyards laid out on pergolas or as separate, low bushes in Burgundian fashion. Vathýpetro itself was a small LM I villa constructed of well-cut limestone ashlars and with the usual Minoan amenities, including a carefully planned drainage system. Situated on a hilltop in the midst of vineyards, olive groves, and the occasional coniferous tree, the site has a glorious, panoramic view across a wide valley to Mount Idi. A unique tripartite "shrine," a short distance north of the "winery," is perfectly aligned with the rising sun as it comes up over an eastern peak during the summer. Another shrine was built on the top of Mount Iouktas to the west.

The Vathýpetro "winery," thus sanctified by its natural surroundings and Minoan tradition, is a small pillared building. Inside, a
stomping area was demarcated on one side of the room. On the other
side, a "bathtub" for more careful grape-pressing had a long spout that
drained into a low basin. In the same corner of the room, a tall jar
without a spout, set at a higher level than the pressing vat, could
have been used to collect and further filter the must. One of the most
curious features of the installation was a specially hollowed-out stone
in front of the basin, with a drainage channel leading away from it,
going under the higher jar, and presumably emptying into the main
sewage line. It was suggested that this shallow "pool" was used for
washing off the grape-trodders' feet after they had finished. A piece
of a "horned altar" was also recovered from the room.

The juice was fermented in a nearby large building, where 17
pithoi could be seen half-buried in the clay floor. An examination of
other parts of the settlement revealed many other small pressing vats.
Perhaps, as at Myrtos, the whole community shared in the enterprise,
then jointly prepared and aged their wine in the large storehouse.
The parallels to what I had observed in the winemaking regions
of modern Georgia and Armenia, where households still keep their
wines underground in large *kwevris* and *karas* (chapter 2), were startling. One wonders whether larger pressing floors exist nearby, perhaps hewn out of the rock, away from the villa and closer to the
vineyards.

In the Early Minoan "wineries" at Myrtos, many jugs with long,
upturned and cut-away spouts ("beak-spouted jugs") were found in
the same rooms as the vats and pithoi and would have been ideal in
scooping out floating debris from the must inside the large-mouthed
pithoi or in transferring the wine at the different stages of fermentation, storage, serving, and drinking. Similar jugs occur earlier in EBA
Anatolia and are the forerunners of bronze specimens with intricate
devices for sieving liquids later in the Iron Age (chapters 8 and 11).
A filter could have been improvised by tying a cloth over the spout
or plugging it with a piece of wool, grass, or other fine material.

High, narrow-mouthed jars with two vertical loop handles at mid-
body, sometimes called "noble jars" because of their elegant piriform
shape, would have been ideal for storing and shipping the wine. In

style and capacity, they can hardly be distinguished from the earlier wine jars in the tomb of Scorpion I at Abydos (chapter 5) that had been exported there from the southern Levant. Flat lids with perforated knobs served as stoppers for the Myrtos jars. Any wine that was not exported was available for local consumption. Numerous cups at the site, variously shaped like tumblers and footed goblets and sometimes with high arching handles, were well suited for drinking.

The importance of wine to the community extended into the religious sphere. In a room in the southwestern sector of the village, pottery vessels had been set out in front of a low stand ("altar"). The vessels may once have contained food and beverage offerings for the strange pottery figurine that originally stood on the stand. Dubbed the "Goddess of Myrtos," a large bell-shaped body is topped by a long, stalklike neck that merges into a head with detailed facial features. The breasts are small applied lumps of clay, and criss-cross bands of dark paint define the pubic triangle and perhaps clothing and a necklace. The main preoccupation of the figurine is with a jug, which she holds tightly in the crook of her left arm and stabilizes by extending her other spindly arm across her upper body to grab onto its handle. The jug has a cut-away, upturned spout like its real-life counterparts used in processing and serving wine.

A spouted bowl in a room next to the "shrine" was full of grape pomace, and if there were any doubt about what this room was used for, a spouted tub, spouted jugs, and pithoi rounded out the pottery repertoire of a standard winemaking facility. Another storeroom between this workshop and the shrine proper was piled high with vessels, mainly used in storing and serving wine. The success of any ancient craft or technology hinged on many unknowable factors, which only a god could allay in a prescientific age. In winemaking, a stuck fermentation—in which the yeast are killed off by high temperatures or a lack of nutrients—is especially dreaded. Pouring out a libation of the precious liquid and invoking the goddess might guarantee success.

As we have seen for Mesopotamia, Egypt, and Anatolia (chapters 6–8), human and divine females played key roles in the origin and promulgation of fermented beverages. A tutelary or household goddess is well-attested in later Bronze Age palaces—the shrine of the

Double Axes at Knossos is one example—where she ensured the steady day-to-day performance of domestic activities and, in more dire circumstances, the provision of enough food and water to survive. Her earliest appearance in Greece is at Myrtos, and her association with winemaking shows that this craft was of the utmost importance to the EBA village. A male companion, like Dionysos in later periods, is noticeably absent.

The sophisticated wine production at Myrtos pointed toward earlier developments in Greece. Is it possible that wine was already being made there in Neolithic times? Unfortunately, the Greek project did not address this issue. Pottery from only one Neolithic site—Gerani—was investigated by Curt Beck's laboratory at Vassar College. When Holley Martlew had first broached the idea of getting involved in the Greek project, I suggested bringing Curt on board, because of his expertise in using gas chromatography–mass spectrometry (GC-MS) to investigate a range of ancient organic materials, especially amber and raw and processed pine resins. The GC-MS separation method operates on the same principals as those for LC-MS (liquid chromatography–mass spectrometry), except that the sample is volatilized and converted to a gas and then sent through a long separation column, usually 100 meters in length. Because compounds must be converted to their gaseous state before they thermally disintegrate, generally only compounds with a molecular weight up to around 500 can be detected. Although more compounds go into solution and can be detected by LC-MS, large databases of some 250,000 compounds now exist for GC-MS, and search programs are easily run to determine what compound best explains the mass spectral data. Curt has been especially avid in tracking down some of the fingerprint compounds for Greek foods and beverages, perhaps partly because his wife, Lily, is Greek and they spend their winters in Athens. Although there was evidence of animal and vegetable fats, as well as olive oil, in the Gerani vessels—possibly components of stews—there was no sign of what was drunk.

Seeds of the wild Eurasian grape (*Vitis vinifera sylvestris*) have been recovered from the Franchthi Cave in the Argolid of the Peloponnese, dating to the late Palaeolithic/Mesolithic periods (ca. 11,000 B.C.), and many later Neolithic sites throughout Greece have yielded comparable evidence. One site in northern Greece that is broadly dated to the Late

Neolithic period (ca. 4300–2800 B.C.)—Dimitra in East Macedonia—has grape pips whose size, shape, and other features place them squarely within the domesticated species (*Vitis vinifera vinifera*). Until other evidence of winemaking is forthcoming from this region and pending future chemical analyses, it is best to reserve judgment about how early and under what stimuli viniculture developed there.

In other parts of Greece, unquestionably domesticated grape pips do not make their appearance until the EBA, ca. 2500 B.C., at the same time that Myrtos was flourishing. Domesticated pips are reported from Syros, Amorgos, and Naxos in the Cyclades, all of which yielded cup and bowl bases with impressions of grapevine leaves. In the Argolid, a *Vitis* leaf impression was also observed on a vessel base from Synoro, and domesticated grape seeds and their impressions on pottery were found at Lerna. But the most significant Early Helladic botanical find on the mainland to date is the domesticated grape pips from inside a pithos from House I at Aghios Kosmas in Attica, about 20 kilometers south of Athens near the coast. As did some of the pithoi at Myrtos, the vessel from Kosmas had a hole near the base. Here was definitive evidence for a shared technology and sophisticated winemaking in Crete and on the mainland.

A cogent argument can be made that the impetus for viniculture in Greece came from western Anatolia or the Balkans, whether by land through Macedonia or by sea. Domesticated grape pips, dating to the mid-third millennium B.C., have been reported from Troy in the Dardanelles (Hellespont), which was excavated by the "Father of Greek Archaeology," Heinrich Schliemann. Farther south at Beycesultan along the Upper Meander River, comparable evidence of the same date was found in the vicinity of a "horned altar," set in front of two stelae believed to represent male and female deities, along with offering vessels, barley, and lentils. Pithoi which still held barley, wheat, and lentils, lined one room of another building here. Two jars, which were partly buried in the floor of an attached room, were believed to have contained wine, which was dispensed across a mudbrick counter to customers; perhaps it was poetic justice, but eight skeletons were sprawled on the other side of the counter in the midst of drinking paraphernalia and knucklebones used in a game of chance. This evocative scene is a snippet of what must still lay buried in this important region of Anatolia, where many other ancient sites probably lie hidden under modern towns. Opposite the Hellespont on the island of Lemnos, Poliochni was even larger and more prosperous than Troy, and its elegantly shaped cups with a pair of high-arching side handles would have admirably served the drinking of wine. These so-called *depata amphikypella* (Greek "two-handled cups"), according to Schliemann's terminology, ranged in size from low, shallow cups to high, everted goblets and are especially characteristic of EBA western Anatolia. As Colin Renfrew had already observed in the 1970s, such vessels were probably imitations of metal prototypes that were already popular among the wealthy for drinking wine.

In previous chapters, we saw that a "wine culture" had emerged in the Near East by around 6000 B.C. in the mountainous regions of eastern Anatolia, the Caucasus, and northwestern Iran and then radiated out from there in time and space. The adoption of winemaking and the successive transplantation or cloning of the domesticated grapevine in areas where even the wild grape had never grown were encouraged by the prestige exchange of wine and special wine-drinking ceremonies among elite individuals. In Greece, this phenomenon is best exemplified by the classical Greek *symposion* (chapter 12), but its roots can be traced back to Middle Minoan (MM) times and Mycenaean palace life. Although the wild Eurasian grape grew in Greece, winemaking is a relative late-comer, and an independent domestication of the plant is therefore less likely.

Another theory for the transference of viticulture and retsina to Greece is that they came from Egypt via Crete. Egypt's winemaking industry had already been operating for centuries (chapter 5). One of the Egyptian hieroglyphs for "grape, vineyard, or wine" is very similar to the Linear A and B signs of LM and Mycenaean times. The vocabulary of a technology such as winemaking—the actual script in this instance—very often follows along with its transference from one culture to another. The Greek signs, like their Egyptian counterparts, are extremely detailed in how they depict a trellised vine. Although the reason for the similarity between the Greek and Egyptian signs is contested, their resemblance is difficult to explain unless one was derived from the other. Moreover, trellised vines on Crete appear to have been more the exception than the rule, according to Linear B tablets in which fig trees are tabulated alongside grapevines in garden holdings. The most natural interpretation of these texts is that the vines were trained up the trees. Like the word for "wine," which is represented by the same root in numerous, widely dispersed language groups (chapter 2)—*wo-no* in Linear B, οἶνος in later Greek—written signs for the beverage were probably highly conservative.

Nevertheless, the earliest Linear A and Cretan Hieroglyphic logograms for "wine" occur several hundred years later than the earliest evidence for retsina from Myrtos. If the domesticated grapevine, along with winemaking, had already been transplanted to Crete from Egypt by at least 2200 B.C., then supporting archaeological evidence should exist. Stone vases, scarabs, hippopotamus tusk ivory, and other artifacts do attest to trade contacts between Egypt and Crete, but they are not directly related to viniculture and pale in significance compared with the goods that were transported during the heyday of internationalism in the Late Bronze Age (LBA). On the other hand, Myrtos, on the southern shore of Crete, is located on a natural landfall and at the terminus of a well-traveled maritime route for ships crossing the Mediterranean to and from Egypt.

Some archaeologists have been struck by the proliferation of small cups that appear suddenly, as it were, in the middle of the third millennium B.C. at sites such as Knossos. Excavations at Knossos by Peter Warren also uncovered a "bathtub" winepress of the same date, like those he found at Myrtos belonging to a later phase of the EBA. The introduction of a new beverage, such as wine, would call for new drinking vessels. Because much of this evidence is unpublished, the final verdict is still pending. Yet, the timing of this upsurge in drinking cups fits with what we already know about winemaking at Myrtos-Phournou Koryphe. This site, together with others throughout Crete and the southern Greek mainland, might well have supplied the beverage and other foods to the emerging urban centers.

Wine Mellowed with Oak

The next glimpse of ancient retsina in Greece, according to our Greek project analyses, comes some 500 years later at Monastiraki, about 1700 B.C., during the Protopalatial period. The site, excavated by Athanasia Kanta of the University of Rethymnon, is a MM IIB palatial center, located along the main north-south road through the Amari valley of Crete. It was probably dependent upon if not directly controlled by the major palace at Phaistos, farther south and closer to the coast. Over 100 pithoi of a type remarkably similar to those at Myrtos, with red-painted trickle patterns running down their body and with upper and lower handles, were recovered from some 80 storerooms. A lack of rope decoration is the main feature that sets the Monastiraki jars apart from the Myrtos pithoi. Grape pips and even the pomace of skins and stems were recovered from some of the vessels, and chemical analysis of one pithos by my laboratory confirmed the presence of a resinated wine.

Retsina had also found its way into a tripod cooking pot at Monastiraki, a globular vessel with three tall legs for straddling it over a fire. A cooking pot was an unlikely candidate for finding any ancient organic evidence, let alone a grape product such as wine, because high temperatures will degrade or destroy organic materials. But our chemical evidence, as well as that of Curt's laboratory, showed that the vessel had once held a grape product.

Curt's GC-MS analysis identified a tree resin in the cooking pot. Specific diterpenoid compounds were characteristic of pine, and the presence of benzoic acid further narrowed the possible pine species down to the Aleppo pine (*Pinus halepensis*). Because tree resins were most commonly added to wine, the grape product in the cooking pot was most likely a resinated wine. Perhaps a mulled wine had been prepared in the vessel, as the Cretans did in the second century A.D. according to *The Deipnosophists* ("The Philosophers at Dinner" or "The Gastronomers") by Athenaeus (11.783). Another ancient organic compound detected by Curt—2-octanol—has medicinal benefits, as do wine and tree resins, and was probably derived from castor beans or oil. Because the "cooking pot" lacked carbon soot on its exterior, which can be expected to have built up over time if it had been used for cooking, this vessel might have been a special container for a medicinal wine.

Another very curious component associated with the resinated wine in this vessel was identified by Curt: an alkyl-γ-lactone, most likely β-methyl-γ-octalactone. It is derived principally from oak wood or resin and is referred to as whiskey or cognac lactone because

FIGURE 10.4. (Left) Cooking pot from Apodoulou on Crete (Greece), a Middle Minoan II village destroyed around 1700 B.C. A contemporaneous vessel of the same type from nearby Monastiraki contained a resinated wine laced with an oak-derived lactone, suggesting that it was intentionally aged in oak barrels. (Right) Conical cup from Apodoulou that contained a wine resinated with terebinth tree resin.

the distinctive flavor and aroma of this compound are imparted to Irish whiskey and French cognac by ageing in oak barrels or adding oak chips. The concentration of this lactone is enhanced if the oak wood has been toasted, as is done in bending the staves of barrels. This is an amazing finding, because it implies that MM winemakers intentionally introduced an oak flavorant, something that we also enjoy today in a fine Cabernet or Scotch, either directly by adding chips or oak resin itself (which was also used in the tanning of leather) or indirectly by stomping out the grapes in oaken wine-presses or, more impressively, "ageing" the wine in oak barrels.

Thus, the long-standing European tradition of ageing wine in oak barrels might have a much earlier pedigree. California winemakers have "rediscovered" in the last few decades how French oak can add "more complexity" to the wine than American oak, especially by "mellowing" out the tannins, polyphenolic compounds found in grape skins and pips that give wine much of its taste. Because no barrels have yet been recovered from a MM site on Crete and the earliest possible literary reference to barrels by Herodotus is dubious (Chapter 8), most scholars argue that coopering was later invented by the Celts or Gauls and passed along to the Romans. With their sophisticated technology of shipbuilding, MM craftsmen must have had a knowledge of toasting oak staves to bend them and perhaps put that knowledge to the purpose of constructing oak barrels for keeping or ageing wine.

Oak-laced wine inside a cooking pot at Monastiraki dramatically illustrates winemaking during the Protopalatial period. At the same time, the canonical wine set of classical times—a large krater, ladle, and variously sized and shaped cups—also makes its first appearance in Greece, at Dendra—in silver, no less. It is not known whether water was being mixed with wine in the krater, as civilized practice dictated later, but Minos and his cohorts would have needed suitable drinking paraphernalia to display in their newly erected palaces, which also showcased the explosion in other visual arts.

Apodoulou, another MM site included in the program of Greek analyses, lay somewhat closer to the palace at Phaistos along the north-south road. As was Monastiraki, it was occupied in MM II and destroyed around 1700 B.C. Excavated by Yannis Tzedakis and Louis Godart, Apodoulou was probably a small village or trading center serving Phaistos. The analysis of a conical cup from this site by my laboratory showed that it been used to pour out libations or to drink retsina, specifically a wine laced with a terebinth tree resin additive. Curt's GC-MS analysis gave the same result, identifying a specific triterpenoid component—oleanonic acid. Terebinth tree resin was added to Neolithic wines (chapter 4) and was one of the most widespread and popular additives to wine in the ancient world for thousands of years.

"Greek Grog": A Revolution in Beverage Making

If the Greek project had not already provided enough surprises, the next one was even more mind-boggling. Maria Andreadaki-Vlazaki had excavated an LM IA "cultic area," with many

FIGURE 10.5. (Top) A conical cup from a "cultic area" at Chania on Crete (Greece), which contained "Greek grog." (Bottom) The careful planning and fine masonry of the shrine at Chania, dating to the Late Minoan IA period (ca. 1600–1480 B.C.), is seen here from above.

"altars" surrounded by the burnt remains of sheep, goat, and cattle, along Splanzia and Daskaloyiannis Streets in the city of Chania on the northwestern coast of Crete (ancient Kydonia). Holley and Yannis provided my laboratory with four conical cups, and we began work. Our chemical analyses showed that a different kind of beverage was being drunk or ceremonially presented in conical cups and other pottery types in LM IA (ca. 1600–1480 B.C.) than in the MM II period. The beverage combined resinated wine, barley beer and honey mead—that is, it was a kind of "Greek grog."

Although the occasional conical cup, with its gently contoured sides contrasting with an ungainly stub base, occurred earlier (e.g., at Apodoulou), it came into its own in LM IA. The cup was mass-produced by "throwing off-the-hump," in which one vessel after another was thrown on a potter's wheel from a large mass of clay and cut off sequentially until the clay was depleted. Incredibly large numbers of conical cups have been excavated at LM IA sites, particularly from what are believed to have been cultic contexts. Because its purpose is unknown, the conical cup has been dubbed a "nightmare vessel." The chemical analyses have now taken away some of its mystery. In tests by the Vassar College and MASCA laboratories of some 20 conical cups, all except one (likely containing olive oil) held the mixed fermented beverage of wine, beer, and mead.

We know that wine was an important commodity in both Proto-palatial and Neopalatial times, because the wine ideogram appears often in Cretan Hieroglyphic and Linear A texts at Chania itself, Knossos, Phaistos, Kato Zakros, and several other sites on Crete. Between about 1375 and 1200 B.C., the Linear B texts, whose large archives are restricted to Knossos and two sites on the mainland (Pylos and Mycenae), record the assessment of wine "taxes" from vineyards in the vicinities of the palaces and their distribution to the royal household, as rations, and for special occasions. The quantity of wine in some instances is extraordinary. One tablet devoted solely to wine from Nestor's palace at Pylos records nearly 12,000 liters (measured according to the standard amphora capacity of 28.8 liters) that had been consigned to nine outlying communities, probably for a festival. In the so-called Wine Magazine at the site, three rows of 25 pithoi, with room for another 10 vessels, were set into the floor of the main room. A full complement of jars, filled to capacity, could have held only about 9000 liters, and other storage facilities must have stood ready to handle such large shipments.

Barley beer has been and continues to be a highly controversial issue in Greek archaeology. In his *Palace of Minos*, Sir Arthur Evans threw down the gauntlet: "It is probably that . . . beer brewed from barley malt was drunk in Minoan Crete from a very early epoch, though its use may have been supplemented in LM times by wine from the juice of the grape." Archaeobotanical specimens from Myrtos-Phournou Koryphe and elsewhere on Crete leave no doubt that domesticated barley was being grown on the island. Moreover, if the domesticated grapevine and winemaking were transferred from Egypt to Crete, then barley bread and beer, in particular, which was the most popular beverage in Egypt, would likely have followed the same route and been known to the Minoans. These inferences are borne out by the later Linear A and B tablets in which various signs are translated as "beer," "flour," and "barley." In one text, as much as 800 tons of grain are involved. Barley plants are also depicted on painted jugs from Akrotiri on the island of Thera, north of Crete, suggesting that the vessels contained beer.

A combination of archaeological and chemical reasoning is needed to determine whether an ancient pottery vessel once contained barley beer. The "fingerprint" compound for ancient barley beer—calcium oxalate or so-called beerstone—occurs in low amounts in many plants. It is most concentrated in spinach and rhubarb, which grow in the Near East and Greece, but these can usually be ruled out as major food sources. If a pottery type can be argued to be a processing, storage, serving, or drinking vessel for liquids and calcium oxalate is detected inside it, then a case can be made for its having contained barley beer.

Two of the Myrtos pithoi, which tested positive for calcium oxalate, illustrate the importance of proceeding cautiously in interpreting the evidence. The excavator, Peter Warren, noted that room 20, in which one of the jars was found, had also yielded barley chaff and good evidence for grain processing, consistent with beer making. The same jars, however, had also held resinated wine. Several interpretations of the evidence were possible: (1) the pithos had been reused;

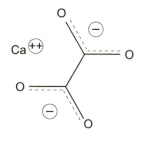

Figure 10.6. Calcium oxalate ("beerstone"), a
bitter compound, collects inside vessels used for
fermenting and drinking barley beer.

(2) barley grains had been intentionally or accidentally added to fermenting wine; (3) because calcium oxalate is widespread in nature, it could derive from another source; or (4) a true mixture of the two beverages had been prepared.

The molecular archaeological results for the LM IA conical cups from Chania, as well as a range of other pottery types from sites elsewhere on Crete ranging in date down to the end of the LBA, consistently showed the presence of calcium oxalate. The infrared and liquid chromatographic results also closely matched a well-defined mixed fermented beverage from the Midas Mound at Gordion in Turkey (chapter 11). The inference was clear: the calcium oxalate was almost always found in vessels intended for liquids and associated with other compounds characteristic of fermented beverages, and thus most likely represented "beerstone" from barley beer fermentation.

The "Greek grog" also included honey, one of the few natural sources of simple sugars in antiquity. This marvelously delicious and fragrant natural product is made only by a range of bee species living in temperate climates around the world. In Greece, the important species is the European honey bee, *Apis mellifera*. Although the sugars in honey rapidly degrade, another product of bees—beeswax—is virtually impossible to filter out completely when processing honey, and its long hydrocarbons and related acids and esters can be very well preserved. These compounds, together with the principal organic acid in honey—gluconic acid—were detected in the Chania samples. When diluted down to 30 percent honey and 70 percent water, osmophilic yeast in the honey will start the fermentation and produce mead. Yeast on the grape skins and, less predictably, air-borne yeast would have aided the fermentation process. Delicious honeys derived from thyme, wild flowers, and pine "honeydew" (chapter 4) are produced today on Crete.

Two words in the Linear B corpus, used to modify the "wine" ideogram, may be related to the Greek grog. In the Wine Magazine at Pylos, one of the large number of clay nodules, which had been impressed with the consignors' seal and had originally been attached by strings to the pithoi, bore the "wine" ideogram and the word *me-ri-ti-jo*. The latter is probably the genitive form of "honey" (Greek μέλι), implying that honey was either fermented together with or mixed with the wine. A similar difficulty arises in later classical texts with οἶνος μέλι, although Columella (*On Agriculture and Trees* 12.39–40) gives a recipe for *mulsum* in which honey and grape must are fermented together. The second word that modifies the "wine" ideogram occurs on a Linear B tablet from Knossos. *De-re-u-ko*, probably related to later Greek γλεῦκος meaning a sweet substance such as grape must, is associated with a principal ingredient in perfumes, perhaps a tree resin, in the same text. Perhaps, the mixed fermented beverage, which has now been confirmed by chemical analysis, is in view in one or both of these tablets.

Three large stirrup jars—two made of a coarse ware and the third of a fine fabric characteristic of other examples marked with Linear B signs—were analyzed from the excavations at the Kastelli hill and its environs at Chania, carried out by a Greek-Swedish team under the direction of Yannis Tzedakis and Eric Hallager. A palace complex of Neopalatial LM IA times and later was revealed here in the old town. The chemical evidence from all three vessels supported the interpretation that they contained the Greek grog. This was a surprising result, because stirrup jars have been argued to have been transport containers for perfumed oils.

A later parallel for the Greek grog is the Homeric *kykeon*, which was served up to a wounded soldier at a later stage in the battle of Troy by Nestor's mistress, Hecamede, when the Greeks were being routed (*Iliad* 11.628–643). An elaborate gold cup with attached figures of doves is described in the text, very similar to an actual example excavated from Grave IV in Grave Circle A, dating to the sixteenth century B.C., at Mycenae in the northeast Peloponnese. Homer's kykeon was composed of Pramnian wine, barley meal, probably honey, with goat's cheese grated on top. It is significant that pottery graters are known from the Middle and Late Bronze periods in Greece and that bronze graters were a standard burial item in Iron Age warrior tombs in Greece and Italy. Kykeon is probably best translated as "mixture," and a range of ancient Greek texts, extending down to Plato and the Eleusinian Mysteries, suggest that many ingredients (herbs, spices, wine, milk, honey, oil, and water) were tossed into the brew.

The pharmacological properties of this brew—whether analgesic or psychoactive is unclear, but certainly exceeding what can be attributed to a high alcoholic content—are implied in the Nestor account, as well as elsewhere in Homer. For example, in the *Odyssey* (10.229–243), Circe changed Odysseus's companions into pigs with *kykeon* and a *pharmakon* that she had prepared. One can argue whether the Pramnian wine, which goes into kykeon, is an herbal wine or even a kind of Italian grappa (although distillation is a very remote possibility); whether the barley is raw, roasted, or fermented; and so forth. The main point is that the mixed fermented beverage, or "Minoan ritual cocktail," which has now been identified chemically, probably bears some relationship to the kykeon of Greek heroic times. As yet, no spice or herb has been chemically identified in the Greek grog, although references to such in the Linear A and B texts and the probable presence of rue, a narcotic and stimulant, in a cooking pot from Mycenae (described later in this chapter) are highly suggestive. Other narcotic substances—such as henbane, mandrake, or opium, which have been proposed as additives for a mixed beverage from farther north in Europe—have also not been confirmed chemically or botanically. Minoan frescoes in which crocus flowers are being gathered, perhaps for their saffron, and a Postpalatial female figurine, crowned with poppy seed capsules whose contents could have been processed into opium, appear to go beyond an artistic or botanical fascination with these plants.

Wine and "Greek Grog" during the Heroic Age

The popularity of the Greek grog was most evident by Mycenaean and LM times, especially in the period from about 1400 to 1130 B.C., when it was being stored, prepared, served, poured out, and drunk in a wide variety of vessels, including rhyta, *kylikes*, the so-called beer mugs, stirrup jars, cooking pots, and cups of various types.

At Armenoi, the largest known LM IIIA/B (ca. 1400–1200 B.C.) cemetery on Crete, excavated by Yannis Tzedakis, burial pits and *dromoi* (entrance ramps) were full of fragmented *kylikes* (goblets), cups, and cooking pots. Both kylikes and cups were analyzed and found to have contained the Greek grog. Yannis has proposed that the vessels were used in a funerary ritual and banquet. This conclusion is supported by a wide array of archaeological, textual, and pictorial evidence from Crete and mainland Greece and bears importantly on a proper understanding of the "King Midas funerary feast" (chapter 11).

The kylikes are of special interest, because they are depicted being "held high" on fresco scenes at Knossos and Pylos and on special objects that have clear ceremonial or religious significance. The "Camp-stool Fresco" at Knossos is the parade example; it gets its name because several men are shown sitting on what appear to be collapsible chairs. One figure holds the traditional chalice of Minoan Crete, which occurs by the hundreds in pottery and stone at outdoor "sanctuaries," such as at Syme and Ayia Triada on the south coast of Crete. Unburnt animal bones in the vicinity of the vessels suggest that feasting, rather than sacrificing per se, was most important to the celebrants. Perhaps this attitude extended to the beverage, and only a symbolic libation would have been made before it was quaffed down. At Palaikastro, cupboards full of hundreds of chalices and jugs were found in the entrance halls to most of the houses, within easy reach for socializing, toasting, and feasting. A second figure on the "Camp-stool Fresco" holds up a kylix, the traditional drinking cup of mainland Greece. Until our analyses were carried out, it was generally assumed that both drinking vessels held wine. Now, we can say that it was almost certainly the Greek grog that is the focal point of the ritualistic toast, which is also represented on Mycenaean kraters and clay sarcophagi from both Crete and the mainland.

The intermingling of pottery types in the same drinking ceremony suggests a relatively peaceful exchange between the Minoans and mainlanders. Perhaps, what had begun as a client–customer relationship in which the Mycenaeans served as mercenaries or palace functionaries for the Minoans gradually shifted in favor of the main-

FIGURE 10.7. (Top) Cemetery of Armenoi on Crete (Greece), with *dromoi*, or entrance ramps, leading down to the tombs, dating to the Late Minoan IIIA/B period (ca. 1400–1200 B.C.). (Bottom) *Kylix*, or drinking cup, which had been deposited in a *dromos*. It contained "Greek grog," a mixture of wine, barley beer, and mead.

FIGURE 10.8. Silver vessels from a tomb at Dendra in the Peloponnesus of Greece, Middle Helladic Period, ca. 1800–1700 B.C. A large krater, ladle, and a variety of cups provide the earliest evidence of the classical wine set.

landers. By the time the Mycenaeans had gained the upper hand early in the LBA, they had also absorbed a great deal of Minoan culture, including the etiquette of drinking. Wine had already begun to be produced on the mainland in Early Helladic times at Aghios Kosmas, and domesticated grape pips were recovered from Middle Helladic Orchomenos in Boeotia and Nichoria in Messenia. The wine service of cups, goblets or kylikes, jugs, and kraters was also well represented at Tsoungiza, north of Mycenae, and a tablet from Pylos employed the actual shapes of several of these vessels to list the gold offerings presented to a veritable pantheon of deities and heroes. The story for barley beer and mead is less certain. The origin of the mixing of all three together is even more mysterious and may have something to do with the conical cup or the movements of new peoples into Greece, bringing a new beverage with them (chapter 11).

The "Campstool Fresco" is elaborated upon in a series of scenes in a monumental pillared building (a *megaron*) at Pylos in the southwestern Peloponnese, where storehouses of goods stood ready to provide for the needs of the palace, including festivals to Poseidon and possibly Dionysos. A huge bull is the centerpiece of one scene, with line upon line of male and female attendants carrying jugs and other items to the innermost part of the "sanctuary." There, although the actual drinking vessels are unfortunately cut off and missing, figures similar to those at Knossos are seen sitting on their "stools," while a musician plays the lyre and a hoopoe-like bird flies overhead. In the same room, two basins connected by a channel, next to a throne, might have received the liquid libation, unless this gave old Nestor a surreptitious way to dispose of old wine gone bad. One is reminded of how Nestor mixed sweet 11-year-old wine from his cellars at the beginning of the *Odyssey* for Telemachus, the protagonist's son. Miniature kylikes were also found strewn on the floor of the throne-room. Elsewhere in the palace, as many as 600 kylikes had been smashed on the floor of only one small room.

Another vessel type that may well shed light on Greek grog is the *rhyton*. Soon after the Athens exhibit, I received an urgent call from a former fellow student, Robert Koehl, who had done his doctoral dissertation on the Mycenaean pottery from Sarepta in Lebanon, the same site that had yielded the earliest Royal Purple dye (chapters 1 and 3). Bob is now a professor at Hunter College in New York City, and his main area of research since he left Penn has been the rhyton, particularly its significance and function in the Minoan and Mycenaean cultures. When he saw the exhibit on Greek Bronze Age beverages and food, he was struck by the fact that an analysis of a fourteenth- or thirteenth-century B.C. rhyton from Midea, near Mycenae in the Peloponnesus, had shown the presence of both wine and barley beer. Bob saw this finding as confirmation of his proposal that rhyta had been used to filter barley beer in a probable brewing facility at Akrotiri on Thera. This idea met with a relatively cold reception at the third symposium on the archaeology and geology of that island, which is best known for the volcanic eruption that transformed it into a water-filled caldera and buried its Bronze Age civilization under a mass of lava.

Although our laboratory had not analyzed the rhyton in the exhibit—the tests had been carried out by John Evans, an archaeochemist at the University of East London and a third member of the Greek project's ancient organic team—Bob was insistent. He wanted to know more about our findings on ancient Greek beverages and whether it might not be possible to analyze additional rhyta in the University of Pennsylvania Museum collections. As program chairman for the New York Aegean Prehistory seminar, Bob said that there was still an opening for the last session of the year that would provide an ideal setting to broadcast and discuss the exciting discoveries. I agreed, and as a result of the lecture, discussions with Bob and others, and more research, I began to see that the rhyton was of more than passing interest. I had contracted, as Bob put it, a minor case of "rhyton flu."

The rhyton is not a vessel of the usual type. It is not meant to hold anything, because, by definition, it always has a hole at its bottom. In his publications, Bob illustrates rhyta that are conical, globular, or ovoid, with a wide or a narrow mouth and variously decorated with geometric or marine designs, such as the tentacles of an octopus. The most splendid examples are in the form of an animal's head, with the bottom hole exiting through the mouth of the creature. For example, as many as six bull's-head rhyta can be reconstructed from the pottery and stone fragments that have been found at Knossos. The black steatite example from the Little Palace, with its high-arching gold horns that were reconstructed on the basis of a similar rhyton from a royal tomb at Mycenae, is one of the artistic masterpieces in the Herakleion Museum (color plate 11). The details of the bull's head are finely carved; its muzzle is accentuated with inlaid shell, and the pupils, irises, and whites of the eyes are composed of different-colored stones. As one traverses the Minoan collection in this museum, one is struck by an astonishing array of decorated rhyta, from the ornate floral designs of the earliest palace at Phaistos (in the so-called Kamares style) to the unending succession of types from Palaikastro and Kato Zakros in later times.

The bull was a formidable presence in Minoan life and cult, whether paraded, hunted, slaughtered, or seemingly toyed with, as agile acrobats leaped over it in the fresco scenes. We have already observed how the bull is identified with Dionysos and other gods in Greek religion, and how some of the later rites involved partaking of a sacrificial meal, including the blood and meat of the animal. The polychrome, elaborate frescos on a sarcophagus from Neopalatial Ayia Triada, exhibited in the Herakleion Museum, illustrate the centrality of the bull sacrifice in Minoan funeral rites (color plate 12). As the blood flows from the neck of the slaughtered animal and is collected in a jug, a man plays a double-reeded flute, a procession of mourners approaches the table on which the bull lies, and a woman "priestess" presents food and a beak-spouted jug of beverage before a horned altar surmounted by the "tree of life," double axes, and a bird. Red wine was a particularly apt symbol for blood (see chapters 5 and 9), so it is not surprising that many scholars have proposed that rhyta were used to pour out libations of wine, if not blood itself.

The scholars' surmise that wine was poured through the rhyta was at least partly correct. But barley beer had also passed through the Midea specimen, and who was to say whether mead might not have been run through the vessel, as well, thus giving a full complement of Greek grog. If the liquid had been poured relatively quickly through a rhyton, the small amount of beeswax in honey might have been minimally retained by the pottery ware and not detected.

Bob Koehl presents strong evidence that liquids were transferred and filtered by rhyta. The narrower-mouthed types can be used like chemical pipettes, to draw up and hold liquids in place by simply placing a hand or a thumb over the upper opening. Parallels can be drawn to the medieval English "toddy-lifter," which has antecedents as far back as the third millennium B.C. in Syria and is quite similar to the later *klepsydra* of sixth-century B.C. Greece. Some of the rhyta also have an interior strainer.

Now that we know that a mixed fermented beverage was being served and poured out as libations in Mycenaean and LM times, it can be argued that the rhyta were also used to filter this beverage or one of its components, and perhaps even to pour the beverage into cups in a flourishing and difficult manner as shown on later classical vases depicting the symposion. For the rhyta without an interior sieve, a piece of wool or cloth might have been inserted to serve as a filter. If some added flavor or stimulant were desired, a spice or herb could be sprinkled on the filtering material or strainer. Bob Koehl successfully demonstrated how this might be done using a replica rhyton, passing wine through a coriander-sprinkled wool insert. He describes the final product after tasting it, which is the "ultimate test," as lightly scented and flavored with coriander.

A reasonable supposition is that one of many herbs and spices available to the Mycenaeans might have been added to retsina or the Greek grog. In the Linear B tablets, coriander, cumin, sage, fennel, mint, safflower, and even sesame, usually thought to be of South

FIGURE 10.9. The bichrome-painted Hubbard Amphora, probably from Vartivounas in northeastern Cyprus and perhaps belonging to the ninth century B.C. This side of the unique jar shows a female deity or ruler sitting and drinking a mixed fermented beverage with a long "straw."

Asian or East African origin, are mentioned. Curt Beck found two ketones specific to the herb genus *Ruta* (rue) in a vessel from the citadel of Mycenae, home to Homer's Agamemnon, dated to early Late Helladic (LH) or Mycenaean IIIC (ca. 1190–1130 B.C.). Although archaeobotanical evidence for wild or domesticated rue is yet to be reported from a Greek archaeological site, the herb was later used as a narcotic and medicinal agent. Its bitterness might have also served to offset the sweetness of grape sugars, barley malt, or honey in the "grog."

The Hubbard Amphora, a unique early Iron Age painted jar from northeastern Cyprus, throws many of the peculiarities that have been described—the mixed fermented beverage, herbs and spices, special drinking vessels, and so on—into high relief. On one side of the vessel, four women, naked to the waist and holding strange plants, dance to the song of a lyre player. Their performance is intended for the enthroned female on the opposite side of the jar, who is similarly attired except that she wears a flowing, diaphanous skirt. In front of the "queen" or "goddess" are two tables. On one is mounted a storage jar, similar to the painted amphora itself. On the other table sit three juglets. Another three juglets, which might be refills, are held by a female attendant, who approaches the seated figure and with the other hand extends yet another juglet toward the mouth of the amphora. Mounted on the wall behind the attendant is a bull's head, perhaps a rhyton. The beneficiary of all these activities, seated on her throne, draws a long drinking tube from the amphora to her mouth. The conjunction of motifs, even though they are not explicitly explained with text and their precise meanings will probably never be known, are evocative of the mixed fermented beverage, or Greek grog, liberally dosed with suitable herbs and spices.

Amphoras containing terebinth-resinated wine, pure and simple, have already been mentioned on board the Uluburun merchantman (chapter 6). This shipment might have been headed toward the Greek mainland when it went down. A similar amphora type was excavated from the Room with the Fresco in the Cult Centre (area 36) at Mycenae, dating to Mycenaean IIIB1 (ca. 1340–1250 B.C.), and it also contained retsina according to our analysis. This room in "Agamemnon's Palace" clearly had a ceremonial function, with its altar, numerous vessels associated with food and drink, and special objects made of ivory and Egyptian faience. In a back storeroom called "The Shrine," a partial fresco shows a woman holding barley or wheat sheaves, with a lion frolicking about her.

The cereal motif of the Shrine fresco may be connected to Greek grog, even though it is divorced from a ceremonial drinking context per se on the fresco. Elsewhere on the Citadel of Mycenae and in the settled areas strung around its periphery, many so-called beer mugs were excavated (although traditional scholarly opinion maintains that the Mycenaeans never drank beer!). The MASCA and Vassar College laboratories analyzed one of these cups, dated to ca. 1370–1340 B.C., and arrived at complementary results to show that it contained the Greek grog. It is not unreasonable to propose that the famous Golden Cup of Nestor from Grave Circle A at the site con-

FIGURE 10.10. (Left) "Beer mug" from the Citadel at Mycenae (Greece), dating to Mycenaean IIIB1 (ca. 1340–1250 B.C.). An analyzed vessel of the same type contained "Greek grog." (Right) The golden cup of Nestor, as described in Homer's *Iliad* (11.631–636), was similar to this gold vessel from Grave IV in Grave Circle A at Mycenae (Greece), sixteenth century B.C. Note the small doves splayed out on the handle tops. On the basis of chemical analyses of contemporaneous vessels similar to the beer mug seen here, the *kykeon* in Nestor's cup was a mixed fermented beverage of wine, beer, and mead (Greek grog).

tained the same potable. Two sieved dippers from the House of Sphinxes, as well as rhyta, provided the tools for straining the beverages and adding the condiments.

With the expansion of a wine industry in Crete and then throughout the southern Greek mainland in Mycenaean times, trade in the precious commodity must have intensified. A glimpse of this commerce is gleaned from a compound "wine" ideogram, otherwise known only from Kato Zakros on the eastern tip of Crete, that had been incised on a local jug found on the island of Kea in the Cyclades, close to the Attic coastline. Already by around 1500 B.C., Kato Zakros had some of the largest pressing facilities for making wine in the Aegean. Trade and emulation of the elite ensured its passage to the mainland, possibly via Kea. The stunning jugs with clusters of deep red grapes from Thera, also belonging to the sixteenth century B.C., show that viniculture had won its way into the hearts and palates of the Aegean islanders. The fine wines of the Levant, Near East, and Egypt also came to be appreciated and were imported in amphoras, the successor to the Middle Bronze Age "Canaanite Jar" (chapter 6).

CHAPTER 11

A Beverage for King Midas and at the Limits of the Civilized World

IT IS not known whether the "Greek grog" (chapter 10) was still being produced during the "Dark Age" from the late twelfth century down to the eighth B.C. When the curtain rises again, a tomb on the central Anatolian plateau at the famous capital city of Gordion provides provocative testimony to its continued popularity in an area more than 1100 kilometers away from the Crete and the Greek mainland and 500 years later.

King Midas and "Phrygian Grog"

Completely by chance and in a study unrelated to the Greek project (chapter 10), my laboratory had embarked on a study of the ancient organic residues inside the famous Midas Mound at Gordion in the winter of 1997–1998. Again, it was a phone call that started the research ball rolling, which eventually led to the amazing discovery that a beverage very similar to the "Greek grog" was likely offered in a libation to Matar, the great Phrygian mother goddess, and drunk at a funerary feast for King Midas himself. The call came from another fellow student during my graduate school days at Penn, Elizabeth Simpson, now a professor at the Bard Graduate Center for Studies in the Decorative Arts in New York City. Elizabeth had written her doctoral dissertation on the extremely well preserved, inlaid wood furniture from the Midas Mound at Gordion, and over the last 20 years, she has devoted herself to preserving what is considered to be one of the best collections of ancient Near Eastern furniture ever found and culling its construction techniques and artistic motifs for clues about the cultural life and foreign relations of ancient Phrygia, the kingdom that Midas ruled.

Elizabeth told me that other ancient organic materials had been recovered from the tomb, when it was excavated by Rodney Young, then professor of Classical Archaeology at the University of Pennsylvania, in 1957. The residues, weighing more than 2 kilograms, were found inside drinking and eating vessels and probably constituted the "left-overs" of a feast for the king before he was buried and ushered into the afterlife.

Two kilograms is an extraordinary amount of ancient organics to contemplate, let alone to have available for analysis. We can get good analytical results from milligrams, even micrograms. Moreover, there were no complicated export procedures to go through or special arrangements to make. It was by far the easiest excavation I have ever been on. The excavators of the tomb had understood the importance of these residues in 1957 and had had the foresight to send them all back to Philadelphia. According to Elizabeth, the residues still sat in their original paper bags in the museum office of Ellen Kohler, who had been the registrar and conservator for the excavation and now oversaw the Gordion Archives in the Museum. Ellen's office was one floor above my laboratory. I simply had to walk up the stairs and explain to Ellen that we were interested in carrying out chemical analyses of the ancient residues. Elizabeth traveled down from New York to index and repackage the ancient samples, and, in very short order, our investigation had begun. The timing was right; a new program to promote technological innovation in archaeological research at the Museum had been initiated by the Kaplan Fund of New York, and an initial grant was made to my laboratory. It went toward the "King Midas Project," which proceeded hand in glove with our Greek analytical program. We came to see just how closely related they were.

The ancient organic residues from Gordion did not look particularly appetizing—any food had long since decayed and the liquids had evaporated—but they held the key to unlocking the molecular secrets of what the ancient Phrygians had eaten and drunk on that momentous occasion around 700 B.C. Though microorganisms had been at work from the instant the tomb was sealed up, the oxygen and water vapor that they needed to survive were soon depleted, and their activity stopped. The tomb was essentially a hermetically sealed time capsule, which had remained closed for more than two and a half millennia.

The burial chamber, the earliest known intact wooden structure in the world, was defined by a double wall of juniper logs and cut pine planks. Only about 5 by 6 meters in area, the chamber was buried beneath a 45-meter-high mound of soil and stones (color plate 13). This artificial feature, still known as the Midas Mound by local people (Tumulus MM in archaeological parlance), was erected after the burial of the king and is the most prominent landmark at Gordion today. Located well above the water table and under tons of soil, the tomb provided the best possible conditions for the long-term preservation of ancient organics.

The huge mound had also kept tomb robbers at bay. Rodney Young's team needed a drilling rig to bore deeply into the mound until they hit the hard stone composite above the wooden chamber. Some 40 meters below the upper surface, the tomb was then reached by excavating a long trench horizontally into the tumulus.

After cutting a hole through the wall, the Penn excavators looked in on an amazing sight, like Howard Carter's first glimpse into Tutankamun's tomb. At their feet was the body of a male, aged 60–65, laid out in state on a thick pile of dyed textiles inside a unique log coffin (color plate 14). These textiles in fact showed how remarkable the preservation conditions inside the tomb were. Although the body of the king had disintegrated, patterns of purple and brown dyes could be discerned, which unfortunately began to fade as soon as the tomb was opened to light and air. A sample of a textile brought back to Philadelphia, however, did yield indigo blue in an analysis carried out in my laboratory. And, of course, blue and purple are the colors of royalty.

In the recesses of the tomb, the excavators saw the outlines of burial goods piled up within its narrow confines. Fourteen furniture pieces, with intricate geometric patterns inlaid in a variety of woods, were later shown by Elizabeth Simpson to be serving and dining tables for the funerary banquet. The coffin itself, she argued, had been reassembled imprecisely inside the burial chamber, showing that it must first have been used in a public viewing ceremony outside the tomb.

From my point of view, the most exciting finds were the 157 bronze vessels that constitute the largest, most comprehensive Iron Age drinking set ever found. Perhaps surprisingly, in view of Midas's legendary "golden touch," these vessels were made of bronze, not gold. Yet, once the accumulated layers of greenish oxidation had been removed, the bronze gleamed like the precious metal. We will probably never know the origins of the Midas legends involving gold—like those of Croesus, the sixth-century B.C. king of Lydia. One romantic possibility is that a wandering Greek of the Dark Age was treated to a dinner in Midas's palace at Gordion. Impressed by the bronze drinking paraphernalia, he returned to Greece with stories of Midas's richness and "touch of gold." Later Greek bards and writers elaborated upon the tale, which reached its fullest expression in Ovid's *Metamorphoses*, written in Rome in the early first century A.D. Midas's alchemical gift might have paved the way to unlimited wealth, but the ruler was also condemning himself to death by starvation—when he picked up a piece of bread or took a sip of wine, it instantly became solid or liquid gold.

The reader may be surprised to learn that a real historical character lurks behind the legends. In fact, contemporaneous Assyrian inscriptions describe a rebellious ruler named Mita who controlled Mushki—Phrygia to the Greeks—in eastern Anatolia and was a friend to Carchemish and Tabal, who posed a more immediate threat to Assyria. After his defeat at the hands of the Assyrians in 716 B.C., Mita or Midas, as he was known to the Greeks and Romans, became an ally of this major Near Eastern power along the Euphrates River in northern Mesopotamia. Taking into consideration the dating of the tomb (ca. 740–700 B.C.) by radiocarbon and dendrochronological determinations, the age and sex of the deceased, the stylistic affiliations of the tomb's rich contents, and a large palace of the same period at Gordion, some scholars believe that the burial chamber

FIGURE 11.1. Large bronze vat or cauldron from the Midas Mound (Tumulus MM) at Gordion (Turkey), ca. 700 B.C. It was used to prepare a mixed fermented beverage of wine, beer, and mead ("Phrygian grog").

beneath the Midas Mound is the final resting place of King Midas. If not him, then a similarly powerful and wealthy ruler, such as Gordius (the father of Midas), must have been buried in such splendor.

The largest vessels in the drinking set were three vats or cauldrons, each with a capacity of about 150 liters and mounted on iron tripod stands. Even before our analyses were carried out, they could be shown to have been the principal containers for the beverage that was served at the feast. Large vats are graphically depicted on wall reliefs in the palace of the Assyrian king Sargon II (722–705 B.C.) at his new capital of Khorsabad (ancient Dur Sharrukin), In this instance, a royal banquet to celebrate a military victory, rather than a funeral, is in view, but the protocol at the two events must have been similar. The vat shown on the relief is similar to those from the Midas Tomb, and a lion-headed *situla* from the burial is nearly an exact replica of those carried by Sargon's attendants on the reliefs.

The lion-headed situla, a companion ram-headed situla (color

FIGURE 11.2. Wall relief from the palace of the Assyrian king Sargon II (722–705 B.C.) at Khorsabad (ancient Dur Sharrukin) in northern Iraq. Attendants, probably young males, dip lion-headed *situlae* into a large vat, like the *situla* found in the "Midas Tomb" (figure 11.3; also compare color plate 15). The funerary feast of the Phrygian king thus followed standard Near Eastern protocol, even though the beverage served was "Phrygian grog" and the occasion was a burial rather than a military victory.

plate 15), two jugs with long, sieved spouts, and 19 juglets served to transfer the beverage to 5-liter round-bottomed buckets, which were inset into unique serving tables. From there, it was ladled into exactly 100 finely wrought bronze drinking bowls. These bowls, which are of the Near Eastern handleless type, are perfectly proportioned to wrap one's hand around the outside, grab onto the indentation (*omphalos* or "belly button") in the base, and drink. Their capacity was about a liter, but for those with greater thirst and perhaps higher status, 19 large two-handled bowls, holding twice as much, were also recovered from the tomb.

The drinking-set vessels may have been made of bronze, but the real "gold," as far as I was concerned, is what they contained. The excavators noted a dark, shiny material in a yellowish matrix lying on the bottom of the vessels and lining their sides. Could these be the organic remains of the beverage, after the mourners had quenched their thirst, or perhaps a special stock for the king in the afterlife?

After the residues had been brought back to Philadelphia in 1957,

FIGURE 11.3. "Phrygian grog" was served with this bronze lion-headed *situla* or bucket from the "Midas Tomb" (compare color plate 15).

they were examined by the museum's chemist, Eric Parkinson. Like the early investigations of the Neolithic wine jars at Hajji Firuz Tepe, which came up empty-handed (chapter 4), his results were largely negative, because highly sensitive analytical instruments, now the routine tools of molecular archaeology, were not available. For example, Parkinson determined how much organic material was present in the samples by burning them and taking the difference between the original weight and what was left. Unfortunately, the sample was destroyed in the process. In fairness, it should be said that he identified carbon, nitrogen, and other elements characteristic of organic compounds.

The funerary feast can now be reconstructed in minute detail by employing infrared spectroscopy, liquid chromatography (LC), gas chromatography (GC), and mass spectrometry. More traditional wet-chemical tests also had their place in our analytical barrage in identifying several simpler organic acids and salts. The extraction of an ancient 5-gram sample with an organic solvent (chloroform or methanol) gave a 20 percent yield, or about 1 gram, of the ancient food or

FIGURE 11.4. The most common type of drinking bowl in the "Midas Tomb" has a petal design and is a tour-de-force example of repoussé metalwork and fine chasing. The bottom indentation (*omphalos*, or "belly button") enabled it to be grasped easily for drinking.

beverage. Because 1 milligram is adequate for Fourier-transform infrared spectrometry, and a thousandth of that amount (1 microgram) is sufficient for gas or liquid chromatography coupled to a mass spectrometer, we had an embarrassment of riches. My laboratory had the luxury of carrying out multiple runs on the same sample, while reserving most of the original samples for the future when even more advanced methods will be available.

The analytical results complemented one another and gave an extremely consistent picture of what was eaten and drunk on that momentous occasion 2700 years ago. Like the "Greek grog" (chapter 10), the beverage was a mixture of grape wine, barley beer, and honey mead. Our analyses focused on identifying fingerprint compounds for specific natural products. In the case of grape wine, tartaric acid and its salt, calcium tartrate, were detected in all the ancient organic residues from the drinking-set vessels that were analyzed (see chapters 3 and 4). Barley beer was marked by the presence of calcium oxalate, or "beerstone," which settles out at the bottom and along the sides of beer fermentation and drinking vessels (chapter 7). A single vessel often served the same purpose in the ancient Near East, so it was difficult to eliminate this bitter-tasting substance from the brew. Although calcium oxalate is widespread in nature, high levels such as were detected in the Midas Tomb drinking vessels are unusual. These vessels most likely held a liquid, and barley beer is the best candidate. The jugs with long, sieved spouts would have been especially well suited to filter out any spent grains or other debris from the brewing process.

Finally, the fermented beverage concoction was rounded off with honey mead. The long-chain, saturated carbon compounds of beeswax, which can be preserved for centuries, provided the tell-tale evidence. Beeswax, a valuable commodity in its own right, was also applied to the outside of several large drinking bowls from the Midas Tomb, and short inscriptions were incised onto it.

I had become interested in honey and mead after several sojourns in Scandinavia, as a Fulbright scholar in Stockholm and a visiting professor at the Universities of Uppsala and Copenhagen. Upon returning to the United States, I got in touch with a long-time friend of my family's when we lived in Ithaca, New York. At the time, Roger Morse was a retired professor of apiculture from Cornell University, where I had studied chemistry as an undergraduate. Roger got me started on the molecular archaeological study of ancient honey and mead by providing our laboratory with an excellent collection of reference materials. He sent along orange blossom, clover, and basswood honey from the Archbold Biological Station in Florida, where he spent the winters, a honeydew honey from Alaska, and a eucalyptus and coffee honey from Brazil. One of the more unusual samples that he provided was a specimen of honey and beeswax from Groton, New York, a small town not far from Ithaca, dated to 1899. The sample was a little darker and more viscous from age than modern honey, but it was still edible and showed how rich in antioxidants honey is. No wonder Alexander the Great's body had been preserved in the liquid!

The upshot of my research on modern honey and mead and a

FIGURE 11.5. Pottery jars filled with the spicy lamb or goat and lentil stew can be seen inside one of the large cauldrons of the "Midas Tomb." They were placed there after the "Phrygian grog," which they originally contained, had been emptied for libations and toastings at the funerary banquet. The food "leftovers" might have been intended to sustain the ruler in the afterlife.

chemical investigation of the ancient beverage residues was that a "Phrygian grog," nearly identical to that which had been the common drink of Mycenaean Greece hundreds of years earlier (chapter 10), had been drunk at the "King Midas funerary banquet." But if a mixed fermented beverage had been served at the funeral, was there also an entrée, or at least hor d'oeuvres, to go with it?

Eighteen pottery jars had been placed inside the large vats. These jars—handleless *dinoi* and small "amphoras"—each contained as much as 150 grams of a spongiform and brownish material, quite unlike the shiny, dark residues in a yellowish matrix found inside the bronze drinking vessels. The jars were also surrounded by large "clumps" of a similar-looking material, which at 80× magnification appeared to be a congealed, homogeneous biomass lacking cell walls. These residues looked suspiciously like a thick liquid that had congealed.

The archaeology of death, or biodegradation, had been at work, and microorganisms had broken down many of the original proteins, carbohydrates, and lipids to simpler compounds. Yet the infrared results from one sample to the next were like carbon copies of one another: the same absorption lines, pointing to the same group of compounds, were present. Liquid chromatography–mass spectrometry (LC-MS) analysis carried out by Robert Moreau and Alberto Nuñez at the Eastern Regional Research Center of the U.S. Department of Agriculture in Wyndmoor, Pennsylvania, identified specific fatty acids and lipids characteristic of sheep or goat fat were identified. The presence of intact triglycerides, which are stored as a prime energy source in fat globules (adipocytes) of animal tissue, further attested to the extraordinary preservation conditions inside the tomb.

Bob Moreau has pioneered the use of HP (high-performance)-LC in lipid analysis, including the development of a new cholesterol-lowering corn oil. In searching for the nonpolar lipid fraction of an ancient sample, he typically runs a hexane solution through a moderately nonpolar column during a period of 40 minutes to over an hour, following a specific protocol for how long each eluent—hexane, isopropanol, and acetic acid—is run through the column (so-called gradient elution). Using a recently developed detection system, based on the nebulization and light-scattering properties of droplets formed from the sample as it comes off the column, he is able to measure precisely the retention time of specific compounds as compared with those of modern reference samples, in particular triglycerides and terpenoids.

The exact identity of the compounds was then obtained by the MS determinations carried out by Alberto Nuñez. The same HP-LC column and conditions are used, but now the fractions coming off the column are fed into a coupled mass spectrometer.

Bob and Alberto were able to show that triglycerides were very prominent in the Midas Tomb food remains, but not in the beverage samples. The fact that both triglycerides and oleic acid were preserved in the ancient food samples highlighted how good the preservation conditions were inside the tomb over the last 2700 years. Generally, the triglycerides are one of the first things to go—being readily hydrolyzed by water breaking up the ester bonds to yield the free acids; the double-bond in oleic acid is also readily oxidized to produce degradation products such as C_9 or nonanoic acid.

These findings dovetailed nicely with those of Curt Beck of Vassar College and Eric Butrym of Scientific Instrument Services, who detected caproic, caprylic, and capric acids using GC-MS. These short-chain acids, whose common names are derived from the Latin root *caper/capra* meaning "goat," have a very distinctive, even rancid, odor. Eric uses a special method that is especially sensitive for volatile compounds. A thermal desorption technique enables very low molecular weight compounds to be volatilized and trapped on a resin medium. When heated up to around 250°C, the compounds are re-evolved (purged) onto the GC column, and their masses measured.

In addition to sheep or goat meat, a variety of other ingredients were detected in the ancient food residues. Phenanthrene, a stable aromatic hydrocarbon, and cresol, a phenol derivative, implied that the meat had first been barbecued. No bones were recovered from the residues, so the meat must then have been cut off the bone. Honey, wine, and olive oil, which might have been used to marinate or barbecue the meat or to add their own distinctive flavors, were respectively represented by gluconic, tartaric, and oleic and elaidic acids (the *cis-* and *trans-* forms of the C_{18} fatty acid, with a double-bond at the C_9 position). Besides large amounts of cholesterol, which would be expected in a meat dish, a high-protein pulse—most likely, lentils—was present, as revealed by a related plant steroid, chondrillasterol, and the triglyceride 2-oleodistearin. Indeed, large stocks of lentils and cereals were found in storage jars in the kitchens of buildings across the street from what is almost certainly Midas's palace on the Gordion citadel.

The finishing touches to this stew were provided by herbs and spices: anisic acid (characteristic of anise or fennel) and α-terpineol and terpenoids found in various spices were identified. Whether the ancient Phrygians imported real pepper from the Indian subcontinent this early is unknown. A colleague of mine in MASCA, Naomi Miller, who is a paleoethnobotanist and a long-time member of the Gordion team, reports that pulses of some domesticated and wild legumes, including bitter vetch (*Vicia*) and wild fenugreek (*Trigonella*), which grow around Gordion today, have a very bitter taste. They may have been used as flavoring agents.

How did the Phrygians eat such a stew, lacking forks and possibly spoons? Knives were certainly used to cut up meat into small chunks, which could be speared with the tip of a blade and eaten. Metal and pottery spoons occur as early as the Neolithic period throughout the Near East. However, none were found in the Midas Tomb or on the citadel. Hands and pieces of bread probably served as the main "utensils," as attested by ancient texts and still a common practice today. Bread has the advantage that leftover juices and sauces can be sopped up. One might then envision some of the mourners dipping their flat bread into the wide-mouthed pottery jars or, more conveniently, spreading the stew out on a piece of cloth or leather. Any leftovers were left in the jars or bound up to form the large clumps, which had been carefully placed in the vats before the tomb was sealed. Ten large bronze jugs, which hung by nails on the walls, had probably held water for washing before and after the meal.

Our chemical findings reveal that the main entrée at the funerary feast of "King Midas" was most likely a spicy lentil and barbecued sheep or goat stew. Roasted whole suckling lamb or kid was also a great favorite in antiquity, as were skewered meats (like modern Greek *souvlaki*). Their preparation is described in the Homeric epics (*Iliad* 9.202–217, and 23.29–56), which were composed in the same century that Midas ruled or somewhat earlier. Indeed, many other archaeological details of the Midas Tomb have close parallels in Homer: multilayered textile bedding, a mound of earth built over a tomb, and funerary feasts for famous personages that included libations and meat sacrifices (*Iliad* 23.29–56; 24.645–646, 660–667, 801–803; compare 23.194–198 and 218–221).

Although some meat and vegetables might have been sacrificed before the funeral banquet, as the Homeric epics and other ancient texts tell us, the lion's share of the ingredients were homogenized into a scrumptious stew for the royal funerary banquet, as shown by almost identical chemical results from all the analyses, irrespective of which pottery jar was sampled. The absence of bones, olive pits, or other seeds and grains also fits best with a well-prepared stew, now attested in the cult center of thirteenth B.C. at Mycenae in mainland Greece and at many Bronze Age sites on Crete. In other words, it is not just the "grog" that is shared by the two "cultures," separated in time and space, but also their basic cuisines.

The decomposed body of "King Midas," lying in state in his coffin, might be viewed as the just reward for his overindulgence. Yet he

FIGURE 11.6. The head of the occupant of the "Midas Tomb," as reconstructed from his skull.

had lived to the ripe old age of 60 or 65, far exceeding the average life expectancy of the time. If his funerary feast reflects what he ate and drank in life, he benefited from a high-protein diet and the enhanced antioxidant and nutritional value of a fermented beverage. He does not appear to have died from starvation or to poisoned himself, as legend would have it. Even his "golden touch" is belied by the lack of any gold in the tomb. He was wealthy and famous, reasons enough that fantastic stories should grow up around his name.

Re-creating an Ancient Anatolian Beverage and Feast

Our investigation of the "King Midas funerary feast" is the first time that an ancient banquet has been reconstructed primarily from the chemical evidence. Until now, ancient recipes and cookbooks, frescoes and drawings have been the primary resources for scholars and writers investigating ancient foods. A great deal is already known about the cuisines of the ancient Near East, Greece, and Rome. Nevertheless, texts can be differently interpreted, and artwork can be too standardized or inept to reveal the specific details of an ancient meal. There is no substitute for the actual physical remains of what was eaten and drunk. As the techniques of molecular archaeology become more widely available and applied, it can anticipated that the cuisines of the ancient Near East and the Mediterranean, as well as many others around the world, will become better known and possibly resuscitated.

The "King Midas funerary feast" was an instant hit among the media, and public interest ran high. The idea dawned on me that re-creating the beverage and entrée could satisfy the desire to experience the past. This is experimental archaeology at its best; you learn about an ancient technology by trying to replicate the process today.

An annual beer event at the Penn Museum brings Michael Jackson, the beer writer not the entertainer, here each March. Many microbrewers are also in attendance, so I took the opportunity to propose a competition. Starting with the basic ingredients of our chemical reconstruction—grape wine, barley beer, and honey mead—could they produce a historically accurate and drinkable beverage in time for a gala event on September 23, 2000?

Many processing decisions had to be made in preparing such an experimental beverage. A very important consideration was whether the wine, the beer, and mead were made separately and then mixed together at the end of the process, or whether all the ingredients were thrown into the pot and fermented together. In making the mixed beverage or mead by itself, there might be advantages to using a whole beehive in the fermentation process. The bee brood, propolis, and pollen all can provide nutrients for the yeast. As far as the yeast was concerned, had the brewer relied on the natural yeast found on the skins of grapes or the osmophilic yeast in honey, or had he or she waited for the rare air-borne species to settle in on the brew or perhaps have isolated some yeast from a previous brew?

The possibilities and permutations were endless. If the king had died in the fall, fresh grapes with quantities of yeast could have been collected, as is still done at an elevation of 1200 meters above sea level in villages near Gordion. At other times of the year, the beverage maker might have used aged wine, raisins, or a concentrated grape syrup. Moreover, a bittering agent was clearly needed to offset the sweet honey, grape sugar, and barley malt. Although the ancient beverage residues were intensely yellow, we had not been able to determine what had caused the color. Perhaps, it was due to an added herb or spice, that still grows in the area of Gordion today or was mentioned in contemporaneous texts, such as wild fenugreek, safflower, coriander, or saffron.

Most of the crucial questions were unanswerable. The time of year that Midas died is not known. No ancient beverage-making facilities have been discovered at Gordion that might help to elucidate the conditions and what ingredients were added at each stage in the process.

The microbrewers went away excited and ready to experiment. Although the predilections of the ancient Phrygian upper class might not have been the same as ours, they would have appreciated a fine bouquet and known the difference between an overly sweet or dry beverage. The final test, then, would be in the tasting.

Within two months, bottles of the experimental brews began arriving at my home. Whether anise-flavored, lightly scented with coriander and cumin, or simply an unadulterated mixture of the three main ingredients, none were turned away and all the entries were assessed for their drinkability.

The microbrewer who emerged triumphant from the competition was Sam Calagione of Dogfish Head Brewery in Milton, Delaware, who is already well known for his historical, hand-crafted beers. Sam opted for a single brew in making his rendition of the "Phrygian grog." Rather than throw a beehive en masse into the brew pot, he chose to use a delectable, filtered honey made from thyme, with the flavor and aroma of the herb. He helped the natural yeast of the grapes and honey along by adding a dry mead yeast. Yellow muscat was selected as the grape varietal, because it has been shown by DNA analysis to be related to the earliest cultivated grapes in the Middle East. The grapes were added late in the brewing process at a lower temperature, to give a fresh, natural aroma. In keeping with the golden Midas touch, yellow saffron was the bittering agent for Sam's re-creation. This native Turkish spice is gleaned from the female stigmas of the crocus flower. Some 5000 flowers are needed to produce one ounce of the spice, making it one of the most expensive spices in the world. It has a wonderful fragrance and a distinctive, slightly bitter taste. It also has mild analgesic and psychotropic effects. The best saffron in antiquity is said to have come from the Corycian cave of Cilicia in southeastern Turkey, where a natural spring gushed from a rock cavern to water the crocus.

The final result was a delectable potion, a golden-hued drink with reddish highlights, "fit for King Midas." It was truly in a class by itself—not a beer, not a mead, not a wine—but a combination of all three, with layers of muscat aroma and a saffron taste that caught at the back of your throat and drew you back for more.

The "Midas Touch" beverage was drunk for the first time at a "re-creation" of the larger feast at a gala event on September 23, 2000, in the Upper Egyptian gallery of the University of Pennsylvania Museum. It was served after the entrée—a delicious, spicy barbecued lamb stew, prepared by chef Pam Horowitz of the Museum Catering Company, in keeping with the ancient chemical evidence and modern Turkish cuisine. Everyone at the dinner was amazed at how good the beverage tasted, and, after the dinner, requests to try the beverage began pouring in. Barely three months after the re-creation of the funerary banquet at the Museum, Sam and I decided to make "Midas Touch" commercially available. As any ancient beverage maker probably would have appreciated, the exact processing method is a closely guarded secret. Whether the beverage will catch on and continue to sell after the initial novelty has worn off remains to be seen. Even if it fails, the challenge of translating an ancient drink, on the basis of molecular archaeological findings, from the past into the present will have been worth the effort.

To the Hyperborean Regions of the North: "European Grog"

The large, comprehensive drinking set from the Midas Tomb, which was used to serve the Phrygian grog, has an importance that extends well beyond "Midas" and his funerary feast. Intriguingly, later Greek writers and gourmands dismissed beer as a barbarian drink, which may partly account for why archaeologists have been so reluctant to accept any archaeological or chemical evidence for its production there (chapter 10). The Greeks of classical times (chapter 12) preferred resinated wine diluted only with water; they would have turned up their nose at a "grog." Yet, as we have seen, the ancient Mycenaeans gladly drank the beverage and considered it fit for their gods.

What was the origin of the mixed fermented beverage that was served at the funerary feast of "King Midas" around 700 B.C., and does it have any relationship to the earlier "Greek grog"? A direct connection between the two versions of the same drink is unlikely, because the wine in the Phrygian grog was not resinated. The earliest wine from Greece is *retsina,* and this tradition prevailed throughout the ancient Near East, including Anatolia, for millennia. Although more archaeological reconnaissance and confirmatory molecular archaeological evidence are needed, a resinated wine was probably produced in the region from which the Phrygians are believed to have emigrated from during the "Dark Age"—northern Greece or the Balkans—at least as early as the third millennium B.C. (see chapter 10). The Phrygians thus came from and entered an area where vintners were accustomed to making resinated wine and where it was even the preferred beverage. Because of their role in the cult and social customs of ancient peoples, beverages are usually one of the most recalcitrant elements to change in any culture. Innovation cannot be ruled out, and special stresses, the unique individual, or a particularly ebullient time—such as the Heroic Age of Mycenaean Greece is imagined to be—might lead to new beverages. Conservatism in drink, however, more often prevails. Adding tree resins to wine is also motivated by the very practical goal of preserving the beverage. In other words, everything went against the idea that the Phrygians would have reverted to making nonresinated wine.

The answer to this seeming contradiction may lie farther north, in Europe. There, a mixed fermented beverage, as odd as it seems to us today, was a long-standing tradition, going back to at least 2000 B.C. and probably much earlier, and extending as far as the Orkney Islands off the northern tip of Scotland. Honey, wheat, barley, and various fruits (cranberry, apple, perhaps even lingonberry or cloudberry) had been fermented together and sometimes laced with meadowsweet and even henbane (*Hyoscyamus niger*) and deadly nightshade (*Atropa belladona*), which have hallucinatory properties.

Sets of numerous cups (sometimes in the form of jars or "beakers," holding as much as 5 liters), found together with a jug or a pitcher, attest to a "drinking culture" that spread across Europe during the fourth and third millennia B.C. The main stimulus for this development appears to have come from Anatolia to the southeast, where a rich and diverse tradition of fermented beverages had already existed for thousands of years (chapter 8). Beautifully burnished Funnel Beakers (German *Trichterbecher*) of the fourth millennium, with incised decoration accentuated by graphite, red paint, and white inlay, are found across central Germany and up into Denmark. Farther south, the "Baden culture" held sway in third-millennium B.C. Germany and the Carpathian basin of Hungary and Romania. Its standard drinking set, best represented in tombs, is a cup, jug, and small beaker; a reasonable inference is that the jug and beaker held different beverages and were used to fill the drinking cup. From the "Baden culture," other affiliated "drinking cultures" radiated out, like so many spokes on a wheel. Later in the second millennium, "Bell Beakers" are found in an arc stretching from the Czech Republic to Spain, with localized "beaker" cultures on the periphery. Although their names differ and their dates vary, these peoples are tied together by common artifactual traditions and, presumably, a similar kind of beverage.

The argument that Phrygian grog has a different origin from the Greek grog carries with it the proposal that these beverages were probably introduced separately at different times to southern Europe and Anatolia. The immigrants to each region could have been Indo-European groups who had migrated from a broadly contiguous region of central Europe that shared a similar tradition of a mixed fermented beverage for millennia. One group of newcomers could have entered Greece in the Middle Bronze Age. They accommodated their "grog" tradition with the preferred beverage—*retsina*—of the native peoples they met by incorporating it into their mixed fermented beverage. Similarly, over 500 years later during the early Iron Age, the Phrygians probably entered a sparsely inhabited region of Anatolia, where they chose to use the plentiful supply of grapes as their main fruit component in their version of the mixed fermented beverage.

Whatever the reason, "grog" found new life in Phrygia after the "Dark Age." Mead is known to have remained a specialty of the Phrygians until at least the first century of our era, according to Pliny the Elder (*Natural History* 14.113). The Phrygians were also notorious for their beer, which they sometimes drank out of large pots with tubes while engaged in contorted sexual acts like those illustrated in Mesopotamia centuries earlier (chapter 7). As the seventh-century Greek lyric poet Archilochos caustically put it: "He has intercourse with her, like a Thracian or a Phrygian drinking his beer through a tube" (see Athenaeus, *The Deipnosophists* 10.447).

As vines continued to proliferate and winemaking improved in the centuries to follow, varietal wines from particular regions became a mark of "civilized" life and "barbaric" beer and mead were again pushed to the sidelines. By classical times, "grog," or *kykeon* (chapter 10) had been confined to esoteric religious ceremonies.

CHAPTER 12

Molecular Archaeology, Wine, and a View to the Future

THE HISTORY of civilization, in many ways, is the history of wine. Economically, religiously, socially, medically, and politically, the domesticated grapevine has intertwined itself with human culture from at least the Neolithic period and probably long before that. We recapitulate that history every time we pick up a glass of wine and savor the fruit of a Eurasian plant that has been cloned, crossed, and transplanted again and again from its beginnings in the Near East more than 7000 years ago.

Most histories of wine begin where this one leaves off. They focus primarily on Greek and Roman literary texts, which are remarkable in themselves, beginning with Homer and Hesiod in the eighth century B.C. By the turn of the millennium, many principles of good vineyard management and wine production, still followed today, had been codified by Mago of Carthage, Varro, Cato, Pliny the Elder, and the Spaniard Columella. These careful observers and historians, however, built on the work of countless unnamed individuals and societies that had gone before them. This book attempts to illuminate the crucial but largely hidden "prehistory" of the vinicultural record and then to follow these developments down through the Bronze and Iron Ages to the coming of the Greeks and Romans.

Where It All Began

By the time the first glimmerings of a literate humanity had dawned in Mesopotamia and Egypt around 3000 B.C., most of the important advances in viniculture had already been made. *Vitis vin-*

ifera vinifera—the domesticated hermaphroditic vine—had been transplanted over thousands of kilometers and was already being carefully irrigated, trained, and tended in trellised vineyards. Grapes were gently treaded out in vats, the pomace separated from the must in settling basins, and wine made in stoppered jars with fermentation locks. The owners of the wineries were the rich and powerful of their day—pharaohs, priests, royal functionaries, doctors, and merchants— who could afford to wait five years or more for the first vintage before recouping their heavy investment in land, facilities, and labor. Their success, with thanks to the gods, was celebrated at grand feasts, served up with liberal quantities of wine in special vessels and accompanied by music, dance, and other entertainment.

The only way to peel back the veil that hides enological prehistory before 3000 B.C. is to examine and critically evaluate archaeological remains from around the world. The emphasis here should be on "critically evaluate." Too often, the historians of wine and other fermented beverages have not had a firm grounding in the science and art of archaeological interpretation. It is not enough to take the word of the excavator that his or her site dates to such and such a period; that a winemaking installation or a wine storehouse, cellar, or shop has been found; or even that domesticated grape seeds have been recovered. As much as possible, one must master the various sciences that underlie modern archaeology—radiocarbon and thermoluminescent dating methods, geology, botany and molecular biology, chemistry, and so on—and independently assess the grounds for the archaeologist's conclusions. Because only a small fraction of the original evidence has been preserved, there is a great temptation to fill in the gaps in our knowledge with unwarranted inferences drawn from modern ethnographic analogies, historical precedent, or "common sense." Inaccuracies are then taken for facts, and errors are perpetuated from one book to the next.

I cannot claim to have avoided all the pitfalls in the way of reconstructing an enological prehistory. Nor can a single investigator keep abreast of the rapid pace of discovery. I have hit the high points of the archaeological evidence in my estimation, moving from the Caucasus to Egypt to Greece to the far north of Europe and beyond. Predictably, I have focused on discoveries in my laboratory and others that have contributed to the emergent discipline of molecular archaeology. Some of the most important, new discoveries in "wine history" have occurred by applying microchemical techniques to ancient archaeological residues. These findings have shown that resinated wine was being produced in the highlands of northwestern Iran as early as 5400 B.C. They have revealed that wine was just as important as barley beer in the earliest stages of Mesopotamian civilization and that wine was often mixed with beer, honey, and herbs and spices in many, if not most, ancient societies of the Old World.

I have tentatively projected the very limited, current knowledge of the familial DNA relationships between *Vitis vinifera* varietals back in time and have proposed that a single domestication area in the eastern Taurus Mountains or Transcauscasia will eventually be delimited. I propose that, from there, the domesticated Eurasian grapevine was transplanted to other parts of the world, interbreeding with wild *Vitis* as it went, and sometimes producing even more exciting gustatory pleasures in the fruit and wine than what had gone before. I have tied this "Noah Hypothesis" to the gradual spread of the domesticated vine, winemaking, and wine drinking from the northern mountainous regions of the Near East to the south, east, and west. I have invoked modern proto-Indo-European linguistic analysis and a dramatic geological event of the in-filling of the Black Sea around 5600 B.C. to bolster a scenario that is consistent with the presently available evidence.

A definitive archaeological or scientific discovery could come at any time to disprove or, at least, shift the emphasis of my scenario. For example, a mass of grape remains inside a leather bag from a post–Ice Age cave, high in the Pyrenees, might provide prima facie evidence for exploitation of the wild vine on the western periphery of its modern distribution and strengthen the case for early domestication and winemaking there. Unequivocal ancient DNA evidence could be forthcoming to show that the Eurasian vine or another grape species, perhaps in China or the New World, was taken into cultivation independent of any contact with the Near East or exchange of germ plasm.

Increasingly, the archaeological, linguistic, botanical, and other scientific data point to eastern Turkey as where the earliest permanent human settlements, based on the domestication of the "founder plants," emerged during the Neolithic period. A DNA study of einkorn wheat has traced its beginnings back to the Karacadağ range of the Taurus Mountains, and chickpea and bitter vetch are also believed to have been domesticated in this general region, extending northward to Mount Ararat (Büyük Agri Daği) and the headwaters of the Tigris and Euphrates Rivers.

Many fruits, including the grape, and nuts still grow wild in eastern Turkey and the Caucasus. Horticultural techniques could have been developed there at an early date, especially if other plants were being experimented with and cultivated. Research is now in progress to compare extracted modern DNA from the wild and domesticated grapevines of Anatolia and Transcaucasia with European cultivars. Will this work bear out my hypothesis or stand at odds with it? Further work in the Near East and Egypt is also needed to fill out the picture.

Consumed by Wine

A unifying concept that runs throughout this book is that of a "wine culture." Where the domesticated grapevine and wine have taken hold, whole cultures have usually been enveloped in their grasp. A trip today to Georgia in the Caucasus Mountains or to one of the countries of southern Europe—France, Italy, Spain, or Greece—will convince one of wine's strong allure. Vineyards cover the hillsides; the main meals of the day would not be complete without a bottle of wine; and special events of all kinds, both religious and secular, are celebrated by toasting and ceremonially presenting wine.

The phenomenon of a wine culture probably had its beginnings in the earliest Neolithic communities in the northern mountainous area of the Near East. By domesticating various plants and animals, humans had taken hold of their destiny. Surplus food could be produced, and this freed up time for other activities and a greater division of labor among the population. More resources could be accumulated, especially as trade developed. Certain individuals inevitably rose to the top of the socioeconomic pyramid, since leaders were needed in a more complex society and opportunities for accumulating wealth or gaining a higher position would be seized upon by some.

Once in control, the "upper classes" had the resources and leisure to adopt what may be called a vinicentric approach to life and the world. They could plant vineyards and make wine, even if it took years, and they could enjoy wine whenever they wanted—daily at meals, certainly, and at every important social occasion and significant event in one's life from the cradle to the grave, as well. Such a special beverage also cried out for special serving and drinking vessels, which underscored their owners' status, and artisans supplied these in clay, metals, stone, wood, and leather.

As a Neolithic wine culture took shape, it played upon all the strengths and weaknesses of the human condition. Wine's color, aroma, and taste were a perceptual delight to the senses. It was a "social lubricant," easing relations with others, and a good way to "come down" from the workday and block out a humdrum existence—even Neolithic man and woman could appreciate those benefits. Moreover, it eased physical pain and helped cure diseases of the body. The most important effects of wine, however, operated at different, often unconscious levels of the mind. The relatively high alcoholic content of wine made it a mind-altering drug. When drunk in moderation, it caused elation and even mental acuity; when drunk in excess, the results were highly unpredictable. Some people fell into a stupor, others went emotionally out of control, and a few even claimed to have communicated with the gods.

Early humans must have been astounded when they first experienced wine's tangible and seemingly other-worldly potency. Metaphorically, the lush, full-bodied clusters of the grapevine represented nature's fecundity, and it was not much of a leap to associate the juice of its fruit with the red liquid, blood, that filled and nourished the human body. If it was the preferred beverage of elite humans, wine must also be the drink of the gods. It was an elixir nonpareil.

Of course, what early humans actually thought about wine and where their unconscious leanings took them can only be inferred from the archaeological record. We sift through the remains of Neolithic settlements and find grape remains and ancient organic compounds of a liquid grape product, probably wine, inside storage vessels and special serving and drinking vessels. The "wine services" are mainly found in public buildings, which were strangely decorated, and therefore probably served a ritualistic function. On the basis of what we now know about wine's sensory, medical, and psychoactive effects, the most parsimonious, straightforward interpretation of the data is that wine was a central part of the life and religion of early humans in the Near East, at least going back to the Neolithic period.

The prestige exchange of wine and special wine-drinking ceremonies were likely the motive forces in the spread of Neolithic wine culture. How else can one explain its inexorable march to Mesopotamia and Shiraz, to Palestine and Egypt, across the northern rim of the Mediterranean, up the Rhone and down the Rhine in the first centuries of our era, and in the last 20 years to the West Coast of the United States? Often, the evidence is there for all to see and understand. Egyptian pharaohs, Elamite rulers and their queens, Assyrian despots, the Bacchic poets of Iran, and the cult winemakers are shown celebrating their victories and giving thanks to their gods, as they drink their cups of wine under arbors of grapevines.

The same social forces that encouraged people to center their lives around wine were just as much at work in later literate civilizations, continuing up to the present, as they were in the Neolithic period. In temperate, upland regions where the grapevine thrived, wine cultures had a high probability of spreading from the top of the socioeconomic ladder down to the small landowner or entrepreneur. Small tracts of land could be planted with a few grapevines at first. With each succeeding generation, cuttings from the older plants could be established, until enough fruit was being produced to make wine for a small family unit. Where the grapevine was less easily grown, such as in the great riverine cultures of Egypt and Mesopotamia which depended on irrigation agriculture, the tentacles of a "democratized wine culture" did not take hold.

What is especially remarkable about an integrated wine culture is that production cannot keep up with demand. Prices fall, and wines are imported even into a country that is already awash with the beverage. By the time the curtain falls on this history of wine in the late Iron Age, ships from Phoenicia, North Syria, Cyprus, and the Greek isles were plying the Mediterranean Sea, loaded down with amphoras of wine. They competed for market share in the other wine-producing countries and traded with the less fortunate who were not yet making their own wine. Like the coals brought to Newcastle, Greek wine poured into Egypt and the Holy Land during the Hellenistic period.

Why Alcohol and Why Wine?

Why have cultures around the world had a millennia-long love affair with wine, once they have been introduced to it? The short answer to this question is that ethyl alcohol has been the most effective drug of all time. And before the discovery of distillation, a potent form of this compound could be most expeditiously obtained from grapes by making wine.

You do not need a degree in pharmacology or great powers of observation to see how the alcohol in wine acts as a drug. It is an analgesic, disinfectant, and general remedy all rolled into one. Moreover, it has profound mind-altering effects, including the release of natural opiate-like "pleasure compounds"—endorphins and enkephalins—in our brain. Social or cultic life has sometimes focused on other psychotropic drugs, such as coca and peyote in the Americas or opium and hashish in the Old World, but in a head-to-head confrontation, they cannot compete with wine as an all-purpose drug.

Wine was the prime medicinal agent of the ancient, medieval, and early modern worlds, up to the nineteenth century. Then, other curative compounds, which were isolated and purified by chemical methods or synthesized, began to displace it. It was the most common ingredient in ancient Egyptian, Mesopotamian, and Syrian medicines, which was readily administered by drinking or external application.

Most important, people who drank alcoholic beverages, as opposed to straight water, in antiquity were more likely to live longer and reproduce more. As Paul advised Timothy (I:5.23): "No longer drink only water, but take a little wine for the sake of your stomach and your frequent ailments." Ancient armies were "inoculated" against disease by mixing wine with the uncertain water supplies that they came upon in their journeys. In addition to the alcohol, the polyphenolic aromatic compounds in wine have antiseptic properties. These antioxidants, including resveratrol, cyanidin, and quercetin, are stronger even than the chemically related phenol or carbolic acid, the antiseptic that the English surgeon Joseph Lister introduced in the late nineteenth century. They also scavenge free radicals, thereby lowering cholesterol and protecting humans against cancer and other ailments.

Because of its high alcoholic content, wine is also an excellent medium or vehicle for dispensing other medicinal agents. In the ancient world, a panoply of remedies was recommended. For example, in ancient Egypt, the testicles of an ass were ground up and steeped in wine to treat epilepsy. According to the Jewish Talmud, impotence could be cured by a hot toddy of wine and ground forest saffron. Pliny the Elder advocated wine and rue for every kind of sting and bite. Hot wine made from Ashkelon wine of the Holy Land, mixed with parsley, fennel, cumin, and pepper, was said to cure a stomachache. Of course, not all of these herbs, spices, or other additives have proven medical benefits.

Ancient humans did not understand the "germ theory of disease" or the inner workings of the cell. To survive in the world, however, they did need to discern cause-and-effect relationships, some of which have stood the test of time. Wine is arguably their greatest legacy to the modern world. Its psychotropic effects and medicinal value, owing to alcohol, largely accounted for its central role in society, religion, and the economy. The fermentation process made it more nutritious than grapes. Finally and more subtly, wine's preeminence in world history can be traced to its array of chemical compounds, which titillate the senses and challenge human imagination. Widespread use of wine by a population, however, was a two-edged sword. Persons who indulged in wine were likely to carry genes that predisposed their descendants to alcoholism.

The discovery and rediscovery of how to make a fermented beverage from a natural or derived source of simple sugars has occurred in many places and at many times. Before the modern period, only the Eskimos, the peoples of Tierra del Fuego at the southern tip of South America, and the Australian aborigines apparently lived out their lives without the solace and medical benefits of alcohol. The polar regions lacked good resources for monosaccharides; bear meat and

seal fat may degrade and go rancid, but they do not ferment. Temperate parts of the globe, by contrast, were blessed with honey and fruit,
above all the grape, and the tropics were awash in sugar-rich plants.

The reader might ask why fermented beverages made from other
natural products, which were sometimes richer in sugar than grapes,
were not adopted and passed as readily as wine from culture to culture. After all, honey is produced by bees in temperate climates all
over the world and has one of the highest concentrations of simple
sugars (60 percent to 80 percent by weight) of any natural product.
Fruits, other than grape, range from the higher-sugar varieties of the
tropics (e.g., dates, pineapples, and bananas) to the less sweet berries
of the northern tundra. If the fruit is dried, its sugar content is accentuated. Even plant juices and tree resins—the agave and the saguaro
cactus in the New World and palm tree resin in the Old World
spring to mind—were sweet enough to ferment directly.

One advantage of the grape over these other sugar sources, all of
which can and have been made into delicious fermented beverages, is
that it can be established under the most adverse environmental conditions and still produce quantities of fruit. Indeed, it thrives and
produces its best fruit in soils that are of little use for growing anything else. Most tellingly, it is easily processed into wine by simply
squeezing the grapes, collecting the must—gravity methods were sufficient at first—and letting the marvelous process of fermentation
take over.

The Lowly Yeast to the Forefront

Beyond knowing where to find a simple sugar source,
ancient humans had to get the fermentation process started and keep
it going. They could not see the microscopic organism, *Saccharomyces
cerevisiae*, but its effects were obvious: the evolution of carbon dioxide, a froth forming on the surface of the liquid, and a final product
that was noticeably smoother, warmer, and sweeter than the starting
material. It is still a mystery why varieties of this yeast live on the
skins of certain fruits, especially grape, or in honey, where they are
able to tolerate high sugar levels. Insects, such as bees and wasps,
probably inadvertently transport the yeast, perhaps from their nests

or hives, when they feed on the sweet juice oozing out of damaged fruit. However explained, honey, grapes, apples, dates, figs, and other fruits harbor *S. cerevisiae*.

Wine was a step ahead of other ancient fermented beverages, because of the ease with which it could be made by letting *S. cerevisiae* do what came naturally. Grapes, when their juices have been exuded, provide the ideal breeding ground for the yeast to multiply and convert the sugars into carbon dioxide and alcohol. The must has just the right amount of water and nutrient mix, so it does not require dilution as do sugar-rich honey and the juices of more fibrous fruits. Moreover, once an alcoholic content of 5 percent by volume has been reached, detrimental microorganisms, which can produce off-flavors, odors, and even disease, are killed off, while *S. cerevisiae* survives to continue the fermentation and produce a beverage with more than twice that amount of alcohol.

Cereals and vegetables, which provide the starting materials for different kinds of beer, are made up mostly of polysaccharides. Ancient humans eventually learned how to break down the complex sugars into simpler ones, primarily by malting barley in the Near East and by saccharifying rice and other grains using molds in China. Nevertheless, these processes do not yield as much sugar as the Eurasian grape does naturally, and a suitable fermenting yeast does not live on cereals and vegetables. The beer-maker either had to wait for an adventitious organism to float into his wort vat on the air currents, as the Belgian lambic producers do today, or introduce it directly. *Saccharomyces cerevisiae* is not air-borne, and microclimates, with the exception of the barns in Brussels, can be very unpredictable, so the best course of action was to add yeast from a guaranteed natural source, such as grapes. Not surprisingly, grapes were included in the earliest "recipe" for barley beer, the Mesopotamian "Hymn to Ninkasi" (chapter 7).

Mixing Things Up

According to classical sources, only the very best wines were aged and drunk neat. More commonly, something was added to the wine. It might be water, which merely blunts the sensory, medicinal, and psychoactive effects of wine. Other additives were a good deal stronger: pepper, wormwood (*Artemisia absinthum*), capers, saffron, and many other herbs and spices. The idea was not just to cover up the signs of a deteriorating wine, although that was an added incentive, but to keep the wines for a longer time and produce new, exciting tastes for jaded palates. Cocktails, grogs, and punches have always had their place in the barman's stock and trade.

The analyses of ancient wine samples in my laboratory have shown that classical practices and predilections stand at the end of a long and complex skein of traditions. Tree resins were among the earliest additives to wine. We have seen how ancient humans probably made several intuitive leaps that led to this development: if a tree oozed resin to heal a cut in its bark, then applying resin to a human wound should serve to cure it, and, by extension, drinking a wine laced with a tree resin could both help to treat internal maladies and prevent the dreaded "wine disease." Because there was little that could be done to prevent oxygen from leaking through a porous earthenware vessel, other methods for preserving wine had to be found.

Modern chemical investigation has shown that many of the pragmatic observations of the fledgling winemakers at the dawn of history were correct up to a point. Tree resins, including terebinth, pine, and cedar, impede the reproduction of *Acetobacter* and other bacteria that convert ethanol to acetic acid or vinegar, and some of the important compounds in tree resins, as well as in the strong, bitter herbs and spices of classical times, have antioxidant properties that prevent these organisms from multiplying. Although their effectiveness did not approach that of sulfur dioxide, the most important antioxidant in the arsenal of the modern winemaker, they helped to stretch out the life of a wine and added special flavors and aromas that were clearly appreciated at the time. Otherwise, the most expensive wine in the Roman world, made with myrrh imported from distant Arabia, would not have continued to command a high price.

Humans have a propensity for sugar and chocolate. Ancient peoples, except in central America, did not have the latter, and their prospects for satisfying their sweet tooth were also limited. Sweet wines were thus the ultimate indulgence. By raisining the grapes and cooking down the wine, ancient beverage makers could prepare even sweeter concoctions. Chalk, lime from marble and shells, and sea water were added to wine to make it more mellow by binding up the acids and accentuating the sugar. In classical times, boiling in lead containers and adding high-lead constituents had the same effect. Honey, always expensive and with different flavors and aromas depending on its origin, was the ultimate sweetener. An equally important reason for choosing a sweet wine over a dry one was that it was less likely to go bad because of its higher sugar content.

In the heyday of discovering how to make wine and other fermented beverages, which I propose is the Neolithic period, an early experimenter would have been less likely to tinker with his drink by adding something at the end of the process than he or she would have been to try to see which natural materials could be fermented from the start and what range of sensory and mental effects they produced. I can imagine an isolated Neolithic town in the mountains of eastern Turkey or in Transcaucasia where some enterprising soul had an intense, even violent fermentation going in a large pottery vat. The process had started with grapes, the most prevalent fruit in the region that harbored the all-important wine yeast. It was the base beverage, the sine qua non for any experimentation. Once things had got going, some pomegranates and plums were tossed in, then a handful of raspberries or hackberries, some spices and herbs, and for good measure, a complete beehive from a nearby forest to finish off the "brew." Temperatures were raised and lowered to see what effect heat had on the fermentation; the ingredients were added at different stages in the process, and the liquid was strained through a coarse woven cloth or a clump of grass into another pottery vessel. Then the village was assembled to pass judgment on the beverage. What did it taste like? How did it make them feel?

We have no idea how often or how intensively ancient humans pursued this line of investigation: that is, testing all the various permutations and combinations of materials and processing steps for making a fermented beverage. We can be sure that at some point social convention and religious taboo stepped in to constrain choice and channel the use of fermented beverages. The Neolithic period lasted thousands of years, and communities were largely independent of one another. If the domestication of a range of plants and animals had proved successful, especially in the mountainous region of eastern Turkey, then why should not the development of new fermented beverages, based on the new domesticates, have kept pace with those developments? Undoubtedly, it did, and other emerging crafts and industries, including pottery making, metallurgy, even cookery, stood to benefit from new and better-crafted beverages.

The experimental phase of fermented beverage creation did not end with the Neolithic period in the Near East. As the new domesticates spread across Europe in the millennia to follow, different native plants of other climatic zones were brought into the "mix." Northern Europe, in particular, did not have natural sources of sugar-rich materials available to the extent that the southern part of the continent did. Wild grapes grew there, but they were sour and it was difficult to establish the domesticated *Vitis vinifera* in the cold climate. Therefore, the northerners did not have the luxury of focusing on just one beverage and consigning everything else, particularly beer, to the barbarian hinterland. They were the heathen, and they had to make do with whatever sweet substances they could glean from their environment. Honey was best, but it was limited to the wealthy. Berries, apples, barley malt, and other grains were more widespread and cheaper. Using a variety of sugar sources made it easier to start fermentations and coax the maximum amount of alcohol out of the limited natural resources. Less sugar, however, meant a beverage lower in alcoholic content and poorer preservation for these "mixed beverages."

Low-alcohol drinks were the standard fare for most European folk, so the higher-alcohol beverages—pure mead or mixed mead-fruit-and-grain concoctions—served at celebrations and feasts were like manna from heaven. When a long-sought-after food or drink has been denied someone or is rarely available and then is brought out in profusion, the tendency is to overindulge. The European "barbarians" were roundly excoriated by the Greeks and Romans for their binging. In its wake, northern Europeans developed a higher genetic propensity for alcoholism than southern Europeans, who drank wine in moderate amounts on a regular basis from a young age.

The tradition of a "mixed fermented beverage" has never died out. Wine connoisseurs may turn up their nose at even the thought of adding a tree resin, honey, barley malt, or an herb or a spice to a fine varietal. Yet the Italians and French today make exquisite apéritifs that are "vermouthed" with tree barks and roots, orange peels, flower extracts, and an array of herbs and spices that are macerated and infused into wine. The harsh tannic edges of fine wines are tamed and "improved" by ageing in oak barrels, which essentially means adding a tree resin, even if it is not called *retsina*. In order to appreciate how common mixed fermented beverages are in Western culture, all you need to do is visit your neighborhood watering hole. Drinking fads, whether the martini of the 1950s, whiskey sours, or the Singapore Sling, come and go. Absinthe, a liqueur made from wormwood, anise, and other aromatics, is making a comeback on the European continent. Wormwood, one of the most bitter substances known and also psychoactive, was banned by many countries a century ago. Gruit and meadowsweet ales have gained a following in the United States and Scotland. Meaderies have begun to open around the world. The holiday seasons, which coincide with ancient harvest festivals and celestial events, are still the times when such drinks are apt to be prepared and served. For example, glögg—a spiced red wine and brandy concoction—is a yuletide tradition in Sweden. In short, the prospects for mixed fermented beverages appear never to have been better.

Wine, the Perfect Metaphor

With molecular archaeology having come of age in the last several decades, the study of ancient organics is poised for takeoff. Ancient wine, one of the most important "discoveries" of the human race with far-reaching cultural consequences, provides a paradigm for how other organic materials in the archaeological record can be resuscitated and traced through time up to the present. We as humans and most of what we surround ourselves with are organic— our bodies, our brains, our clothing and houses, our food. Each is the end-result of a historical process, which can be fully understood only by retracing the steps in its "creation." Although much of the evidence has been swallowed up by the earth and destroyed by inexorable chemical processes, certain signposts can be recovered along the way. The hiatuses can be filled in by a careful and often intuitive sifting and assessment of the genetic, environmental, social, and individual forces at work.

There is now no question that ancient organic materials can survive relatively intact for centuries, even millennia, depending on how stable they are and what they are exposed to environmentally. The best circumstances for long-term preservation are dry deserts, deep-sea and waterlogged contexts, such as bogs, in which oxygen levels are low, and the extremely cold mountains and polar regions of the world. The principal inorganic material, fired clay or pottery, that was most often used to make ancient containers for organics is virtually indestructible, and it ties up the more fragile compounds in the interstices of its polar silicate structure, where they are less apt to break down than in an exposed environment. Ancient humans themselves helped to guarantee a better outcome for the survival of ancient organics by using preservatives and disinfectants to preserve the bodies of their dead and the offerings that accompanied them into eternity. Burial chambers, like the Midas Mound, were built with an eye to concealing them from mortals, and, in the process, they were hermetically sealed off from the environment. Even when compounds have degraded, microchemical techniques are increasingly able to tease out the available evidence and work backward to reconstruct the original material.

In the spirit of an unending scientific quest, the next generation of molecular archaeological exploration must plot a course that will lead us asymptotically toward a better understanding of ancient wine. With persistence and ever-improving archaeological and scientific tools, who is to say what is the limit of our knowledge. Perhaps Bob Ballard will locate and recover a Neolithic boat from the floor of the Black Sea, over 1800 meters below sea level, with its shipment of wine and other goods still intact. Such a finding, which is not beyond the realm of possibility, would open a window onto the past from which earlier and later stages in the history of wine could be assessed. Rather than hypothesizing about the earliest cultivar on the basis of limited ancient DNA evidence, we might be able to say that it was definitely related to a muscat, a Georgian Saperavi, a Turkish Boğazkere, or some other grape. Careful observation, taste tests (if they were allowed), and analyses would further inform us as to whether red or white grapes, or boths, had been pressed, what yeast was used to ferment the beverage, and how the final product measured up in terms of its acidity, sweetness, astringency, and alcoholic level. Additives and preservatives could be identified. Someday, it may even be possible to say whether the ancient winemaker had an appreciation for ageing, malolactic fermentation, and other subtleties of the production process.

There are still many gaps in our understanding of how wine cultures and viniculture spread across the ancient world. One of the most intriguing puzzles, yet to be resolved, is whether the wine cultures of the Near East and China, separated by over 2000 kilometers and the mountains and deserts of central Asia, were in contact with one another during the earliest phases of their development. The earliest Chinese fermented beverage thus far attested to, according to unpublished molecular archaeological evidence from my laboratory, is from Jiahu in Henan Province (color plate 16). The analyzed jars for storing, serving, and, presumably, drinking a beverage, date to about 7000 B.C., when the first winemaking experiments with lasting consequences were probably also taking place in the Near East. Our analyses showed that the eastern and western Neolithic beverages were similar in containing an added or infused tree resin or herb. In addition, although rice (*Oryza sativa*) was the main constituent of the Chinese beverage, a large amount of tartaric acid or tartrate pointed to grape as a likely ingredient. How could this be, when most scholars have argued that the many wild grape species of China were never exploited and that winemaking was introduced to China as late as the second century B.C. and then only because the Eurasian grape was transplanted there (chapter 1)?

At first, I was troubled by the chemical evidence from the Jiahu jars. I could imagine both Neolithic peoples independently discovering and using tree resins or herbs; that scenario has been documented elsewhere around the world. But, if grapes were involved in the earliest experimentation in fermented beverages in both places, then the likelihood of contact increased. The more I thought about it, the more sense it made that an early Chinese beverage would contain a grape constituent. Before the Chinese developed their unique saccharification system for breaking down polysaccharides, they would have needed a sure source of yeast for fermentation, and that could not be obtained from rice. The many wild grape species could have filled the breach, since they were literally there for the picking and some are sweet enough that wine is made from them today (e.g., *Vitis amurensis* in the north and *V. quinquangularis* Rahd and *V. pentagona* Diels and Gilg. in the south). My surmise has recently gained support from an archaeobotanical study of the ancient plant remains at Jiahu. Zhijun ("Jimmy") Zhao of the Institute of Archaeology in Beijing is engaged in a far-flung investigation of plant exploitation and ecology in ancient China, in which soils are intensively floated, sieved, and examined for microscopic remains. Jimmy was startled to find, in addition to some of the earliest domesticated rice, many wild grape seeds at Jiahu, and pips have begun showing up at other prehistoric sites as well. Perhaps, it is coincidental that a fermented beverage, using grapes and tree resins, was "discovered" in two distant regions some 9000 years ago, especially since humans, left to their own devices, often arrive at comparable solutions to a given problem. On the other hand, our findings could point the way to a revolutionary reassessment of east-west connections in Asia during the early Neolithic period, powered by a common appreciation of and desire for wine.

Each culture has its own story to tell about its relationship with wine and the vine. Together, they form a truly remarkable history of a truly remarkable plant, and its product, intertwining itself with human culture throughout the world. Humans have learned how to make an infinite range of tastes and bouquets from a single Eurasian grape species, which probably began to be cultivated in the mountains of eastern Turkey or the Caucasus and was transplanted over and over again. The story of the ancient "culture of the vine," however, has not yet been fully told. The full genetic and social potential of *Vitis vinifera vinifera* and the many other grape species around the world can be realized only by tracing them back to their "homeland," where they first thrived and were uniquely suited to their habitats. Call it the vinicultural Garden of Eden, if you will. The archaeological and chemical hunt continues.

SELECTED BIBLIOGRAPHY

ONE can hardly do justice to the literature on a subject as vast as that of ancient wine, and many references are scattered throughout specialized archaeological and scientific journals. The interested reader will be able to track down supporting information on many of the archaeological sites, artifacts, and arguments presented in this book by consulting the detailed bibliography in P. E. McGovern, S. J. Fleming, and S. H. Katz, eds., *The Origins and Ancient History of Wine* (Luxembourg: Gordon and Breach, 1996; reprinted, with new foreword, 2000). General information is also available on my websites:

> *http://www.sas.upenn.edu/~mcgovern/*
> *http://www.upenn.edu/museum/Wine/wineintro.html*
> *http://www.museum.upenn.edu/Midas/intro.html*
> *http://www.museum.upenn.edu/Midas/recipes.html*
> *http://www.upenn.edu/museum/News/beer.html*

General

Amerine, M. A., H. W. Berg, R. E. Kunkee, C. S. Ough, V. R. Singleton, and A. D. Webb. 1980. *The Technology of Wine Making.* 4th ed. Westport, CN: Avi Publishing.

Amouretti, M.-C., and J. P. Brun, eds. 1993. *La Production du vin et de l'huile en Méditerranée. Bulletin de correspondance hellénique* (suppl. 26). Athens: Ecole française d'Athènes.

Baldy, M. W. 1997. *The University Wine Course: A Wine Appreciation Text and Self Tutorial.* San Francisco: Wine Appreciation Guild.

Dayagi-Mendels, M. 1999. *Drink and Be Merry: Wine and Beer in Ancient Times.* Jerusalem: Israel Museum.

Farkaš, J. 1988. *Technology and Biochemistry of Wine.* 2 vols. New York: Gordon and Breach.

Frankel, R. 1999. *Wine and Oil Production in Antiquity in Israel and Other Mediterranean Countries. Journal for the Study of the Old Testament.* American Schools of Oriental Research Monograph Series, no. 10. Sheffield, England: Sheffield University.

Hyams, E. 1965. *Dionysus: A Social History of the Wine Vine.* New York: Macmillan.

Johnson, H. 1989. *Vintage: The Story of Wine.* New York: Simon and Schuster.

Lutz, H. F. 1922. *Viticulture and Brewing in the Ancient Orient.* Leipzig: J. C. Hinrichs.

Milano, L., ed. 1994. *Drinking in Ancient Societies: History and Culture of Drinks in the Ancient Near East.* Padua: Sargon.

Mills, J. S., and R. White. 1994. *The Organic Chemistry of Museum Objects.* 2nd ed. Oxford: Butterworth-Heinemann.

Murray, O., and M. Tecuşan, eds. 1995. *In Vino Veritas.* London: British School at Rome.

Phillips, R. 2001. *A Short History of Wine.* London: Penguin.

Seltman, C. 1957. *Wine in the Ancient World.* London: Routledge & Kegan Paul.

Unwin, T. 1991. *Wine and the Vine: An Historical Geography of Viticulture and the Wine Trade.* London: Routledge.

Warner Allen, H. 1962. *A History of Wine: Great Vintage Wines from the Homeric Age to the Present Day.* New York: Horizon Press.

Younger, W. 1966. *Gods, Men, and Wine.* London: Wine and Food Society.

Chapter 1. Stone Age Wine

Adams, L. D. 1990. *The Wines of America.* 4th ed. New York: McGraw-Hill.

Huang, H.-T. 2000. *Biology and Biological Technology.* Part V, *Fermentations and Food Science.* Vol. 6, *Science and Civilisation in China,* by J. Needham. Cambridge: Cambridge University.

McGovern, P. E., and R. H. Michel. 1990. Royal Purple Dye: The Chemical Reconstruction of the Ancient Mediterranean Industry. *Accounts of Chemical Research* 23:152–58.

Vandiver, P. B., O. Soffer, B. Klima, and J. Svoboda. 1989. The Origins of Ceramic Technology at Dolni Vestoniče, Czechoslovakia. *Science* 246: 1002–8.

Zhang, F., F. Luo, and D. Gu. 1990. Studies on Germplasm Resources of Wild Grape Species (*Vitis* spp.) in China. Pages 50–57 in *Proceedings of the 5th International Symposium on Grape Breeding, Sept. 12–16, 1989, St. Martin, Pfalz, Germany. Vitis* (special issue).

Zohary, D., and P. Spiegel-Roy. 1975. Beginning of Fruit Growing in the Old World. *Science* 187:319–27.

Chapter 2. The Noah Hypothesis

Bar Yosef, O., and R. H. Meadow. 1995. The Origins of Agriculture in the Near East. Pages 39–94 in *Last Hunters—First Farmers: New Perspectives on the Prehistoric Transition to Agriculture*, ed. T. D. Price and A. B. Gebauer. Sante Fe: School of American Research.

Bowers, J. E., and C. P. Meredith. 1997. The Parentage of a Classic Wine Grape, Cabernet Sauvignon. *Nature Genetics* 16:721–24.

———. 1999. Historical Genetics: The Parentage of Chardonnay, Gamay, and Other Wine Grapes of Northeastern France. *Science* 285:1562–65.

Burney, C. A. 1971. *The Peoples of the Hills: Ancient Ararat and Caucasus.* London: Weidenfeld and Nicolson.

Diamond, J. 1997. Location, Location, Location: The First Farmers. *Science* 278 (5341): 1243–44.

Foster, B. R., D. Frayne, and G. Beckman, eds. 2001. *The Epic of Gilgamesh: A New Translation, Analogues, Criticism; The Sumerian Gilgamesh Poems; The Hittite Gilgamesh.* New York: Norton.

Gamkrelidze, T. V., and V. V. Ivanov. 1990. The Early History of Indo-European Languages. *Scientific American* 262:110–16.

———. 1995. *Indo-European and the Indo-Europeans: A Reconstruction and Historical Analysis of a Proto-Language and a Proto-Culture*, ed. W. Winter, trans. J. Nichols. 2 vols. Berlin: M. de Gruyter.

Heun, H., R. Schafer-Pregl, D. Klawan, R. Castagna, M. Accerbi, B. Borghi, and F. Salamini. 1997. Site of Einkorn Wheat Domestication Identified by DNA Fingerprinting. *Science* 278(5341): 1312–14.

Miller, N. F. 1991. The Near East. Pages 133–61 in *Progress in Old World Palaeoethnobotany: A Retrospective View on the Occasion of 20 Years of the International Work Group for Palaeoethnobotany*, eds. W. van Zeist, K. Wasylikowa, and K.-E. Behre. Rotterdam: Balkema.

Núñez, D. R., and M. J. Walker. 1989. A Review of Palaeobotanical Findings of Early *Vitis* in the Mediterranean and of the Origins of Cultivated Grape-Vines, with Special Reference to New Pointers to Prehistoric Exploitation in the Western Mediterranean. *Review of Palaeobotany and Palynology* 61:205–37.

Renfrew, C. 1988. *Archaeology and Language: The Puzzle of Indo-European Origins*. New York: Cambridge University.

Ryan, W., and W. Pitman. 1998. *Noah's Flood: The New Scientific Discoveries about the Event That Changed History*. New York: Simon and Schuster.

Sefc, K. M., M. S. Lopes, F. Lefort, R. Botta, K. A. Roubelakis-Angelakis, J. Ibáñez, I. Pejić, H. W. Wagner, J. Glössl, and H. Steinkellner. 2000. Microsatellite Variability in Grapevine Cultivars from Different European Regions and Evaluation of Assignment Testing to Assess the Geographic Origin of Cultivars. *Theoretical and Applied Genetics* 100:498–505.

Zohary, D., and M. Hopf. 2000. *Domestication of Plants in the Old World: The Origin and Spread of Cultivated Plants in West Asia, Europe, and the Nile Valley*. 3rd ed. Oxford: Oxford University.

Chapter 3. The Archaeological and Chemical Hunt for the Earliest Wine

Badler, V. 1991. Travels with "Jarley": A 4th Millennium B.C. Wine Jar from Godin Tepe. *Archaeological Newsletter, Royal Ontario Museum*, 2d ser., 44:1–4.

Biers, W. R., and P. E. McGovern, eds. 1990. *Organic Contents of Ancient Vessels: Materials Analysis and Archaeological Investigation*. MASCA Research Papers in Science and Archaeology 7. Philadelphia: Museum Applied Science Center for Archaeology.

Haevernick, Th. E. 1963. Beiträge zur Geschichte des antiken Glases:

X. Römischer Wein. *Jahrbuch des Römisch-Germanischen Zentralmuseum Mainz* 10:118–22.

Lambert, J. B. 1997. *Traces of the Past: Unraveling the Secrets of Archaeology through Chemistry*. Reading, MA: Addison-Wesley.

McGovern, P. E., ed. 1995. Science in Archaeology: A Review. *American Journal of Archaeology* 99:79–142.

Michel, R. H., J. Lazar, and P. E. McGovern. 1992. Indigoid Dyes in Peruvian and Coptic Textiles of the University Museum of Archaeology and Anthropology. *Archeomaterials* 6:69–83.

Michel, R. H., P. E. McGovern, and V. R. Badler. 1993. The First Wine and Beer: Chemical Detection of Ancient Fermented Beverages. *Analytical Chemistry* 65:408A–13A.

Weiss, H., and T. C. Young Jr. 1975. The Merchants of Susa: Godin V and Plateau-Lowland Relations in the Late Fourth Millennium B.C. *Iran* 13:1–17.

Chapter 4. Neolithic Wine!

Kushnareva, K. K. 1997. *The Southern Caucasus in Prehistory: Stages of Cultural and Socioeconomic Development from the Eighth to the Second Millennium B.C.*, trans. H. N. Michael. University Museum Monograph 99. Philadelphia: University Museum.

Majno, G. 1975. *The Healing Hand: Man and Wound in the Ancient World*. Cambridge: Harvard University.

McGovern, P. E., U. Hartung, V. R. Badler, D. L. Glusker, and L. J. Exner. 1997. The Beginnings of Winemaking and Viniculture in the Ancient Near East and Egypt. *Expedition* 39(1): 3–21.

McGovern, P. E., M. M. Voigt, D. L. Glusker, and L. J. Exner. 1986. Neolithic Resinated Wine. *Nature* 381 (June 6): 480–81.

Mellaart, J. 1965. *Earliest Civilizations of the Near East*. New York: McGraw-Hill.

Mills, J., and R. White. 1989. The Identity of the Resins from the Late Bronze Age Shipwreck at Ulu Burun (Kaş). *Archaeometry* 31:37–44.

Renfrew, C. 1973. *Before Civilization: The Radiocarbon Revolution and Prehistoric Europe*. New York: Knopf.

Voigt, M. M. 1983. *Hajji Firuz Tepe, Iran: The Neolithic Settlement*. Philadelphia: University Museum.

Chapter 5. *Wine of the Earliest Pharaohs*

Cavalieri, D., P. McGovern, D. Hartl, R. Mortimer, and M. Polsinelli. In press. Evidence for *S. cerevisiae* Fermentation in Ancient Wine. *Journal of Molecular Evolution*.

Grüss, J. 1932. Kleinere Mitteilungen III: Zwei altgermanische Trinkhörner mit Bier-und Metresten. *Prähistorische Zeitschrift* 22:180–91.

Hartung, U. 2001. *Importkeramik aus dem Friedhof U in Abydos (Umm el-Qaab) und die Beziehungen Ægyptens zu Vorderasien im 4. Jahrtausend v. Chr*. Archäologische Veröffentlichungen der Deutschen Archäologischen Instituts, Abteilung Kairo 92. Mainz: P. von Zabern.

Lucas, A. 1962. *Ancient Egyptian Materials and Industries*. 4th ed., rev. and enl. by J. R. Harris. London: E. Arnold.

Leonard, A., Jr. 2000. Food for Thought: Saqqara Tomb 3477 Revisited. *Near Eastern Archaeology* 63:177–79.

McGovern, P. E. 1998. Wine for Eternity. *Archaeology* 5(4): 28–34.

Poo, M.-C. 1995. *Wine and Wine Offering in the Religion of Ancient Egypt*. London: Kegan Paul International.

Spindler, K. 1994. *The Man in the Ice: The Discovery of a 5,000-Year-Old Body Reveals the Secrets of the Stone Age*, trans. E. Osers. New York: Harmony Books.

Chapter 6. *Wine of Egypt's Golden Age*

Bass, G. F., C. Pulak, D. Collon, and J. M. Weinstein. 1989. The Bronze Age Shipwreck at Uluburun: 1986 Campaign. *American Journal of Archaeology* 93:1–29.

Bietak, M. 1985. Ein altägyptischer Weingarten in einem Tempelbezirk (Tell el-Dab'a 1. März bis 10. Juni 1985). *Anzeiger der philosophisch-historischen Klasse der Österreichischen Akademie der Wissenschaften* 122:267–78.

Hayes, W. C. 1951. Inscriptions from the Place of Amenhotep III. *Journal of Near Eastern Studies* 10: 35–56, 82–111, 156–83, 231–42.

Kitchen, K. A. 1992. The Vintages of the Ramesseum. Pages 115–23 in *Studies in Pharaonic Religion and Society in Honour of J. Gwyn Griffiths*, ed. A. B. Lloyd. Occasional Publications, no. 8. London: Egypt Exploration Society.

Lesko, L. H. 1977. *King Tut's Wine Cellar*. Berkeley: B.C. Scribe.

McGovern, P. E. 1997. Wine of Egypt's Golden Age: An Archaeochemical Perspective. *Journal of Egyptian Archaeology* 83:69–108.

———. 2000. *The Foreign Relations of the "Hyksos": A Neutron Activation Study of the Middle Bronze Pottery from Tell el-Dab'a (Ancient Avaris)*. British Archaeological Reports International Series, vol. 888. Oxford: Archaeopress.

Oren, E. D., ed. 1997. *The Hyksos: New Historical and Archaeological Perspectives*. University Museum Monograph 96. Philadelphia: University of Pennsylvania Museum.

Stager, L. E. 1991. *Ashkelon Discovered: From Canaanites and Philistines to Romans and Moslems*. Washington, DC: Biblical Archaeology Society.

Chapter 7. Wine of the World's First Cities

Badler, V. R., P. E. McGovern, and D. L. Glusker. 1996. Chemical Evidence for a Wine Residue from Warka (Uruk) inside a Late Uruk Period Spouted Jar. *Baghdader Mitteilungen* 27:39–43.

Boehmer, R. M. 1995. Mehrtüllengefässe im Grabkult. *Baghdader Mitteilungen* 26:47–63.

Green, M. W., and Nissen, H. J. 1987. *Zeichenliste der Archaischen Texte aus Uruk*. Berlin: Mann.

Jacobsen, T. 1976. *The Treasures of Darkness: A History of Mesopotamian Religion*. New Haven: Yale University.

Katz, S. H., and M. M. Voigt. 1986. Bread and Beer: The Early Use of Cereals in the Human Diet. *Expedition* 28(2): 23–34.

Kramer, S. N. 1969. *The Sacred Marriage Rite: Aspects of Faith, Myth, and Ritual in Ancient Sumer*. Bloomington: Indiana University.

Mallowan, M. E. L. 1965. *Early Mesopotamia and Iran*. New York: McGraw-Hill.

Michel, R. H., P. E. McGovern, and V. R. Badler. 1992. Chemical Evidence for Ancient Beer. *Nature* 360:24.

Woolley, L. 1965. *Excavations at Ur: A Record of Twelve Years' Work.* New York: Crowell.

Chapter 8. *Wine and the Great Empires of the Ancient Near East*

Alp, S. 2000. *Song, Music, and Dance of Hittites: Grapes and Wines in Anatolia during the Hittite Period,* trans. Y. Eran. Ankara: Kavaklıdere Cultural.

Barnett, R. D. 1985. Assurbanipal's Feast. *Eretz-Israel* 8:1*–6*.

Harden, D. 1963. *The Phoenicians.* 2nd ed. New York: F. A. Praeger.

Hoffner, H. A. 1974. *Alimenta Hethaeorum: Food Production in Hittite Asia Minor.* American Oriental Series, vol. 55. New Haven, CN: American Oriental Society.

Kinnier Wilson, J. V. 1972. *The Nimrud Wine Lists.* London: British School of Archaeology in Iraq.

Lloyd, S. 1967. *Early Highland Peoples of Anatolia.* New York: McGraw-Hill.

Matthiae, P. 1981. *Ebla: An Empire Rediscovered.* Garden City, NY: Doubleday.

Özdoğan, M., and N. Başgelen. 1999. *Neolithic in Turkey, The Cradle of Civilization: New Discoveries.* 2 vols. Istanbul: Arkeoloji ve Sanat Yayınları.

Özguç, T. 1988a. *Inandi: An Important Cult Center in the Old Hittite Period.* Türk Tarih Kurumu Yayınları 5, no. 43. Ankara: Türk Tarih Kurumu.

———. 1988b. *Kültepe-Kanis II: New Researches at the Trading Center of the Ancient Near East.* Türk Tarih Kurumu Yayınları 5, no. 41. Ankara: Türk Tarih Kurumu.

———. and N. Özguç 1950. *Ausgrabungen in Kültepe 1949.* Türk Tarih Kurumu Yayınları 5, no. 10. Ankara: Türk Tarih Kurumu.

Salje, B. 1996. Becher für die Toten? Bronzende Trinksets und ihre Bedeutung im Grabkult. *Baghdader Mitteilungen* 27:429–46.

Seeher, J. 1999. *Hattusha-Guide: A Day in the Hittite Capital.* Deutsches Archäologisches Institut, Boğazköy-Expedition. Istanbul: Ege Yayınları.

Chapter 9. *The Holy Land's Bounty*

Alon, D. 1976. Two Cult Vessels from Gilat. *'Atiqot* 11:116–20.

Amiran, R. 1986. A New Type of Chalcolithic Ritual Vessel and Some Implications for the Nahal Mishmar Hoard. *Bulletin of the American Schools of Oriental Research* 262:83–87.

Bartlett, J. R. 1983. *Jericho*. Cities of the Biblical World. Grand Rapids, MI: W. B. Eerdmans.

Broshi, M. 1984. Wine in Ancient Palestine: Introductory Notes. *Israel Museum Journal* 3:21–40.

Dothan, T. K. 1982. *The Philistines and Their Material Culture*. New Haven: Yale University.

James, F. W., and P. E. McGovern. 1993. *The Late Bronze Egyptian Garrison at Beth Shan: A Study of Levels VII and VIII*. University Museum Monograph 85. Philadelphia: University of Pennsylvania Museum.

Johnson, B. L., and L. E. Stager. 1995. Ashkelon: Wine Emporium of the Holy Land. Pages 95–109 in *Recent Excavations in Israel: A View to the West*, ed. S. Gitin. Archaeological Institute of America Colloquia and Conference Papers, no. 1. Dubuque, IA: Kendall/Hunt.

Kenyon, K. M. 1971. *Royal Cities of the Old Testament*. New York: Schocken Books.

Kislev, M. E., D. Nadel, and I. Carmi. 1992. Epipalaeolithic (19,000 BP) Cereal and Fruit Diet at Ohalo II, Sea of Galilee, Israel. *Review of Palaeobotany and Palynology* 73:161–66.

Lewis, T. J. 1989. *Cults of the Dead in Ancient Israel and Ugarit*. Harvard Semitic Monographs 39. Atlanta: Scholars Press.

McGovern, P. E. 1986. *The Late Bronze and Early Iron Ages of Central Transjordan: The Baqʿah Valley Project, 1977–1981*. University Museum Monograph 65. Philadelphia: University of Pennsylvania Museum.

McGovern, P. E., J. Bourriau, G. Harbottle, and S. J. Allen. 1994. The Archaeological Origin and Significance of the Dolphin Vase as Determined by Neutron Activation Analysis. *Bulletin of the American Schools of Oriental Research* 296:31–43.

Mayerson, P. 1992. The Gaza "Wine" Jar and the "Lost" Ashkelon Jar (*Askalônion*). *Bulletin of the American Schools of Oriental Research* 42:76–80.

Pritchard, J. B. 1964. *Winery, Defenses, and Soundings at Gibeon*. Museum Monograph. Philadelphia: University Museum.

Stager, L. E. 1985. The Firstfruits of Civilization. Pages 172–88 in *Palestine in the Bronze and Iron Ages: Papers in Honour of Olga Tufnell*, ed. J. N. Tubb. London: Institute of Archaeology.

———. 1996. Ashkelon and the Archaeology of Destruction: Kislev 604 BCE. *Eretz-Israel* 25:61*–74*.

Ussishkin, D. 1982. *The Conquest of Lachish by Sennacherib*. Tel Aviv: Tel Aviv University.

Walsh, C. E. 2000. *The Fruit of the Vine: Viticulture in Ancient Israel.* Harvard Semitic Monographs 60. Winona Lake, IN: Eisenbrauns.

Yadin, Y. 1972. *Hazor.* Schweich Lectures. London: Oxford University.

Zevulun, U. 1987. A Canaanite Ram-Headed Cup. *Israel Exploration Journal* 37:88–104.

Chapter 10. *Lands of Dionysos: Greece and Anatolia*

Dikaios, P. 1937. An Iron Age Painted Amphora in the Cyprus Museum. *Annual of the British School at Athens* 36–37:56–72.

Hamilakis, Y. 1996. Wine, Oil and the Dialectics of Power in Bronze Age Crete: A Review of the Evidence. *Oxford Journal of Archaeology* 15:1–32.

Koehl, R. B. 1981. The Functions of Aegean Bronze Age Rhyta. Pages 179–87 in *Sanctuaries and Cults in the Aegean Bronze Age*, ed. R. Hägg and N. Marinatos. Stockholm: Svenska institutet i Athen.

———. 1990. The Rhyta from Akrotiri and Some Preliminary Observations on Their Functions in Selected Contexts. Pages 350–60 in *Thera and the Aegean World III*, vol. 1, ed. D. A. Hardy. London: Thera Foundation.

Merrillees, R. S. 1989. Highs and Lows in the Holy Land: Opium in Biblical Times. *Eretz-Israel* 20:148*–54*.

Platon, N. 1971. *Zakros: The Discovery of a Lost Palace of Ancient Crete.* New York: C. Scribner's.

Sakellarakis, Y., and E. Sapouna-Sakellaraki. 1997. *Archanes: Minoan Crete in a New Light.* 2 vols. Athens: Ammos.

Tzedakis, Y., and H., Martlew, eds. 1999. *Minoans and Mycenaeans: Flavours of Their Time.* Athens: Greek Ministry of Culture and National Archaeological Museum.

Wace, A. J. B. 1955. Mycenae 1939–1954, Part 1: Preliminary Report on the Excavations of 1954. *Annual of the British School at Athens* 50:175–89.

Warren, P. 1969. *Minoan Stone Vases.* Cambridge: Cambridge University.

———. 1972. *Myrtos: An Early Bronze Age Settlement in Crete.* British School of Archaeology, suppl. vol. 7. London: Thames and Hudson.

Wiener, M. H. 1984. Crete and the Cyclades in LM I: The Tales of the Conical Cups. Pages 17–26 in *The Minoan Thalassocracy: Myth and Reality*, ed. R. Hägg and N. Marinatos. Skrifter utgivna av Svenska institutet i Athen, no. 32. Stockholm: Svenska institutet i Athen.

Chapter 11. A Beverage for King Midas and at the Limits of the Civilized World

Biel, J. 1985. *Der Keltenfurst von Hochdorf.* Stuttgart: K. Theiss.

Bogucki, P. 1996. The Spread of Early Farming in Europe. *American Scientist* 84:242–53.

Crane, E. 1983. *The Archaeology of Beekeeping.* Ithaca, NY: Cornell University.

Dickson, J. H. 1978. Bronze Age Mead. *Antiquity* 52:108–13.

Dietler, M. 1990. Driven by Drink: The Role of Drinking in the Political Economy and the Case of Early Iron Age France. *Journal of Anthropological Archaeology* 9:352–406.

Goodman, J., P. E. Lovejoy, and A. Sherratt, eds. 1995. *Consuming Habits: Drugs in History and Anthropology.* London: Routledge.

Karageorghis, V. 1969. *The Ancient Civilization of Cyprus.* New York: Cowles Education.

Knapp, A. B. 1991. Spice, Drugs, Grain and Grog: Organic Goods in Bronze Age East Mediterranean Trade. Pages 69–82 in *Bronze Age Trade in the Mediterranean*, ed. N. H. Gale. Jonesered: P. Åström.

McGovern, P. E. 2000. The Funerary Banquet of "King Midas." *Expedition* 42(1): 21–29.

McGovern, P. E., D. L. Glusker, R. A. Moreau, A. Nuñez, C. W. Beck, E. Simpson, E. D. Butrym, L. J. Exner, and E. C. Stout. 1999. A Feast Fit for King Midas. *Nature* 402:863–64.

Morse, R. A. 1980. *Making Mead (Honey Wine): History, Recipes, Methods and Equipment.* Ithaca, NY: Wicwas.

Muscarella, O. W. 1992. Greek and Oriental Cauldron Attachments: A Review. Pages 16–45 in *Greece between East and West: 10th–8th Centuries B.C.*, ed. G. Kopcke and I. Tokumaru. Mainz: P. von Zabern.

Pain, S. 1999. Grog of the Greeks. *New Scientist* 164:54–57.

Rudgley, R. 1998. *The Encyclopedia of Psychoactive Substances.* New York: Little, Brown.

Sams, G. K. 1977. Beer in the City of Midas. *Archaeology* 30:108–15.

Sherratt, A. 1987. Cups That Cheered. Pages 81–114 in *Bell Beakers of the Western Mediterranean*, ed. W. H. Waldren and R. C. Kennard. Oxford: British Archaeological Reports.

———. 1997. *Economy and Society in Prehistoric Europe: Changing Perspectives*. Princeton: Princeton University Press.

Young, R. S. 1967. A Bronze Bowl in Philadelphia. *Journal of Near Eastern Studies* 26:145–54.

———. 1981. *Three Great Early Tumuli*. University Museum Monograph 43. Philadelphia: University of Pennsylvania Museum.

Chapter 12. Molecular Archaeology, Wine, and a View to the Future

Lucia, S. P. 1963. *A History of Wine as Therapy*. Philadelphia: J. B. Lippincott.

Vallee, B. L. 1998. Alcohol in the Western World. *Scientific American* 281: 80–85.

ILLUSTRATION CREDITS

AND OBJECT DIMENSIONS

Color Plates

Color plate 1. Colored engraving by J. J. Plenck, *Icones Plantarum Medicinalium secundum systema Linnaei digestarum* (Vienna: R. Graeffer, 1784).

Color plate 2. Photograph courtesy of W. Pratt, Royal Ontario Museum, Toronto, West Asian Dept., no. Gd. 73-113.

Color plate 3. Photograph courtesy of Hasanlu Project, University of Pennsylvania Museum of Archaeology and Anthropology, Philadelphia, no. 69-12-15, height 23.5 cm.

Color plate 4. Photographs courtesy of University of Pennsylvania Museum of Archaeology and Anthropology, Philadelphia, Egyptian Section, nos. E6943 and 60-15-23, length of jar 66.5 cm.

Color plate 5. Photograph courtesy of British Museum, London, no. 121545, length 4.4 cm.

Color plate 6. Photograph courtesy of University of Pennsylvania Museum of Archaeology and Anthropology, Philadelphia, Near East Section, no. B17694/U.10556, height of head 35.6 cm.

Color plate 7. Photograph courtesy of British Museum, London, no. WA 121201, length ca. 47 cm.

Color plate 8. Photograph courtesy of Museum of Anatolian Civilizations, Ankara, height including handle 8 cm.

Color plate 9. "Autumn: Spies with Grapes from the Promised Land," 1660–1664. Musée du Louvre, Département des Peintures. Photograph from A. Mérot, *Nicholas Poussin* (New York: Abbeville, 1990), p. 246, cat. no. 208.

Color plate 10. Photograph courtesy of Staatliche Antikensammlungen und Glyptothek, Munich, no. 8729.

Color plate 11. Photograph from J. A. Sakellarakis, *Herakleion Museum Illustrated Guide* (Ekdotike Athenon: Athens, 2000), p. 35, no. 1368, height without horns 20.6 cm.

Color plate 12. Photograph from J. A. Sakellarakis, *Herakleion Museum Illustrated Guide* (Ekdotike Athenon: Athens, 2000), p. 115, length 1.37 m.

Color plate 13. Photograph courtesy of Gordion Project, University of Pennsylvania Museum of Archaeology and Anthropology, Philadelphia, no. G381.

Color plate 14. Photograph courtesy of Gordion Project, University of Pennsylvania Museum of Archaeology and Anthropology, Philadelphia, no. G2324.

Color plate 15. Photograph courtesy of Gordion Project, University of Pennsylvania Museum of Archaeology and Anthropology, Philadelphia, nos. G2848/B1080/MM46, length 20.5 cm.

Color plate 16. Photograph courtesy of Juzhong Zhang and Institute of Archaeology, Zhengzhou, nos. M252:1, M482:1, and M253:1 (left to right), height of leftmost juglet 20 cm.

Figures

Figure 2.1. Photograph by P. E. McGovern.

Figure 3.1. Photograph by B. Boyle, courtesy of Royal Ontario Museum, Toronto, West Asian Dept., no. Gd. 73-113, height ca. 55 cm.

Figure 3.3. Photograph by D. E. McGovern.

Figure 4.1. Photograph courtesy of Hasanlu Project, University of Pennsylvania Museum, Philadelphia.

Figure 4.2. Courtesy of State Museum of Georgia, Tblisi, no. XIII-69, length ca. 16 cm. Photograph by P. E. McGovern.

Figure 4.3. Photograph by P. E. McGovern, courtesy of State History Museum of Armenia, Yerevan. Drawing from K. K. Kushnareva, *The Southern Caucasus in Prehistory: Stages of Cultural and Socioeconomic Development from the Eighth to the Second Millennium* B.C. (Philadelphia: University of Pennsylvania Museum, 1997), fig. 48.

Figure 5.1. Photograph courtesy of German Institute of Archaeology, Cairo.

Figure 5.2. Drawings courtesy of German Institute of Archaeology, Cairo;

handleless jar, no. 10-33, height 40.8 cm; two-handled jar, no. 7-35, height 30.2 cm.

Figure 6.1. (Top) Photograph courtesy of J. Huntoon, Tell el-Dabʿa no. 4538, height 48 cm. (Bottom) Photograph courtesy of American School of Classical Studies at Athens, Agora Excavations, nos. SS 8602, SS 7918, P 19120, and SS 7319.

Figure 6.2. Photograph courtesy of D. Frey and Institute of Nautical Archaeology, Texas A&M University, College Station.

Figure 6.3. Plan from W. C. Hayes, *Journal of Near Eastern Studies* 10 (1951), fig. 1; courtesy of The Metropolitan Museum of Art, New York.

Figure 6.4. Photograph courtesy of The Metropolitan Museum of Art, New York, no. 30.4.121 (facsimile painting), Rogers Fund, 1930.

Figure 6.5. Photograph courtesy of Egyptian Expedition, The Metropolitan Museum of Art, New York.

Figure 6.6. Drawings courtesy of Griffith Institute, Ashmolean Museum, Oxford.

Figure 7.1. Photograph courtesy of University of Pennsylvania Museum of Archaeology and Anthropology, Philadelphia, Near East Section, (left to right) nos. B17692/U.10451 (height 8 cm), B17691/U.10453 (height 15.2 cm) and B17693/U.10850 (length 13.1 cm, width 9.4 cm).

Figure 8.1. Drawing courtesy of T. Özgüç and Museum of Anatolian Civilizations, Ankara, height 82 cm.

Figure 8.2. Photograph courtesy of T. Özgüç and Museum of Anatolian Civilizations, Ankara, height 16 cm.

Figure 8.3. Photograph courtesy of R. Gorny.

Figure 8.4. Photograph and drawing courtesy of The Metropolitan Museum of Art, New York, no. 1989.281.10, gift of Norbert Schimmel Foundation.

Figure 8.5. Photograph courtesy of R. Gorny.

Figure 8.6. Drawing from P. E. Botta and E. N. Flandin, *Monument de Ninive* (Imprimerie Nationale, Paris, 1849), I:pl. 140.

Figure 8.7. Photograph courtesy of British Museum, London.

Figure 9.1. Photograph courtesy of The Metropolitan Museum of Art, New York, Rogers Fund and Edward S. Harkness Gift, 1922, no. 22.1.95, height 26.5 cm.

Figure 9.2. Drawing from G. Loud, *The Megiddo Ivories*, Oriental Institute Publications, vol. 12 (Chicago: University of Chicago, 1939), pl. 4.

Figure 9.3. Photograph courtesy of University of Pennsylvania Museum of Archaeology and Anthropology, Philadelphia, Near East Section, no. P.81-6-276, height 24 cm.

Figure 10.1. Photographs on p. 248 and drawing (p. 249; height 21.1 cm) courtesy of P. Warren. Photograph on p. 249 courtesy of Greek Ministry of Culture, from Y. Tzedakis and H. Martlew, eds., *Minoans and Mycenaeans: Flavours of Their Time* (Athens: National Archaeological Museum, 1999), p. 145, cat. no. 127, height 80.7 cm.

Figure 10.2. Photograph courtesy of K. Oehrlein and Martin von Wagner Museum, University of Würzburg, no. L 265.

Figure 10.3. Photograph from N. Platon, *History of the Hellenic World*, ed. G. Phylactopoulos, trans. P. Sherrard (Athens: Ekdotike Athenon, 1974), p. 195.

Figure 10.4. Photographs courtesy of Greek Ministry of Culture, from Y. Tzedakis and H. Martlew, eds., *Minoans and Mycenaeans: Flavours of Their Time* (Athens: National Archaeological Museum, 1999), pp. 91 and 149, cat. nos. 57 and 130. (Left) Rethymnon Museum no. 21189, height ca. 30 cm; (right) Rethymnon Museum no. 6615, height 4.5 cm.

Figure 10.5. Photographs courtesy of Greek Ministry of Culture, from Y. Tzedakis and H. Martlew, eds., *Minoans and Mycenaeans: Flavours of Their Time* (Athens: National Archaeological Museum, 1999), pp. 167 and 103. Cup: cat. no. 153, Chania Museum no. 9378, height ca. 5 cm.

Figure 10.7. Photographs courtesy of Greek Ministry of Culture, from Y. Tzedakis and H. Martlew, eds., *Minoans and Mycenaeans: Flavours of Their Time* (Athens: National Archaeological Museum, 1999), pp. 175 and 176. Cup: cat. no. 167, Rethymnon Museum no. 3459, height ca. 20 cm.

Figure 10.8. Photograph courtesy of Swedish Institute at Athens, and National Archaeological Museum, Athens.

Figure 10.9. Photograph courtesy of Cyprus Archaeological Museum, Nicosia.

Figure 10.10. (Left) Photograph courtesy of E. French and Mycenae Archive, Cambridge, height ca. 19 cm. (Right) Photograph courtesy of National Archaeological Museum, Athens.

Figure 11.1. Photograph courtesy of Gordion Project, University of Pennsylvania Museum of Archaeology and Anthropology, Philadelphia, no. B786/MM2, height 48.5 cm, volume about 150 liters.

Figure 11.2. Drawing from P. E. Botta and E. N. Flandin, *Monument de Ninive* (Imprimerie Nationale, Paris, 1849), I:pl. 64.

Figure 11.3. Photograph courtesy of Gordion Project, University of Pennsylvania Museum of Archaeology and Anthropology, no. G2847/B810/MM465, length 22.5 cm.

Figure 11.4. Photograph courtesy of Gordion Project, University of Pennsylvania Museum of Archaeology and Anthropology, Philadelphia, no. G2484/B889/MM80, diameter of rim 22.2 cm, volume about 1 liter.

Figure 11.5. Photograph courtesy of Gordion Project, University of Pennsylvania Museum of Archaeology and Anthropology, Philadelphia, no. G2393/MM3, height of vat 51.5 cm.

Figure 11.6. Photograph courtesy of R. Neave and J.N.W. Prag, University of Manchester, England, and University of Pennsylvania Museum of Archaeology and Anthropology, Philadelphia.

Maps

Map 2. Map after version prepared by P. Zimmerman, MASCA, University of Pennsylvania Museum of Archaeology and Anthropology, Philadelphia.

Map 4. Map after version prepared by P. Zimmerman, MASCA, University of Pennsylvania Museum of Archaeology and Anthropology, Philadelphia.

INDEX

Page numbers followed by letters *f* and *m* refer to figures and maps, respectively.

saccharides. *See* sugar

Saccharomyces cerevisiae (yeast): complete DNA sequencing of, 25, 103–4; in fermented beverages, 82, 186; grapes as preferred source of, 82, 84; insects as carriers of, 104, 307–8; precursor of, in Scorpion I wine jars, 105–6; role in fermentation, 307–8

Saccharomyces winlocki (yeast), 103

sacred marriage (*hieros gamos*): in Anatolia, 175f, 176; in Assyria, 200; in Israel, 229; in Sumer, 159

sacrifice. *See* animal sacrifice; human sacrifice

saffron: in "Phrygian grog," 295; as wine additive, 235, 268, 309

Sahure (Egyptian pharaoh), pyramid temple of, 137

Salamis (Cyprus), necropolis of, vessels from, 197–98

Samaria (West Bank): excavations at, 228; ivory plaques from, 229; ostraca from, 228; royal banqueting at, 229–30

Samtauro (Georgia), 23

sandarac tree (*Tetraclinis articulata*), 72

Sanskrit, 32

Saqqara (Egypt), 86; tombs of nobles at, 88, 91. *See also* Memphis

Sarepta (Lebanon), 49–50; excavations at, 49, 202; Mycenaean pottery from, 272; purple dye production at, 49–51

Sargon II the Great (Akkadian king), 155, 159

Sargon II (Assyrian king), 191; tomb of queen of, 193; palace at Khorsabad, wall reliefs from, 194–95, 195f, 198, 283, 284f; victories in Urartu, 194; wine cellars at, 195–96

Sayre, Edward, 99

Schliemann, Heinrich, 84, 257–58

Scorpion I tomb (Abydos, Egypt), 91–92, 93f; clay sealings from, 101; INAA study of wine jars from, 100; organic analyses of residues from, 93–94; pottery types from, stylistic parallels in Levant, 96; provenience of

wine jars from, 100–1; wine jars from, 92, 94, 95f, 96; wine labels from, 92–93; yeast DNA from jars from, 104–6

Scotch, oak flavorant in, 261

scuppernong grape, 3

Scybelites or Siræum (Anatolian wine), 187

šdḥ (Egyptian wine), 140

Sea of Galilee, 212

Sea Peoples, 226–27

sea water, as wine additive, 309–10

seal impressions: Egyptian, 85–87; Elamite, 165–66; Hittite, 187; Sumerian, 154–55, 159

secondary fermentation locks, 88; lack on Malkata stoppers, 129–30

sed-festival (Egypt), 124–25

seeds. *See* grape seeds

šekar (Israelite "date wine"), 235–36

Semele (mythological Greek heroine), 242

Sennacherib (Assyrian king), 234

Seth (Egyptian god), 135, 142; temple at Abydos, 142; temple at Avaris, 119–20

Setnakhte (Egyptian pharaoh), 146

Sety I (Egyptian pharaoh), 141–42

Sety II (Egyptian pharaoh), 141; mortuary temple in Thebes, 146

sexual acts: Anatolian ceremonies and, 175f, 176; Phrygian drinking and, 298; Sumerian banqueting and, 158–59. *See also* sacred marriage

Shalmaneser V (Assyrian king), 193

Shamash (Babylonian god), 153, 171, 230

Sharuhen (Hyksos city), 114, 116

Shesmu (Egyptian god), 135

Shiloh (West Bank), Iron Age jug from, 234

shipping: Byblos and, 114; Canaanite Jars and amphoras used in, 110; in Mediterranean trade, 277–78, 304–5; in Mesopotamian trade, 152, 167–68, 170–71. *See also* maritime trade

Shiraz (Iran), 164–66